Excel 2013 for Scientists
by
Dr. Gerard M. Verschuuren

Holy Macro! Books

PO Box 82, Uniontown, OH 44685 USA

Excel 2013 for Scientists

Author: Dr. Gerard M. Verschuuren

Layout: Tyler Nash

Cover Design: Shannon Mattiza 6'4 Productions

Indexing: Nellie J. Liwam

Published by: Holy Macro! Books, PO Box 82, Uniontown, OH 44685 USA

Distributed by: Independent Publishers Group, Chicago, IL

First Printing: December 2013. Printed in USA

ISBN: 978-1-61547-025-9 Print, 978-1-61547-217-8 PDF, 978-1-61547-338-0 ePub, 978-1-61547-117-1 Mobi

LCCN: 2013938521

Contents

About the Author

Dr. Gerard M. Verschuuren is a Microsoft Certified Professional specialized in VB, VBA, VBScript, VB.NET, and C#-NET. He has more than 25 years of experience in teaching at colleges and corporations.

He holds master's degrees in biology (human genetics) and philosophy, as well as a doctorate in the philosophy of science from universities in Europe.

He is the author of *From VBA to VSTO* (2006, Holy Macro! Books), and the author of *Excel Simulations* (2013, Holy Macro! Books).

He is also the author behind the *Visual Learning* series (`www.mrexcel.com/microsoft-office-visual-learning.html`), which includes:

- Your Access to the World (2004)

- Access 2007 VBA (2008)

- Visual C# Express DVD (2008)

- Excel 2007 Expert (2007)

- Excel VBA 2007 (2008)

Introduction

This book can be used on its own or in conjunction with an interactive CD called *Excel 2013 for Scientists*, also available from MrExcel (www.mrexcel.com/2013books/scientist2013cd.html). This book assumes at least some basic knowledge of Excel. Readers new to Excel may want to familiarize themselves with a basic how-to source such as the interactive CD *Excel 2007 Expert*, also available from MrExcel (www.MrExcel.com/excel2007expert.shtml).

Scientists do not want nor do they need verbose explanations. Therefore, I was as concise as possible in the chapters of this book. I also attempted to add some meaningful simple exercises because the proof is still in the pudding. The examples appear at the end of each part, along with their solutions. Because I am a human geneticist myself, most of my simple examples stem from the life sciences.

All files used in this book can be found at www.genesispc.com/Science2013.htm. Each file has an original version (to work in) and a finished version (to check your solutions).

Excel was originally created as a financial application, but it has evolved into a rather sophisticated scientific tool. Although other and perhaps more advanced programs exist, many of those have a steep learning curve. Excel may, therefore, still be your best choice. I hope you will soon discover why.

I also teach the content of this book to scientists. It is a 4-day hands-on course of six hours a day at your own location. To schedule such a class go here: www.genesispc.com/schedule.htm.

Part 1: General Spreadsheet Techniques

Chapter 1: Navigation in Excel

Excel 2013 has plenty of space for your scientific work. Each workbook (or *.xlsx* file) can hold an unlimited number of worksheets (provided that your computer memory permits), and each worksheet has a capacity of 1,048,576 rows by 16,384 columns. Hopefully, you won't use all this space before retirement.

Scientific spreadsheets can be huge—filled with many numbers. So you need ways to quickly navigate around and to create formulas for giant ranges of cells in a swift and efficient way. That's what this chapter is about.

Most sheets in this book have a modest size, so it is easy to practice with them. But in real life, you probably deal with much larger collections of data. The basic techniques discussed in this chapter will benefit you even more when your data sets become larger and larger.

Navigation Shortcuts

The following keystrokes are some important navigation shortcuts:

- *Ctrl+Home* takes you to the origin of the sheet, which is usually cell A1.

- *Ctrl+Arrow* key jumps between section borders. (A border is an empty row and/or column.)

- *Ctrl+Shift+Arrow* key jumps and selects what is between the section borders.

- *Shift+Arrow* key expands or reduces whatever has been selected.

Let's use Figure 1.1 to see how these shortcuts work. Based on Figure 1.1, the following would happen:

	A	B	C	D	E	F	G	H	I	J	K
1		1	1			0.69	0.42				
2		2				0.33	0.83				
3		3				0.63	0.70				
4		4				0.50	0.43				
5		5				0.12	0.23				
6		6				0.10	0.90				
7		7				0.86	0.94				
8		8				0.42	0.98				
9		9				0.41	0.77				
10		10				0.56	0.20				
11					SD						
12											
13			Column								
14		0.38	0.38								
15		0.69	0.69								
16		0.50	0.50								
17		0.03	0.03								
18		0.94	0.94								
19		0.11	0.11								
20		0.78	0.78								
21		0.31	0.31								
22		0.30	0.30								
23		0.12	0.12								
24	COUNTIF >.5										
25											

Figure 1.1

Note

- **Starting in A1:** Pressing *Ctrl+Down Arrow* takes you to A24 and then to A1048576. Pressing *Ctrl+Up Arrow* takes you back, with the same stops on the way.

- **Starting in B1:** Repeatedly pressing *Ctrl+Down Arrow* jumps to B10, B14, B23, and finally the end.

- **Starting in B1:** Pressing *Ctrl+Shift+Down Arrow* selects the entire range B1:B10. Pressing *Shift+Down Arrow* once expands the selection with one more cell. Instead pressing *Shift+Up Arrow* shortens the selection by one cell. The *Shift* key keeps all in-between cells included in the selection.

- **Starting in J1:** Typing J24 in the *Name* box just above column A and then pressing *Shift+Enter* selects all cells between J1 and J24 (thanks to the *Shift* key). With the range J1:J24 selected, typing =ROW() in the *formula bar* and then pressing *Ctrl+Enter* causes all the selected cells to be filled with this formula (thanks to the *Ctrl* key).

Creating Formulas

Figure 1.2 shows an example of how to create formulas:

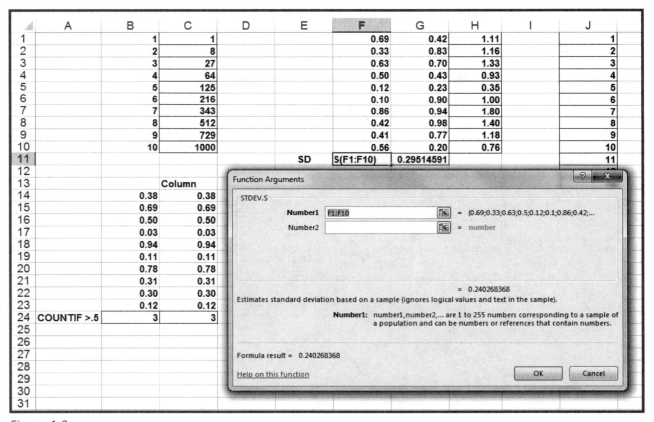

Figure 1.2

1. Select cell F11 and press the f_x button (located just in front of the *formula bar*).

2. Choose the function `STDEV.S` and start the first argument by clicking cell F10 and then pressing *Ctrl+Shift+Up Arrow*; this selects the entire range above cell F11. Often, Excel finds the correct range automatically—but not necessarily so; when it does not, you have to be in charge yourself!

3. Press *OK* in the dialog box, and the cell shows the actual standard deviation of these cells.

4. In cell B24, use the function `COUNTIF` and follow these steps:

    1. For the first argument, click cell B23 and then press *Ctrl+Shift+Up Arrow*.

    2. For the second argument, type *>=5* (which changes into a string: *">=5"*).

    3. Finalize the functions by pressing *Ctrl+Enter*.

Figure 1.3 shows a quick technique for calculating the sum or mean of certain measurements per strain of bacteria and per test:

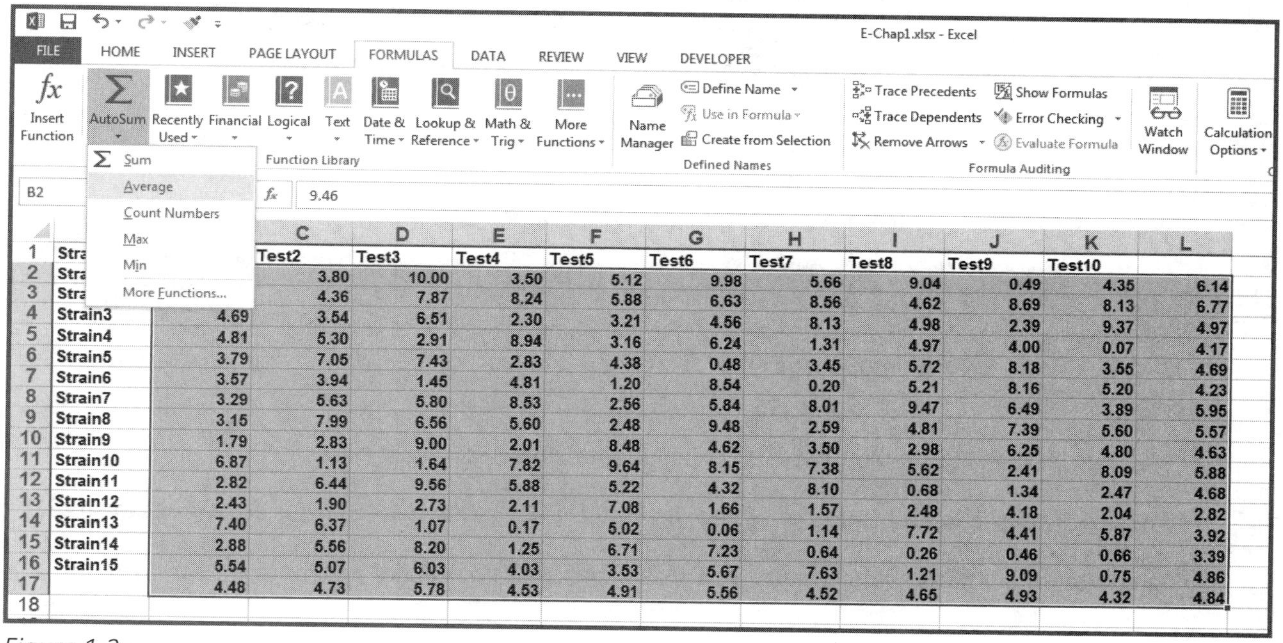

	A	B	C	D	E	F	G	H	I	J	K	L
1	Stra		Test2	Test3	Test4	Test5	Test6	Test7	Test8	Test9	Test10	
2	Stra		3.80	10.00	3.50	5.12	9.98	5.66	9.04	0.49	4.35	6.14
3	Stra		4.36	7.87	8.24	5.88	6.63	8.56	4.62	8.69	8.13	6.77
4	Strain3	4.69	3.54	6.51	2.30	3.21	4.56	8.13	4.98	2.39	9.37	4.97
5	Strain4	4.81	5.30	2.91	8.94	3.16	6.24	1.31	4.97	4.00	0.07	4.17
6	Strain5	3.79	7.05	7.43	2.83	4.38	0.48	3.45	5.72	8.18	3.55	4.69
7	Strain6	3.57	3.94	1.45	4.81	1.20	8.54	0.20	5.21	8.16	5.20	4.23
8	Strain7	3.29	5.63	5.80	8.53	2.56	5.84	8.01	9.47	6.49	3.89	5.95
9	Strain8	3.15	7.99	6.56	5.60	2.48	9.48	2.59	4.81	7.39	5.60	5.57
10	Strain9	1.79	2.83	9.00	2.01	8.48	4.62	3.50	2.98	6.25	4.80	4.63
11	Strain10	6.87	1.13	1.64	7.82	9.64	8.15	7.38	5.62	2.41	8.09	5.88
12	Strain11	2.82	6.44	9.56	5.88	5.22	4.32	8.10	0.68	1.34	2.47	4.68
13	Strain12	2.43	1.90	2.73	2.11	7.08	1.66	1.57	2.48	4.18	2.04	2.82
14	Strain13	7.40	6.37	1.07	0.17	5.02	0.06	1.14	7.72	4.41	5.87	3.92
15	Strain14	2.88	5.56	8.20	1.25	6.71	7.23	0.64	0.26	0.46	0.66	3.39
16	Strain15	5.54	5.07	6.03	4.03	3.53	5.67	7.63	1.21	9.09	0.75	4.86
17		4.48	4.73	5.78	4.53	4.91	5.56	4.52	4.65	4.93	4.32	4.84
18												

Figure 1.3

1. Select cell A1 (or press *Ctrl+Home*).

2. Press *Ctrl+Shift+Down Arrow* and then *Ctrl+Shift+Right Arrow*.

3. You need an extra row and column for the calculations of the means, so to expand the selection with an extra row and column, press *Shift+Down Arrow* and *Shift+Right Arrow*.

4. From the *Formulas* tab, use the drop-down button next to the *Sum* button, and choose the option *Sum*, *Average*, *Min*, or *Max*.

All calculations are done automatically at the end of each numeric row or column. You could do this more tediously; go ahead if you like that route better!

Note

There is also a shortcut key for the `SUM` function: *Alt+=*. There is no such feature for the mean.

Figure 1.4 shows the same data set as Figure 1.3, but this time in the dedicated table structure available in Excel 2013. Follow these steps:

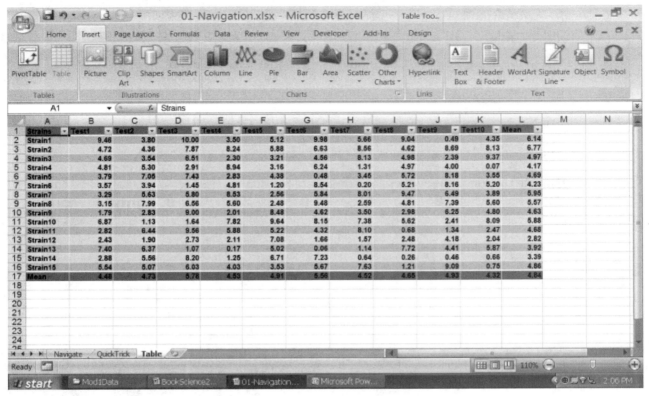

Figure 1.4

1. Click the *Table* button on the *Insert* tab to create a table structure with a striping pattern for easy reading.

2. Specify whether your table has headers (also called labels) on top or not.

3. After the table structure is implemented, use the *Design* tab to change table settings as desired.

4. To create calculations again for sum and mean, use the same technique you used earlier.

Chapter 2: The Fill Handle

One of the best-kept secrets in Excel is the *fill handle*. This tool allows you to copy cells over a contiguous range of cells or to fill such a range with a series of specific values. In addition, it helps you copy formulas over huge ranges.

The *fill handle* is located in the lower-right corner of your selected cell(s). Whenever you move your mouse to that point, the cursor changes to a small + sign (not to be confused with a crosshairs). That very spot holds the *fill handle*.

Figure 1.5 shows examples that help you explore some of the features of the *fill handle*:

	A	B	C	D	E	F	G	H
1	Day	Hours	Day#	+10	+3.3	D*E	Anal.	List
2	Monday	8	1	0	7	0	gmv	gmv
3	Tuesday	8	2	10	10.3	103	tjk	tjk
4	Wednesday	8	3	20	13.6	272	bdo	bdo
5	Thursday	8	4	30	16.9	507	gmv	gmv
6	Friday	8	5	40	20.2	808	tjk	tjk
7	Monday	8	6	50	23.5	1175	bdo	bdo
8	Tuesday	8	7	60	26.8	1608	gmv	gmv
9	Wednesday	8	8	70	30.1	2107	tjk	tjk
10	Thursday	8	9	80	33.4	2672	bdo	bdo
11	Friday	8	10	90	36.7	3303	gmv	gmv
12								

Figure 1.5

- **Cell A2:** Click and drag the *fill handle* downward to cell A6 in order to stop at Friday. If you keep going, the fill handle goes into Saturday, and so on. If you stop at Friday and then start the *fill handle* again (with A2:A6 still selected), you can just copy the previous section by holding the *Ctrl* key down until you are finished.

- **Cell B2:** To insert the number 8 in column B for every day of the week, double-click the *fill handle* of cell B2. A double-click on the *fill handle* copies the content down to the first empty cell in the previous or next column. So the double-click does not work when there is no column with data to the immediate left or right.

- **Cell C2:** Double-clicking the *fill handle* of cell C2 gives you a series of 1s. To change this into an incrementing series, click the button that has popped up and select ⊙*Fill Series*. Now the series increments by 1.

- **Cells D2 and D3:** For a series that needs to increment by a value different from 1, create a pattern in the first two cells, select both cells, and then double-click the *fill handle*.

- **Cell E2:** If you do not want to create a pattern ahead of time, double-click the *fill handle* of the first cell only. Now go to the *Fill* button drop-down (located under the Σ button on the *Home* tab) and then choose the option *Series*. Specify any step value (for example, 2).

- **Cell F2:** To multiply D2 by E2, follow these steps (you will appreciate them someday!):

1. Select cell F2.

2. Type the equals sign (=).

3. Press *Left Arrow* twice to get to D2 (that is, do not type D2).

4. Type the multiplication sign (*).

5. Press the *Left Arrow* key once to get to E2.

6. To finish, press *Ctrl+Enter* (not just *Enter*).

Note

What is the advantage of pressing Ctrl+Enter instead of Enter only? You stay in the same cell, so you can just double-click the fill handle to copy the formula all the way down. (Otherwise, you would have to go back to the previous cell first.) Another advantage is this: When you discover a mistake in your formula—after you have copied the formula down and all the cells are still selected—you just correct your formula in the formula bar once, and hitting Ctr+Enter will propagate the correction in all the selected cells

- **Cell G2:** If you always work with the same analysts in the same order, type their names once, select them all, and double-click the *fill handle*. If you want to use this same list over and over again—especially if it's a long list—use the following technique:

  1. If you have a listing on your sheet already, select that listing first.

  2. Click the *File* tab in the left-top corner.

  3. At the bottom of the new box, select *Options*.

  4. In the left panel, choose *Advanced*.

  5. Click *Edit Custom Lists* (in the section *General*).

  6. Accept the highlighted list.

  7. Click the *Import* button.

  8. Click *OK* twice.

Now you can use this list anywhere in Excel. Just type the first name of this (potentially long) list and double-click the *fill handle*—provided that there is a column with contents to the left or right. Excel does the rest!

Chapter 3: Relative vs. Absolute Cell References

Each cell on a sheet has a certain position. When you copy a cell that contains a formula to another position, the formula's cell references automatically adjust. Those references are called *relative*. Sometimes, you do not want formula references to adapt to their new location; in that case, you "lock" them and make them *absolute*.

To see how relative and absolute cell references work, take a look at Figure 1.6. Cell C1 has a formula in it: =A1*B1. You can copy the formula in cell C1 down by double-clicking because, in this case, you *do* want the cell references to change!

	A	B	C	D	E	F
1	1	2	2			% of mean
2	2	4	8		1	8%
3	3	6	18		2	15%
4	4	8	32		7	54%
5	5	10	50		8	62%
6	6	12	72		16	123%
7	7	14	98		17	131%
8	8	16	128		21	162%
9	9	18	162		22	169%
10	10	20	200		23	177%
11				Mean	13	100%
12						
13		Dilute	0.02	0.04	0.06	0.08
14		2	0.04	0.08	0.12	0.16
15		4	0.08	0.16	0.24	0.32
16		6	0.12	0.24	0.36	0.48
17		8	0.16	0.32	0.48	0.64
18		10	0.20	0.40	0.60	0.80
19		12	0.24	0.48	0.72	0.96
20		14	0.28	0.56	0.84	1.12
21		16	0.32	0.64	0.96	1.28
22		18	0.36	0.72	1.08	1.44
23		20	0.40	0.80	1.20	1.60
24						

Figure 1.6

How can you see all formulas at once? Use the shortcut *Ctrl+~* (the tilde is located under the *Esc* key). Notice that *Ctrl+~* tells us that all cell references are relative here—which means: "Multiply two-cells-over-to-the-left by one-cell-over-to-the-left."

In cell F2, however, you want to find out what the value in cell E2 is, as a percentage of the mean in cell E11, using the formula =E2/E11. You accept the formula by pressing *Ctrl+Enter* and then double-click the *fill handle* downward. This time, you get into trouble! *Ctrl+~* reveals the problem: The reference to E11 should be *absolute*; otherwise, the adjusted formula in the downward cells attempts to divide by empty cells, which is an invalid division-by-zero error.

Let's start over in cell F2:

1. Type the equals sign (=) in cell F2.

2. Press the *Left Arrow* key once to get to E2.

3. Type / (in order to divide).

4. Press the *Left Arrow key* once and then *Ctrl+Down Arrow* to get to E11.

5. Press the *F4* key to make E11 "locked" or absolute (that is, $E$11).

6. Press *Ctrl+Enter*.

As a result, the copy behavior of the cell references is correct now: It is partly relative (E2) and partly absolute ($E$11). $ is a string sign that "locks" the column number and/or the row number, making them absolute. *F4* is a cycle key that works like this:

- Pressing *F4* once changes E11 to $E$11.

- Pressing *F4* twice changes E11 to E$11.

- Pressing *F4* three times changes E11 to $E11.

- Pressing *F4* four times takes changes the cell back to E11.

You select the range C14:F23 in order to calculate what the new concentration of a certain solution is if you dilute certain concentrations (in column B) with a particular factor (in row 13). Then you follow these steps:

1. Enter the formula =$B14*C$13 in cell C14.

2. While building the formula in the *formula bar*, select a cell and press *F4* immediately. If you do this at a later stage, you need to click or double-click the cell address that needs to be changed before you press *F4*.

3. Accept this formula with *Ctrl+Enter* so it goes into all the selected cells, where it behaves partially as relative and partially as absolute.

Another way of creating this kind of tables is using Excel's often overlooked *Data Table* feature as we used it in Figure 1.7. The formula in cell B4 calculates the population size after 30 generations (B3), if the growth rate is 2.3 (B2) and the population starts with 2 organisms (B1): =B1*B2^B3. We could create a two-dimensional table based on the two variables growth rate (in column B) and number of generations (in row 4). Then you follow these steps:

	A	B	C	D	E	F	G	H	I
1	Population	2							
2	Growth rate	2.3							
3	Generations	10							
4	Size	8285	5	10	15	20	25	30	generations
5		2.0	64	2,048	65,536	2,097,152	67,108,864	2,147,483,648	
6		2.1	82	3,336	136,245	5,564,369	227,254,433	9,281,300,578	
7		2.2	103	5,312	273,760	14,108,590	727,104,808	37,472,306,040	
8		2.3	129	8,285	533,270	34,323,117	2,209,153,514	142,188,697,582	
9		2.4	159	12,681	1,009,715	80,399,774	6,401,931,729	509,761,752,308	
10		2.5	195	19,073	1,862,645	181,898,940	17,763,568,394	1,734,723,475,977	
11		2.6	238	28,233	3,354,519	398,562,978	47,354,766,002	5,626,397,802,570	
12		2.7	287	41,178	5,908,625	847,823,166	121,653,357,543	17,455,927,136,176	
13		2.8	344	59,239	10,195,311	1,754,650,492	301,981,806,790	51,972,180,241,581	
14		2.9	410	84,141	17,258,377	3,539,891,523	726,072,424,725	148,925,796,883,350	
15		3.0	486	118,098	28,697,814	6,973,568,802	1,694,577,218,886	411,782,264,189,298	
16		rate							
17									

Figure 1.7

1. Select the entire table: B4:H15.

2. Make sure there is a formula at the origin (B4).

3. Go to: *Data* tab | *What-if Analysis* | *Data Table*.

4. Set in the dialog box the *row input cell* to B3 and the *column input cell* to B2.

5. Click the *OK* button

The end result is fabulous. All calculations are done in accordance with the formula at the origin of the table. The table itself (C5:H15) has an array formula in it: {=TABLE(B3,B2)}. Do not type the formula, nor its braces. Each cell is now part of an array and cannot be deleted or changed on its own. You will use Excel's feature of *Data Table* extensively in Chapter 47.

Chapter 4: Range Names

A cell address is like a street number—and both can be difficult to remember. You might want to replace a cell number with a more meaningful address: a cell *name*. A cell *name* basically acts like an absolute cell address, but when used in formulas, it may be more informative. You can also name a range of cells. So you can have cell names and range names, but because a cell is basically also a range, though consisting of only one cell, the term *range name* is more comprehensive.

The top of Figure 1.8 shows a list of readings that several analysts found during several tests. The bottom table marks each combination of a specific analyst and a specific test with a plus sign (+) if that reading was above the grand mean. Instead of comparing each individual reading with the grand mean in $G$12, you could also give cell G12 a more meaningful name—a range *name*. Here's how you do it:

	A	B	C	D	E	F	G
1	Readings	Test1	Test2	Test3	Test4	Test5	Means
2	Analyst1	3.83	5.06	6.08	4.36	8.37	5.54
3	Analyst2	9.83	8.75	7.21	4.85	1.84	6.50
4	Analyst3	9.20	4.07	3.36	6.52	4.76	5.58
5	Analyst4	9.71	3.51	1.19	4.66	3.48	4.51
6	Analyst5	7.29	9.10	9.46	9.05	3.11	7.60
7	Analyst6	6.61	4.53	0.22	0.41	0.31	2.42
8	Analyst7	9.80	7.55	4.62	8.14	9.19	7.86
9	Analyst8	9.73	5.63	0.49	9.22	1.14	5.24
10	Analyst9	3.19	4.20	8.27	4.06	6.21	5.19
11	Analyst10	3.09	1.57	1.07	2.93	5.16	2.76
12	Means	7.23	5.40	4.20	5.42	4.36	5.32
13							
14	>Mean	Test1	Test2	Test3	Test4	Test5	
15	Analyst1			+		+	5.3198
16	Analyst2	+	+	+			5.3198
17	Analyst3	+			+		5.3198
18	Analyst4	+					5.3198
19	Analyst5	+	+	+	+		5.3198
20	Analyst6	+					5.3198
21	Analyst7	+	+		+	+	5.3198
22	Analyst8	+	+		+		5.3198
23	Analyst9			+		+	5.3198
24	Analyst10						5.3198
25							

Figure 1.8

1. Select cell G12.

2. In the *Name* box, found to the left of the *formula bar*, type `GrandMean`. Here are a few rules for naming:

   ◦ Don't include spaces in a range *name*; underscores are okay.

- Names are not case-sensitive, so GrandMean is the same as grandmean, GRANDMEAN, and so on.

- Unique names function in the entire workbook. If you create a duplicate name, the second name will be assigned only to the specific sheet you are in.

3. Press *Enter*. If you don't, the range *name* does not exist.

Now the *name* GrandMean has become official, so you can access the cell *GrandMean* through the drop-down list of the *Name* box—no matter where you are in this workbook—and Excel will take you there!

From now on, you should be able to call the IF function in cell B15. Its first argument is B2>GrandMean. You can just type the new range *name*, or you can click cell G12 to have Excel insert its *name* automatically. The end result in cell B15 is this: =IF(B2>GrandMean,"+","").

Unfortunately, the previously installed range *name* does not kick in when you select multiple cells to fill them with the same formula. You must use an absolute cell address again, or you could use an extra tool: the *Use in Formula* drop-down located on the *Formulas* tab.

Try getting a copy of the grand mean in the cells G15:G24. When you just type the formula in the *Formula bar*, notice that the range *name* nicely pops up once you start typing =Gr…

To find all your range *names* listed, follow these steps:

1. Select the *Formulas* tab.

2. Click the *Name Manager* button.

3. Select the *name* of your choice.

4. Delete that *name* (using the button to the right) or expand/change its reference (at the bottom).

Figure 1.9 shows that you can also name ranges of multiple cells. For example, you could name the first range *Analysts*, the second one *Strains*, and the third one *Readings*. Instead of doing all this manually, you can use a handy Excel tool:

	A	B	C	D	E	F	G
1	Analysts	Strains	Readings			Count	Means
2	Analyst1	Strain1	1.22		Analyst1	5	5.48
3	Analyst1	Strain2	5.19		Analyst2	5	5.13
4	Analyst1	Strain2	8.81		Analyst3	5	5.85
5	Analyst1	Strain3	5.71		Analyst4	5	6.20
6	Analyst1	Strain3	6.46				
7	Analyst2	Strain1	1.23				
8	Analyst2	Strain1	8.22				
9	Analyst2	Strain2	1.70			Count	Means
10	Analyst2	Strain2	6.96		Strain1	6	6.35
11	Analyst2	Strain3	7.54		Strain2	7	5.22
12	Analyst3	Strain1	9.44		Strain3	7	5.52
13	Analyst3	Strain1	9.86				
14	Analyst3	Strain2	2.41				
15	Analyst3	Strain3	0.67				
16	Analyst3	Strain3	6.86				
17	Analyst4	Strain1	8.14				
18	Analyst4	Strain2	1.80				
19	Analyst4	Strain2	9.65				
20	Analyst4	Strain3	5.48				
21	Analyst4	Strain3	5.92				
22							

Figure 1.9

1. Select the entire data set by selecting A1, pressing *Ctrl+Shift+Down Arrow*, and then pressing *Ctrl+-Shift+Right Arrow*.

2. From the *Defined Names* section of the *Formulas* tab, select *Create Names from Selection*.

3. Select *Create Names from Values* in ☑ *Top Row*

4. Check the *Name* box to ensure that the three new names have appeared.

Now try counting in cell F2 how many readings *Analyst1* has—by using the COUNTIF function: =COUNTIF(Analysts,E2). You can do something similar in cell G2 with the SUMIF function: =SUMIF(Analysts,E2,Readings). To find the mean in cell H2, you need both previous columns—or you could use the Excel function AVERAGEIF. Then you can do something similar for the second table: =COUNTIF(Strains,E10) and =SUMIF(Strains,E10,Readings).

There is another interesting feature about range *names* that you may benefit from. Instead of using a formula like =SUM(Readings), you can use the word *Readings* as it is displayed somewhere in a cell. However, you need the function INDIRECT to change the word into a *name*. For example, if cell A1 holds the word *Readings*, the formula =SUM(INDIRECT(A1))   would deliver the same results as =SUM(Readings). Why would you want to make such a detour? The answer is simple: Sometimes you want the headers of a summary table somewhere else in your book to be used in your formulas. One of the exercises at the end of this part offers an example of such a scenario.

Range *names* are great. However, the problem with range *names* is that a new row added at the end of a table, column, or row is not automatically incorporated into the range *name*—so formulas based on that range ignore the new entries. You can solve this problem by either inserting cells inside the range or manually fixing the range reference through the *Name Manager*. Neither solution is ideal.

Figure 1.10 shows how you can handle this problem in a better way, by using Excel's *table* structure. First of all, the table itself has automatically been given a default name (as you can see in the *Name* box). When you want to "talk" to the *table* structure from outside the *table*, you must use this *name*. You just type something like the following somewhere in a cell outside the *table*: = `Table1[`. Yes, the keystroke at the end is a bracket, not a parenthesis! As soon as you type the first bracket, several range *names* pop up:

	A	B	C	D	E	F	G
	F2			f_x	=COUNTIF(Table1[Analysts],E2)		
1	Analysts	Strains	Readings			Count	Means
2	Analyst1	Strain1	1.22		Analyst1	5	5.478
3	Analyst1	Strain2	5.19		Analyst2	5	5.13
4	Analyst1	Strain2	8.81		Analyst3	5	5.848
5	Analyst1	Strain3	5.71		Analyst4	5	6.198
6	Analyst1	Strain3	6.46				
7	Analyst2	Strain1	1.23				
8	Analyst2	Strain1	8.22				
9	Analyst2	Strain2	1.70			Count	Means
10	Analyst2	Strain2	6.96		Strain1	6	6.351666667
11	Analyst2	Strain3	7.54		Strain2	7	5.217142857
12	Analyst3	Strain1	9.44		Strain3	7	5.52
13	Analyst3	Strain1	9.86				
14	Analyst3	Strain2	2.41				
15	Analyst3	Strain3	0.67				
16	Analyst3	Strain3	6.86				
17	Analyst4	Strain1	8.14				
18	Analyst4	Strain2	1.80				
19	Analyst4	Strain2	9.65				
20	Analyst4	Strain3	5.48				
21	Analyst4	Strain3	5.92				
22							

Figure 1.10

- *Analysts* (A2:A21 in this example)

- *Strains* (B2:B21 in this example)

- *Readings* (C2:C21 in this example)

- *#All* (A1:C21 in this example)

- *#Data* (A2:C21 in this example)

- *#Headers* (A1:C1 in this example)

- *#Totals* (missing in this example)

A great feature of a *table* name is that it adjusts to a new range whenever you use its "drag button" in the right-lower corner. Be careful, though! When you have selected the last cell, the drag button is hidden behind the *fill handle* of the selected cell. So you must select another cell first in order to make the drag button accessible.

Now let's tackle the formulas in the two summary tables to the right. This time, you manually type the COUN-TIF formula in cell F2. (Notice how much help you get here.) You end up with the following two formulas: =COUNTIF(Table1[Analysts],E2) and =SUMIF(Table1[Analysts],E2,Table1[Readings]).

But what can you do if you don't want to create a *table* structure? Is there another way of making range names automatically expand when new rows or columns have been added at the end? Yes, there is! Although it is not an easy way, it is sometimes highly advantageous. You use the OFFSET function in the *Name Manager*. The OFFSET function has the following syntax: =OFFSET(*start-cell, row-offset, col-offset, number-of-rows, number-of-columns*). To assign a dynamic *name* to the table in the columns A:C, you take these steps:

1. Open *Name Manager* on the *Formulas* tab.

2. Type a new *name* for the table, such as MyTable, MyColumn, or MyRow.

3. In the *Refers To* box, type =OFFSET($A$1,0,0,COUNTA($A:$A),COUNTA($1:$1)). This is how the formula works:

   ◦ The *name*'s reference starts in A1.

   ◦ You want to keep that cell as a starting point, so you offset by 0 rows and 0 columns.

   ◦ You find the height of the range by counting all non-empty cells in column A. You need to make sure there are no hidden cells below the table.

   ◦ You find the width of the range by counting all non-empty cells in row 1. You need to make sure there are no hidden cells to the right of the table (which is not the case here!).

Whenever rows or columns are added to the data set or deleted, the two COUNTA functions inside OFFSET automatically take care of the size of the adjusted range.

Chapter 5: Nested Functions

Formulas in Excel contain calculations and/or functions. What is the difference between them?

- Calculations work with operators such as `()`, `^`, `*`, `/`, `+`, and `−` (in this order of precedence). So whereas `2+4/2` is 4 in Excel, `(2+4)/2` returns 3. To create the square root of the number 4 by using operators, you need parentheses as well: `=4^(1/2)`.

- Functions are built-in operations, such as `=SUM(A1:A3)`, which is equivalent to the calculation `=A1+A2+A3`. Most functions accept or require one or more arguments inside their parentheses. For instance, the square root of 4 done with a function would require one argument: `SQRT(4)`.

- Formulas can be a combination of calculations and functions. There can be calculations inside functions (for instance, `=SUM(A1:A3)*0.05`), and there can be functions inside calculations (for example, `=ROUND(A1/B1,1)`).

- Formulas can also nest functions inside functions (for example, `=ROUND(SUM(A1:A3), 2)`). In this case, the SUM function is nested inside the ROUND function.

You can just type these formulas into a cell, but don't forget to start with an equals sign if you do so. When you type functions, you receive some help as to their syntax: which arguments there are and in which order. Notice also that some arguments are shown in bold, which means they are required for the function to work; the functions that are not bold are optional and can be skipped most of the time.

To get more extensive help, you should use one of these three options:

- The f_x button on the *Formula bar*

- The Σ drop-down button on the *Home* tab

- One of the buttons on the *Formulas* tab

Figure 1.11 shows the use of two different functions: in column A, the function RAND (generating a random number between 0 and 1) and in column B, the function ROUND (to round RAND to two decimals). You could combine these two operations into one column (column C) by using a nested function. Here's how you do it:

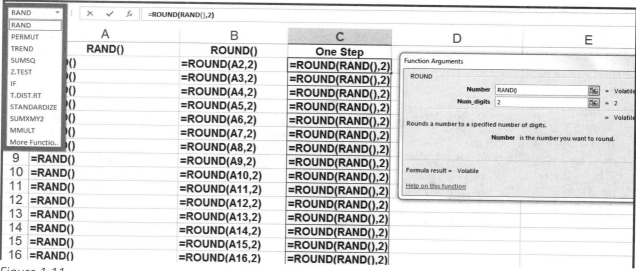

Figure 1.11

1. Start the ROUND function, this time from the f_x button.

2. Ensure that the first argument of the ROUND function is a nested RAND function. You get this second function from a new drop-down section located where the *Name* box used to be (probably

under *More Functions*). When you do so, the ROUND function dialog box gets replaced by the RAND function dialog box.

3. Do **not** click *OK* because you are not yet done with ROUND. You get back to ROUND by clicking its name in the *Formula bar* (not in the *Name* box). When you are back in the ROUND box, you can complete the second argument, and then click *OK* (or *Ctrl+Enter*, if you have multiple cells selected).

Figure 1.12 shows a spreadsheet in which you mark each analyst with a plus sign if both tests came out above the mean; otherwise, there is no marker. In this case, you need two functions: the function IF to test for values above the mean and the function AND to check for both tests at the same time; in other words, AND should be nested inside IF. Here's how it works:

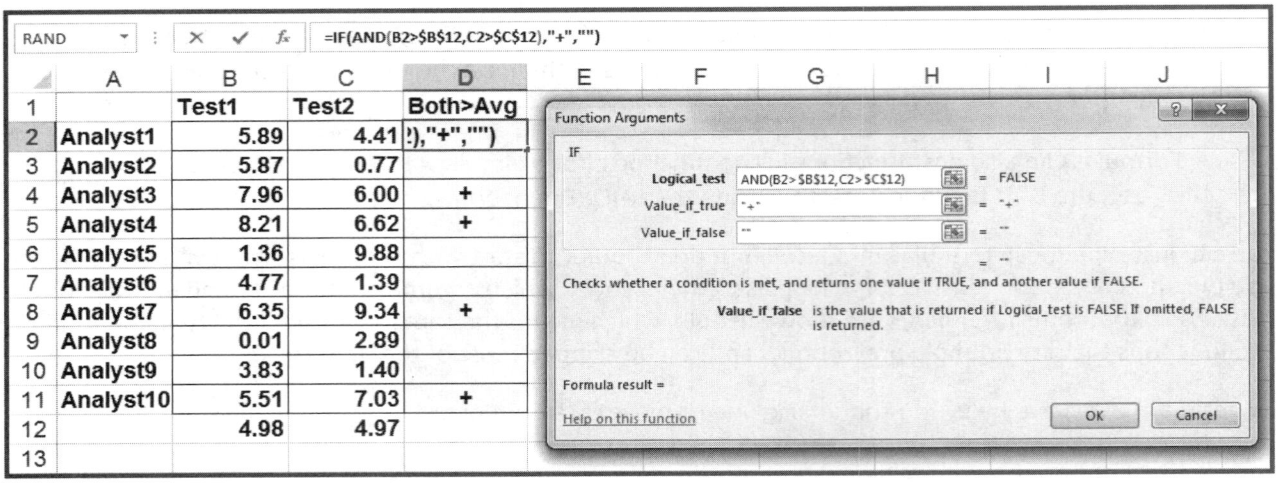

Figure 1.12

1. Call the function IF from f_x.

2. Give the first argument an AND function from the former *Name* box:
AND(B2>$B$12,C2>$C$12).

3. Instead of clicking *OK*, click the word IF in the formula bar.

4. When you are back in IF, finish the formula: =IF(AND(B2>$B$12,C2>$C$12),"+","").

Could you just type this formula from scratch? Sure you could, but when the syntax gets more complicated, those function dialog boxes protect you from making mistakes, and they provide more help when you are dealing with a function you are not familiar with.

<u>Note</u>

In addition to the AND function, there is also an OR function. Whereas AND returns TRUE when all its arguments are true, OR returns TRUE if at least one of its arguments is true. Then there is also a function XOR. The difference between OR and XOR is a follows: OR is inclusive and XOR is exclusive. For instance, OR(A,B) is true if A is true, or B, or both. But *XOR(A,B)* is like either-or; it is only true if A is true, or if B is true, but not both at the same time. To give an example, if A stands for high-HDL and B for high-LDL, the formula *XOR(A,B)* would only spot those who have either a high-HDL or a high-LDL, but not both at the same time.

Figure 1.13 shows the same spreadsheet as in figure 1.12 (with two named ranges), but this time with a table structure. Here are the steps to implement the formulas:

	A	B	C	D
1	Analysts	Test1	Test2	Both>Avg
2	Analyst1	5.89	4.41	
3	Analyst2	5.87	0.77	
4	Analyst3	7.96	6.00	+
5	Analyst4	8.21	6.62	+
6	Analyst5	1.36	9.88	
7	Analyst6	4.77	1.39	
8	Analyst7	6.35	9.34	+
9	Analyst8	0.01	2.89	
10	Analyst9	3.83	1.40	
11	Analyst10	5.51	7.03	+
12				

Figure 1.13

1. Start typing in cell D2: `=IF(AND(`.

2. Use the *Left arrow* twice, which inserts `B2`.

3. Notice what pops up: `Table1[[#ThisRow],[Test1]]`

4. Finish the formula and notice how the formula nicely permeates the column.

5. When you drag the button in the right lower corner of the table one row down, you can add a new record. Once you enter data in A12:C12, the formula in D12 will automatically kick in.

Now that you know these basic techniques, you can use them when dealing with the analysis of scientific data—whether you're doing data analysis (discussed in Part 2), data plotting (Part 3), regression analysis (Part 4), or statistical analysis (Part 5). Read on!

Part 1 Exercises

You can download all the files used in this book from www.genesispc.com/Science2013.htm, where you can find each file in its original version (to work on) and in its finished version (to check your solutions).

1. The Fill Handle

1.1. Make column D completely identical to column A by using just the *fill handle* (and, if needed, the *Ctrl* key).

1.2. Make column E completely identical to column B by using just the *fill handle* (and, if needed, the *Ctrl* key).

	A	B	C	D	E	
1	Plate1	Cycle1		Plate1	Cycle1	
2	Plate1	Cycle2				
3	Plate1	Cycle3				
4	Plate1	Cycle4				
5	Plate1	Cycle5				
6	Plate1	Cycle6				
7	Plate1	Cycle7				
8	Plate1	Cycle8				
9	Plate1	Cycle9				
10	Plate1	Cycle10				
11	Plate2	Cycle1				
12	Plate2	Cycle2				
13	Plate2	Cycle3				
14	Plate2	Cycle4				
15	Plate2	Cycle5				
16	Plate2	Cycle6				
17	Plate2	Cycle7				
18	Plate2	Cycle8				
19	Plate2	Cycle9				
20	Plate2	Cycle10				
21						

2. Relative vs. Absolute Cell References

2.1. Select the range D4:H15 and implement the equation shown below the table in a single step. (Note: The value 1.96 features in cell B2, so use its "locked" cell reference.)

2.2. Do the same for range L4:P15 but this time with the value 1.65 (in cell J2).

	A	B	C	D	E	F	G	H	I	J	K	L	M	N	O	P
1																
2		1.96				margin/mean				1.65				margin/mean		
3				0.01	0.02	0.05	0.1	0.25				0.01	0.02	0.05	0.1	0.25
4			0.1	384	96	15	4	1			0.1	272	68	11	3	0
5			0.2	1537	384	61	15	2			0.2	1089	272	44	11	2
6			0.3	3457	864	138	35	6			0.3	2450	613	98	25	4
7			0.4	6147	1537	246	61	10			0.4	4356	1089	174	44	7
8			0.5	9604	2401	384	96	15			0.5	6806	1702	272	68	11
9		SD/mean	0.6	13830	3457	553	138	22		SD/mean	0.6	9801	2450	392	98	16
10			0.7	18824	4706	753	188	30			0.7	13340	3335	534	133	21
11			0.8	24586	6147	983	246	39			0.8	17424	4356	697	174	28
12			0.9	31117	7779	1245	311	50			0.9	22052	5513	882	221	35
13			1	38416	9604	1537	384	61			1	27225	6806	1089	272	44
14			2	153664	38416	6147	1537	246			2	108900	27225	4356	1089	174
15			3	345744	86436	13830	3457	553			3	245025	61256	9801	2450	392
16																

$$n = \left(\frac{1.96}{margin \: / \: \mu} \right)^2 \left(\frac{SD}{\mu} \right)^2$$

3. Data Tables

3.1. We calculate a confidence margin in cell B5: `=CONFIDENCE(B4,B2,B3)`.

3.2. In cell B6 are the two confidence limits: `=ROUND(B1-B5,2) & " - " & ROUND(B1+B5,2)`. The ampersand (&) "hooks" entities together.

3.3. Implement a *Data Table* by using different standard deviations in C6:I6 and different sample sizes in B7:B15.

	A	B	C	D	E	F	G	H	I	J
1	Mean	40								
2	SD	2.5								
3	Sample size	30								
4	2-tailed error level	5%								
5	confidence margin	0.895								
6	95% confidence limits	39.11 - 40.89	2.0	2.5	3.0	3.5	4.0	4.5	5.0	SD
7		30	39.28 - 40.72	39.11 - 40.89	38.93 - 41.07	38.75 - 41.25	38.57 - 41.43	38.39 - 41.61	38.21 - 41.79	
8		35	39.34 - 40.66	39.17 - 40.83	39.01 - 40.99	38.84 - 41.16	38.67 - 41.33	38.51 - 41.49	38.34 - 41.66	
9		40	39.38 - 40.62	39.23 - 40.77	39.07 - 40.93	38.92 - 41.08	38.76 - 41.24	38.61 - 41.39	38.45 - 41.55	
10		45	39.42 - 40.58	39.27 - 40.73	39.12 - 40.88	38.98 - 41.02	38.83 - 41.17	38.69 - 41.31	38.54 - 41.46	
11		50	39.45 - 40.55	39.31 - 40.69	39.17 - 40.83	39.03 - 40.97	38.89 - 41.11	38.75 - 41.25	38.61 - 41.39	
12		55	39.47 - 40.53	39.34 - 40.66	39.21 - 40.79	39.08 - 40.92	38.94 - 41.06	38.81 - 41.19	38.68 - 41.32	
13		60	39.49 - 40.51	39.37 - 40.63	39.24 - 40.76	39.11 - 40.89	38.99 - 41.01	38.86 - 41.14	38.73 - 41.27	
14		65	39.51 - 40.49	39.39 - 40.61	39.27 - 40.73	39.15 - 40.85	39.03 - 40.97	38.91 - 41.09	38.78 - 41.22	
15		75	39.55 - 40.45	39.43 - 40.57	39.32 - 40.68	39.21 - 40.79	39.09 - 40.91	38.98 - 41.02	38.87 - 41.13	
16		sample size								
17										

4. Range Names

4.1. Use Excel's handy and quick *Name* tool to name each column in the left section with its label name.

4.2. In the table in H2:K5, calculate the correlation between any two variables used in the data set to the left. Use the labels of your correlation table in combination with the functions CORREL and INDIRECT.

	A	B	C	D	E	F	G	H	I	J	K
1	Age	Weight	Height	FVC				Age	Weight	Height	FVC
2	55	1.84	1.41	2.67			Age	1	-0.122390	-0.778753	-0.980487
3	59	1.80	1.41	2.80			Weight	-0.122390	1	0.328697	0.069172
4	44	1.53	1.50	3.21			Height	-0.778753	0.328697	1	0.775915
5	37	1.50	1.54	3.32			FVC	-0.980487	0.069172	0.775915	1
6	50	1.57	1.54	2.87							
7	48	1.90	1.55	3.01							
8	45	1.89	1.56	2.96							
9	40	1.50	1.57	3.21							
10	26	1.73	1.57	3.56							
11	52	1.92	1.60	2.82							
12	56	1.64	1.41	2.74							
13	44	1.66	1.46	3.14							
14	53	1.88	1.51	2.82							
15	36	1.78	1.54	3.39							
16	46	1.71	1.56	2.98							
17	35	1.71	1.60	3.41							
18	31	1.98	1.65	3.44							
19	23	1.77	1.67	3.73							
20	36	1.71	1.73	3.30							
21	27	1.51	1.74	3.67							
22	37	1.93	1.75	3.28							
23	28	1.99	1.75	3.63							
24	23	1.96	1.77	3.73							
25	21	1.73	1.78	3.77							
26	40	1.79	1.78	3.38							
27	30	1.98	1.82	3.46							
28	24	1.74	1.91	3.77							
29	30	1.72	1.91	3.60							
30	31	1.99	1.91	3.46							
31	22	1.87	1.95	3.71							
32											

5. Nested Functions

5.1. In cell B2, use the function ADDRESS with the nested functions ROW and COLUMN to get the address of cell A1.

5.2. In cell F2, use the function CONCATENATE with the nested functions LEFT and RIGHT. Because you want to get the number 10 in cells F11 and F21 (instead of 0), you may have to also use the function LEN nested inside RIGHT.

	A	B	C	D	E	F
1		**Address**				**Combine**
2	1	$A$2		Plate1	Cycle1	Pla1-Cy1
3	2	$A$3		Plate1	Cycle2	Pla1-Cy2
4	3	$A$4		Plate1	Cycle3	Pla1-Cy3
5	4	$A$5		Plate1	Cycle4	Pla1-Cy4
6	5	$A$6		Plate1	Cycle5	Pla1-Cy5
7	6	$A$7		Plate1	Cycle6	Pla1-Cy6
8	7	$A$8		Plate1	Cycle7	Pla1-Cy7
9	8	$A$9		Plate1	Cycle8	Pla1-Cy8
10	9	$A$10		Plate1	Cycle9	Pla1-Cy9
11	10	$A$11		Plate1	Cycle10	Pla1-Cy10
12	11	$A$12		Plate2	Cycle1	Pla2-Cy1
13	12	$A$13		Plate2	Cycle2	Pla2-Cy2
14	13	$A$14		Plate2	Cycle3	Pla2-Cy3
15	14	$A$15		Plate2	Cycle4	Pla2-Cy4
16	15	$A$16		Plate2	Cycle5	Pla2-Cy5
17	16	$A$17		Plate2	Cycle6	Pla2-Cy6
18	17	$A$18		Plate2	Cycle7	Pla2-Cy7
19	18	$A$19		Plate2	Cycle8	Pla2-Cy8
20	19	$A$20		Plate2	Cycle9	Pla2-Cy9
21	20	$A$21		Plate2	Cycle10	Pla2-Cy10
22						

6. Nested Functions

6.1. In column C, round the standard deviation of the two values to the left to two decimals by using the function `STDEV` (or `STDEV.S`) nested inside the function `ROUND`.

6.3. You receive errors in column C, so improve your formula in column G by nesting the previous formula inside an `IF` function that tests for standard deviation errors by using the function `ISERROR`, or use its shorter version, the function `IFERROR`.

	A	B	C	D	E	F	G
1			SD errors				Correct
2	0.45	6.32	4.15		0.45	6.32	4.15
3	10.63	5.86	3.37		10.63	5.86	3.37
4	8.92		#DIV/0!		8.92		
5	8.77	14.22	3.85		8.77	14.22	3.85
6	1.02	6.64	3.97		1.02	6.64	3.97
7		3.90	#DIV/0!			3.90	
8	9.06	9.71	0.46		9.06	9.71	0.46
9	8.96	11.83	2.03		8.96	11.83	2.03
10	1.85	3.85	1.41		1.85	3.85	1.41
11	5.27	10.80	3.91		5.27	10.80	3.91
12			#DIV/0!				
13	3.70	4.70	0.71		3.70	4.70	0.71
14	0.88	2.44	1.10		0.88	2.44	1.10
15	12.36	2.09	7.26		12.36	2.09	7.26
16	9.45	13.37	2.77		9.45	13.37	2.77
17	6.90	3.74	2.23		6.90	3.74	2.23
18	1.20	11.85	7.53		1.20	11.85	7.53
19	10.40	0.12	7.27		10.40	0.12	7.27
20	1.48	13.67	8.62		1.48	13.67	8.62
21	12.57	12.30	0.19		12.57	12.30	0.19
22	Mean SD		#DIV/0!		Mean SD		3.58
23							

7. Nested Functions

7.1. Use the *Name* tool to name B2:B11 *Test1* and C2:C11 *Test2*.

7.2. Mark column D with a plus for analysts who have both tests between mean-minus-SD and the mean-plus-SD. This is going to be a heavily nested function: STDEV inside AVERAGE inside AND inside another AND inside IF.

7.3. You can do this by typing the entire formula or by stepping from dialog box to dialog box starting with f_x.

7.4. If the *Formula bar* becomes too cramped, click the expand button to the right of the bar.

	A	B	C	D
1		Test1	Test2	-SD<X>+SD
2	Analyst1	5.89	4.41	+
3	Analyst2	5.87	0.77	
4	Analyst3	7.96	6.00	
5	Analyst4	8.21	6.62	
6	Analyst5	1.36	9.88	
7	Analyst6	4.77	1.39	
8	Analyst7	6.35	9.34	
9	Analyst8	0.01	2.89	
10	Analyst9	3.83	1.40	
11	Analyst10	5.51	7.03	+
12				
13		both named		
14				

Part 2: Data Analysis

Chapter 6: Auto-numbering

To make record keeping easier, it may be wise to implement a good numbering system for each row or record in your data set on your spreadsheet. You need to know about some of Excel's dedicated tools and functions before you take on your records' numbering system.

Figure 2.1 provides an overview of Excel's rounding functions. All numbers in the top row have been rounded with various functions—some always round down; others round toward zero, depending on whether they are in the positive or negative range; and so on.

	5.8378581	6.3023967	5.6891037	0.7981612	5.2418008	-7.9780912	-3.5669476
ABS	5.8378581	6.3023967	5.6891037	0.7981612	5.2418008	7.97809123	3.56694757
INT	5	6	5	0	5	-8	-4
TRUNC	5	6	5	0	5	-7	-3
QUOTIENT	2	3	2	0	2	-3	-1
MOD	1.8378581	0.3023967	1.6891037	0.7981612	1.2418008	0.02190877	0.43305243
FLOOR(..., 0.5)	5.5	6	5.5	0.5	5	-8	-4
FLOOR(..., -0.5)	#NUM!	#NUM!	#NUM!	#NUM!	#NUM!	-7.5	-3.5
CEILING(..., 0.5)	6	6.5	6	1	5.5	-7.5	-3.5
CEILING(..., -0.5]	#NUM!	#NUM!	#NUM!	#NUM!	#NUM!	-8	-4
EVEN	6	8	6	2	6	-8	-4
ODD	7	7	7	1	7	-9	-5
ROUND(..., 2)	5.84	6.3	5.69	0.8	5.24	-7.98	-3.57
ROUNDDOWN	5.83	6.3	5.68	0.79	5.24	-7.97	-3.56
ROUNDUP	5.84	6.31	5.69	0.8	5.25	-7.98	-3.57
ROUNDEVEN	-	-	-	-	-	-	-
n signif. digits	1	2	3	4	5	6	7
ROUNDn	6.00000000	6.30000000	5.69000000	0.79820000	5.24180000	-7.97809000	-3.56694800

(side legend: up — 3, 2, 1, 0, -1, -2, -3 — toward 0 — down)

Figure 2.1

This chapter focuses on four of the rounding functions:

- **INT:** This function returns the integer part of a number but rounds down; for example, INT(7/2) returns 3, but INT(-7/2) returns -4.

- **TRUNC:** This function returns the integer part of a number but rounds toward zero; for example, TRUNC(7/2) returns 3, and TRUNC(-7/2) returns -3.

- **QUOTIENT:** This function returns the integer part of a number after division; for example, QUOTIENT(7,2) returns 3.

- **MOD:** This function returns the remainder of a division; for example, MOD(7,2) returns 1

- There is one more function you should know about in this context—the ROW function:

  ○ =ROW() returns the number of the row the formula is located in.

  ○ =ROW(A1) returns the row number of cell A1, which is 1. When you copy the formula downward, the reference to A1 automatically updates to A2, and so on.

Figure 2.2 shows you some fancy automatic numbering systems:

	A	B	C	D	E	F	G	H	I
1	1		001		1000		1		1
2	2		002		1001		2		1
3	3		003		1002		3		1
4	4		004		1003		4		1
5	5		005		1004		5		1
6	6		006		1005		1		2
7	7		007		1006		2		2
8	8		008		1007		3		2
9	9		009		1008		4		2
10	10		010		1009		5		2
11	11		011		1010		1		3
12	12		012		1011		2		3
13	13		013		1012		3		3
14	14		014		1013		4		3
15	15		015		1014		5		3
16	16		016		1015		1		4
17	17		017		1016		2		4
18	18		018		1017		3		4
19	19		019		1018		4		4
20	20		020		1019		5		4

Figure 2.2

- **A1:** =ROW()

- **C1:** =RIGHT("000" & ROW(),3). The ampersand (&) is a string connector to hook things together. The function RIGHT takes the last three digits in this case.

- **E1:** =ROW(A1000). The ROW function's argument allows you to start at a higher number, and it adjusts to copying.

- **G1:** =MOD(ROW()-1,5)+1. After each fifth row, the number starts all over again.

- **I1:** =QUOTIENT(ROW()-1,5)+1. The number repeats itself five times.

Here are three important steps to use in implementing an auto-numbering system:

- You can select the entire numbering range at once. To do so, you click in the start cell (for example, A1), then in the *Name* box, type the address of the end cell (for example, A1000), and press *Shift+Enter* to select the entire range in between.

- Now you can just start your function or formula, which automatically ends up in the start cell; then you press *Ctrl+Enter* to place that formula in all the selected cells

- Finally, you can change the formulas into real numbers by copying the entire section with *Copy*, then selecting *Paste Special*, and choosing ⊙ *Values Only*.

Figure 2.3 shows a different kind of auto-numbering system: It places a series of values (A1:E20) into a number of bins (in column I). In cell G2, you can determine how many bins you would like (from 5 to 30). Note the following about Figure 2.3:

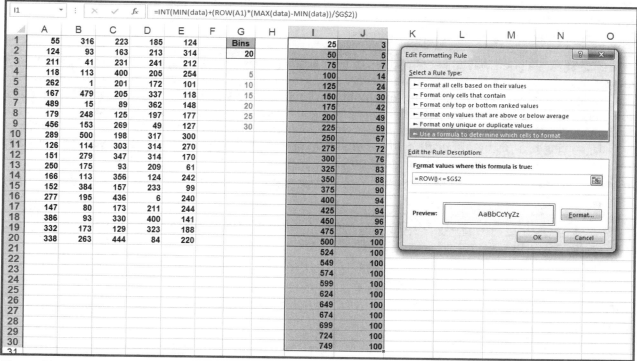

Figure 2.3

- The range of the series of values has been named *data*.

- Cell G2 allows you to change the number of bins with a drop-down box: *Data | Data Validation | Allow*: List | *Source*: =$G$4:$G$9.

- When you change the number of bins, the frequency bins adjust automatically, thanks to a formula in the cells I1:I30 that uses the functions INT, ROW, MIN, and MAX: =INT(MIN(-data)+(ROW(A1)*(MAX(data)-MIN(data))/$G$2)). This is not the perfect formula yet, but good enough for now.

- In column J, we list the frequency of each bin. To do so, select the entire range J1:J30 at once, insert the formula =FREQUENCY(data,I1:I30), but accept it with *Ctrl+Shift+Enter* (this is required because we are dealing with an array function; more on this later).

- Range I1:J30 changes its colored range according to cell G2. To do so select the entire range: *Home | Conditional Formatting | New Rule | Use a Formula |* =ROW()<=$G$2 | Select a format.

Chapter 7: Subtotals

A common step in data analysis is to create subtotals for specific subsets of records. Subtotals can be sums, means, standard deviations, and similar summary calculations. This step can become a tremendous task in large spreadsheets if you're not familiar with the right tools to do so quickly and efficiently. As you'll learn in this chapter, you have to follow a few basic rules.

Figure 2.4 shows a good way of keeping track of your readings, measurements, observations, or what have you. Of course, in your real life, the number of records is much, much larger than is shown here. In addition, you would not want to repeat recurring information in each record as is done here because that would be a time-consuming job—and also a potential source of error. However, the advantage of not replicating repetitive information turns into a grave disadvantage when you need to reshuffle records. If you have incomplete records, sorting records by a specific column would change a neat list into a mess. (So if you have tried to sort, undo the sorting before the power goes off!)

	A	B	C	D	E	F	G	H
1	Plate ID	Analyst	50 ng/mL	%CV	25 ng/mL	%CV	10 ng/mL	%CV
2	8696p08a	gmv	52.3	1.0	26.5	2.0	12.2	2.0
3			49.7	2.0	25.0	1.0	11.2	3.0
4		ksm	56.4	12.0	29.1	11.0	12.8	9.0
5			51.3	2.0	26.9	1.0	11.7	1.0
6	8696p08b	bdo	52.9	3.0	27.5	6.0	13.1	9.0
7			50.1	1.0	26.8	3.0	12.1	2.0
8		ksm	51.0	1.0	26.1	1.0	12.3	2.0
9			48.6	1.0	24.8	0.0	11.4	2.0
10	8697p58b	tjk	47.5	0.0	22.7	2.0	9.6	8.0
11			47.5	1.0	22.9	3.0	9.4	0.0
12		tkm	43.2	4.0	22.6	3.0	9.4	4.0
13			44.3	3.0	22.6	3.0	9.4	6.0
14	8877p58a	gmv	47.7	2.0	22.7	0.0	10.3	0.0
15			48.7	3.0	23.0	3.0	10.0	0.0
16		tjk	49.3	0.0	23.0	1.0	10.4	3.0
17			45.9	2.0	22.9	1.0	9.8	1.0
18	8877p58b	bdo	43.2	4.0	22.6	3.0	9.6	4.0
19			44.3	3.0	20.7	3.0	9.7	6.0
20		tkm	47.5	0.0	22.7	2.0	9.6	8.0
21			45.9	1.0	22.9	3.0	9.4	0.0
22								

Figure 2.4

Apparently, you really need to fill all those blank cells. Here is an easy, quick, and efficient way to select all blank cells in this list and fill them with the same data contained in the previous cell:

1. Select columns A and B

2. Click *Find & Select* on the *Home* tab.

3. Select *Go To Special*.

4. Choose ⊙ *Blanks*.

5. Now all blank cells have been selected. Do not lose what you have selected but just start typing (automatically in the active cell B3): =B2 (or just press the *Up Arrow* so you go to the cell above where you are).

6. Press *Ctrl+Enter* to place this formula in all selected cells.

7. Replace the formulas with their values by selecting *Copy, Paste Special,* ⊙ *Values Only*.

Figure 2.5 shows the completed list with subtotals. Say that you want to calculate the standard deviations per plate and per analyst who worked on that plate. The first step is to ensure that the list or data set is properly sorted for this purpose. This is an example of multilevel sorting, which you can achieve by following these steps:

	A	B	C	D	E	F	G	H
1	Plate ID	Analyst	50 ng/mL	%CV	25 ng/mL	%CV	10 ng/mL	%CV
2	8696p08a	gmv	52.3	1.0	26.5	2.0	12.2	2.0
3	8696p08a	gmv	49.7	2.0	25.0	1.0	11.2	3.0
4		gmv StdDev	1.838478		1.06066		0.707107	
5	8696p08a	ksm	56.4	12.0	29.1	11.0	12.8	9.0
6	8696p08a	ksm	51.3	2.0	26.9	1.0	11.7	1.0
7		ksm StdDev	3.606245		1.555635		0.777817	
8	8696p08a StdDev		2.858175		1.693861		0.684957	
9	8696p08b	bdo	52.9	3.0	27.5	6.0	13.1	9.0
10	8696p08b	bdo	50.1	1.0	26.8	3.0	12.1	2.0
11		bdo StdDev	1.979899		0.494975		0.707107	
12	8696p08b	ksm	51.0	1.0	26.1	1.0	12.3	2.0
13	8696p08b	ksm	48.6	1.0	24.8	0.0	11.4	2.0
14		ksm StdDev	1.697056		0.919239		0.636396	
15	8696p08b StdDev		1.79722		1.15181		0.699405	
16	8697p58b	tjk	47.5	0.0	22.7	2.0	9.6	8.0
17	8697p58b	tjk	47.5	1.0	22.9	3.0	9.4	0.0
18		tjk StdDev	0		0.141421		0.141421	
19	8697p58b	tkm	43.2	4.0	22.6	3.0	9.4	4.0
20	8697p58b	tkm	44.3	3.0	22.6	3.0	9.4	6.0
21		tkm StdDev	0.777817		0		0	
22	8697p58b StdDev		2.211146		0.141421		0.1	

Figure 2.5

1. Click anywhere inside your data set.

2. Click the *Sort* button on the *Data* tab.

3. Add the first level: *Plate ID*.

4. Add the second level: *Analyst*.

When the sorting order is correct, do the following:

1. Click *Subtotal* on the *Data* tab.

2. *At Each Change in*: Plate ID.

3. Use the STDEV function.

4. Select the three columns for which you want subtotals.

Not only do you get beautiful subtotals, you also get a great outlining tool to the left of the sheet: #1 shows only the grand total(s); #2 shows only subtotals; #3 shows all the details as well. If you want to change the format of the subtotals row only, do the following:

1. Select the #2 level. *(NL1)*

2. Select all the cells you want to format. However, this includes also the hidden rows (7-10, 12-15, etc.)

3. Therefore, we need to take extra steps: *Find & Select | GoTo Special | ⊙ Visible cells only*.

4. Now choose the format you want; it will not be applied to the hidden rows.

To add another level of subtotals, you follow these steps:

1. Click *Subtotal* again.

2. *At Each Change in*: *Analyst*.

3. Make sure the option *Replace* is checked off—unless you do want to replace the current ones.

Note

If you ever want to get rid of the subtotals, do this: *Data* tab | *Subtotals* | Click the button *Remove All*. Be aware, though, that there is no *Undo* option, so you may have to start all over if you want subtotals again.

If you prefer Excel's *Table* structure over the list or data set shown in Figure 2.5, be aware that the *Subtotal* tool does not work on a *Table* structure. Since subtotals are really handy, you may decide to change the Excel *table* back into a regular list. Follow these steps:

1. Click inside the *table*.

2. Click the *Design* tab.

3. Select *Convert to Range*. You're now back in a regular set of rows, so you can create your subtotals.

Note

The terminology may be a bit confusing at this point. When we speak of a series of records, I use the words "list," "data set," or "database." In addition, Excel also uses the term "table,"which is a list or data set with a "table" structure, including alternating rows and some fancy editing tools. Finally, we discussed already in Chapter 3 that Excel also offers a "Data Table" that has usually a formula at its origin and manipulates this formula. Let us try to keep the terminology straight.

Figure 2.6 shows a list that has columns that were created in the "wrong" order. Changing their order—especially if you have a large number of columns—would be another enormous job. But you can use the following trick:

	A	B	C	D	E	F	G	H	I
1	1	2	7	8	5	6	3	4	⇒
2	Plate ID	Analyst	50 ng/mL	%CV	25 ng/mL	%CV	10 ng/mL	%CV	
3	8877p58a	gmv	47.7	2.0	22.7	0.0	10.3	0.0	
4	8877p58a	gmv	48.7	3.0	23.0	3.0	10.0	0.0	
5	8877p58a	tjk	49.3	0.0	23.0	1.0	10.4	3.0	
6	8877p58a	tjk	45.9	2.0	22.9	1.0	9.8	1.0	
7	8877p58b	tkm	47.5	0.0	22.7	2.0	9.6	8.0	
8	8877p58b	tkm	45.9	1.0	22.9	3.0	9.4	0.0	
9	8877p58b	bdo	43.2	4.0	22.6	3.0	9.6	4.0	
10	8877p58b	bdo	44.3	3.0	20.7	3.0	9.7	6.0	
11	8696p08a	ksm	56.4	12.0	29.1	11.0	12.8	9.0	
12	8696p08a	ksm	51.3	2.0	26.9	1.0	11.7	1.0	
13	8696p08a	gmv	52.3	1.0	26.5	2.0	12.2	2.0	
14	8696p08a	gmv	49.7	2.0	25.0	1.0	11.2	3.0	
15	8696p08b	bdo	52.9	3.0	27.5	6.0	13.1	9.0	
16	8696p08b	bdo	50.1	1.0	26.8	3.0	12.1	2.0	
17	8696p08b	ksm	51.0	1.0	26.1	1.0	12.3	2.0	
18	8696p08b	ksm	48.6	1.0	24.8	0.0	11.4	2.0	
19	8697p58b	tjk	47.5	0.0	22.7	2.0	9.6	8.0	
20	8697p58b	tjk	47.5	1.0	22.9	3.0	9.4	0.0	
21	8697p58b	tkm	43.2	4.0	22.6	3.0	9.4	4.0	
22	8697p58b	tkm	44.3	3.0	22.6	3.0	9.4	6.0	
23									

Figure 2.6

1. Create a dummy row by inserting an empty row before row 1.

2. Give each column a rank number (in the order in which you want the columns to appear).

3. Go here: *Data* tab | *Sort* | Sort by Row 1 | *Options* | ⊙ *Sort Left to Right*.

4. Now you can delete the dummy row.

Figure 2.7 shows the number of colonies growing on 2x10 Petri dishes with two different nutrient levels. The list to the left has totals in the row 15, 26, and 27—which is great for data analysis but not for record keeping. That's what the section to the right is for. So you need to transfer the data from the left into the right section. To do so, use the following technique:

	A	B	C	D	E	F	G	H	I
1	Colonies on 10 Petri Dishes						pH<6	pH 6-8	pH>8
2						1000 mg/L	34	60	27
3						2000 mg/L	66	50	20
4	Nutrient	pH<6	pH 6-8	pH>8					
5	1000 mg/L	1	4	2					
6	1000 mg/L	2	5	2					
7	1000 mg/L	2	5	2					
8	1000 mg/L	4	6	2					
9	1000 mg/L	4	6	2					
10	1000 mg/L	4	6	3					
11	1000 mg/L	4	6	3					
12	1000 mg/L	4	7	3					
13	1000 mg/L	4	7	3					
14	1000 mg/L	5	8	5					
15	1000 mg/L	34	60	27					
16	2000 mg/L	5	3	0					
17	2000 mg/L	6	4	1					
18	2000 mg/L	6	4	1					
19	2000 mg/L	6	5	2					
20	2000 mg/L	6	5	2					
21	2000 mg/L	7	5	2					
22	2000 mg/L	7	5	2					
23	2000 mg/L	7	6	3					
24	2000 mg/L	7	6	3					
25	2000 mg/L	9	7	4					
26	2000 mg/L	66	50	20					
27	Grand Tota	100	110	47					
28									

Figure 2.7

1. Collapse the left list to its subtotals only.

2. Select B15:D26 (subtotals only).

3. Select *Home* | *Find & Select* | *Go To Special* | ⊙ *Visible Cells Only* (otherwise, you would copy all that's in between as well).

4. Press *Ctrl+C* (to copy what is visible).

5. Select G2 and press *Ctrl+V* (to paste the subtotals only).

Now you can remove the subtotals from the list on the left. The only problem is that the values on the right are hard coded, so they don't update when the values to the left change. Chapter 16 discusses a way to copy the formulas instead.

Chapter 8: Summary Functions

Data analysis often requires summary functions that provide summary information for a particular subset of records only. Excel calls these functions *D-functions*. Their names always start with a *D* (e.g. DSUM) and they supply regular summary operations, according to conditions you have specified somewhere. *D-functions* require filters that identify the criteria for filtering the "database," using the list's labels as identifiers.

The rules for filters are pretty simple:

- A list must have labels or headers on top (usually in row 1).

- A list cannot contain completely empty rows or columns inside.

- The filter uses labels, which are usually identical to the list's labels.

- Criteria in the filter that appear on the same row act as an AND condition.

- Criteria in the filter that appear in the same column act as an OR condition.

- A filter cannot contain completely empty rows or columns either.

Figure 2.8 shows a list named *Data* and three filters named *Filter1*, *Filter2*, and *Filter3*. In cell K4, the function DAVERAGE would calculate the mean of the age (K1), weight (L1), and systolic blood pressure (M1) for records in *Data* according to *Filter1*. This is the formula: =DAVERAGE(Data,K$1,Filter1). You just copy the formula downward and then change DAVERAGE into DSTDEV and DCOUNT. Now you can copy K4:K7 to the right.

	A	B	C	D	E	F	G	H	I	J	K	L	M	N
1	Patient	Gender	DOB	Age	Weight	Systolic		Patient	Gender	DOB	Age	Weight	Systolic	
2	Bush	M	1/3/1975	38	160	178					>50		>140	
3	Carter	F	10/22/1937	75	192	151								
4	Clinton	M	7/15/1971	41	171	175		Mean			72	169	161	
5	Eisenhower	F	11/24/1934	78	154	128		SD			7	22	23	
6	Ford	M	2/9/1950	63	164	141		Count			5	5	5	
7	Johnson	F	6/13/1965	47	152	125								
8	Kennedy	M	11/27/1973	39	165	193		Patient	Gender	DOB	Age	Weight	Systolic	
9	Lincoln	M	8/1/1972	40	188	166					>60			
10	Nixon	F	9/15/1930	82	189	146					<40			
11	Reagan	M	3/28/1939	74	140	170								
12	Roosevelt	M	9/29/1945	67	159	196		Mean			65	165	163	
13	Truman	F	10/20/1962	50	151	139		SD			17	17	25	
14	Washington	F	10/15/1963	49	209	180		Count			8	8	8	
15														
16								Patient	Gender	DOB	Age	Weight	Systolic	Systolic
17													>140	<180
18														
19								Mean			59	172	161	
20								SD			19	19	15	
21								Count			7	7	7	
22														

Figure 2.8

According to *Filter1* in Figure 2.8, the mean age of people older than 50 with a systolic blood pressure over 140 is 72. Any changes in the settings of *Filter1* are automatically reflected in the results of the summary calculations. The same thing happens when you implement the two other filters. Note that *Filter2* is set up as an OR filter, and *Filter3* acts as an AND filter.

The real power of these filters is that they can include filter fields that contain formulas. You can just expand a filter with a newly invented field name that holds a formula for an even more customized filter. The idea behind the formula is that if the formula evaluates to TRUE, the record qualifies for the filtered subset. You should know, though, that the formula you create in a filter always works on the first record, but internally it runs through all records in the data set.

Figure 2.9 has a formula in its filter to select all records that have a systolic blood pressure above the mean systolic blood pressure: `=F2>AVERAGE($F$2:$F$14)`. You need to make sure this formula checks the first record (F2) and compares it with the mean of the entire, absolute range ($F$2:$F$14). Calculated or computed filters always evaluate to `TRUE` or `FALSE`. They actually show the evaluation for the first record—which happens to be `TRUE` in this case because 178 is in fact greater than the mean of 161. Notice that the database functions in the summary section (D19:F21) reflect the subset they are based on, and they follow the same rule: If the formula evaluates to `TRUE`, the record qualifies.

	A	B	C	D	E	F	G
1	Patient	Gender	DOB	Age	Weight	Systolic	
2	Johnson	F	6/13/1965	47	152	125	
3	Eisenhower	F	11/24/1934	78	154	128	
4	Truman	F	10/20/1962	50	151	139	
5	Ford	M	2/9/1950	63	164	141	
6	Nixon	F	9/15/1930	82	189	146	
7	Carter	F	10/22/1937	75	192	151	
8	Lincoln	M	8/1/1972	40	188	166	
9	Reagan	M	3/28/1939	74	140	170	
10	Clinton	M	7/15/1971	41	171	175	
11	Bush	M	1/3/1975	38	160	178	
12	Washington	F	10/15/1963	49	209	180	
13	Kennedy	M	11/27/1973	39	165	193	
14	Roosevelt	M	9/29/1945	67	159	196	
15							
16	Patient	Gender	DOB	Age	Weight	Systolic	>Mean SBP
17							FALSE
18							
19	Mean			50	170	180	
20	SD			15	22	11	
21	Count			7	7	7	
22							

Figure 2.9

The following are examples of some other filters:

- A filter for weights between the 25th and 75th percentiles: `=AND(E2>=PERCEN-TILE($E$2:$E$14,0.75),F2>=PERCENTILE($F$2:$F$14,0.75))`

- A filter that excludes records with missing systolic blood pressure readings: `=F2<>""`

- An alternative filter for the same purpose: `=ISBLANK(F2)=FALSE`

- A filter that skips non-numeric entries: `=ISERROR(F2)=FALSE`

Note

Non-numeric entries such as `NA` or `#N/A` would interfere with most calculations.

Filter formulas cannot use references outside the data range of the list. So you cannot compare the cell A2 of the first record with cell A1 (which is its label) or with cell A15 (which is below the list you are filtering). In cases like these, you may have to expand your formula with functions such as `IF`.

Chapter 9: Unique Lists

Summary overviews often depend on listings of **unique** entries. Duplicate readings may have to be skipped, for they would affect the calculation of the mean and the standard deviation. When you add or import records coming from an external data source, you may end up with duplicates that need to be eliminated in order to avoid miscalculations. In all these cases, you need lists of unique values or records. You can often create unique lists by removing duplicates.

Excel has a simple tool for removing duplicates. Say that you want to remove all records that have duplicate readings for the same plate. This is what you do:

1. On the *Data* tab, click *Remove Duplicates*.

2. Select only those columns that you want to check for duplicates.

Note

To remove completely identical records, you must select all columns. If you want to keep the original list, you need to make a copy first, of course.

Figure 2.10 shows a case in which you want to create a summary (to the right) based on unique entries in the records (to the left). These are the steps:

	A	B	C	D	E	F	G	H	I
1	Date	Plate ID	Analyst	C Value			etv	kpm	luv
2	09/14/01	8696p08b	etv	62.5		8696p08b	1	1	1
3	09/14/01	8696p08b	kpm	73.6		8877p63b	1	1	1
4	09/14/01	8696p08b	luv	63.3		8877p70d	2	1	1
5	09/26/01	8877p63b	etv	47.5		8877p78b	1	1	1
6	09/14/01	8877p63b	kpm	50.2		8877p84b	1	2	1
7	09/26/01	8877p63b	luv	45.4					
8	09/19/01	8877p70d	etv	79.4					
9	09/20/01	8877p70d	kpm	58.4					
10	09/21/01	8877p70d	luv	65.8					
11	09/18/01	8877p70d	etv	39.8					
12	09/21/01	8877p78b	kpm	60.8					
13	09/25/01	8877p78b	luv	78.4					
14	09/25/01	8877p78b	etv	64.9					
15	10/03/01	8877p84b	kpm	62.5					
16	09/12/01	8877p84b	luv	58.3					
17	09/11/01	8877p84b	etv	64.8					
18	09/11/01	8877p84b	kpm	70.2					
19									

Figure 2.10

1. Copy and paste the *Plates* column to F1 and the *Analysts* column to H1. Make sure the copied *Plates* column and *Analysts* column are surrounded by an empty column on either side, so Excel treats them as isolated lists.

2. Make sure you also copy the labels, since filters always work with those labels.

3. On the *Data* tab, click *Remove Duplicates*.

4. To turn the *Analysts* column by 90 degrees, we could use the *Transpose* feature. Select the unique Analysts entries, use *Copy*, click where you want the transposed version, then use *Paste Special* and choose ☑ *Transpose*. Now you have a two-dimensional summary table with row entries and column entries.

5. Use the function COUNTIFS in G2: =COUNTIFS($B$2:$B$18,$F2,$C$2:$C$18,G$1).

Note

Figure 2.11 shows another situation. Sometimes you receive lists with updated records, and you need to compare what has changed in the list to the left and what has changed in the list to the right. Here's what you do:

	A	B	C	D	E	F	G
1	Patient	SBP			Patient	SBP	
2	Bush	120			Bush	120	
3	Carter	139	145		Carter	145	139
4	Clinton	160			Clinton	160	
5	Eisenhower	148			Eisenhower	148	
6	Ford	167	159		Ford	159	167
7	Johnson	145			Johnson	145	
8	Kennedy	137			Kennedy	137	
9	Lincoln	123			Lincoln	123	
10	Nixon	155	140		Nixon	140	155
11	Reagan	137			Reagan	137	
12	Truman	145			Truman	145	
13							

Figure 2.11

1. Enter the following formula in C2: =IF(B2=F2,"",F2).

2. Enter the following formula in G2: =IF(B2=F2,"",B2).

Figure 2.12 shows a case that's a bit more complicated. To determine whether there is a new name in the list that is missing in the other list, do the following:

	A	B	C	D	E	F	G
1	Patient	SBP	New		Patient	SBP	New
2	Bush	120			Bush	120	
3	Carter	139			Carter	139	
4	Clinton	160			Clinton	160	
5	Eisenhower	148			Eisenhower	148	
6	Ford	167			Ford	167	
7	Johnson	145			Johnson	145	
8	Kennedy	137			Kennedy	137	
9	Lincoln	123	Lincoln		Nixon	155	
10	Nixon	155			Reagan	137	
11	Reagan	137			Roosevelt	131	Roosevelt
12	Truman	145	Truman		Washington	139	Washington
13							

Figure 2.12

1. Enter the following formula in C2: =IF(COUNTIF($E$2:$E$12,A2)=0,A2,"").

2. Enter the following formula in G2: =IF(COUNTIF($A$2:$A$12,E2)=0,E2,"").

Chapter 10: Data Validation

Good data analysis depends on reliable records. Of course, no one can prevent inaccurate data entry, but you do have the power to subject data entry to some kind of validation check. A list of records without data validation may contain very unreliable information.

With Excel, you can set up your own rules for checking data entry. For instance, if dates are important to you, you want to make sure no one can enter a date in the past or somewhere in the future. This is where data validation comes in. You can apply validation by using the button *Data Validation* on the *Data* tab. This activates a dialog box with three tabs:

- The first tab is for what you want to allow. The default option is *Any Value*. The most flexible option is *Custom* because you can use it to implement your own formulas.

- The second tab creates a message that kicks in whenever the user enters a validated cell; the use of this setting is usually annoying for users.

- The third tab implements a specific error alert when date entry violates the rule.

<u>Caution</u>

Validation settings can be deleted by *Copy* and *Paste* operations, for a regular *Paste* also replaces the cell's validation settings with the validation settings of the copied cell. Therefore, invalid entries that were pasted may elude detection. Data validation applied later on to a column that already has invalid entries does not detect those violations until you click *Circle Invalid Data* (under the *Validation* drop-down button).

You can apply data validation in two different ways:

- **Selecting the entire column:** This is a great option when you keep adding records at the bottom of the list, but it takes more memory in your file.

- **Selecting a specific range of data:** If you ever need to find out later where your validation range ended, you can use either of the following routes:

  ◦ From the *Home* tab, select *Find & Select*, then *Data Validation*

  ◦ From the *Home* tab, select *Find & Select*, *GoTo Special*, then ⊙ *Data Validation*. You can then choose between highlighting all ranges and highlighting just the one around your selected cell(s).

Again, you can also use your own formulas for data validation; for example, you can use the formula =LEN(B2)=3 when you want a text length of exactly three characters. Formulas always deal with the first selected cell (B2, in this case) but adjust to all selected cells (so B2 should be relative). The idea behind the validation formula is that if the formula evaluates to TRUE, the entry is valid. (Unfortunately, you can only type the formula manually; other help, such as f_x, is not available here.)

Figure 2.13 shows many candidates for data validation:

	A	B	C	D	E	
1	Date	Analyst	Plate ID	50 ng/mL	Plate ID	
2	1/3/2006	gmv	2321a	47.7	2321a	
3	1/4/2006	gmv	2321b	48.7	2321b	
4	1/5/2006	tjk	2322a	49.3	2322a	
5	1/6/2006	tjk	2322b	45.9	2322b	
6	1/9/2006	tkm	2323a	47.5	2323a	
7	1/10/2006	tkm	2323b	45.9	2323b	
8	1/11/2006	bdo	2324a	43.2	2324a	
9	1/12/2006	bdo	2324b	44.3	2324b	
10	1/13/2006	ksm	2325a	56.4	2325a	
11	1/16/2006	ksm	2325b	51.3	2325b	
12	1/17/2006	gmv	2326a	52.3	2326a	
13	1/18/2006	gmv	2326b	49.7	2326b	
14	1/19/2006	bdo	2327a	52.9	2327a	
15	1/20/2006	bdo	2327b	50.1	2327b	
16	1/23/2006	ksm	2328a	51.0	2328a	
17	1/24/2006	ksm	2328b	48.6	2328b	
18	1/25/2006	tjk	2329a	47.5	2329a	
19	1/26/2006	tjk	2329b	47.5	2329b	
20	1/27/2006	tkm	2330a	43.2	2330a	
21	1/30/2006	tkm	2330b	44.3	2330b	
22						

Figure 2.13

In column A, you accept only dates between a certain date in the past and the current date. The settings are *Allow Date* and *Between* any start date and =TODAY().

- In column B, you want to make sure that each analyst has a three-character designation. You could use the option *Text* or choose *Custom* and enter the formula =LEN(B2)=3.

- In column C, you want to prevent duplicate plate numbers, so each plate number can only be used once. The custom setting would be =COUNTIF($C$2:$C$21,C2)=1.

- In column D, say that you've never found readings outside the range 40–60. You can use the following formula to trap any values outside the range 40–60: =AND(D2>40,D2<60).

- In column E, you want to validate for five characters and no duplicates. This should work: =AND(LEN(E2)=5,COUNTIF($E$2:$E$21,E2)=1).

Some of these settings could be achieved in a simpler way, but the *Custom* option is always more flexible—and often your only choice.

Figure 2.14 may not look like a validation issue, but it actually is. In column B, the user can only choose from a list of names that is located somewhere else on this sheet or on another sheet in this workbook. Using this list as a validation tool prevents typos during data entry and thus guarantees more reliable data analysis later on. To get to this point, you do the following:

	A	B	C	D	E
1	**Date**	**Patient**	**New SBP**		
2	5/16/2013	Bush	127		**Bush**
3	5/15/	Bush	152		**Carter**
4	5/14/	Carter / Clinton	165		**Clinton**
5	5/13/	Eisenhower	180		**Eisenhower**
6	5/10/	Ford / Johnson	158		**Ford**
7	5/9/	Kennedy	160		**Johnson**
8	5/8/2013	Nixon	142		**Kennedy**
9	5/7/2013	Nixon	190		**Nixon**
10	5/6/2013	Reagan	125		**Reagan**
11	5/3/2013	Bush	141		
12	5/2/2013	Carter	191		
13	5/1/2013	Clinton	155		
14	4/30/2013	Eisenhower	160		
15	4/29/2013	Ford	141		
16	4/26/2013	Johnson	132		
17	4/25/2013	Kennedy	139		
18	4/24/2013	Nixon	147		
19	4/23/2013	Reagan	151		
20					

Figure 2.14

1. Select the list in E2:E10 and name the range *Patients* (naming is required if the list is on another sheet than where you use it).

2. Select either B2:B19 or the entire column.

3. Select: *Data* tab | *Data Validation* | Set *Allow* to *List* | *Source*: =Patients (do not forget the equal sign, so it refers to a range *name* instead of a word).

4. Once you click *OK*, you see a button when you enter any of the validated cells. Only entries from the list are accepted.

Figure 2.15 shows another validation example applied to temperature readings per week. Later, we'll discuss other features of this sheet—for instance, how the graph adjusts automatically to new settings. For now, take a look at cells E2 and E4, which regulate where to start the plot and where to end the plot in the chart:

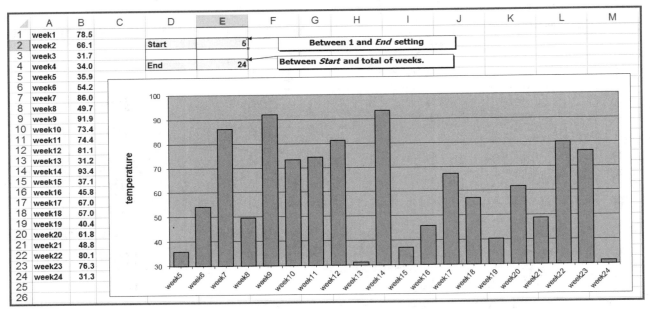

Figure 2.15

- The validation setting of cell E2 is rather obvious: It is a whole number *between* 1 and =E4-1.

- The setting for cell E4 could be a whole number *between* =E2+1 and =COUNTA(A:A).

Chapter 11: Conditional Formatting

Among the numerous details in a spreadsheet, you may want to flag, mark, or highlight specific values that should stick out for some reason. Conditional formatting allows you to do this according to particular rules you set up yourself. You are the master of your sheets.

Figure 2.16 shows some examples of conditional formatting that you can practically do automatically, thanks to Excel's new tools:

	A	B	C	D	E	F	G
1	Plate ID	Date	Analyst	Max OD	C-Value	SD	
2	8696p08d	09/14/01	cod	2.3	59.9	7.9	
3	8877p63a	09/14/01	cod	2.8	45.0	2.2	
4	8877p120e	10/03/01	ejs	1.5	62.5	7.4	
5	8877p66b	09/26/01	ejs	2.6	47.5	7.1	
6	8877p78b	09/21/01	ejs	2.8	60.8	7.0	
7	8696p08b	09/14/01	etv	2.4	62.5	7.6	
8	8877p60a	09/12/01	etv	3.2	58.3	0.9	
9	8877p71b	09/19/01	etv	2.5	79.4	4.4	
10	8877p84b	09/25/01	etv	1.9	78.4	0.3	
11	8877p70c	09/18/01	gmv	1.4	57.1	1.3	
12	8877p83a	09/25/01	gmv	2.0	83.7	2.0	
13	8696p08e	09/14/01	kpm	2.5	73.6	7.3	
14	8877p58a	09/11/01	kpm	2.6	64.8	4.0	
15	8877p63b	09/14/01	kpm	2.7	50.2	7.5	
16	8877p75b	09/20/01	kpm	1.7	58.4	8.3	
17	8696p08f	09/14/01	luv	2.4	63.3	4.7	
18	8877p66a	09/26/01	luv	2.8	45.4	0.2	
19	8877p78a	09/21/01	luv	2.6	65.8	8.2	
20	8877p58b	09/11/01	tjk	2.2	70.2	8.6	
21	8877p70d	09/18/01	tjk	1.1	39.8	7.0	
22	8877p83b	09/25/01	tjk	1.7	64.9	1.3	
23							

Figure 2.16

- **Column D:** You can "grade" values by simply selecting *Home, Conditional Formatting, Data Bars* or *Color Scales.*

- **Column E:** You can flag all values that are above (or below) the mean by selecting *Home, Conditional Formatting, Top/Bottom Rules, Above Average.*

- **Column F:** You can flag even maximum and minimum values by using the top or bottom one item.

- **Column B:** You flag duplicate (or unique) values by selecting *Highlight Cells Rules, Duplicate Values.*

Excel's options are extremely rich, but you may sometimes need your own formulas, especially for scientific work. With formulas, the sky is the limit. The idea behind formulas should be familiar by now: If a formula evaluates to TRUE, the conditional format is applied. The steps are simple:

1. From the *Home* tab, select *Conditional Formatting*.

2. Select *New Rule* (which is almost at the bottom).

3. Choose the last option: *Use a formula*.

4. Type the formula, making sure to correct the default absolute cell reference if necessary.

5. Determine the format you would like.

Note

If you discover a mistake later on, do not go to *New Rule* (that would add another rule); instead, go to *Manage Rules* (where you can add, edit, and delete rules).

Figure 2.17 offers some interesting examples:

	A	B	C	D	E	F	G
1	Plate ID	Date	Analyst	C-Value	Max OD	SD	
2	8877p70d	09/18/01	tjk	39.8	1.1	7.0	
3	8877p63a	09/14/01	cod	45.0	2.8	2.2	
4	8877p66a	09/26/01	luv	45.4	2.8	0.2	
5	8877p66b	09/26/01	ejs	47.5	2.6	7.1	
6	8877p63b	09/14/01	kpm	50.2	2.7	7.5	
7	8877p70c	09/18/01	gmv	57.1	1.4	1.3	
8	8877p60a	09/12/01	etv	58.3	3.2	0.9	
9	8877p75b	09/20/01	kpm	58.4	1.7	8.3	
10	8696p08d	09/14/01	cod	59.9	2.3	7.9	
11	8877p78b	09/21/01	ejs	60.8	2.8	7.0	
12	8877p120e	10/03/01	ejs	62.5	1.5	7.4	
13	8696p08b	09/14/01	etv	62.5	2.4	7.6	
14	8696p08f	09/14/01	luv	63.3	2.4	4.7	
15	8877p58a	09/11/01	kpm	64.8	2.6	4.0	
16	8877p83b	09/25/01	tjk	64.9	1.7	1.3	
17	8877p78b	09/21/01	luv	65.8	2.6	8.2	
18	8877p58b	09/11/01	tjk	70.2	2.2	8.6	
19	8696p08e	09/14/01	kpm	73.6	2.5	7.3	
20	8877p84b	09/25/01	etv	78.4	1.9	0.3	
21	8877p71b	09/19/01	etv	79.4	2.5	4.4	
22	8877p63a	09/25/01	gmv	83.7	2.0	2.0	
23							

Figure 2.17

- To mark the C-values between the 25th and 75th percentiles, the formula is quite long: `=AND(D2>PERCENTILE($D$2:$D$22,0.25),D2<PERCENTILE($D$2:$D$22,0.75))`.

- To flag the analysts in column C who have more than three readings, you use `=COUNTIF($C$2:$C$22,C2)>3`. Don't forget to "unlock" the 2nd C2 and to set `COUNTIF` to >3.

- When you try to mark values in columns D and E that are above the 50th percentile in the range, you may encounter a surprise: `=AND(D2>PERCENTILE($D$2:$D$22,0.5),E2>PERCENTILE($E$2:$E$22,0.5))` formats only the left column. To correct, this you use `=AND($D2>PERCENTILE($D$2:$D$22,0.5),$E2>PERCENTILE($E$2:$E$22,0.5))`. See the difference? Cells D2 and E2 need an absolute column reference!

Note

The functions `PERCENTILE` and `QUARTILE` work fine when you have large samples, for everyone can agree where each quartile occurs. However, in samples of small sizes, you may have to interpolate to find a value between two values in the data set. The new functions `PERCENTILE.EXC` and `QUARTILE.EXC` do a better job. The old method is still available in `QUARTILE.INC` and `PERCENTILE.INC`.

Figure 2.18 shows a similar problem: The left database (A:E) simply places a border line in column C before a new analyst. But the right database (G:K) does this for the entire record. This is how you do it:

	A	B	C	D	E	F	G	H	I	J	K
1	Plate ID	Date	Analyst	C Value	Max OD		Plate ID	Date	Analyst	C Value	Max OD
2	8696p08d	09/14/01	cod	59.9	2.3		8696p08d	09/14/01	cod	59.9	2.3
3	8877p63a	09/14/01	cod	45.0	2.8		8877p63a	09/14/01	cod	45.0	2.8
4	8877p120e	10/03/01	ejs	62.5	1.5		8877p120e	10/03/01	ejs	62.5	1.5
5	8877p66b	09/26/01	ejs	47.5	2.6		8877p66b	09/26/01	ejs	47.5	2.6
6	8696p08b	09/14/01	etv	62.5	2.4		8696p08b	09/14/01	etv	62.5	2.4
7	8877p60a	09/12/01	etv	58.3	3.2		8877p60a	09/12/01	etv	58.3	3.2
8	8877p84b	09/25/01	etv	78.4	1.9		8877p84b	09/25/01	etv	78.4	1.9
9	8877p70c	09/18/01	gmv	57.1	1.4		8877p70c	09/18/01	gmv	57.1	1.4
10	8877p83a	09/25/01	gmv	83.7	2.0		8877p83a	09/25/01	gmv	83.7	2.0
11	8696p08e	09/14/01	kpm	73.6	2.5		8696p08e	09/14/01	kpm	73.6	2.5
12	8877p58a	09/11/01	kpm	64.8	2.6		8877p58a	09/11/01	kpm	64.8	2.6
13	8877p63b	09/14/01	kpm	50.2	2.7		8877p63b	09/14/01	kpm	50.2	2.7
14	8877p75b	09/20/01	kpm	58.4	1.7		8877p75b	09/20/01	kpm	58.4	1.7
15	8696p08f	09/14/01	luv	63.3	2.4		8696p08f	09/14/01	luv	63.3	2.4
16	8877p66a	09/26/01	luv	45.4	2.8		8877p66a	09/26/01	luv	45.4	2.8
17	8877p78a	09/21/01	luv	65.8	2.6		8877p78a	09/21/01	luv	65.8	2.6
18	8877p58b	09/11/01	tjk	70.2	2.2		8877p58b	09/11/01	tjk	70.2	2.2
19	8877p70d	09/18/01	tjk	39.8	1.1		8877p70d	09/18/01	tjk	39.8	1.1
20	8877p83b	09/25/01	tjk	64.9	1.7		8877p83b	09/25/01	tjk	64.9	1.7
21											

Figure 2.18

- For C2:C20 (do not start in C1!), use `=C2<>C1`. Format with a top border.

- For G2:K20 (again, not G1!), use `=$C2<>$C1`. Make sure you "lock" the column reference. Format with a top border.

Figure 2.19 may not look like it is a conditional formatting issue, but it is. You could reach this striping effect by using Excel's *table* structure, but you might not always want to do so. Instead, you can use conditional formatting based on a formula with the MOD function, as discussed in Chapter 6: `=MOD(ROW(A1),2)=1`. An advantage of using this formula is that you can make the striping alternate at any step, such as at every fifth row. This is something Excel's *table* structure cannot achieve.

	A	B	C	D	E	F
1	Plate ID	Date	Analyst	C Value	Max OD	
2	8696p08d	09/14/01	cod	59.9	2.3	
3	8877p63a	09/14/01	cod	45.0	2.8	
4	8877p120e	10/03/01	ejs	62.5	1.5	
5	8877p66b	09/26/01	ejs	47.5	2.6	
6	8696p08b	09/14/01	etv	62.5	2.4	
7	8877p60a	09/12/01	etv	58.3	3.2	
8	8877p84b	09/25/01	etv	78.4	1.9	
9	8877p70c	09/18/01	gmv	57.1	1.4	
10	8877p83a	09/25/01	gmv	83.7	2.0	
11	8696p08e	09/14/01	kpm	73.6	2.5	
12	8877p58a	09/11/01	kpm	64.8	2.6	
13	8877p63b	09/14/01	kpm	50.2	2.7	
14	8877p75b	09/20/01	kpm	58.4	1.7	
15	8696p08f	09/14/01	luv	63.3	2.4	
16	8877p66a	09/26/01	luv	45.4	2.8	
17	8877p78a	09/21/01	luv	65.8	2.6	
18	8877p58b	09/11/01	tjk	70.2	2.2	
19	8877p70d	09/18/01	tjk	39.8	1.1	
20	8877p83b	09/25/01	tjk	64.9	1.7	
21						

Figure 2.19

In Figure 2.20, it would be nice if the number of bins in columns I and J would be highlighted according to the number of bins chosen in cell G2. Here is the simple formula for making this happen in the cells I1:J30: =ROW()<=$G$2. In addition, you may want to hide the cells below the last bin (in our example, I21:J30). To do so, add another conditional format: =$I1>MAX(data). The secret of hiding the values in the bottom cells is the setting of the *Number* format to *Custom*: ; ; ; (yes, just type three semicolons there). One more trick: If you want to flag all cells that have formulas in it, so users cannot inadvertently delete or change them, do the following: Select all cells on the sheet (*Ctrl+A* twice) and assign conditional formatting with this formula: =ISFORMULA(A1).

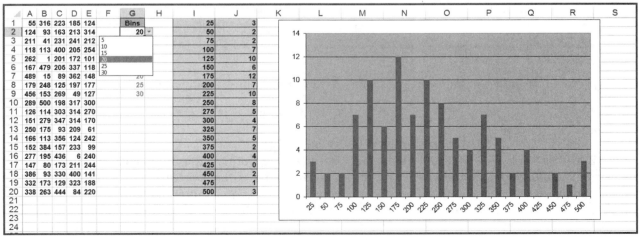

Figure 2.20

Chapter 12: Filtering Tools

In the chapters up to this point, you have marked a subset of records inside the total collection, so the entire set of records remains visible and may thus obscure the specific records you want to focus on. Filtering tools allow you to display just the filtered subset on its own, so you can study and analyze the subset without being distracted by the immense surroundings. These tools help you combat the famous forest and trees problem.

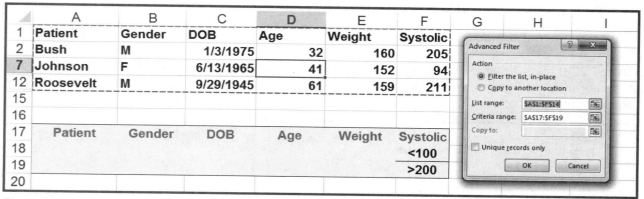

Figure 2.21

Say that in Figure 2.21, you forgot to validate the systolic blood pressure values as being between 100 and 200 mmHg. You can correct this by applying an advanced filter, similar to the one you used earlier for summary or database functions. This filter creates a subset of invalid records (in this case, below 100 or above 200 mmHg) so they can be corrected or deleted. These are the steps:

1. Create the correct settings in the filter (A17:F19) for violations; OR conditions should be in separate rows (F18 and F19).

2. Click inside the database first (so Excel can automatically detect its borders).

3. On the *Data* tab, click the *Advanced* button. The *List Range* is already displayed, thanks to step 2.

4. Select the *Criteria* range A17:F19.

5. Click *OK* and watch the subset of "violators":

- If you want to correct the filtered violators, do so.

- If you want to delete the filtered violators, select all their rows and then select the *Home* tab, *Find & Select*, *Go To Special*, ⊙ *Visible Cells Only*; then right-click these rows and select *Delete Rows*.

- If you want all records back, click the *Clear* button in the *Sort & Filter* group of the *Data* tab.

As with summary filters, you can use computed criteria with a formula as well. If the formula evaluates to TRUE, the record qualifies for the subset. Here are some examples of possible filters:

- For blood pressures above the mean in column F, starting in F2: =F2>AVERAGE($F$2:$F$14).

- For records that have no weight or no systolic blood pressure values: =OR(E2<>"",F2<>"").

- For values that you want to hide, use a *Custom Number* conditional format: ;;; (3 semicolons).

You can also place filters on a sheet separate from the database itself in order to gather several filtered subsets on separate sheets. If you regularly use specific filters, you can place each one on its own sheet. Be aware, though, that unlike D-functions, filters do not automatically update. You must apply the filter again.

When using filters on a separate sheet, you must perform the following actions:

1. Click inside the filter first (not in the database).

2. Start the *Advanced* filter.

3. Highlight the database or type its name.

4. Mark ⊙ *Copy to Another Location*.

5. Specify the location of the copied subset.

Figure 2.22 shows a database on its own sheet; it has been named *Data*. (Do not name a database *Database* because Excel uses that name internally for its filters.) On separate sheets, you could use the following filters, among many others:

	A	B	C	D	E	F
1	Plate ID	Date	Analyst	C Value		
2	8877p70d	09/18/01	tjk	39.7		
3	8877p63a	09/14/01	cod	45.0		
4	8877p66a	09/26/01	luv	45.3		
5	8877p66b	09/26/01	ejs	47.4		
6	8877p63b	09/14/01	kpm	50.2		
7	8877p70c	09/18/01	gmv	57.1		
8	8877p60a	09/12/01	etv	58.3		
9	8877p75b	09/20/01	kpm	58.4		
10	8696p08d	09/14/01	cod	59.9		
11	8877p78b	09/21/01	ejs	61.5		
12	8877p120e	10/03/01	ejs	62.5		
13	8696p08b	09/14/01	etv	63.3		
14	8696p08f	09/14/01	luv	63.3		
15	8877p58a	09/11/01	kpm	64.8		
16	8877p83b	09/25/01	tjk	64.2		
17	8877p78a	09/21/01	luv	65.8		
18	8877p58b	09/11/01	tjk	70.2		
19	8696p08e	09/14/01	kpm	73.5		
20	8877p84b	09/25/01	etv	78.3		
21	8877p71b	09/19/01	etv	79.3		
22	8877p83a	09/25/01	gmv	83.6		
23						
24						
25						

NotValid   AboveMean   Up>5   **Separate**   Filter1   Filter2   Filter3   ⊕

Figure 2.22

- =Separate!D2>AVERAGE(Separate!$D$2:$D$22)

- =AND(Separate!D2>PERCENTILE(Separate!$D$2:$D$22,0.25),Separate!D2<PERCENTILE(Separate!$D$2:$D$22,0.75))

- =Separate!D2=MEDIAN(Separate!$D$2:$D$22)

- =Separate!D2=MODE(Separate!$D$2:$D$22)

- =Separate!D2=AVERAGE(Separate!$D$2:$D$22) (but this record will probably never be found unless it has a value that happens to have the exact same value as the mean).

After working with all these examples, you should have a better understanding of how to use formulas for filtering, validation, and conditional formatting.

Chapter 13: Lookups

Because data analysis depends on using reliable data, it also depends on the use of lookup functions, which allow you to quickly and efficiently locate specific data in another list and to automatically ensure that you are using the correct and latest information.

The most common solution is to look up the information in a lookup table. Why is this a great solution? First, the use of a lookup function guarantees correct information. Second, changes in the lookup table will immediately cascade through your records. To look up information in a vertical way, you can use the VLOOKUP function; if the table is horizontally structured, you use HLOOKUP instead. VLOOKUP is the most common one and has the following syntax: =VLOOKUP(*lookup_value, table, column#, T/F*).

VLOOKUP's last argument (*T/F*) determines whether your *lookup-value* has an exact match in the lookup table (0 or FALSE), or not (1 or TRUE). If you go for an exact match, the first column of the lookup table doesn't have to be sorted; VLOOKUP can find an answer anyway. If you cannot guarantee an exact match, the first column must be sorted in ascending order because VLOOKUP may have to go for the previous closest match in ascending order.

Figure 2.23 shows an example of a simple lookup situation: finding the group to which a specific analyst has been assigned. Column D finds its answer in the lookup table to the right (or wherever). In cell D2, you look up information for analyst *kpm* (C2) in a vertically structured lookup table (G2:H10), and you find an exact answer (0 or FALSE) in column 2 (yes, this requires a column **number**) of the table: =VLOOKUP(C2,$G$2:$H$10,2,0). You can now perform analysis operations such as creating subtotals per group of analysts. If someone were assigned to the wrong group, updates in the lookup table would automatically permeate the records as well.

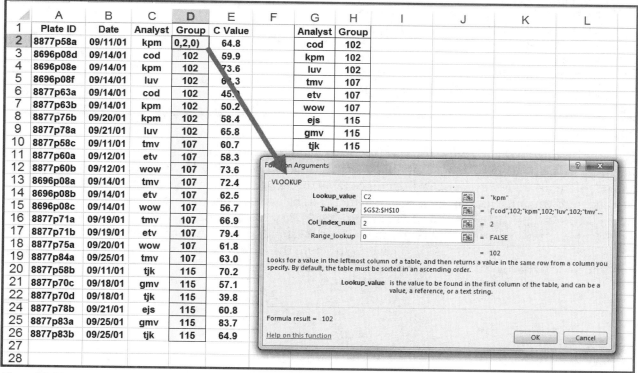

Figure 2.23

Figure 2.24 presents a different situation. Cell H13 has a dropdown box to select a specific *Plate ID*. The row below it displays the corresponding record. Cell G15 has this formula: =VLOOKUP($H$13, $A$2:$E$25, – COLUMN(A1), 0). The nested function COLUMN(A1) returns the number 1 for the lookup table column number. Copied to the right (H15:K15), COLUMN(A1) changes into COLUMN(B1), which returns the number 2 (for B1 is in column 2), and so on.

	A	B	C	D	E	F	G	H	I	J	K
1	Plate ID	Date	Analyst	Group	C Value		Analyst	Group			
2	8877p58a	09/11/01	kpm	102	64.8		cod	102			
3	8696p08d	09/14/01	cod	102	59.9		kpm	102			
4	8696p08e	09/14/01	kpm	102	73.6		luv	102			
5	8696p08f	09/14/01	luv	102	63.3		tmv	107			
6	8877p63a	09/14/01	cod	102	45.0		etv	107			
7	8877p63b	09/14/01	kpm	102	50.2		wow	107			
8	8877p75b	09/20/01	kpm	102	58.4		ejs	115			
9	8877p78a	09/21/01	luv	102	65.8		gmv	115			
10	8877p58c	09/11/01	tmv	107	60.7		tjk	115			
11	8877p60a	09/12/01	etv	107	58.3						
12	8877p60b	09/12/01	wow	107	73.6						
13	8696p08a	09/14/01	tmv	107	72.4		Plate ID	8877p60a			
14	8696p08b	09/14/01	etv	107	62.5						
15	8696p08c	09/14/01	wow	107	56.7		887		etv	107	58.29
16	8877p71a	09/19/01	tmv	107	66.9						
17	8877p71b	09/19/01	etv	107	79.4						
18	8877p75a	09/20/01	wow	107	61.8						
19	8877p84a	09/25/01	tmv	107	63.0						
20	8877p58b	09/11/01	tjk	115	70.2						
21	8877p70c	09/18/01	gmv	115	57.1						
22	8877p70d	09/18/01	tjk	115	39.8						
23	8877p78b	09/21/01	ejs	115	60.8						
24	8877p83a	09/25/01	gmv	115	83.7						
25	8877p83b	09/25/01	tjk	115	64.9						
26											

Figure 2.24

Figure 2.25 shows a slightly different case. You have measured the forced vital capacity (*FVC*; a pulmonary function) in relationship to gender and body length, and you would like to compare each individual with known reference values, as found in a reference table to the right. This time, you need to distinguish values by gender, so you must look in the proper column by using an IF function nested inside a VLOOKUP function: =VLOOKUP(A3, $H$2:$J$18, IF(B3="F",2,3),1). Because VLOOKUP cannot always find an *exact* match in the lookup table, it searches for the closest previous value in an ascending list by having its last argument set to 1 or TRUE. So you have to structure the lookup table in such a way that the first category can handle the lowest value (in this case, 1.50 to 1.52).

	A	B	C	D	E	F	G	H	I	J	
1	Pulmonary Function Forced Vital Capacity (FVC)							Length/m	F	M	
2	Length/m	Gender	FVC/L	Reference	Ratio			1.50	2.3		
3	1.77	F	3.9	4.9	80%			1.52	2.5		
4	1.80	M	3.7	5.4	69%			1.54	2.7		
5	1.80	M	5.0	5.4	93%			1.56	2.9	3.0	
6	1.71	F	2.8	4.3	65%			1.58	3.1	3.2	
7	1.56	F	3.5	2.9	121%			1.60	3.3	3.4	
8	1.58	F	3.7	3.1	119%			1.62	3.5	3.6	
9	1.71	F	2.3	4.3	53%			1.64	3.7	3.8	
10	1.80	M	3.4	5.4	63%			1.66	3.9	4.0	
11	1.75	F	3.1	4.7	66%			1.68	4.1	4.2	
12	1.75	F	2.5	4.7	53%			1.70	4.3	4.4	
13	1.55	F	3.3	2.7	122%			1.72	4.5	4.6	
14	1.73	M	2.8	4.6	61%			1.74	4.7	4.8	
15	1.58	M	2.0	3.2	63%			1.76	4.9	5.0	
16	1.78	M	2.4	5.2	46%			1.78		5.2	
17	1.65	M	2.5	3.8	66%			1.80		5.4	
18	1.62	M	2.9	3.6	81%			1.82		5.6	
19	1.78	M	1.6	5.2	31%						
20	1.76	M	3.9	5.0	78%						
21	1.71	M	3.6	4.4	82%						
22	1.54	F	2.2	2.7	81%						
23											

Figure 2.25

So far, you have mostly used a hard-coded column number for VLOOKUP to find the proper answer. However, there is also a function that can find column and row numbers on its own: MATCH. The MATCH function finds the relative position of a row or column in a range. Thanks to MATCH, columns can still be located, even after they have been moved around. Its syntax is =MATCH(*lookup_value, table*, −1/0/1). Figure 2.26 shows how the last argument in this syntax works:

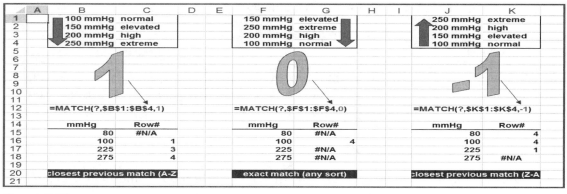

Figure 2.26

- **1:** Finds the closest previous match in ascending, A–Z, order. (If there is none, the result is #N/A.) In Figure 2.26, MATCH has found every row number except for 80 because there is no previous match before 100.

- **0:** Finds an exact match. In Figure 2.26, this is possible only for 100 mmHg. All other cases are not found: #N/A.

- **−1:** Finds the closest previous match in a descending, Z–A, order. In Figure 2.26, MATCH has found every row number except for 275 mmHg because there is no previous match before 250 (therefore, #N/A).

In Figure 2.27, you use a drop-down box in cell I1 to select a patient's name (see Chapter 10). Based on that selected name, you can locate all other information in the main database by using MATCH nested inside VLOOKUP:

	A	B	C	D	E	F	G	H	I
1	Patient	Gender	DOB	Age	Weight	Systolic		Patient	Reagan
2	Bush	M	1/3/1975	32	160	205		Gender	M
3	Carter	F	10/22/1937	69	192	151		DOB	3/28/1939
4	Clinton	M	7/15/1971	35	171	175		Age	67
5	Eisenhower	F	11/24/1934	72	154	128		Weight	140
6	Ford	M	2/9/1950	57	164	141		Systolic	170
7	Johnson	F	6/13/1965	41	152	94			
8	Kennedy	M	11/27/1973	33	165	193			
9	Lincoln	M	8/1/1972	34	188	166			
10	Nixon	F	9/15/1930	76	189	146			
11	Reagan	M	3/28/1939	67	140	170			
12	Roosevelt	M	9/29/1945	61	159	211			
13	Truman	F	10/20/1962	44	151	139			
14	Washington	F	10/15/1963	43	209	180			
15									

Figure 2.27

- The function MATCH in cell I2 would find the column number of *Gender* (H2) in the main table's headers (A1:F1) with this formula: =MATCH(H2,$A$1:$F$1,0). This returns column number 2 in the database.

- The entire formula in I2 would be as follows: =VLOOKUP($I$1,$A$2:$F$14,– MATCH(H2,$A$1:$F$1,0),0).

- When you copy this formula down to I6, H2 inside MATCH will change into H3, and so on.

- You may have to adjust the date format in cell I3 manually.

Note

An advantage of not using a hard-coded column number in VLOOKUP's third argument is that you could change the order of columns in the database without affecting the outcome of the VLOOKUP function. But you cannot change the column's labels or headers in row 1, unless you change them accordingly in column H as well!

VLOOKUP works great, but it has two big limitations:

- It can only search in the first column of a table and then find corresponding information in the next columns to the right. So VLOOKUP cannot find corresponding information in columns located before the one we search in. Of course, you could move columns around.

- It accepts column numbers (which can be done with MATCH), but it does not acknowledge row numbers. In other words, you could never offset a row number by a certain amount when using VLOOKUP.

Fortunately, Excel has a function without these limitations: `INDEX`. Its syntax is much more flexible than that of VLOOKUP: `=INDEX(table, row#, col#)`. `INDEX` needs to know the row position and the column position, which is usually a nice challenge for the `MATCH` function. Then it can search in any row and in any column to find a value at their intersection. When calling the function `INDEX`, you find out that it has two versions: One version returns the **value** at a certain intersection; the other one returns the **reference** of the cell at that intersection (the address of the intersection, not its value). You normally use the first version, but we will use the second version later on.

Note

Interestingly enough, `INDEX` can also return an entire record if you set *Column_num* to 0. Make sure you place the formula in a horizontal range of multiple cells and accept the formula with *Ctrl+-Shift+Enter*, for now we are dealing with an array formula (more on this in Chapter 17).

Figure 2.28 shows an example of the `INDEX` function. `VLOOKUP` could never find the ID in cell J1 because it is located in a column located before the *lookup_value* column. Obviously, you could move that column to the right, but users could still inadvertently move it back to its original position.

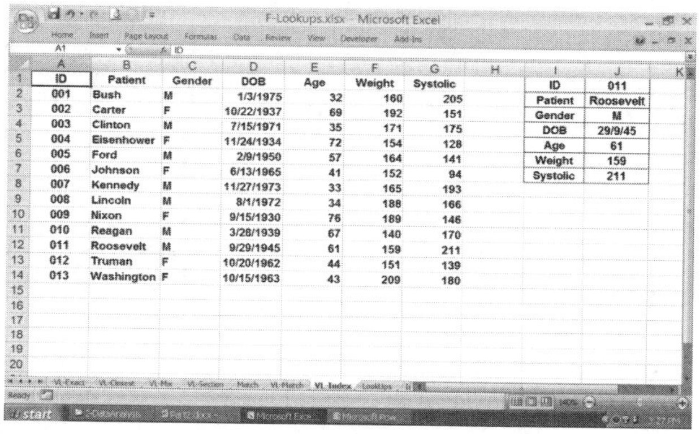

ID	Patient	Gender	DOB	Age	Weight	Systolic
001	Bush	M	1/3/1975	32	160	205
002	Carter	F	10/22/1937	69	192	151
003	Clinton	M	7/15/1971	35	171	175
004	Eisenhower	F	11/24/1934	72	154	128
005	Ford	M	2/9/1950	57	164	141
006	Johnson	F	6/13/1965	41	152	94
007	Kennedy	M	11/27/1973	33	165	193
008	Lincoln	M	8/1/1972	34	188	166
009	Nixon	F	9/15/1930	76	189	146
010	Reagan	M	3/28/1939	67	140	170
011	Roosevelt	M	9/29/1945	61	159	211
012	Truman	F	10/20/1962	44	151	139
013	Washington	F	10/15/1963	43	209	180

ID	011
Patient	Roosevelt
Gender	M
DOB	29/9/45
Age	61
Weight	159
Systolic	211

Figure 2.28

1. Use the `INDEX` function in cell J2 to find the *ID* information for a specific *Patient* chosen in cell J1: =INDEX($A$2:$G$14,MATCH($J$2,$B$2:$B$14,0),MATCH(I1,$A$1:$G$1,0)).

2. The first `MATCH` finds row 11 for *Roosevelt*.

3. The second `MATCH` finds column 1 for the *ID* field.

4. At the intersection of row 11 and column 1, `INDEX` finds the *ID* number 011. The leading 0 is missing, so you need a *Custom* format: 000.

Note

All `MATCH` positions are relative, so row 12 on the sheet is row 11 within range A2:G14.

Another function, `INDIRECT`, can make your life easier here. As discussed briefly in Chapter 4, `INDIRECT` returns the value of a cell referenced by its *name*. Here are some examples:

- `INDIRECT("A1")` returns *Plate ID* (or whatever is in the cell named A1).
- `INDIRECT("E4")` returns 60.7 (or whatever is in the cell named E4).
- `INDIRECT(Total)` returns whatever is in the cell named *Total* (notice no quotes this time).

Figure 2.29 shows INDIRECT in action. If you give cell H2 the name *cod*, the formula `INDIRECT(cod)` returns the value of cell H2, which happens to be 102. So let's give the cells H2:H10 the names from the cells to their left (G2:G10). Here is an easy way to do so:

	A	B	C	D	E	F	G	H
1	Plate ID	Date	Analyst	Group	C Value		Analyst	Group
2	8877p58a	09/11/01	kpm	102	64.8		cod	102
3	8877p58b	09/11/01	tjk	115	70.2		kpm	102
4	8877p58c	09/11/01	tmv	107	60.7		luv	102
5	8877p60a	09/12/01	etv	107	58.3		tmv	107
6	8877p60b	09/12/01	wow	107	73.6		etv	107
7	8696p08a	09/14/01	tmv	107	72.4		wow	107
8	8696p08b	09/14/01	etv	107	62.5		ejs	115
9	8696p08c	09/14/01	wow	107	56.7		gmv	115
10	8696p08d	09/14/01	cod	102	59.9		tjk	115
11	8696p08e	09/14/01	kpm	102	73.6			
12	8696p08f	09/14/01	luv	102	63.3			
13	8877p63a	09/14/01	cod	102	45.0			
14	8877p63b	09/14/01	kpm	102	50.2			
15	8877p70c	09/18/01	gmv	115	57.1			
16	8877p70d	09/18/01	tjk	115	39.8			
17	8877p71a	09/19/01	tmv	107	66.9			
18	8877p71b	09/19/01	etv	107	79.4			
19	8877p75a	09/20/01	wow	107	61.8			
20	8877p75b	09/20/01	kpm	102	58.4			
21	8877p78a	09/21/01	luv	102	65.8			
22	8877p78b	09/21/01	ejs	115	60.8			
24	8877p83a	09/25/01	gmv	115	83.7			
25	8877p83b	09/25/01	tjk	115	64.9			
26	8877p84a	09/25/01	tmv	107	63.0			
27								

Figure 2.29

1. Select G2:H10.

2. Click *Create from Selection* on the *Formulas* tab.

3. Check ☑ *Left Column*.

4. Click *OK*. Notice all the names that were given to H2:H10 in the *Name* box

5. Call each group number through its *name* (for example, in cell D2: `=INDIRECT(C2)`).

Figure 2.30 shows a similar situation. In cell I3, you can use `INDIRECT` to find the reading for a specific strain (selected in cell I1) and a specific test (selected in cell I2). As you can see in this example, `INDIRECT` finds this reading at the intersection of the ranges named *Strain5* and *Test3*:

	A	B	C	D	E	F	G	H	I
1		Test1	Test2	Test3	Test4	Test5		Strain	Strain5
2	Strain1	1.49	1.23	1.01	1.60	1.88		Test	Test3
3	Strain2	1.11	1.01	1.94	1.97	1.74		Reading	1.45
4	Strain3	1.79	1.21	1.04	1.58	1.68			
5	Strain4	1.04	1.29	1.41	1.19	1.68			
6	Strain5	1.70	1.65	1.45	1.59	1.86			
7	Strain6	1.01	1.74	1.34	1.99	1.15			
8	Strain7	1.22	1.13	1.23	1.75	1.13			
9	Strain8	1.97	1.73	1.09	1.75	1.85			
10	Strain9	1.21	1.30	1.47	1.89	1.74			
11	Strain10	1.49	1.40	1.58	1.99	1.54			
12	Strain11	1.39	1.40	1.89	1.31	1.13			
13	Strain12	1.65	1.52	1.29	1.81	1.21			
14	Strain13	1.46	1.27	1.77	1.93	1.39			
15	Strain14	1.09	1.14	1.42	1.39	1.72			
16	Strain15	1.86	1.25	1.77	1.45	1.34			
17									

Figure 2.30

1. Select A1:F16.

2. Click *Create from Selection* for both ☑ *top row* and ☑ *left column*.

3. Use in cell I3 the row and column labels that were chosen in the cells I1 and I2 by using `INDIRECT` and separating the two `INDIRECT` functions with a *space*:
    `=INDIRECT(I1) INDIRECT(I2)`.

Note

The *space* keystroke (spacebar) acts as an intersection operator. There is one more situation where you may want to use `INDIRECT`: When you type in a cell a formula such as `ROW(1:10)`, this formula will change into `ROW(2:11)` when you insert a cell above it. To avoid such changes, use `ROW(INDIRECT("1:10"))`. Make sure *1:10* is a string placed inside double quotes.

Chapter 14: Working with Trends

Based on values that you have observed, you might want to predict values you have not observed. Predictions are an issue of curve fitting and regression analysis, as discussed in Part 4. Here we focus only on how we may have to look up existing, observed values first.

Let's use Figure 2.31 as an example. (This sheet has many features we don't discuss yet: *Controls* are discussed in Chapter 42; and graphs and charts are discussed in Part 3.) The scroll-bar *control* in A19:B19 regulates C19, which determines D19 through a formula, so in turn the graph gets updated. The values you have measured and observed show a rather clear trend: When the percentage of *C-G* bonds in DNA goes up, the temperature of denaturation goes up as well—according to the formula $y = 42.97x + 69.50$ (more on this later).

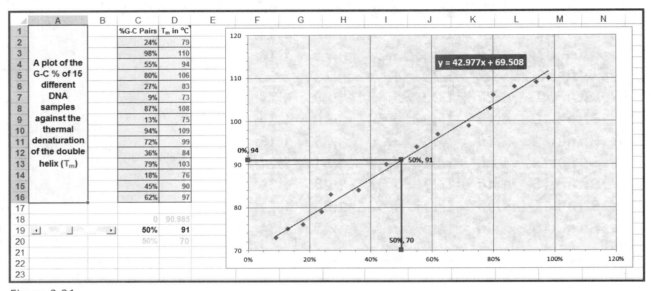

Figure 2.31

You have a relatively easy situation here because you know the formula, so you can predict for any (unobserved) x-value what the corresponding y-value would be. Cell D19 uses that formula based on the value in cell C19 (and C19 in turn is regulated by the *control* to its left). The graph shows where that point is by using 3 sets of coordinates shown in C18:D20.

Figure 2.32 shows an example of *EC50* determination, where you do not yet have a formula (more on this in Chapter 36). To predict an unobserved x-value, you need a linear trend between the two nearest observations. In other words, you need to locate the two nearest observations—for -9.75, these would be -9.52 and -10—plus their corresponding mean values. VLOOKUP cannot do the job because it does not work with a row number (only a column number). Instead, you need a combination of INDEX and MATCH. These are the formulas you need, based on the range names *Logs* for B2:B10, *Means* for C2:C10, and *Determ* for the entire data set:

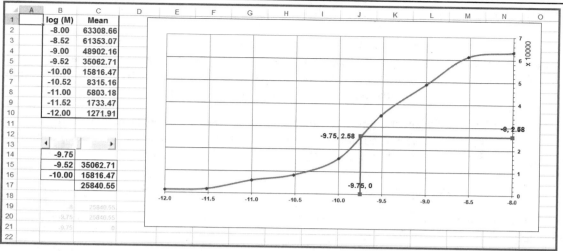

Figure 2.32

- **Cell B15:** Search in column 1 of the data set *Determ*: `=INDEX(Determ,-MATCH($B$14,Logs,-1),1)`.

- **Cell B16:** Do the same but go one row farther: `=INDEX(Determ,-MATCH($B$14,Logs,-1)+1,1)`.

- **Cell C15:** Search in column 2 of the table: `=INDEX(Determ,MATCH($B$14,Logs,-1),2)`.

- **Cell C16:** Do the same again but down one row: `=INDEX(Determ,-MATCH($B$14,Logs,-1)+1,2)`.

Now that you know the nearest observations in the table, you can predict the y-value that corresponds with the new x-value of -9.75—by using the `TREND` function: `=TREND(C15:C16,B15:B16,B14)`. Thanks to `TREND`, `INDEX`, and `MATCH`, you can predict new values by just manipulating the scroll-bar *control*. The insert in the graph is based on 3 sets of coordinates shown in B19:C21.

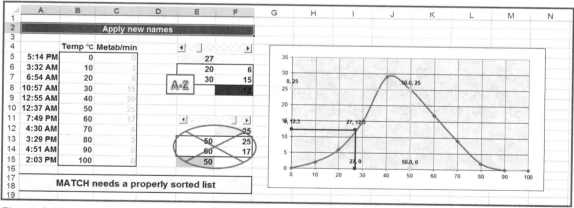

Figure 2.33

Caution

The first *control* on Figure 2.33 doesn't work until column B is sorted in an ascending order (A-Z). Remember that `MATCH` often needs a sorted range. But the second *control* does not work when column B is sorted because column C then has an ascending section followed by a descending section. If you sort column C in an ascending order, the predicted value follows an "imaginary" path that connects the dots in a zigzag way. (In addition, the first *control* would be in trouble.) The bottom line is that you need to be careful when you use `INDEX`, `MATCH`, and `TREND` together. `MATCH` cannot handle certain situations; when that's the case, you must find the formula behind the trend, which you will learn about in Part 4 when we discuss curve fitting.

Chapter 15: Fixing Numbers

Sometimes you want your values to look a bit different, and yet you need them to be numeric for calculation purposes. On the other hand, your figures might look great, but you cannot use them for calculations. Yet, it may be very helpful, especially when you have many columns with numeric entries, to show which column uses which kind of measurement units. How do you handle situations like these in your data analysis?

Figure 2.34 shows two lists. The list on the left is perfect, from a mathematical point of view, but for some reason—perhaps to clearly indicate what kind of measurement units you are dealing with in each column—you would rather have columns look like the ones on the right. There are bad solutions and good solutions. Here's what you can do:

	A	B	C	D	E	F	G	H	I	J	K	L
1	Plate ID	Analyst	Group	50 ng/mL	%CV	25 ng/mL	%CV		50 ng/mL	CV	25 ng/mL	CV
2	8877p58b	bdo	105	43.2	4	22.6	3		43.2 ng/mL	4%	22.6 ng/mL	3%
3	8877p58b	bdo	105	44.3	3	20.7	3		44.3 ng/mL	3%	20.7 ng/mL	3%
4	8696p08b	bdo	105	52.9	3	27.5	6		52.9 ng/mL	3%	27.5 ng/mL	6%
5	8696p08b	bdo	105	50.1	1	26.8	3		50.1 ng/mL	1%	26.8 ng/mL	3%
6	8877p58a	gmv	107	47.7	2	22.7	0		47.7 ng/mL	2%	22.7 ng/mL	0%
7	8877p58a	gmv	107	48.7	3	23.0	3		48.7 ng/mL	3%	23.0 ng/mL	3%
8	8696p08a	gmv	107	52.3	1	26.5	2		52.3 ng/mL	1%	26.5 ng/mL	2%
9	8696p08a	gmv	107	49.7	2	25.0	1		49.7 ng/mL	2%	25.0 ng/mL	1%
10	8696p08a	ksm	121	56.4	12	29.1	11		56.4 ng/mL	12%	29.1 ng/mL	11%
11	8696p08a	ksm	121	51.3	2	26.9	1		51.3 ng/mL	2%	26.9 ng/mL	1%
12	8696p08b	ksm	121	51.0	1	26.1	1		51 ng/mL	1%	26.1 ng/mL	1%
13	8696p08b	ksm	121	48.6	1	24.8	0		48.6 ng/mL	1%	24.8 ng/mL	0%
14	8877p58a	tjk	113	49.3	0	23.0	1		49.3 ng/mL	0%	23.0 ng/mL	1%
15	8877p58a	tjk	113	45.9	2	22.9	1		45.9 ng/mL	2%	22.9 ng/mL	1%
16	8697p58b	tjk	113	47.5	0	22.7	2		47.5 ng/mL	0%	22.7 ng/mL	2%
17	8697p58b	tjk	113	47.5	1	22.9	3		47.5 ng/mL	1%	22.9 ng/mL	3%
18	8877p58b	tkm	209	47.5	0	22.7	2		47.5 ng/mL	0%	22.7 ng/mL	2%
19	8877p58b	tkm	209	45.9	1	22.9	3		45.9 ng/mL	1%	22.9 ng/mL	3%
20	8697p58b	tkm	209	43.2	4	22.6	3		43.2 ng/mL	4%	22.6 ng/mL	3%
21	8697p58b	tkm	209	44.3	3	22.6	3		44.3 ng/mL	3%	22.6 ng/mL	3%
22												
23	Mean			48.4	2	24.2	3		#DIV/0!	2%	24	3
24												

Figure 2.34

- Say that in cell I2, you want to show 43.2 as 43.2 *ng/mL*. Instead of using CONCATENATE, you could apply the ampersand as a concatenation operator in your formula: =D2&" ng/mL". Generally, the ampersand operator (&) is easier to use than CONCATENATE. The price you pay is that the entry has become text, so summary calculations at the bottom are not possible.

- In column J, you want to add a percentage sign without losing the possibility of calculating totals. So do not use the ampersand (not =E2&"%"), but =E2/100 and then apply the percentage format. Formatting does not change the number itself.

- A similar solution was applied to cell K2 and the rest of the column: =F2, followed by a *Custom* format: 0.0 "ng/mL". (The number of zeros determines the number of decimals; do not use & here, because this is not a formula.) Again, formatting does not affect the number itself, but things may still look better.

- In column L, you can use the same technique (instead of =E2/100 with a percentage format). Just use =E2 followed by a *Custom* format: 0"%" (again, no & here).

Unfortunately, oftentimes, some columns contain non-numeric entries to begin with, so they have to be changed into numeric entries. You may have received such "values" through e-mail or through another program that does not work with real numbers. How can you fix them so you can perform calculations? There are basically two solutions: You can use Excel functions or you can apply an Excel tool. Let's look at both options.

Figure 2.35 shows how to fix some troubled "values" by using functions. The columns D, F, H, and J may appear to hold real numbers but they were forced into text and then right aligned. In the columns to their right, the problem was solved this way:

	A	B	C	D	E	F	G	H	I	J	K
1	Plate ID	Analyst	Group	50 ng/mL	50 ng/mL	CV	CV	25 ng/mL	25 ng/mL	CV	CV
2	8877p58a	gmv	105	47.7 ng/mL	47.7	2%	2	22.7 ng/mL	22.7	0%	0
3	8877p58a	gmv	105	48.7 ng/mL	48.7	3%	3	23 ng/mL	23.0	3%	0.03
4	8877p58a	tjk	105	49.3 ng/mL	49.3	0%	0	23 ng/mL	23.0	1%	0.01
5	8877p58a	tjk	105	45.9 ng/mL	45.9	2%	2	22.9 ng/mL	22.9	1%	0.01
6	8877p58b	tkm	107	47.5 ng/mL	47.5	0%	0	22.7 ng/mL	22.7	2%	0.02
7	8877p58b	tkm	107	45.9 ng/mL	45.9	1%	1	22.9 ng/mL	22.9	3%	0.03
8	8877p58b	bdo	107	43.2 ng/mL	43.2	4%	4	22.6 ng/mL	22.6	3%	0.03
9	8877p58b	bdo	107	44.3 ng/mL	44.3	3%	3	20.7 ng/mL	20.7	3%	0.03
10	8696p08a	ksm	121	56.4 ng/mL	56.4	12%	12	29.1 ng/mL	29.1	11%	0.11
11	8696p08a	ksm	121	51.3 ng/mL	51.3	2%	2	26.9 ng/mL	26.9	1%	0.01
12	8696p08a	gmv	121	52.3 ng/mL	52.3	1%	1	26.5 ng/mL	26.5	2%	0.02
13	8696p08a	gmv	121	49.7 ng/mL	49.7	2%	2	25 ng/mL	25.0	1%	0.01
14	8696p08b	bdo	113	52.9 ng/mL	52.9	3%	3	27.5 ng/mL	27.5	6%	0.06
15	8696p08b	bdo	113	50.1 ng/mL	50.1	1%	1	26.8 ng/mL	26.8	3%	0.03
16	8696p08b	ksm	113	51.0 ng/mL	51.0	1%	1	26.1 ng/mL	26.1	1%	0.01
17	8696p08b	ksm	113	48.6 ng/mL	48.6	1%	1	24.8 ng/mL	24.8	0%	0
18	8697p58b	tjk	209	47.5 ng/mL	47.5	0%	0	22.7 ng/mL	22.7	2%	0.02
19	8697p58b	tjk	209	47.5 ng/mL	47.5	1%	1	22.9 ng/mL	22.9	3%	0.03
20	8697p58b	tkm	209	43.2 ng/mL	43.2	4%	4	22.6 ng/mL	22.6	3%	0.03
21	8697p58b	tkm	209	44.3 ng/mL	44.3	3%	3	22.6 ng/mL	22.6	3%	0.03
22											
23				#DIV/0!	48.365	#DIV/0!	2.3	#DIV/0!	24.2	#DIV/0!	0.026
24											

Figure 2.35

- In cell E2, you can use the function LEFT as follows: =LEFT(D2,4). Although this cuts off the text part, the remaining part is still a text string—until you nest LEFT inside the VALUE function: =VALUE(LEFT(D2,4)). In addition to using VALUE, you could also multiply the result by 1: =1*LEFT(D2,4). This forces the text value into a numeric value.

- In column G, the LEFT function cannot just take the first character because there may be more than one digit. To get around this problem, you also need the LEN function, which determines the length of the string: =LEFT(F2,LEN(F2)-1). And, of course, you must nest all of this inside the VALUE function.

- Cell I2 needs a similar formula: =VALUE(LEFT(H2,LEN(H2)-6)).

- In column K, you use the bare VALUE function—and nothing else. It can handle simple situations such as VALUE("5%") and VALUE("$5").

Figure 2.36 shows how to fix troubled "values" by using an Excel tool, *Text to Columns*, instead of functions. You find the *Text to Columns* tool on the *Data* tab. Say that someone had combined the series number and its sub-IDs into a single *Plate ID*, so you cannot sort properly. You take these steps to split the *ID*:

	A	B	C	D	E	F
1	Plate ID	Sub ID	Date	Analyst	Group	C Value
2	8877p58a		09/11/01	kpm, 102		64.8
3	8877p58b		09/11/01	tjk, 115		70.2
4	8877p58c		09/11/01	tmv, 107		60.7
5	8877p60a		09/12/01	etv, 107		58.3
6	8877p60b		09/12/01	wow, 107		73.6
7	8696p08a		09/14/01	tmv, 107		72.4
8	8696p08b		09/14/01	etv, 107		62.5
9	8696p08c		09/14/01	wow, 107		56.7
10	8696p08d		09/14/01	cod, 102		59.9
11	8696p08e		09/14/01	kpm, 102		73.6
12	8696p08f		09/14/01	luv, 102		63.3
13	8877p63a		09/14/01	cod, 102		45.0
14	8877p63b		09/14/01	kpm, 102		50.2
15	8877p70c		09/18/01	gmv, 115		57.1
16	8877p70d		09/18/01	tjk, 115		39.8
17	8877p71a		09/19/01	tmv, 107		66.9
18	8877p71b		09/19/01	etv, 107		79.4
19	8877p75a		09/20/01	wow, 107		61.8
20	8877p75b		09/20/01	kpm, 102		58.4
21	8877p78a		09/21/01	luv, 102		65.8
22	8877p78b		09/21/01	ejs, 115		60.8
24	8877p83a		09/25/01	gmv, 115		83.7
25	8877p83b		09/25/01	tjk, 115		64.9
26	8877p84a		09/25/01	tmv, 107		63.0
27						

Figure 2.36

1. Make sure you have a receptacle ready for each section you cut off. In this case, you need an empty column to the right of column A—by right-clicking on column C, followed by *Insert*.

2. Choose *Text to Columns* from the *Data* tab.

3. Because, in this case, you are dealing with a *Fixed Width* situation—all IDs have the same length—you split column A after five characters.

4. Repeat steps 1–3 for column D, and don't forget to create an empty column for the second part of the split. This time, however, choose *Delimited Text* with both ☑ *comma* and ☑ *space* as delimiters.

Figure 2.37 shows another way to fix numbers. Let's pretend that the instruments of some analysts needed calibration, and that some correction factor is required for two analysts. Instead of using formulas in extra columns, you can multiply directly by using the *Paste Special* tool. These are the steps:

	A	B	C	D	E	F	G	H	I
1	Plate ID	Analyst	50 ng/mL	%CV	25 ng/mL	%CV		gmv	1.1
2	8877p58b	bdo	43.2	4	22.6	3		tkm	0.9
3	8877p58b	bdo	44.3	3	20.7	3			
4	8696p08b	bdo	52.9	3	27.5	6			
5	8696p08b	bdo	50.1	1	26.8	3			
6	8877p58a	gmv	52.5	2	25.0	0			
7	8877p58a	gmv	53.6	3	25.3	3			
8	8696p08a	gmv	57.5	1	29.2	2			
9	8696p08a	gmv	54.7	2	27.5	1			
10	8696p08a	ksm	56.4	12	29.1	11			
11	8696p08a	ksm	51.3	2	26.9	1			
12	8696p08b	ksm	51.0	1	26.1	1			
13	8696p08b	ksm	48.6	1	24.8	0			
14	8877p58a	tjk	49.3	0	23.0	1			
15	8877p58a	tjk	45.9	2	22.9	1			
16	8697p58b	tjk	47.5	0	22.7	2			
17	8697p58b	tjk	47.5	1	22.9	3			
18	8877p58b	tkm	42.8	0	20.4	2			
19	8877p58b	tkm	41.3	1	20.6	3			
20	8697p58b	tkm	38.9	4	20.3	3			
21	8697p58b	tkm	39.9	3	20.3	3			
22									

Figure 2.37

1. Copy I1 (which is the correction factor for *gmv*).

2. Select the readings done by *gmv* (e.g. C6:C9 and E6:E9).

3. Use *Paste Special*, selecting the option ⊙ *Multiply*.

4. Repeat steps 1–3 for analyst *tkm* (e.g. C18:C21 and E18:E21).

This trick works quickly and efficiently.

Figure 2.38 tackles the rounding issue besides. The table on the right has the correction factors for each analyst. Here's what you could do:

	A	B	C	D	E	F	G	H	I	J	K
1	Plate ID	Analyst	50 ng/mL	50 Corr.	%CV	25 ng/mL	25 Corr.	%CV		bdo	0.9
2	8877p58b	bdo	43.2	38.90000	4	22.6	20.30000	3		gmv	1.1
3	8877p58b	bdo	44.3	39.90000	3	20.7	18.60000	3		ksm	1.0
4	8696p08b	bdo	52.9	47.60000	3	27.5	24.80000	6		tjk	0.8
5	8696p08b	bdo	50.1	45.10000	1	26.8	24.10000	3		tkm	0.9
6	8877p58a	gmv	47.7	52.50000	2	22.7	25.00000	0			
7	8877p58a	gmv	48.7	53.60000	3	23.0	25.30000	3			
8	8696p08a	gmv	52.3	57.50000	1	26.5	29.20000	2			
9	8696p08a	gmv	49.7	54.70000	2	25.0	27.50000	1			
10	8696p08a	ksm	56.4	56.40000	12	29.1	29.10000	11			
11	8696p08a	ksm	51.3	51.30000	2	26.9	26.90000	1			
12	8696p08b	ksm	51.0	51.00000	1	26.1	26.10000	1			
13	8696p08b	ksm	48.6	48.60000	1	24.8	24.80000	0			
14	8877p58a	tjk	49.3	39.40000	0	23.0	18.40000	1			
15	8877p58a	tjk	45.9	36.70000	2	22.9	18.30000	1			
16	8697p58b	tjk	47.5	38.00000	0	22.7	18.20000	2			
17	8697p58b	tjk	47.5	38.00000	1	22.9	18.30000	3			
18	8877p58b	tkm	47.5	42.80000	0	22.7	20.40000	2			
19	8877p58b	tkm	45.9	41.30000	1	22.9	20.60000	3			
20	8697p58b	tkm	43.2	38.90000	4	22.6	20.30000	3			
21	8697p58b	tkm	44.3	39.90000	3	22.6	20.30000	3			
22											

Figure 2.38

1. In cell D2, use the formula =ROUND(C2*VLOOKUP(B2,$J$1:$K$5,2,0),1).

2. In cell G2, use the formula =ROUND(F2*VLOOKUP(B2,$J$1:$K$5,2,0),1).

3. Change the formulas into values before you get rid of the previous, old columns. Increasing the number of decimals through formatting should no longer have any effect.

Note

If you ever wonder how precise and reliable Excel's calculations are, be aware that numeric precision in most computer programs is limited by a maximum of 15 digits (beyond 15, all digits are 0). In addition, there is another problem with computer calculations: Decimal values (10-based) have to be converted into binary values (2-based) and back. That's where things can go wrong. Try the following:

- =1/9000 returns 0.000111111111111111 (15 digits followed by 0s)

- Add 1 to the result: 1.00011111111111 (15 digits followed by 0s)

- Subtract 1 again: 0.000111111111111173 (15 digits again, but the last two are incorrect). Is this troubling? Usually not, but there might be circumstances when an error kicks in, which might propagate when used elsewhere.

Figure 2.39 shows a sheet with figures that were copied from an e-mail message or that were manipulated with text functions such as LEFT. No matter how you obtained them, they are text, and, therefore, cannot be used in calculations. Of course, you could create a new column with the function VALUE, as you did before. But there is actually a quicker solution: Make sure you type the number 1, as a multiplier, somewhere on the sheet, copy it, select the cells with text entries, and then use *Paste Special* to perform an operation based on either ⊙ *multiplication* or ⊙ *division*. This forces the cell entries to become numeric, so you can use them in calculations.

	A	B	C	
1	Plate ID	Analyst	C-Value	
2	8877p58a	gmv	47.7	
3	8877p58a	gmv	48.7	
4	8877p58a	tjk	49.3	
5	8877p58a	tjk	45.9	
6	8877p58b	tkm	47.5	
7	8877p58b	tkm	45.9	
8	8877p58b	bdo	43.2	
9	8877p58b	bdo	44.3	
10	8696p08a	ksm	56.4	
11	8696p08a	ksm	51.3	
12	8696p08a	gmv	52.3	
13	8696p08a	gmv	49.7	
14	8696p08b	bdo	52.9	
15	8696p08b	bdo	50.1	
16	8696p08b	ksm	51	
17	8696p08b	ksm	48.6	
18	8697p58b	tjk	47.5	
19	8697p58b	tjk	47.5	
20	8697p58b	tkm	43.2	
21	8697p58b	tkm	44.3	
22				
23		Mean	#DIV/0!	
24		SD	#DIV/0!	
25				

Figure 2.39

Note

Sometimes cells that hold numbers as text have a green marker in the left top corner. This marker is only there if that option is turned on: *File | Options | Formulas | Error Checking | ⊙ Enable background error checking*. If this is the case, you can select the cell, click on the icon in front of it, and select *Convert to Number*. But this has to be done for each cell individually, so the above trick is a better choice.

Chapter 16: Copying Formulas

Copying formulas can be a tedious process. When you copy a formula, its relative, "unlocked" cell references adjust to their new location. Sometimes, that's great. If formulas (with relative references) did not adjust to their new locations, you would never be able to copy your formulas downward in the columns of your spreadsheets—which you have probably been doing for years. You can even use this formula behavior to your advantage when creating a transposed version of a list: Copy the list (*Ctrl+C*), select a new location, *Paste Special*, ☑*Transpose*. The transposed list will be nicely "rotated" by 90 degrees, and all formulas will beautifully adjust. So you should be grateful for such performance.

However, "unlocked" references are not so great when you want a formula pasted into another location to come up with the same formula result as the original formula. Is such a thing possible? Yes, it is. Although it is not easy to reach this result, you may need to do it at times.

Figure 2.40 shows different ways of copying formulas that should keep the formulas' result the same (that is, if you want copies of formulas that do not change their references):

	A	B	C	D	E	F	G
1			**Mean**				**Copy Mean**
2							
3	$ 213.45	$ 119.97	$ 333.42	Copy/Paste			$ -
4							
5							
6	$ 213.45	$ 119.97	$ 333.42	Absolute/Copy/Paste			$ 333.42
7							
8							
9	$ 213.45	$ 119.97	$ 333.42	Copy/Paste as Link			$ 333.42
10							
11							
12	$ 213.45	$ 119.97	$ 333.42	Copy FormulaBar/Paste			$ 333.42
13							
14							
15	$ 213.45	$ 119.97	$ 333.42	Direct Link			$ 333.42
16							
17							
18	$ 213.45	$ 119.97		Cut/Paste (but only 1x)			$ 333.42
19							

Figure 2.40

- Row 3 shows that *Copy* and *Paste* are not going to work in cell G3. Fortunately, there are alternatives (but don't expect miracles).

- Row 6 uses absolute cell references. So cell C6 has the formula =SUM($A$6:$B$6), which remains unchanged in the *Copy* and *Paste* process.

- Row 9 uses the *Paste Link* option from the *Paste* command on the *Home* tab (located in the left lower corner of the dialog box). This automatically creates the following reference in cell G9: =$C$9. This is great, but now you can never delete the original cell(s).

- In row 12, you apply a copying technique through the *formula bar* (not the cell itself): Select C12's formula in the *formula bar*, copy it, press *Esc*, and paste it into cell G12. The formula does not update this time in its new location, because you copied it from the *formula bar*.

- In row 15, you create your own link. Just type the following in G15: =C15 or =$C$15. Again, the original cell cannot be deleted without affecting its link.

- If you use the *Cut* option, the formula of cells that you cut and paste does not adjust either, but the *Paste* operation works only once, and you lose the original. Sometimes, that's a high price to pay.

What is the best method? It depends on your preferences, but the *formula bar* method is often the best.

Figure 2.41 revisits a situation we discussed earlier. The summary section on the right needs to be created from records on the left. The easiest way to get started is to use the Subtotal tool. Next you collapse the table to its subtotals and copy only the visible cells into the summary table on the right (refer to Chapter 7). But no matter how you paste them, there isn't an ideal solution here: The link would no longer work when you decide to delete the subtotals, and the values would not update when records on the left are altered. The best solution is not so ideal in terms of time and work:

	A	B	C	D	E	F	G	H	I
1							pH<6	pH 6-8	pH>8
2	Colonies on 10 Petri Dishes					1000 mg/L	34	60	27
3						2000 mg/L	66	50	20
4	Nutrient	pH<6	pH 6-8	pH>8					
5	1000 mg/L	1	4	2					
6	1000 mg/L	2	5	2					
7	1000 mg/L	2	5	2					
8	1000 mg/L	4	6	2					
9	1000 mg/L	4	6	2					
10	1000 mg/L	4	6	3					
11	1000 mg/L	4	6	3					
12	1000 mg/L	4	7	3					
13	1000 mg/L	4	7	3					
14	1000 mg/L	5	8	5					
15	1000 mg/L Total	34	60	27					
16	2000 mg/L	5	3	0					
17	2000 mg/L	6	4	1					
18	2000 mg/L	6	4	1					
19	2000 mg/L	6	5	2					
20	2000 mg/L	6	5	2					
21	2000 mg/L	7	5	2					
22	2000 mg/L	7	5	2					
23	2000 mg/L	7	6	3					
24	2000 mg/L	7	6	3					
25	2000 mg/L	9	7	4					
26	2000 mg/L Total	66	50	20					
27	Grand Total	100	110	47					
28									

Figure 2.41

1. Copy the first formula (B15) from the *formula bar*.

2. Press *Esc*.

3. Paste the copy into G2.

4. Use the *fill handle* to copy G2 to the right.

5. Repeat steps 1–4 for B26.

6. Now you can delete the subtotals to the left, and cell references adjust automatically. In addition, changes made to the table on the left replicate to the table on the right.

Chapter 17: Multi-cell Arrays

Most of the time, a formula returns a single value or result. Some formulas, though, return multiple values at the same time. Consequently, these array formulas, called *multi-cell array formulas*, need multiple cells to display their formula results. With these formulas, you need to select multiple cells ahead of time and accept each formula by pressing *Ctrl+Shift+Enter* (not just *Enter* or even *Ctrl+Enter*). If you forget that final step, you receive a #VALUE error. To correct that error, you click in the formula bar and then press *Ctrl+Shift+Enter*.

Figure 2.42 shows an example of a multi-cell array formula. As you learned in Chapter 8, filters work through labels or headers that need to be exact replicas of the database labels. Each one of these filters is a perfect candidate for a multi-cell array formula. You use one as follows:

	A	B	C	D	E	F	G	H	I	J	K
1	Patient	DOB	Age	Weight	Systolic		Patient	DOB	Age	Weight	Systolic
2	Bush	7/20/1976	36	152	126				>50		
3	Carter	2/24/1946	67	179	151						
4	Clinton	11/21/1982	30	185	160						
5	Eisenhower	9/19/1977	35	163	138		Patient	DOB	Age	Weight	Systolic
6	Ford	8/21/1955	57	172	144						>150
7	Johnson	7/20/1965	47	156	128						
8	Kennedy	3/28/1947	66	145	120						
9	Nixon	1/23/1955	58	165	140		Patient	DOB	Age	Weight	Systolic
10	Reagan	10/21/1961	51	159	132				>50		>150
11											

Figure 2.42

1. Select multiple cells, such as G1:K1, or G5:K5, or G9:K9.

2. Delete the contents of these cells.

3. Type =A1:E1. (A multi-cell array formula does not need absolute cell references.)

4. Press *Ctrl+Shift+Enter*.

When you press *Ctrl+Shift+Enter*, Excel adds braces to your formula: ={A1:E1}. You should never actually type these braces; they appear when you press *Ctrl+Shift+Enter*, and they change the formula into an array formula. Using an array formula has two advantages: First, no one can delete or change part of the array; second, when the database headers change, the filter labels change accordingly.

Because parts of an array cannot be deleted, arrays are a nice tool for protecting certain cells from being changed inadvertently. To take advantage of this tool, you select the cell with a formula that you want to protect plus an empty cell next to it, click in the formula bar, and then press *Ctrl+Shift+Enter*. You probably want to hide the contents of the neighboring cell by making its font color white (to match its background). Now, unaware users (including yourself) cannot inadvertently delete the visible formula because it is attached to the neighboring cell.

Not only can you make your own array formulas, but there are also some preexisting array functions in Excel. The most important ones are TRANSPOSE, FREQUENCY, TREND, and INDEX. There are a few more; we discuss some of them in Chapters 37 and 40.

Figure 2.43 shows how Excel's built-in multi-cell array functions work. Let's start with TRANSPOSE:

	A	B	C	D	E	F	G	H	I	J
1	Patient	DOB	Age	Weight	SBP$_{obs}$	SBP/Wgt$_{pred}$			Field	Value
2	Bush	7/20/1976	36	152	126	126			Patient	Bush
3	Carter	2/24/1946	67	179	151	152			DOB	7/20/76
4	Clinton	11/21/1982	30	185	160	158			Age	36
5	Eisenhower	9/19/1977	35	163	138	137			Weight	152
6	Ford	8/21/1955	57	172	144	146			SBPobs	126
7	Johnson	7/20/1965	47	156	128	130				
8	Kennedy	3/28/1947	66	145	120	119			Age	Freq
9	Nixon	1/23/1955	58	165	140	139		Age to 30	30	1
10	Reagan	10/21/1961	51	159	132	133		30 to 40	40	2
11								40 to 50	50	1
12								50 to 60	60	3
13								60 to 70	70	2
14	Bush	7/20/76	36	152	126	126				0
15										

Figure 2.43

1. Select I2:I6.

2. Type or call the function TRANSPOSE, whose range is A1:E1 (that is, no absolute references needed): =TRANSPOSE(A1:E1).

3. Press *Ctrl+Shift+Enter* to get a transposed copy.

Then you follow these steps to find the frequencies per age category:

1. Select J9:J14. Notice the extra cell at the bottom, which serves as a bin for cases not covered by the previous categories (if the last cell is not 0, you must have overlooked some higher values—in this case, ages over 70).

2. Type or call FREQUENCY, whose data range is C2:C10 and the bins range is I9:I13.

3. Press *Ctrl+Shift+Enter* to get the frequencies per category: =FREQUENCY(C2:C10,I9:I13). The total should be 10, of course.

Next, say that you want to predict what the systolic blood pressure would be if there is a linear relationship between systolic blood pressure and weight. You can easily achieve this by using the multi-cell array function TREND:

1. Select F2:F10.

2. Type or call TREND, using the formula =TREND(E2:E10,D2:D10).

3. Press *Ctrl+Shift+Enter* to get predictions based on a linear regression line. Notice how close the predicted values are to the observed values, so there seems to be a linear relationship in this case.

Finally, you want to display the full record of the person that was selected in cell J2. This can be done with the INDEX function, but this time as an array function that returns multiple cells.

1. Select A14:F14.

2. Type or call INDEX, using the formula =INDEX(A2:F10,MATCH(J2,A2:A10,0),0). By setting the argument *Column_num* to 0, the function returns all columns in a horizontal array. (When *Row_num* is set to 0, the function returns a vertical array of values.)

3. Press *Ctrl+Shift+Enter* to get the entire record for the person shown in cell J2.

Figure 2.44 shows the linear relationship between hemoglobin percentage and red blood cell count. Column E uses the multi-cell array function TREND. In column F, you calculate the *residuals*—the difference between observed and predicted values. You could do this the conventional way per individual cell (e.g. =C2-E2), but a custom multi-cell array formula would be a good alternative:

	A	B	C	D	E	F	G
1	Patient	DOB	Weight	Systolic BP		SBP Top 5	
2	Bush	7/20/1976	152	120		167	
3	Carter	2/24/1946	179	139		160	
4	Clinton	11/21/1982	185	160		155	
5	Eisenhower	9/19/1977	163	148		148	
6	Ford	8/21/1955	172	167		145	
7	Johnson	7/20/1965	156	145			
8	Kennedy	3/28/1947	145	137			
9	Nixon	1/23/1955	165	155			
10	Reagan	10/21/1961	159	137			
11							

Figure 2.44

1. Select F2:F20.

2. Type the following formula: =C2:C20-E2:E20. (Or: =(C2:C20)-(E2:E20).)

3. Press *Ctrl+Shift+Enter*, which adds the braces.

What are the advantages of using an array formula in situations like these? First, you get one consistent formula. Second, you cannot delete individual cells. Third, you replace numerous formula with just one, which creates a smaller file size.

Custom multi-cell array formulas can get very complicated. Fortunately, there is a great way of testing them piece by piece:

1. Highlight one part in the *formula bar*; make sure it is an inclusive part (no missing parenthesis, etc.).

2. Press the *F9* key to run that part and watch the outcome. Select another part and hit *F9* again.

3. When done, do not hit *Enter*, but *Esc*—otherwise you would replace the formula with its values.

Figure 2.45 displays the top five values for systolic blood pressure in a pilot study. You can do so by using the LARGE function. Its second argument specifies the position from the top. So for five different positions, we could include a sub-array with the numbers 1 through 5: {1,2,3,4,5}.

	A	B	C	D	E	F	G
1	Patient	DOB	Weight	Systolic BP		SBP Top 5	
2	Bush	7/20/1976	152	120		167	
3	Carter	2/24/1946	179	139		160	
4	Clinton	11/21/1982	185	160		155	
5	Eisenhower	9/19/1977	163	148		148	
6	Ford	8/21/1955	172	167		145	
7	Johnson	7/20/1965	156	145			
8	Kennedy	3/28/1947	145	137			
9	Nixon	1/23/1955	165	155			
10	Reagan	10/21/1961	159	137			
11							

Figure 2.45

1. Select F2:F6.

2. Implement the array formula: =LARGE(D2:D10,{1,2,3,4,5,}). Instead of an inserted array, you could also use a nested ROW function: =LARGE(D2:D10,ROW(1:5)). To avoid that *1:5* could change when the cells get inserted downwards, you could protect the function: =LARGE(D2:D10,ROW(INDIRECT("1:5"))).

3. Press *Ctrl+Shift+Enter*, which adds the braces.

Figure 2.46 shows a situation where array functions can help you solve equations—for instance two equations with two unknown X's or three equations with three unknown X's. The Y-values you want to equate to are shown in column G. To get these solutions for the unknown X's, you need three different functions: `MINVERSE` (to invert the matrix *[A]* of all *a*-values), `MMULT` (to multiply 2 matrices: *Inv[A] * [Y]*), and `TRANSPOSE` (because `MMULT` always return a vertical array, whereas you need a horizontal one in C6:D6 and C14:E14).

	A	B	C	D	E	F	G	H	I
1		2 equations with 2 unknown X's:			$Y = a_1X_1 + a_2X_2$				TEST
2									
3			a_1	a_2					
4	2 equations with 2 unknowns		9.375	3.042		Y	9.231		9.231
5			3.042	6.183		Y	8.202		8.202
6		X's	0.659	1.002					
7									
8		3 equations with 3 unknown X's:			$Y = a_1X_1 + a_2X_2 + a_3X_3$				
9									
10			a_1	a_2	a_3				
11	3 equations with 3 unknowns		9.375	3.042	-2.437	Y	9.231		9.231
12			3.042	6.183	1.216	Y	8.202		8.202
13			-2.437	1.216	8.443	Y	3.931		3.931
14		X's	0.896	0.765	0.614				
15									
16									

Figure 2.46

1. Select C6:D6.

2. Implement the array formula: `=TRANSPOSE(MMULT(MINVERSE(C4:D5),G4:G5))`, followed by Ctr+Sh+Enter.

3. Do something similar for C14:E14: `=TRANSPOSE(MMULT(MINVERSE(C11:E13),G11:G13))`.

Column I shows you that the equations were correctly solved. Cell I4, for instance, uses this formula: `=C4*$C$6+D4*$D$6`. The results in column I are completely identical to the Y-values in column G.

Chapter 18: Single-cell Arrays

Whereas a multi-cell array formula returns multiple values, a single-cell array formula returns a single value. But in order to calculate this single value, a single-cell array formula needs to work with arrays in the background; it can therefore perform calculations that are otherwise impossible.

Figure 2.47 shows a situation in which you might want to use a single-cell array because, following the rules of significant digits, the sum of the diluted volumes is not correct anymore: It should be 23.1 (E7) and not 23.2 (C7). In order to correct for this, you need a new column E that rounds all volumes to one digit first, before you calculate the total in column F. A single-cell array formula could do all this work in the background by rounding the values in a "hidden" array and then performing a sum operation on the values from this rounded array. It's all done in one formula of the single-cell array type.

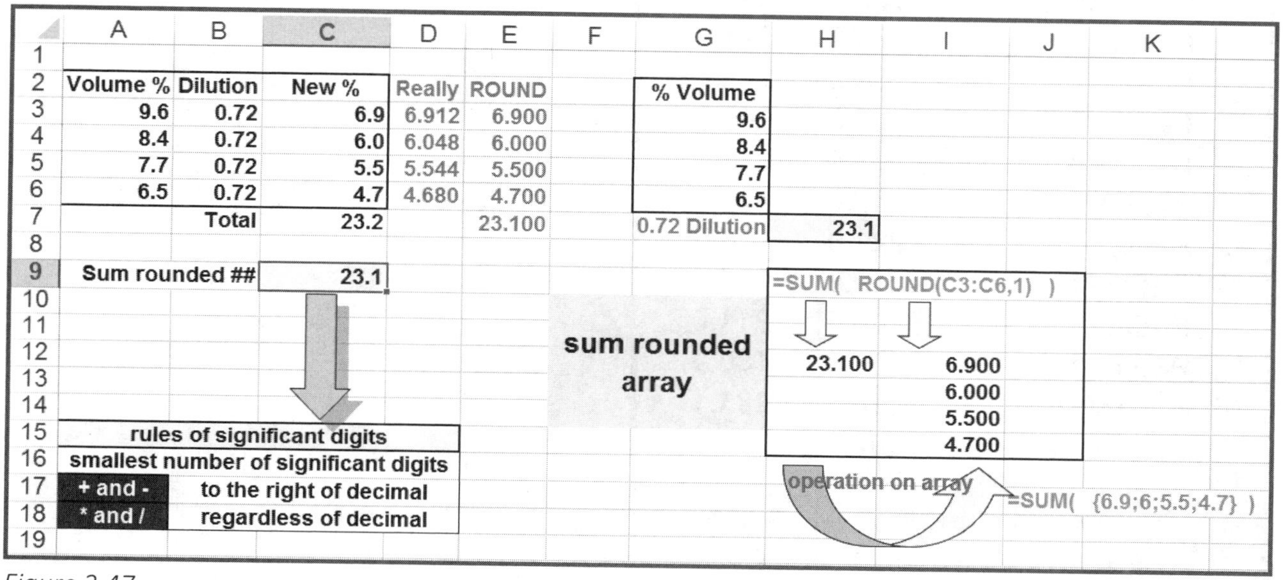

Figure 2.47

This is the array formula for cell C9: =SUM(ROUND(C3:C6,1)). Don't forget to accept the formula by pressing *Ctrl+Shift+Enter*. If you want to check how the formula actually performs, you can do the following:

1. Highlight the ROUND(…) part of the formula in the formula bar. Make sure you don't highlight more or fewer characters.

2. Press *F9* to run the formula, and you get the rounded array.

3. Press *Esc* to stop the run.

4. Highlight the SUM(…) part of the formula and press *F9* to get the sum of this array.

5. Press *Esc*. (If you don't, you replace the ranges with values. If you press *Enter* instead of *Esc*, use *Undo*.)

Note

In this case, the single-cell array formula combines (and, therefore, eliminates) intermediate columns by using internal arrays instead. You could skip even more columns! In cell H7, you could use one single-cell array formula based on only one column of figures: =SUM(ROUND((G3:G6)*0.72,1)).

Figure 2.48 presents a similar situation. In this case, the effect of a diet pill was measured for 16 participants in the study. You could use extra columns for in-between calculations, but all you need is some summary information. So you can use single-cell array formulas instead:

	A	B	C
1		Before	After
2	Patient1	213.4	200.1
3	Patient2	225.0	216.4
4	Patient3	217.0	195.6
5	Patient4	183.7	175.0
6	Patient5	197.2	202.3
7	Patient6	223.6	214.8
8	Patient7	224.2	215.7
9	Patient8	215.2	200.7
10	Patient9	202.4	211.7
11	Patient10	217.7	216.1
12	Patient11	221.0	208.5
13	Patient12	219.9	188.4
14	Patient13	205.4	211.4
15	Patient14	195.1	180.9
16	Patient15	218.0	184.1
17	Patient16	207.6	202.3
18			
19	Mean Change		-10.15
20	Largest Pos. Change		9.3
21	Largest Neg. Change		-33.9
22	Mean Negative Change		-14.06
23			

Figure 2.48

- In cell C19, calculate the mean change with =AVERAGE((C2:C17)-(B2:B17)).

- In cell C20, calculate the largest positive change with =MAX((C2:C17)-(B2:B17)).

- In cell C21, calculate the largest negative change with =MIN((C2:C17)-(B2:B17)).

- In cell C22, calculate the mean negative change with
=AVERAGE(IF((C2:C17)-(B2:B17)<0,(C2:C17)-(B2:B17))).

Figure 2.49 shows another example. Instead of using column E (as we did in the previous chapter with a multi-cell array formula), we use single-cell array formulas in D21, D22, and D23:

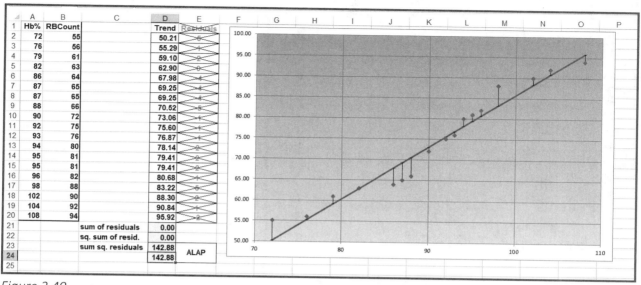

Figure 2.49

- In cell D21, calculate the sum of residuals with =SUM(B2:B20-D2:D20) (in one formula, followed by *Ctrl+Shift+Enter*). The sum should be 0.

- In cell D22, calculate the *squared sum of residuals* with =SUM(B2:B20-D2:D20)^2 (in one formula, followed by *Ctrl+Shift+Enter*). The sum should be 0.

- In cell D23, calculate the *sum of squared residuals* with =SUM(((B2:B20)-(D2:D20))^2) (in one formula, followed by *Ctrl+Shift+Enter*). This is an important number for curve fitting (see Part 4).

- In cell D24, use a dedicated Excel function called SUMXMY2. It is a regular function equivalent to the previous array formula: =SUMXMY2(B2:B20,D2:D20), **not** followed by *Ctrl+Shift+Enter*).

Figure 2.50 shows another case. You have a series of samples, each with a different number of replicas. The mean of these means is not 23.83, but 23.67—which is a *weighted* mean that takes into account the number of replicates. A weighted mean can be calculated with a single-cell array formula in cell B14. To do so, you sum all the multiplications of each mean with its number of replicates, and then divide this total by the total number of replicates: =SUM(B2:B11*C2:C11)/SUM(C2:C11). Again, this can also be done with a regular Excel function called SUMPRODUCT, which does **not** require Ctrl+Shift+Enter: =SUMPRODUCT(B2:B11,C2:C11)/SUM(C2:C11).

	A	B	C
1	**Sample**	**Mean**	**# Replicates**
2	Sample1	24.97	2
3	Sample2	20.54	4
4	Sample3	21.17	3
5	Sample4	27.99	2
6	Sample5	27.27	4
7	Sample6	19.59	3
8	Sample7	28.00	4
9	Sample8	22.86	6
10	Sample9	24.77	6
11	Sample10	21.15	5
12			
13	Mean	23.83	incorrect
14	Mean	23.67	array formula
15	Mean	23.67	XL function
16			

Figure 2.50

Figure 2.51 shows a very common situation. Calculating the standard deviation at the bottom of column C will never work here because some observations were marked as #NA. You could solve this problem by creating extra columns: first a column D that checks for errors by using the function ISERROR or IFERROR, and then a column E that uses IF to replace error values with no value ("″"). However, a single-cell array formula can do all this in one step: =STDEV.S(IFERROR(C2:C11,"″"))—or the longer one: =STDEV.S(IF(ISERROR(C2:C11),"″",C2:C11)).

	A	B	C	D	E
1	**Date**	**Analyst**	**C Value**	IsError	Final
2	09/18/01	tjk	39.8	FALSE	39.80
3	09/14/01	cod	45.0	FALSE	45.00
4	09/26/01	luv	#N/A	TRUE	
5	09/26/01	ejs	47.5	FALSE	47.50
6	09/14/01	wow	50.2	FALSE	50.20
7	09/14/01	kpm	50.2	FALSE	50.20
8	09/18/01	gmv	57.1	FALSE	57.10
9	09/12/01	etv	#N/A	TRUE	
10	09/20/01	kpm	58.4	FALSE	58.40
11	09/14/01	cod	59.9	FALSE	59.90
12	**Standard Deviation**		7.03		7.03
13					

Figure 2.51

Note

Don't forget `""` in the nested `IF` function. Otherwise, `STDEV` or `STDEV.S` will use zeros in its calculations. In addition, you may want to know that Excel 2010 also introduced the `AGGREGATE` function. It allows you to specify in its first argument which summary function to use (including `STDEV.S`, etc.), and in its second argument which cells to ignore (including error values). However, you must specify those choices with numbers. You can solve this problem, by just typing the function in the cell (instead of using f_x) and those choices will nicely pop up.

Single-cell array formulas can do even more. They use three rather unusual operators:

- For `AND`, you use `*`. You cannot use `AND()`.

- For `OR`, you use `+`. You cannot use `OR()`.

- For `CONCATENATE`, you use `&` (without space on either side).

With these operators, you can perform miracles. Summary tables often require Excel functions such as `SUMIFS`, `COUNTIFS`, and `AVERAGEIFS`, but there is **no** such thing as `STDEVIFS`. However, you can create your own single-cell array formula. Thanks to the above-mentioned operators, single-cell array formulas can do anything you want.

Figure 2.52 calls for a summary table. Say that the main table has three named ranges: *Plates* for A1:A25, *Alysts* for B1:B25, and *Readings* for C1:C25. You have two options:

	A	B	C	D	E	F	G	H	I
1	Plate1	Anal1	1.48			Anal1	Anal2	Anal3	MEAN
2	Plate1	Anal2	1.12		Plate1	1.29	1.38	0.89	1.00
3	Plate1	Anal3	0.81		Plate2	0.91	1.69	1.10	1.31
4	Plate1	Anal1	0.39		Plate3	0.49	1.42	1.46	1.49
5	Plate1	Anal2	1.55		MEAN	1.32	1.20	0.95	1.17
6	Plate1	Anal3	1.35						
7	Plate1	Anal1	2.00						
8	Plate1	Anal2	1.46						
9	Plate1	Anal3	0.50						
10	Plate2	Anal1	1.32						
11	Plate2	Anal2	1.30				with *		
12	Plate2	Anal3	0.81						
13	Plate2	Anal1	0.58			Anal1	Anal2	Anal3	
14	Plate2	Anal2	1.95		Plate1	1.29	1.38	0.89	
15	Plate2	Anal3	1.39		Plate2	0.91	1.69	1.10	
16	Plate2	Anal1	0.82		Plate3	0.49	1.42	1.46	
17	Plate2	Anal2	1.83						
18	Plate3	Anal3	1.94						
19	Plate3	Anal1	0.69						
20	Plate3	Anal2	1.54				with &		
21	Plate3	Anal3	1.56						
22	Plate3	Anal1	0.18			Anal1	Anal2	Anal3	
23	Plate3	Anal2	1.30		Plate1	1.29	1.38	0.89	
24	Plate3	Anal3	0.89		Plate2	0.91	1.69	1.10	
25	Plate3	Anal1	0.60		Plate3	0.49	1.42	1.46	
26									

Figure 2.52

- You can use the operator * in cell G14:
  =STDEV.S(IF((Plates=$F14)*(Alysts=G$13),Readings)).

- You can use the operator & in cell G23:
  =STDEV.S(IF($F23&G$22=Plates&Alysts,Readings)).

Figure 2.53 offers another example in which you might want to consider using single-cell array formulas. Suppose you need to compare two lists—a new one versus an old one—in order to find out whether the exact combination of a specific name and specific systolic blood pressure reading can be found anywhere in the other list. To find a specific entry, e.g. A3, in another range, e.g. F3:F13, you could use the OR function in an array formula: =OR(A3=$F$3:$F$13). It returns TRUE if at least one of its components is true (do not confuse this OR function with the + operator in array formulas).

	A	B	C	D	E	F	G
1	new list					old list	
2	Patient	SBP	A=F	AB=FG		Patient	SBP
3	Bush	120				Lincoln	123
4	Carter	139		changed		Bush	120
5	Clinton	160				Kennedy	137
6	Eisenhower	148				Reagan	137
7	Ford	167		changed		Nixon	140
8	Johnson	145				Carter	145
9	Kennedy	137				Johnson	145
10	Nixon	155		changed		Truman	145
11	Reagan	137				Eisenhower	148
12	Roosevelt	131	new	changed		Ford	159
13	Washington	139	new	changed		Clinton	160
14							

Figure 2.53

- In C3: =IF(OR(A3=$F$3:$F$13),"","new")

- In D3: =IF(OR(A3&B3=$F$3:$F$13&$G$3:$G$13),"","changed")

You can use *F9* at any time to test how the formula builds up.

Note

As said before, a great deal of data analysis can also be done with *Pivot Tables*. They are easier to make but not as flexible as your own (array) formulas. *Pivot Tables* are not part of this book, but can be studied from a more general CD on Excel: www.MrExcel.com/excel2007expert.shtml.

Chapter 19: Date Manipulation

If your records require dates, you probably shouldn't skip this chapter. Excel handles dates in a special way—so you can easily calculate with them if you know what is going on in the background.

There are two important Excel date/time functions:

- `TODAY()` returns the current date. It is a volatile function, similar to `RAND()`.

- `NOW()` returns current date and time. It is another volatile function, similar to `RAND()`.

Each time you press *F9* or change something on the sheet, these two functions update to the latest date/time information from your computer system. Obviously, TODAY and NOW are not good for record keeping because they change constantly (and are therefore called *volatile*). For record keeping, on the other hand, you rather need dates that are fixed. To enter them, you use the following shortcut keys:

- *Ctrl+;* returns the current date (fixed).

- *Ctrl+Shift+;* returns the current time (fixed).

- *Ctrl+; [space] Ctrl+Shift+;* returns the current date and time combined.

Excel assigns a serial number, with or without decimals, to each day. For example, January 1, 2014 was day 40164 since Jan 1, 1900. Excel uses these weird numbers because it is easier for Excel to calculate with dates this way. You don't want to see the serial numbers, so Excel lets you simply format them in more human-readable date formats.

Dates can contain time information as well. For example, day 40164 is 1/1/14, and 40164.5 is 1/1/14 12:00 PM So 6:00 PM would be 40164.75. The number 401654 is therefore 12:00 AM on 1/1/14 in terms of time.

Note

If you want to quickly glimpse at the serial numbers behind dates, you use *Ctrl+~*. Sometimes they pop up automatically on your spreadsheet, so you probably want to change their format to *Date/Time*.

Figure 2.54 offers an overview of date manipulation:

	A	B	C	D	E	F	G	H	I	J
1	TODAY()	5/18/2013								
2	NOW()	5/18/2013 10:28								
3										
4	Ctr ;	5/18/2013								
5	Ctr Sh ;	10:18 AM						DATEDIF(earlier,later,"y")		
6	combination	5/18/2013 10:18								
7								d	m	y
8		Monday		Today's date			5/18/2013	0	0	0
9		Tuesday		1 weeks ago			5/10/2013	8	0	0
10		Wednesday		2 weeks ago			4/10/2013	38	1	0
11		Thursday		3 weeks ago			4/9/2012	404	13	1
12		Friday		4 weeks ago			4/9/2011	770	25	2
13		Monday		5 weeks ago			5/19/2010	1095	35	2
14		Tuesday		6 weeks ago						
15		Wednesday		7 weeks ago						
16		Thursday		8 weeks ago						
17		Friday		9 weeks ago						
18		Monday								
19		Tuesday								
20		Wednesday								
21		Thursday								
22		Friday								
23										

Figure 2.54

- Cells B1 and B2 contain formulas that update, whereas cells B4:B6 have fixed dates created with shortcut keys.

- You can fill column B with weekdays in either of two ways:

  ○ Select B8:B12 and copy that section down with the *fill handle* (refer to Chapter 2).

  ○ Select B12, copy downward with a right-mouse drag of the *fill handle*, and choose *Fill Weekdays* from the drop-down.

- You can place in front of today's weekday (column A) a fixed date for the current date.

- You can copy that date upward and downward—but without weekend dates. To do this, you click the drop-down at the bottom and choose ⊙ *Fill Weekdays*.

- You select D9, use the *fill handle*, and copy down to cell D17.

- You can place a fixed current date in cell E8 by using *Ctrl+;*.

- In order to go back in time by 7 days, we need to do more work:

  1. Select E7:E17.

  2. Click the *Fill* button (located under the Σ button) on the *Home* tab.

  3. Choose the *Series* option

  4. Specify a *step value* of -7.

- If it is important for you to find out how long ago a certain date is from now (in days, weeks, months, etc.), you can use the function DATEDIF in H8:J13. Although DATEDIF is nowhere to be found in Excel, you can type it according to the following syntax: =DATEDIF(*earlier*, *later*, *"y"*). The formula in H8, for instance, could be =DATEDIF($G8,TODAY(),H$7).

Figure 2.55 has in column A dates that increase by 365 days. In the columns B:E, you can find an exact replica of the dates in column A—but their looks are rather different. No matter how fancy the looks are, however, the serial number behind them didn't change. You can change the appearance of dates through the *Format* dialog box. Most of the ones used in these columns are preexisting Excel options, except for the last column. Column E has a *Custom* format that is based on the following rules:

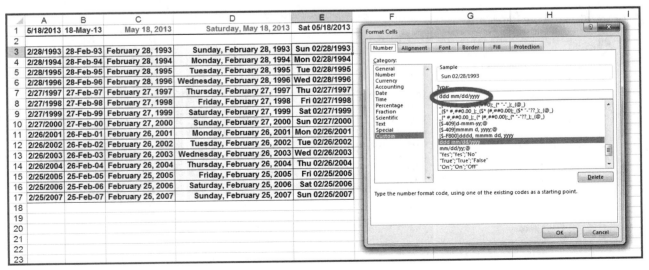

Figure 2.55

- *dd* is 01; *ddd* is Sun; *dddd* is Sunday

- *mm* is 02; *mmm* is Mar; *mmmm* is March

Figure 2.56 starts with "problem" dates in column A. Once in a while, you may still be given records with dates that Excel doesn't recognize—and therefore cannot use in its calculations. There are at least 3 different ways:

	A	B	C	D	E	F	G	H	I
1	990615		99	6	15	06/15/99		990615	06/15/99
2	990616		99	6	16	06/16/99		990616	06/16/99
3	990617		99	6	17	06/17/99		990617	06/17/99
4	990618		99	6	18	06/18/99		990618	06/18/99
5	990619		99	6	19	06/19/99		990619	06/19/99
6	990620		99	6	20	06/20/99		990620	06/20/99
7	981111		98	11	11	11/11/98		981111	11/11/98
8	981112		98	11	12	11/12/98		981112	11/12/98
9	981113		98	11	13	11/13/98		981113	11/13/98
10	981114		98	11	14	11/14/98		981114	11/14/98
11	981115		98	11	15	11/15/98		981115	11/15/98
12	970101		97	1	1	01/01/97		970101	01/01/97
13	970102		97	1	2	01/02/97		970102	01/02/97
14	970103		97	1	3	01/03/97		970103	01/03/97
15	970104		97	1	4	01/04/97		970104	01/04/97
16									

Figure 2.56

- The easiest way to convert these text items into Excel dates is to use the button *Text to Columns* on the *Data* tab. Just skip step 1 and 2, but don't forget to mark in step 3 which type of date format you are dealing with – e.g. 140225 would be *YMD*. This tool will replace the "old" dates with Excel dates.

- If you do use the steps 1 and 2, you have to make sure you have two blank columns waiting so you have space for the three split components. When something like 990615 has been properly split into 99 + 06 + 15, you still do not have a date that Excel understands until you use the DATE function in column F: =DATE(`cellY,cellM,cellD`).

- Instead of using Excel's splitting tool, you could do all this in a single step in column I by using a heavily nested DATE function, such as =DATE(LEFT(H1,2),MID(H1,3,2),RIGHT(H1,2)).

Figure 2.57 uses *conditional formatting* to highlight the current date (refer to Chapter 11). When you know that there are also functions such as DAY, MONTH, and YEAR, you can highlight the current date in a calendar through conditional formatting. The formula would be =AND(ROW()=DAY(TODAY())+1, - COLUMN()=MONTH(TODAY())+1). The +1 addition is needed because rows and columns have headers.

	A	B	C	D	E	F	G	H	I	J	K	L	M
1	Day	Jan	Feb	Mar	Apr	May	Jun	Jul	Aug	Sep	Oct	Nov	Dec
2	1												
3	2												
4	3												
5	4												
6	5												
7	6												
8	7												
9	8												
10	9												
11	10												
12	11												
13	12												
14	13												
15	14												
16	15												
17	16												
18	17												
19	18												
20	19												
21	20												
22	21												
23	22												
24	23												
25	24												
26	25												
27	26												
28	27												
29	28												
30	29												
31	30												
32	31												
33													

Figure 2.57

Chapter 20: Time Manipulation

If the timing of experiments is important to you, you need to know some basics about the way Excel handles time information. You may have to do some manual work before you can perform calculations with your timed data.

Time is a value that ranges from 0 to 0. 999988425925926, representing the times from 0:00:00 (12:00:00 AM) to 23:59:59 (11:59:59 PM). You can see the value of a particular time under *General Format* or by using *Ctrl+~*. The advantage of using decimal values for time is that you can then easily add and subtract them. You can even use functions such as SUM, AVERAGE, and so on.

When the difference in time values is more than 24 hours, the decimal time values go beyond 0.9999999. This causes trouble, for time values beyond 0.9999999 get truncated when forced into the *h:mm:ss* format. If the sum is 1.5, for example, Excel shows only its decimal part, 0.5, which is 12:00:00. To solve this problem, you must change the format of this number from *h:mm:ss* to *[h]:mm.ss*. Then a number such as 1.5 will indeed show up as 1.5 (in the proper time format, of course: 36:00:00). Thanks to the *[h]:mm:ss* format, you can calculate with time values beyond the duration of 1 day, which is usually necessary for sum operations.

Some people prefer to use hours with decimals—where, for example, 13.50 (with a decimal point) is 13 hours and 30 minutes, as opposed to 13:50 (with a colon), which is 13 hours and 50 minutes. To convert these decimals to Excel's time decimals, you need to divide by 24 because Excel works with day units of 24 hours, 60 minutes, and 60 seconds.

Figure 2.58 shows you how to perform calculations with time values:

	A	B	C	D
1	start time	end time	duration	
2	9:09:15	9:10:05	0:00:50	
3	10:10:11	11:10:57	1:00:46	
4	13:13:30	16:14:32	3:01:02	
5		average duration	1:20:53	
6				
7				
8				
9	start date+time	end date+time	duration as day decimal	duration in hrs/mins/secs
10	10/23/2004 10:10:30	10/26/2004 11:30:15	3.055381944	73:19:45
11	10/26/2004 10:10:30	10/27/2004 11:30:15	1.055381944	25:19:45
12		total duration		98:39:30
13				
14				
15				
16		hours with decimals	as day decimal	in hrs/mins/secs
17		13.50	0.5625	13:30:00
18		8.25	0.34375	8:15:00
19		7.75	0.322916667	7:45:00
20	total	29.50	1.229166667	29:30:00
21				

Figure 2.58

- **Cell C2:** Uses a regular subtraction, =B2−A2, and a regular format (<1 day or 24 hours): *h:mm:ss*.

- **Cell C5:** Uses a regular function, =AVERAGE(C2:C4), and a regular format (<1 day): *h:mm:ss*.

- **Cell C10:** Has a regular subtraction as well, but if you want to show decimals greater than 1 in a time notation, you must use the format *[h]:mm:ss*.

- **Cell B17:** Uses a decimal time notation, and you need to convert these decimals to Excel's time system. To do so, you divide by 24. Hence, cell C17 uses the formula =B17/24.

- **Cell D20:** Contains the function =SUM(D17:D19) and the format *[h]:mm:ss* because Excel's time decimal is greater than 1.

Figure 2.59 plots on the Y-axis the values measured in column B after a cumulative period of time calculated in column D on the X-axis:

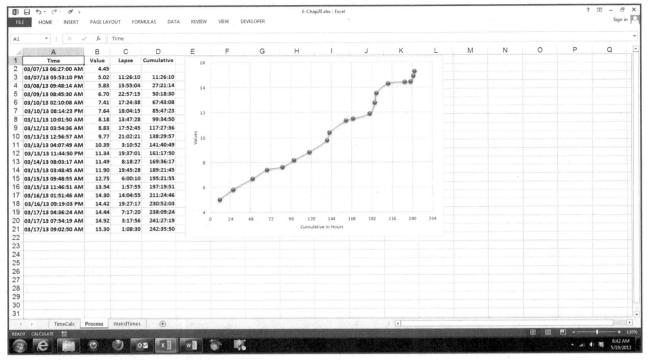

Figure 2.59

- **Cell C3:** Uses a regular subtraction, =A3−A2, and a special format (>1 day or 24 hours): [h]:mm:ss.

- **Cell D3:** Uses a cumulative summing function, =SUM($C$3:C3), and a special format again: [h]:mm:ss.

- The X-axis has the following settings: *Custom Number* format is [h] and *Major Units* 1.0.

Figure 2.60 deals with time information that Excel cannot handle. Excel has no problem with the times in column B because they are done with Excel's time decimals. But column D is another story because those "values" came in as text. You transform them as follows:

	A	B	C	D	E	F	G	H	I	J	K
1		**Fine**				**Trouble**					
2										**Time()**	**TimeValue()**
3		**Excel Time**		**Text Time**		**Day Decs**	**Mins Decs**	**Secs Decs**			
4		98:39:30		98:39:30		4.08333	0.02708	0.00035		2:39:30	2:39 AM
5		29:30:00		29:30:00		1.20833	0.02083	0.00000		5:30:00	5:30 AM
6		56:20:30		56:20:30		2.33333	0.01389	0.00035		8:20:30	8:20 AM
7		35:11:00		35:11:00		1.45833	0.00764	0.00000		11:11:00	11:11 AM
8		14:01:30		14:01:30		0.58333	0.00069	0.00035		14:01:30	2:01 PM
9		16:52:00		16:52:00		0.66667	0.03611	0.00000		16:52:00	4:52 PM
10		19:42:30		19:42:30		0.79167	0.02917	0.00035		19:42:30	7:42 PM
11		22:33:00		22:33:00		0.91667	0.02292	0.00000		22:33:00	10:33 PM
12	**Sum**	292:50:00				12.04167	0.15833	0.00139			
13											
14	**Serial**	12.20139				**Total**	12.20139				
15											
16						**Excel time**	292:50:00				
17											

Figure 2.60

- In column F, you extract the hours part: `=LEFT(D4,2)/24`.

- In column G, you extract the minutes part: `=MID(D4,4,2)/60/24`.

- In column H, you extract the seconds part: `=RIGHT(D4,2)/60/60/24`.

- When you have Excel-time decimals, you can sum each part in F12:H12.

- Calculate the grand total in G14: `=SUM(F12:H12)`. This value should be identical to the value in B14.

- Cell G16 refers to cell G14, but then formatted as `[h]:mm:ss`.

<u>Note</u>

In Chapter 19, you applied the `DATE` function to split text dates. But you cannot apply the `TIME` or `TIMEVALUE` function to manipulate text times because they do not go beyond 1 day. This is shown in the columns J and K.

Part 2 Exercises

You can download all the files used in this book from www.genesispc.com/Science2013.htm, where you can find each file in its original version (to work on) and in its finished version (to check your solutions).

1. Subtotals

1.2. Sort at two levels: per analyst and per plate (in this order).

1.3. Create a summary of means per analyst.

1.4. Give these means a different format.

1.5. Add means per plate—without losing the previous subtotals.

	A	B	C	D	E	F	G	H
1	Plate ID	Analyst	50 ng/mL	%CV	25 ng/mL	%CV	10 ng/mL	%CV
2	8696p08b	bdo	52.9	3.0	27.5	6.0	13.1	9.0
3	8696p08b	bdo	50.1	1.0	26.8	3.0	12.1	2.0
4	**8696p08b Average**		51.5		27.2		12.6	
5	8877p58b	bdo	43.2	4.0	22.6	3.0	9.6	4.0
6	8877p58b	bdo	44.3	3.0	20.7	3.0	9.7	6.0
7	**8877p58b Average**		43.8		21.7		9.7	
8		**bdo Average**	47.6		24.4		11.1	
9	8696p08a	gmv	52.3	1.0	26.5	2.0	12.2	2.0
10	8696p08a	gmv	49.7	2.0	25.0	1.0	11.2	3.0
11	**8696p08a Average**		51.0		25.8		11.7	
12	8877p58a	gmv	47.7	2.0	22.7	0.0	10.3	0.0
13	8877p58a	gmv	48.7	3.0	23.0	3.0	10.0	0.0
14	**8877p58a Average**		48.2		22.9		10.2	
15		**gmv Average**	49.6		24.3		10.9	
16	8696p08a	ksm	56.4	12.0	29.1	11.0	12.8	9.0
17	8696p08a	ksm	51.3	2.0	26.9	1.0	11.7	1.0
18	**8696p08a Average**		53.9		28.0		12.3	
19	8696p08b	ksm	51.0	1.0	26.1	1.0	12.3	2.0
20	8696p08b	ksm	48.6	1.0	24.8	0.0	11.4	2.0
21	**8696p08b Average**		49.8		25.5		11.9	
22		**ksm Average**	51.8		26.7		12.1	

2. Summary Functions

2.1. Implement a calculated filter in cell G17 for patients who are above the 75th percentile for both weight and systolic blood pressure.

2.2. Create the formulas in D19:F21 for age, weight, and systolic blood pressure.

2.3. Create a subset of records in the database by applying the filter.

	A	B	C	D	E	F	G
1	Patient	Gender	DOB	Age	Weight	Systolic	
2	Bush	M	1/3/1975	38	160	178	
3	Carter	F	10/22/1937	75	192	191	
4	Clinton	M	7/15/1971	41	171	175	
5	Eisenhower	F	11/24/1934	78	154	128	
6	Ford	M	2/9/1950	63	164	141	
7	Johnson	F	6/13/1965	47	152	125	
8	Kennedy	M	11/27/1973	39	185	193	
9	Lincoln	M	8/1/1972	40	188	166	
10	Nixon	F	9/15/1930	82	189	146	
11	Reagan	M	3/28/1939	74	140	170	
12	Roosevelt	M	9/29/1945	67	159	196	
13	Truman	F	10/20/1962	50	151	139	
14	Washington	F	10/15/1963	49	209	189	
15							
16	Patient	Gender	DOB	Age	Weight	Systolic	W+SBP 75th
17							FALSE
18							
19	Mean			62	201	190	
20	SD			83	242	233	
21	Count			2	2	2	
22							

3. Summary Functions

3.1. Implement a calculated filter in cell G17 for patients who are above the 75th percentile for both weight and systolic blood pressure.

3.2. Create the formulas in D19:F21 for age, weight, and systolic blood pressure.

3.3. Create a subset of records in the database by applying the filter.

	A	B	C	D	E	F	G	H	I	J
1	Date	Patient	Old SBP	New SBP		Date	Patient	Old SBP	New SBP	Up>10
2	5/24/2006	Ford	167	141						FALSE
3	5/25/2006	Johnson	145	132						
4	5/17/2006	Reagan	137	125						
5	5/11/2006	Ford	167	158			Mean	141	166	
6	5/29/2006	Nixon	155	147			SD	11	19	
7	5/22/2006	Clinton	160	155			Count	8	8	
8	5/26/2006	Kennedy	137	139						
9	5/9/2006	Clinton	160	165						
10	5/15/2006	Kennedy	137	142						
11	5/5/2006	Bush	120	127						
12	5/23/2006	Eisenhower	148	160						
13	5/8/2006	Carter	139	152						
14	5/30/2006	Reagan	137	151						
15	5/12/2006	Johnson	145	160						
16	5/18/2006	Bush	120	141						
17	5/10/2006	Eisenhower	148	180						
18	5/16/2006	Nixon	155	190						
19	5/19/2006	Carter	139	191						
20										

4. Summary Functions

4.1. Implement a calculated filter in cell J2 for cases in which the systolic blood pressure went up by more than 10 mmHg.

4.2. Create the formulas in H5:I7.

4.3. Create a subset of records in the database by applying the filter.

	A	B	C	D	E	F	
1	Date	Patient	Old SBP	New SBP		Up by more than	
2	5/5/2006	Bush	120	127		10	
3	5/18/2006	Bush	120	141			
4	5/8/2006	Carter	139	152			
5	5/19/2006	Carter	139	191			
6	5/9/2006	Clinton	160	165			
7	5/22/2006	Clinton	160	155			
8	5/10/2006	Eisenhower	148	180			
9	5/23/2006	Eisenhower	148	160			
10	5/11/2006	Ford	167	158			
11	5/24/2006	Ford	167	141			
12	5/12/2006	Johnson	145	160			
13	5/25/2006	Johnson	145	132			
14	5/15/2006	Kennedy	137	142			
15	5/26/2006	Kennedy	137	139			
16	5/16/2006	Nixon	155	190			
17	5/29/2006	Nixon	155	147			
18	5/17/2006	Reagan	137	125			
19	5/30/2006	Reagan	137	151			
20							

5. Conditional Formatting

5.1. Mark the cells in columns C:D for cases in which the systolic blood pressure went up by more than 10 mmHg (cell F2)—by using a conditional formatting formula.

5.2. Make sure both cells are marked for each record.

5.3. Locate the section of conditional formatting by using *GoTo*.

	A	B	C	D
1	Date	Patient	Old SBP	New SBP
2	5/5/2006	Bush	120	127
3	5/8/2006	Carter	139	152
4	5/9/2006	Clinton	160	165
5	5/10/2006	Eisenhower	148	180
6	5/11/2006	Ford		
7	5/12/2006	Johnson	145	160
8	5/15/2006	Kennedy	137	142
9	5/16/2006	Nixon	155	190
10	5/17/2006	Reagan		
11	5/18/2006	Bush	120	141
12	5/19/2006	Carter	139	191
13	5/22/2006	Clinton		
14	5/23/2006	Eisenhower	148	160
15	5/24/2006	Ford		
16	5/25/2006	Johnson		
17	5/26/2006	Kennedy	137	139
18	5/29/2006	Nixon		
19	5/30/2006	Reagan	137	151
20				

Part 2: Data Analysis

87

6. Conditional Formatting

6.1. Use a conditional formatting formula to hide systolic blood pressure values if the new value is lower than the old value (the rows 6, 10, 13, 15, 16, and 190.

6.2. Make sure both cells are hidden for each qualifying record (e.g. in row 6, both 167 and 158 are hidden).

	A	B	C	D	E	F	G
1	Patient	Gender	DOB	Age	Weight	Systolic	
2	Bush	M	1/3/1975	32	160	178	
3	Carter	F	10/22/1937	69	192	151	
4	Clinton	M	7/15/1971	35	171		
5	Eisenhower	F	11/24/1934	72	154	128	
6	Ford	M	2/9/1950	57	164	141	
7	Johnson	F	6/13/1965	41			
8	Kennedy	M	11/27/1973	33	165	193	
9	Lincoln	M	8/1/1972	34	188		
10	Nixon	F	9/15/1930	76	189	146	
11	Reagan	M	3/28/1939	67	140	170	
12	Roosevelt	M	9/29/1945	61	159		
13	Truman	F	10/20/1962	44	151	139	
14	Washington	F	10/15/1963	43	209	180	
15							
16							
17	Patient	Gender	DOB	Age	Weight	Systolic	W+SBP
18							TRUE
19							

7. Filtering Tools

7.1. Filter in cell G18 only for records that have readings in both column E and column F (so no rows 4, 7, 9, and 12).

7.2. Apply the filter.

7.3. Do the opposite: Filter for records that have readings missing in column E and/or column F.

	A	B	C	D	E	F	
1	Plate ID	Date	Analyst	C Value	Mean/plate		
2	8696p08e	09/14/01	kpm	73.5	78.7		
3	8696p08e	09/25/01	etv	78.3	78.7		
4	8696p08e	09/19/01	etv	79.3	78.7		
5	8696p08e	09/25/01	gmv	83.6	78.7		
6	8877p66b	09/26/01	ejs	47.4	53.3		
7	8877p66b	09/14/01	kpm	50.2	53.3		
8	8877p66b	09/18/01	gmv	57.1	53.3		
9	8877p66b	09/12/01	etv	58.3	53.3		
10	8877p70d	09/18/01	tjk	39.7	43.3		
11	8877p70d	09/14/01	cod	45.0	43.3		
12	8877p70d	09/26/01	luv	45.3	43.3		
13	8877p75b	09/20/01	kpm	58.4	59.2		
14	8877p75b	09/14/01	cod	59.9	59.2		
15	8877p78b	09/21/01	ejs	61.5	63.1		
16	8877p78b	10/03/01	ejs	62.5	63.1		
17	8877p78b	09/14/01	etv	63.3	63.1		
18	8877p78b	09/14/01	luv	63.3	63.1		
19	8877p78b	09/11/01	kpm	64.8	63.1		
20	8877p83b	09/25/01	tjk	64.2	66.7		
21	8877p83b	09/21/01	luv	65.8	66.7		
22	8877p83b	09/11/01	tjk	70.2	66.7		
23							
24							
25	Plate ID	Date	Analyst	C Value	Mean/plate	Once	
26						TRUE	
27							

8. Filtering Tools

8.1. There are several C-values per plate (column D). Calculate in column E the mean of all C-values for each plate by using `AVERAGEIF`.

8.2. Filter in such a way that you show each plate only once by using the function `COUNTIF` in F26.

8.3. Apply the filter.

	A	B	C	D	E	F	G	H	I	J
1	Plate ID	Date	Analyst	Pre/Post	Group	C Value		Group	Analyst	Pre/Post
2	8877p58a	09/11/01	kpm	pre	102	64.8		102	cod	pre
3	8877p58b	09/11/01	tjk	pre	115	70.2		102	kpm	pre
4	8877p58c	09/11/01	tmv	post	107	60.7		102	luv	post
5	8877p60a	09/12/01	etv	pre	107	58.3		107	tmv	post
6	8877p60b	09/12/01	wow	pre	107	73.6		107	etv	pre
7	8696p08a	09/14/01	tmv	post	107	72.4		107	wow	pre
8	8696p08b	09/14/01	etv	pre	107	62.5		115	ejs	post
9	8696p08c	09/14/01	wow	pre	107	56.7		115	gmv	post
10	8696p08d	09/14/01	cod	pre	102	59.9		115	tjk	pre
11	8696p08e	09/14/01	kpm	pre	102	73.6				
12	8696p08f	09/14/01	luv	post	102	63.3				
13	8877p63a	09/14/01	cod	pre	102	45.0				
14	8877p63b	09/14/01	kpm	pre	102	50.2				
15	8877p70c	09/18/01	gmv	post	115	57.1				
16	8877p70d	09/18/01	tjk	pre	115	39.8				
17	8877p71a	09/19/01	tmv	post	107	66.9				
18	8877p71b	09/19/01	etv	pre	107	79.4				
19	8877p75a	09/20/01	wow	pre	107	61.8				
20	8877p75b	09/20/01	kpm	pre	102	58.4				
21	8877p78a	09/21/01	luv	post	102	65.8				
22	8877p78b	09/21/01	ejs	post	115	60.8				
24	8877p83a	09/25/01	gmv	post	115	83.7				
25	8877p83b	09/25/01	tjk	pre	115	64.9				
26	8877p84a	09/25/01	tmv	post	107	63.0				
27										

9. Lookups

9.1. Leave the lookup table H1:J10 as is, but name ranges if you want to.

9.2. Find in column D whether the analyst is pre- or post- according to the lookup table H1:J10. Use `VLOOKUP`.

9.3. In column E, fill in the group to which the analyst belongs. You must use `INDEX` and `MATCH`.

9.4. Check whether sorting the lookup table differently has any impact.

	A	B	C	D	E	F	G	H	I	J	K
1	Patient	Clearance	Weight	Dosage							
2	Bush	50	85	260			Dosage (µg) by clearance (mL/min/70kg) and weight (kg)				
3	Carter	11	88	180			60	70	80	90	100
4	Clinton	15	85	180		10	125	125	180	188	195
5	Eisenhow	10	70	125		20	125	180	188	195	240
6	Ford	47	80	240		30	180	188	195	240	260
7	Johnson	71	63	240		40	188	195	240	260	280
8	Kennedy	83	78	300		50	195	240	260	280	300
9	Nixon	48	75	195		60	220	260	280	300	325
10	Reagan	12	66	125		70	240	280	300	325	350
11	Bush	51	87	260		80	260	300	325	350	375
12	Carter	48	96	260		90	280	325	350	375	400
13	Clinton	61	65	220		100	300	350	375	400	500
14	Eisenhow	67	84	280							
15	Ford	82	71	300							
16	Johnson	17	90	188							
17	Kennedy	30	80	195							
18	Nixon	58	81	260							
19	Reagan	16	94	188							

10. Trends

10.1. Make the first *control* functional by creating the correct formulas in D4:E6.

10.2. Make the second *control* functional by creating the formulas in D11:E13.

10.3. Move the *controls* (more on *controls* in part 4, Curve Fitting).

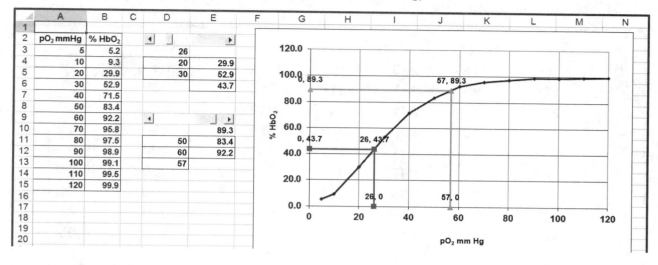

11. Multi-cell Array Formulas

11.1. Calculate in column H the percentage of occurrences per bin by using the functions FREQUEN-CY and COUNT in one formula.

11.2. Make sure no value is overlooked.

11.3. Make sure the total is 100%.

	A	B	C	D	E	F	G	H
1	55	316	223	185	124		Bins	Percent
2	124	93	163	213	314		50	5.0%
3	211	41	231	241	212		100	9.0%
4	118	113	400	205	254		150	16.0%
5	262	1	201	172	101		200	19.0%
6	167	479	205	337	118		250	18.0%
7	489	15	89	362	148		300	9.0%
8	179	248	125	197	177		350	12.0%
9	456	153	269	49	127		400	6.0%
10	289	500	198	317	300		450	2.0%
11	126	114	303	314	270		500	4.0%
12	151	279	347	314	170			0
13	250	175	93	209	61			
14	166	113	356	124	242			
15	152	384	157	233	99			
16	277	195	436	6	240			
17	147	80	173	211	244			
18	386	93	330	400	141			
19	332	173	129	323	188			
20	338	263	444	84	220			
21								

12. Single-cell Array Formulas

12.1. Calculate the mean in cell C27 and include the zero values.

12.2. Calculate the mean again in cell C28, but this time ignore zero readings by using a single-cell array formula.

12.3. Could you have achieved the same result by hiding the rows with a zero value?

	A	B	C
1	Plate1	Anal1	1.48
2	Plate1	Anal2	0.00
3	Plate1	Anal3	0.81
4	Plate1	Anal1	0.39
5	Plate1	Anal2	1.55
6	Plate1	Anal3	1.35
7	Plate1	Anal1	2.00
8	Plate1	Anal2	0.00
9	Plate1	Anal3	0.50
10	Plate2	Anal1	1.32
11	Plate2	Anal2	1.30
12	Plate2	Anal3	0.81
13	Plate2	Anal1	0.00
14	Plate2	Anal2	1.95
15	Plate2	Anal3	1.39
16	Plate2	Anal1	0.82
17	Plate2	Anal2	0.00
18	Plate3	Anal3	1.94
19	Plate3	Anal1	0.69
20	Plate3	Anal2	1.54
21	Plate3	Anal3	0.00
22	Plate3	Anal1	0.18
23	Plate3	Anal2	1.30
24	Plate3	Anal3	0.89
25	Plate3	Anal1	0.60
26			
27	Mean (with 0's)		0.91
28	Mean (no 0)		1.14
29			

13. Single-cell Array Formulas

13.1. Use `INDEX`, `MATCH`, and the `&` operator in cell J8 to find the mean value for a specific plate (J6) and a specific cycle (J7).

13.2. Show in row 19 the entire record for that specific plate and specific cycle by using a multi-cell array formula with the functions `INDEX` and `MATCH`.

	A	B	C	D	E	F	G	H	I	J
1	Plate	Cycle	Anal1	Anal2	Anal3	Anal4	Mean			
2	ab10	cycl1	0.649	0.053	0.119	0.398	0.305			
3	ab10	cycl2	0.268	0.607	0.666	0.736	0.569			
4	ab10	cycl3	0.852	0.553	0.366	0.261	0.508		Array INDEX	
5	ab10	cycl4	0.002	0.229	0.019	0.970	0.305			
6	bc11	cycl1	0.522	0.106	0.865	0.228	0.430		Plate	ab10
7	bc11	cycl2	0.348	0.368	0.097	0.261	0.269		Cycle	cycl2
8	bc11	cycl3	0.662	0.623	0.341	0.685	0.578		Mean	0.569
9	bc11	cycl4	0.291	0.755	0.361	0.725	0.533			
10	de12	cycl1	0.818	0.469	0.399	0.334	0.505			
11	de12	cycl2	0.298	0.552	0.638	0.529	0.504			
12	de12	cycl3	0.529	0.628	0.175	0.634	0.492			
13	de12	cycl4	0.196	0.528	0.129	0.750	0.401			
14	fg13	cycl1	0.400	0.471	0.945	0.324	0.535			
15	fg13	cycl2	0.020	0.783	0.478	0.138	0.355			
16	fg13	cycl3	0.815	0.588	0.118	0.327	0.462			
17	fg13	cycl4	0.812	0.538	0.112	0.981	0.611			
18										
19	ab10	cycl2	0.268	0.607	0.666	0.736	0.56925			
20										

14. Time Manipulation

14.1. Calculate the metabolic rate per hour in column E.

14.2. Calculate the metabolic rate per minute in column F.

14.3. Create the correct units for the X-axis scale in the graph, if you know how to deal with graphs (see Part 3).

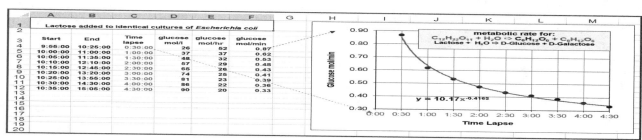

Part 3: Plotting Data

Chapter 21: Types of Charts and Graphs

Excel offers a good array of chart or graph types, all of which fall into four main types: *Pie, Column, Line,* and *XY.* All the other types are essentially subtypes of these four. What are the differences between these four types, and when should you use which type?

Figure 3.1 explains a bit of the terminology related to databases and their charts or graphs:

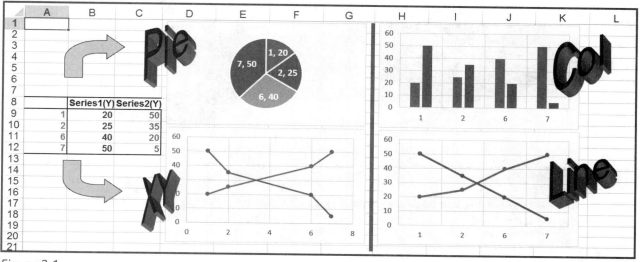

Figure 3.1

- This database has four *categories* (A9:A12); they usually end up on the horizontal axis.

- This database has two *series* of values, or data series (in columns B and C).

- The values of each data *series* are on the vertical axis, if the graph does have axes.

- The labels of the data *series* end up in the *legend*.

Figure 3.1 also shows the four main graph types Excel has to offer (I usually call the first three types charts and the last type graphs, but that is a matter of convention; Excel calls them all charts). Here is an overview of the main characteristics of each major type:

- **Pie (and Doughnut) charts:** These charts have no axes. A *Pie* chart is based on a *category* and is limited to only one data *series*; a *Doughnut* chart may display more than one *Data Series.*

- **Column (and Bar) charts:** These charts have two axes: one for *categories* and one for values. They can display multiple *Data Series.*

- **Line (plus Area and Surface) charts:** These charts have two axes: one for *categories* and one for values. They can display multiple *Data Series.*

- **XY and Scatter graphs:** These graphs have two axes, both of which are for values. An *XY* or *Scatter* graph can display more than one *Data Series,* but each *series* represents pairs of x-values and y-values.

Figure 3.2 deals with the first type, the *Pie* type, and its close "relative" the *Doughnut*. *Pie* and/or *Doughnut* graphs are ideal for showing the contribution of each value to a total (for example, the phases of a cell cycle). To create a *Pie* graph, you follow these steps:

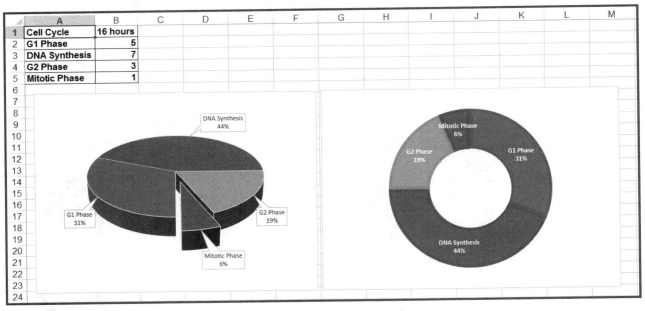

Figure 3.2

1. Select any cell inside the database. By doing so you give the *Chart Wizard* a "clue" as to where the database is located—including its boundaries: the first empty row and column.

2. Select *Insert*, *Pie* dropdown, *Exploded 3D*.

3. If you don't need or like the *title*, select it and press *Delete*.

4. If you want to turn the *Pie* around, R-click inside the chart, choose *3D-Rotation*, and change *X Rotation* with the arrow up button.

You can open and close gaps between pie pieces by dragging them in or out. You need to follow these rules when doing so:

- Click and drag any piece to move all the pieces in or out together.

- Click and drag again to do this for a specific piece only. (The second click selects one piece only.)

- Click outside any piece to deselect the pieces.

- Click twice on any piece to select that piece specifically.

Here's how you add a *Doughnut* chart:

1. Click anywhere inside the database. (Otherwise, you might replace the previous *Pie* chart.)

2. Select *Doughnut* under the *Pie* dropdown button.

3. Change the look of the chart by selecting another *Chart Style* under *Design*. (This option is available only when you are inside the chart.)

4. If you want data labels,

   ◦ Select the chart.

   ◦ Click the *Design* tab.

○ Select *Add Chart Element*, then *Data Labels*.

○ Choose any option, but the last choice, *More…*, gives you the most control.

To fix the labels, click any label once to select all labels and click any label twice to select one only.

Note

To change chart or graph settings, you can either use buttons next to the chart's right border or use the menu *Design Tools* with a *Design* and *Format* tab. You must be inside the chart or graph to have access to these options.

Figure 3.3 lists the DNA components G (guanine), C (cytosine), A (adenine), T (thymine) for some bacteria. The big limitation of *Pie* charts is the fact that they cannot display more than one *Data Series*. In this case, the chosen *Data Series* comes from row 2 rather than from column B because it is more informative. But Excel always takes the *Data Series* from the longest set of values, which in this case is in the column (with five values), not in the rows (with only four values).

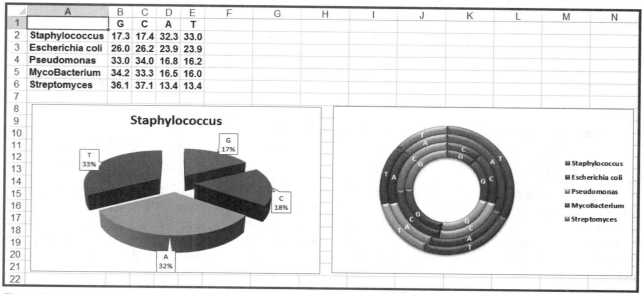

Figure 3.3

When you let Excel decide where to get the *Data Series*, it takes its first and only *series* from column B. That's great if you want to show how the guanine component varies per species—but then a *Pie* chart would not be very appropriate because this type of chart is best for showing contributions to the total. So you should really use the button *Switch Row/Column* to make the chart more instructive; that button is located on the *Design* tab when you are inside the chart.

But what do you do with the other species of bacteria that are not shown in the *Pie* chart? You have two options if you want to stay in this "food" category of charts:

• Create five separate *Pie* charts for each species of bacteria.

• Create one concentric *Doughnut* chart for all species together.

However, *Doughnut* charts are difficult to read and interpret, and they are also difficult to fix. (For instance, if you want to display the *Data Series* values, you must first activate the labels and then select them for each category before you can change them.) So let's go for a better type!

Figure 3.4 shows an example of a *Column* and a *Bar* chart. *Column* and *Bar* charts are best for comparing values across categories. Here are some design options:

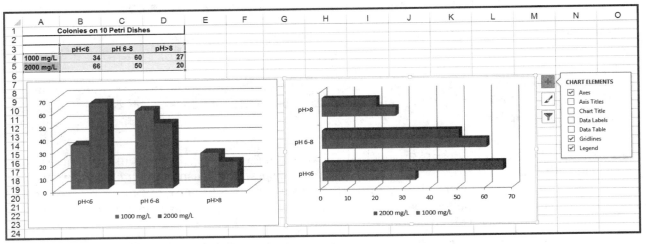

Figure 3.4

- At any time, you can change the type of the left or right chart by clicking the button *Change Chart Type* on the *Design* tab—or right-click inside the chart and select *Change Chart Type*.

- You can exchange the axes of the left or right chart by using the *Row/Column Switch* button, also on the *Design* tab.

- In addition, you can change details with the three tools next to the chart's top-right corner (when inside the chart): the first one is for chart elements; the second one for chart styles; the third one for filtering data series.

Figure 3.5 shows data plotted in so-called *stacked* charts, which are subtypes of the *Column* type. *Stacked* means that they resemble a *Pie* chart in showing contributions to a total: either in values (see the right chart) or in percentages (see the left chart). Which one is best? It depends on your needs or on your hypothesis! The left chart in Figure 3.5, for instance, shows that almost all Ca-ions are in the blood, not in the cells. The right chart, on the other hand, shows that the concentration of Ca-ions is relatively low anyway.

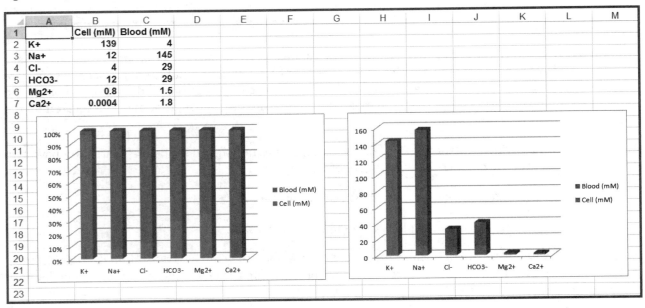

Figure 3.5

Figure 3.6 compares the photosynthetic activity of three different pigments. Sometimes, as you can see in this case, *Line* graphs do a better job than *Column* charts. Let us experiment how the data can be represented:

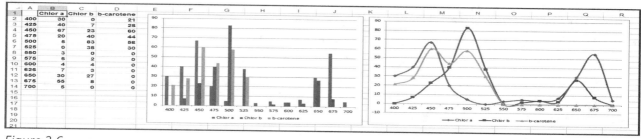

Figure 3.6

1. Create the *Column* chart first: *Insert | Column*. Move its *legend* to the bottom. There are three different ways: You can drag it around in the *plot* area, or you use *Add Chart Elements* on the *Design* tab, or click on the top button outside the chart's right-top border.

2. Create a *Line* chart: *Insert | Line | choose one with markers*. (Be aware that the last two with markers are of the stacked type.). Move the legend to the bottom again.

3. For each *Data Series*, create a smoother line. You do this by right-clicking on any *Data Series* and then selecting *Format Data Series*, *Fill & Line* button on top, *Line*, and finally ☑ *Smoothed Line*. (You can keep the *Format Data Series* box open while selecting the next *Series* curve.)

Note

In this case, a *Line* chart is a better bet than a *Column* chart. There are no clear rules that dictate when to use one type over the other; you simply have to develop a feel for this issue.

Figure 3.7 shows a *Line* chart and two *Area* charts. *Line* type charts are usually great for trends over time. *Area* type charts are their cousins: They emphasize differences over time more clearly. The top right one is a non-stacked *Area* chart. The one below it is a copy of the one above it, but the type was changed into a *3D Area* chart.

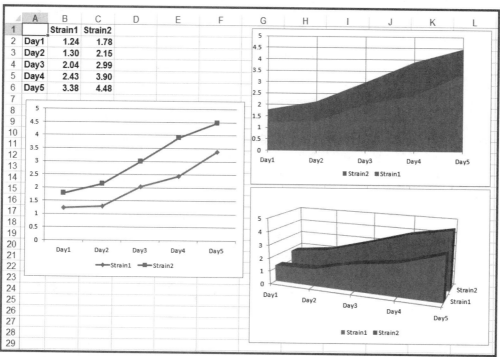

Figure 3.7

Figure 3.8 plots the hemoglobin percentage versus the erythrocyte count of human blood, using the *XY* or *Scatter* type—once with and once without connecting lines. Each dot represents one pair of values: an X-value and a Y-value. So you are dealing here with one *Data Series*, but the series contains pairs of values this time. The right graph (with connecting lines) may look a little better after column A has been sorted. But still, you probably prefer the left graph; it would be even better if it were outfitted with a regression line (as discussed in Part 4). That's why the *XY* type is also called the *Scatter* type.

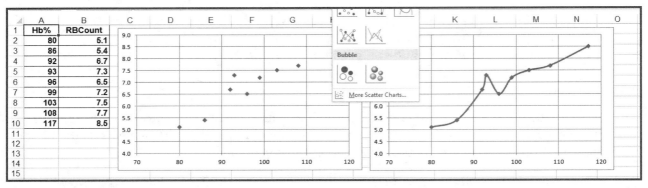

Figure 3.8

Figure 3.9 makes a comparison between *Line* charts (on the left) and XY graphs (on the right). They are almost identical when the intervals in column A are equal, but this time the intervals are unequal, so the left one, *Line*, paints a picture very different from the right one, *XY*. The reason for this difference is very simple: *Line* charts use *categories* on the horizontal axis (they act like labels, even if they are numeric), whereas *XY* graphs use real values on the horizontal axis (so they acknowledge the distances in between).

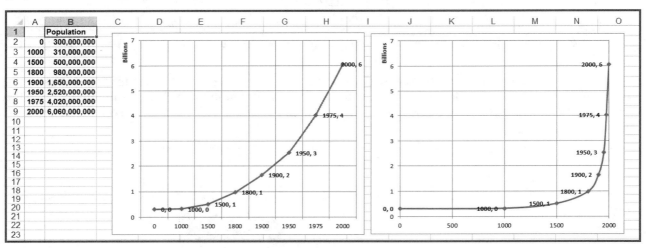

Figure 3.9

Figure 3.10 measures how a person's eyesight changes with age. The left graph shows how the near point (*NP*) changes with age. The right graph shows how the focal power (*=1/NP*) changes with age. You can see that both graphs require the *XY* type because the values in column A have unequal intervals.

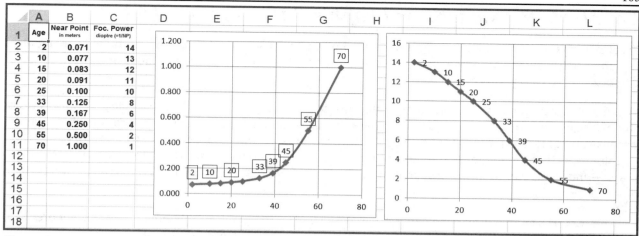

Figure 3.10

Here's how you create the left graph:

1. Select A1:A11 and B1:B11.

2. Select *Insert, Scatter*.

Here's how you create the right graph:

1. Select A1:A11 and C1:C11 (with the *Ctrl* key).

2. Select *Insert, Scatter*.

Here's how you add data labels:

1. While in the graph, select the *Design* tab, *Add Chart Element*, *Data Labels*. Usually the last one, *More Data Label Options*, gives you the most power.

2. Another possibility is using the top button outside the right border of the chart.

Figure 3.11 presents a unique type of chart: the *Radar* type. It is basically a subtype of the *Line* chart, but it works well for very specific occasions—such as the one shown in this figure. A *Radar* chart shows clustering well (left chart), and it can also be good for cyclic events that have a particular pattern (right chart). Remember, though, that *Radar* charts are basically *Line* charts, so they work with *categories*. If you use numbers in the first column, you need to make sure to create equal intervals.

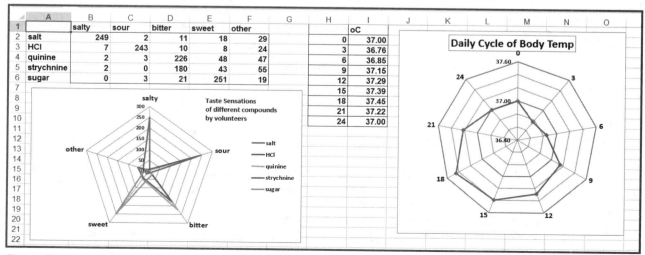

Figure 3.11

Chapter 22: A Chart's or Graph's Data Source

Excel calls the data that a chart or graph is based on the *data source*. Very often, you need to manipulate a graph's data source sometime after you create the graph—in order to correct, add, or remove *series* or *categories*. You can do this easily.

When your *data source* is huge—which is often the case—your graph may get overloaded by the details of the data. One of the simplest ways to eliminate details is to hide certain rows or columns in the database because anything that is hidden in the database is also hidden in the graph. The disadvantage of hiding rows or columns is that the database is affected as well. There must be a way to get the same results just for the graph—and that's where the *data source* comes in. That is where you can remove any series from the graph alone.

Figure 3.12 has a large database that was originally all part of the graph—until most of the *series* were manually removed in the graph itself. You remove series from a graph by using these steps:

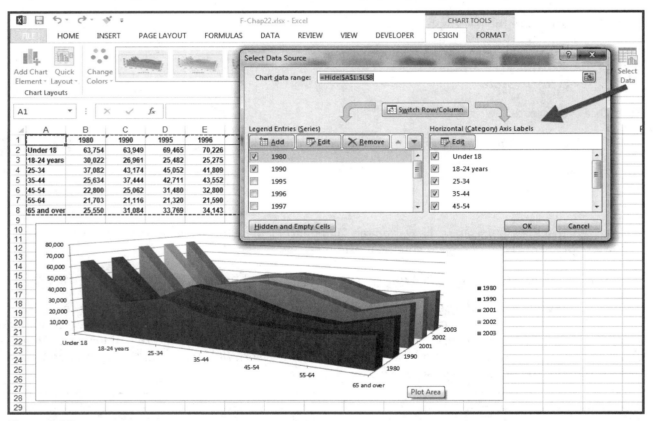

Figure 3.12

1. Click inside the database and select *Insert*, *Area*, then *3D-Area*. (*Area* and *3D-Area* are basically subtypes of a *Line* type.)

2. Select *Switch Row/Column*.

3. To remove any *Data Series*, you have several options:

   ◦ Access the *Data Source* through *Select Data* on the *Design* tab. In its left panel, you can either unmark any specific *Series*, or you can select it and then click *Remove*.

   ◦ Access the *Data Source* through *Select Data* with a right-click inside the graph. In its left panel, you can either unmark any specific *Series*, or you can select it and then click *Remove*.

○ Use the third button outside the graph in the top right corner: Check or uncheck a specific *Series* in the list.

○ Just click on a *Series* in the chart and hit the *Delete* key.

When you are done, the chart has its own number of *Series*, distinct from the number in the database.

Note

Also notice that when you select a *Data Series* in the chart, its corresponding database section becomes highlighted automatically.

Figure 3.13 uses two *Pie* charts to display the composition of inspired and expired air in human respiration. Both charts are based on the same database, so their data source includes both *Data Series*, but each chart can display only one of the *Data Series*, while the other one is hidden. All you have to do is remove one *Data Series* from each chart to make it distinct and appropriate.

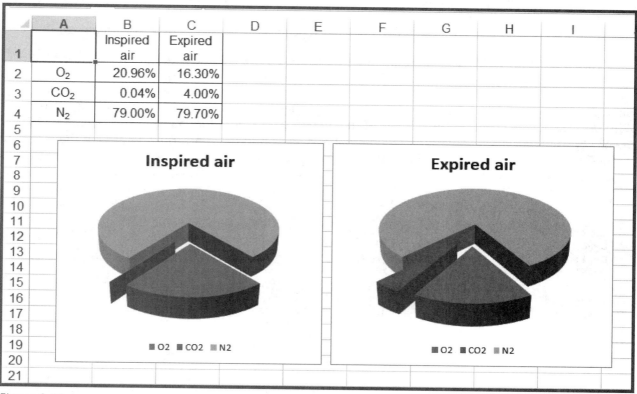

Figure 3.13

Figure 3.14 shows a decline in HbO_2 (in the blood) and MbO_2 (in the muscles) with prolonged diving time. Both charts are of the regular *Line* type, but the left one was created automatically, whereas the right chart is a manually adjusted version. In creating the chart on the left, the *Chart Wizard* assumed that the first column is a *Data Series* and not a set of *categories*, so it made a chart with three *Data Series*, instead of two, and then created its own set of *categories* (labeled 1 to 7). To create the right chart, you make the following changes:

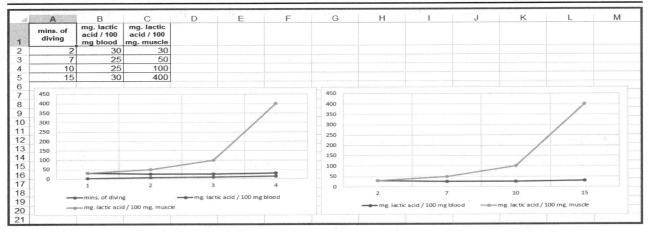

Figure 3.14

    1. Open the *Select Data* dialog box.

    2. In the left panel, remove the first *Data Series* (because those values are really *categories*).

    3. In the right panel, replace the *categories* the *Chart Wizard* created with the *categories* from the first column. Click the *Edit* button and then drag across the cells in Column A.

Figure 3.15 simulates a situation in which the original chart was based on a smaller database. The *Chart Wizard* automatically detected the borders of the original database. After you delete the empty row 7 and the empty column D, the database has been expanded, but no so the chart. How do we add the new data to the chart?

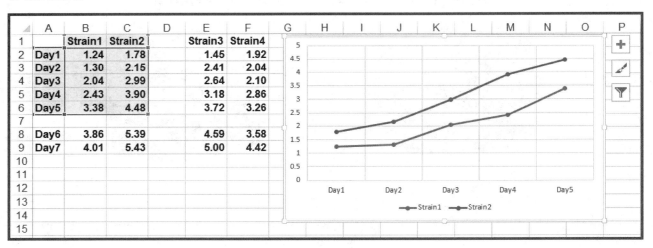

Figure 3.15

    1. Click in the *Plot Area* and notice how the *data source* is automatically highlighted in the database.

    2. Just drag the range marker in the right-lower corner downward to add *Day6* and *Day7*, which automatically expands the chart's *Data Source* (which is much easier and faster than using its dialog box).

    3. To add two new *Data Series* (*Strain3* and *Strain4*) as well, drag the marker to the right or use *Add* in *the Data Source* dialog box.

Figure 3.16 shows a rather complicated situation. Suppose you want only the highlighted database sections to be plotted—columns A, F, H, and J. The *Chart Wizard* cannot figure this out by itself, so you need to start from scratch:

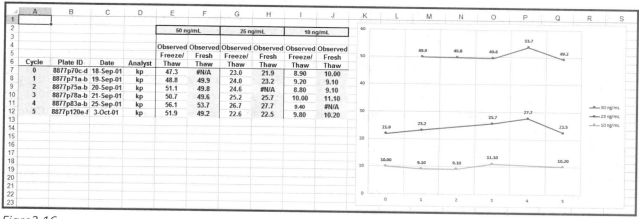

Figre3.16

1. Click in "neutral" territory—nowhere near the database—and choose a regular *Line* graph. Excel adds a blank chart frame to your sheet.

2. Use the *Select Data* dialog box to add three *Data Series* manually (in its left panel).

3. Add the *categories* from the first column (in the right panel).

4. Notice the dips in each line where the series has values that are missing or not available (F7, H9, and J11). Replace those NA entries in the database with a formula based on the function NA: =NA ( ) .

5. If you prefer not to use =NA(), then there is another solution: Leave the cell empty and use in the *Data Source* dialog box the button in the left-lower corner, *Hidden and Empty Cells*: Show empty cells as... (and take your pick).

Note

The advantage of using the NA function is that the chart does not plot these values as zeros. Changing the chart type to "no markers" would hide missing values completely, which is usually not good policy in science because each marker is supposed to represent a real observation. On the other hand, *NA* or *#NA* entries create trouble for calculations, but that can be solved with single-cell array functions (refer to Chapter 18).

By now, you may have discovered why some databases cause so much trouble in creating charts: The culprit is often the header, caption, or label that appears on top of the first column! The problem is that the *Chart Wizard* uses the following built-in rules:

- The longest set of values is considered a *Data Series* (either by row or by column).

- Each longest set of values with headers becomes a *Data Series* (even if they are meant to be *categories*).

In other words, if you want a chart with *categories* (that is, *Line, Column, Bar,* or *Area* charts), you should not give the *category* column (or row) a header. If you prefer to include a header, you have to correct the problems manually through the *Select Data* dialog box. Perhaps it is smarter to leave the first header temporarily empty until the *Chart Wizard* has done its work.

Chapter 23: Combining Chart Types

It is possible—and often desirable—to combine different types of charts into one single chart. It is very common policy, for instance, to add calculations to data plots. However, you don't want calculated values to look the same as observed values in your chart. To visually separate the two types of values, you may have to combine two different chart types.

You cannot just combine any chart types. There are a few important rules. The most important rule is that the axes of the chart types you want to combine should not conflict with each other. In other words, you cannot combine a graph based on two value axes (such as *XY*) with a chart (such as *Line, Bar, Column,* or *Area*) that has two very different axes—a category axis versus a value axis—or no axis at all (*Pie* and *Dough-nut*). Another axis-related rule is that you need to be careful in mixing regular *Stacked* subtypes with *100% Stacked* subtypes because they may fight each other.

Figure 3.17 shows a situation in which calculated values are mixed with observed values. To create a chart that looks like the one shown here, you follow these steps:

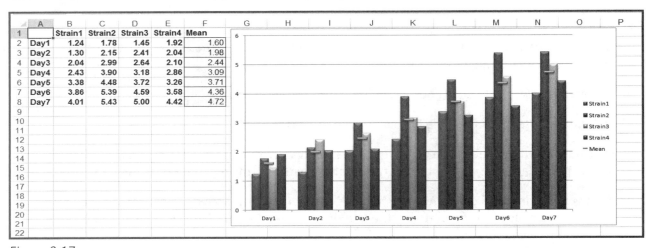

Figure 3.17

1. Calculate the mean of all strains per day in column F.

2. Add the column of means to the chart either by using the *Select Data* dialog and adding a new series, or by clicking in the plot area and expanding the corresponding hairlines in the database to the added column.

3. Right-click one of the columns of the new *Data Series* of means and select *Change Series Chart Type*.

4. The dialog box now defaults to *Combo*. One of the choices for the mean is *Line with Markers* (but don't ever try an *XY* type).

5. Lines usually suggest a development in time, so you may want to take the line itself out and change its markers. You do this by right-clicking the line and selecting *Format Data Series*. Next: *Fill & Line* icon | *Line* section | ⊙ *No Line*. Then: *Select Marker* section | ⊙ *Built-in* | fix everything to your liking.

Figure 3.18 shows the mean per strain (during a seven days period), whereas the previous figure showed the mean per day (for four different strains). These are the steps to take to create this chart:

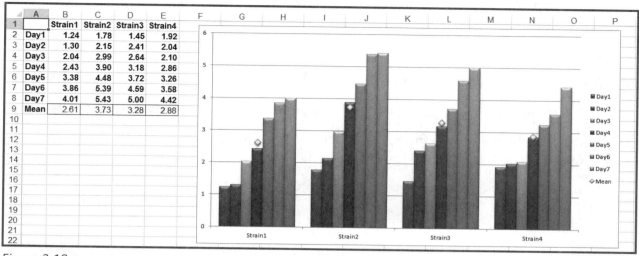

Figure 3.18

1. Calculate the means in row 9.

2. This time we need the *Switch Row/Column* button on the *Design* tab.

3. Add the mean values and change the chart type for this *Data Series* to *Line with markers*.

4. Remove the line itself and fix the markers.

Figure 3.19 shows a chart that is often called a *histogram*. It is a combination of two types: *Column* and *Line*. To create a histogram, you could take the following steps:

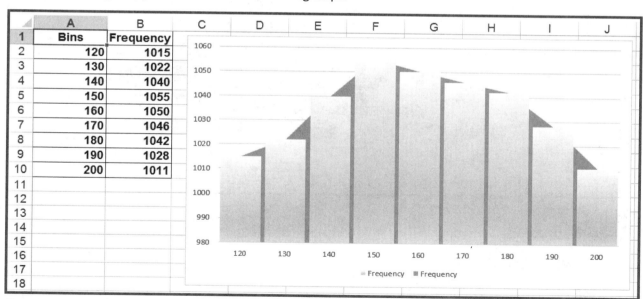

Figure 3.19

1. Insert a *Column* chart.

2. Remove the series *Bins* as a series, by using the *Remove* button in the *Select Data Source* dialog box.

3. Edit the *Categories* so they show the bin values (instead of 1 through 9) by using the *Edit* button.

4. Add the frequency values as a new *Data Series* by using the *Add* button.

5. Change the second *Data Series* into a *Line* or *Area* graph.

6. Make the chart's line style smooth by selecting ☑ *Smoothed line* in the *Format Data Series* dialog (bottom).

7. Give the first *Data Series* a smaller gap width through *Format Data Series* dialog (accessible with a right-click).

<u>Note</u>

Notice there is also a *Combo Chart* option on the *Insert* tab ribbon. When the first cell in the column of categories is empty (no header), this option often works well and fast.

Figure 3.20 shows a *comparative histogram*. Its secret is negative values in the first series. If column B does not have negative values yet, you can multiply those values with -1 (which we discussed in Chapter 15). Here's how you make such a histogram:

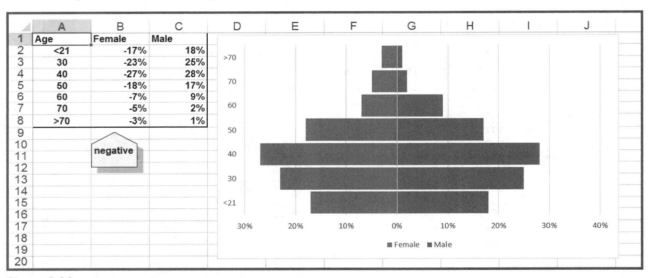

Figure 3.20

1. Create a *Stacked Bar* graph.

2. Move the *legend* to the bottom.

3. Close the gap between the bars.

4. Right-click the vertical axis in the middle of the chart, select *Format Axis, Axis Options*, and set *Label Position* to *Low*.

5. If you don't like the negative percentages on the (horizontal) value axis, right-click the horizontal axis, select *Format Axis, Axis Options*, and *Number*. Assign a *Format Code* like this: *0%;0%;0%*. Finally, click *Add*.

Figure 3.21 shows a new feature in Excel that you might be interested in. It gives you very small graphs and charts located in a single cell. They can easily be made and are sometimes very informative. Here's how you make them:

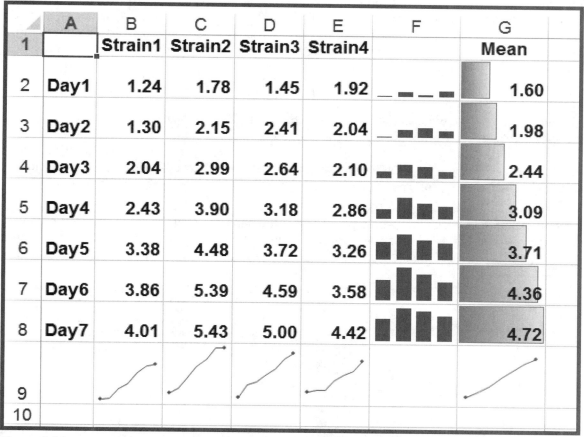

	Strain1	Strain2	Strain3	Strain4		Mean
Day1	1.24	1.78	1.45	1.92		1.60
Day2	1.30	2.15	2.41	2.04		1.98
Day3	2.04	2.99	2.64	2.10		2.44
Day4	2.43	3.90	3.18	2.86		3.09
Day5	3.38	4.48	3.72	3.26		3.71
Day6	3.86	5.39	4.59	3.58		4.36
Day7	4.01	5.43	5.00	4.42		4.72

Figure 3.21

1. Select F2:F8 | *Insert* | *Sparklines* | *Columns* | enter the *Data Range* B2:E8.

2. The top column has the same height in all cells. If you want to see relative values instead: *Design* | *Axis* | ☑ *Same*.

3. Select G2:G8 | calculate the means | apply *Conditional Formatting*.

4. Select B9:G9 | *Insert* | *Sparklines* | *Line* | enter the *Data Range* B2:G8.

5. You probably want to change some settings on the *Design* tab.

Chapter 24: Changing Graph Locations

So far, in most cases, a chart or graph has been located on the same sheet as its data source. When charts get bigger or when you want to combine several charts, it may be better to place them on a separate sheet—called a *chart sheet*. A chart located next to a very detailed database—even if it is a collapsed one—is generally difficult to read and work on, and it takes space away from the database. So you probably want to move it to its own sheet (although you will lose the option of adjusting the chart by dragging ranges manually in the data source).

Note

When moving charts, it helps to know two handy shortcuts: If you decide to keep a chart on a spreadsheet with data, but it's temporarily in the way, you can press *Ctrl+6* (yes *6*, not *F6*) to toggle from visible to hidden charts and reversed. This shortcut does not work on a separate chart sheet, of course. You can press the key *F11* to automatically create a default chart on a separate sheet. Chapter 25 discusses default charts in more detail.

Figure 3.22 is an example in which you would probably want a separate chart sheet. It is based on a very detailed database with a structure of collapsed subtotals (refer to Chapter 7). Here's how you get this result:

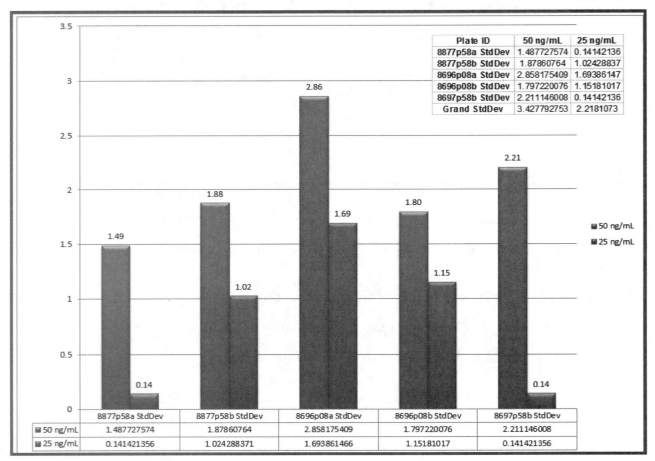

Figure 3.22

1. Insert a *Column* chart on the same sheet as the data source.

2. Click *Move Chart* on the *Design* tab and choose a new (separate) sheet.

Note

You can press *F11* while in the data source to accomplish steps 1 and 2 with one keystroke, but the chart ends up by default on a separate sheet. To keep the chart on the same sheet, use *Alt+F1* (no, not *F11*).

3. Get rid of the grand total by using the *Filter* tool outside the chart in the top right corner.

4. Since the data source is out of sight, you may want to add labels in the chart; do so on the *Layout* tab.

5. To add the original figures to the bottom of the graph in some kind of table format, click the *Data Table* button on the *Layout* tab.

6. If desired, add a picture of the table. You do so as follows:

    ○ In the database, you select *Copy As Picture* (perhaps for visible cells only).

    ○ In the chart, you select *Paste As Picture*. (Note that pictures don't update.)

Figure 3.23 shows a situation in which you would want to combine several charts—perhaps to show the data in four different views. You can do this easily, as follows:

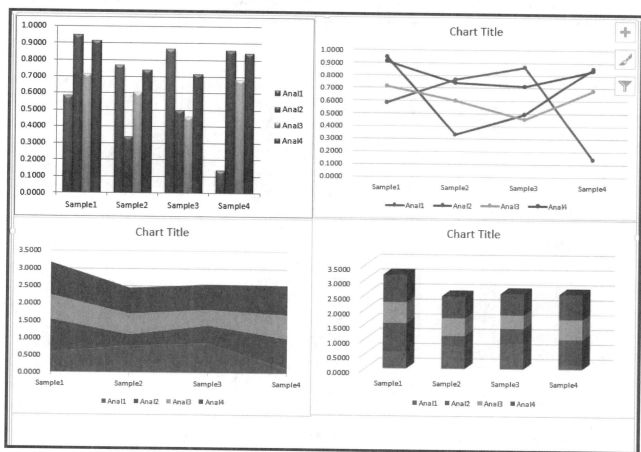

Figure 3.23

1. Click outside the database and press *F11*. This creates an empty chart sheet as a receptacle.

2. Select the chart next to the data source and move it into the empty receptacle by using *Move Chart* from the *Design* tab.

3. For each of the other three charts, follow these steps:

    ○ Click inside the data source first.

    ○ Click *Insert*, and choose the type of chart you want.

    ○ Move the chart into the receptacle on the chart sheet, like you did in step 2.

4. Rearrange the four graphs on the chart sheet, if necessary.

Note

You may want to try to copy and paste the first graph onto this sheet, but don't do it. Or, if you want to see what happens, do try it!

Figure 3.24 shows a situation where the readings before and after some treatment are so far apart that it might be better to use a broken axis. Because Excel does not provide such an option, you must instead work with two charts: one for the top section and another one for the bottom section. Here's how you could do it:

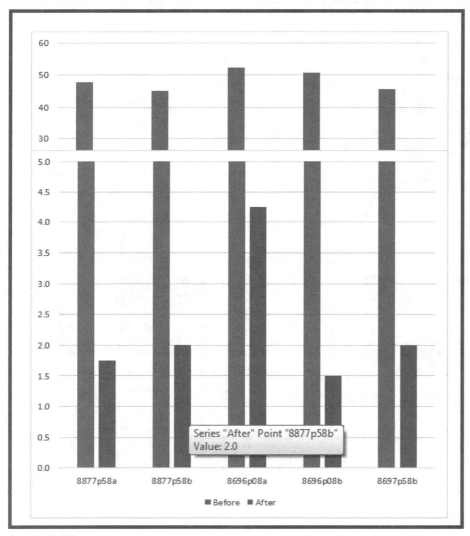

Figure 3.24

1. Click outside the database and press *F11*.

2. Move two identical charts into the empty chart sheet.

3. Set the maximum value for the value axis of the bottom chart to, say, 5. You do this by right-clicking the value axis, *Format Axis*, *Axis Options*, and set the *Maximum* to 5.

4. Manually fine-tune the charts by moving borders and so on.

Note

There is another, probably better, way of creating a broken axis. We will discuss this in Chapter 27.

Chapter 25: Templates and Defaults

If you often use the same type of chart, you can make it your *default* chart. If you have a favorite chart type that you have heavily customized to meet your needs, you can save that chart as a chart template (*.crtx*) in the charts *template* folder and then reuse it whenever you need it.

Earlier, we discussed the fact that when you press *F11* while in a database, a chart of that data source is placed on a separate chart sheet—or *Alt+F1* (not *F11*) for a chart on the same sheet as the data source. The graph that appears is of the *default chart type*, which in Excel is initially a *Column* chart that has a particular Microsoft layout.

If you rather make another type the default chart—for instance, an *XY* graph—do the following: Right-click on the chart | *Change Chart Type* | select the second tab, *All Charts* | choose your favorite type | right-click on its icon on top | *Set as Default*.

Figure 3.25 shows how you can completely customize your own charts and then save them as templates, like so:

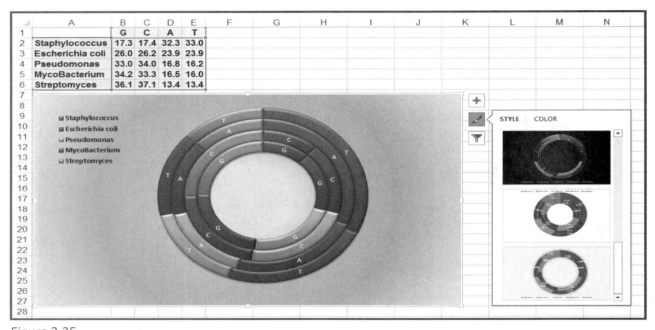

Figure 3.25

1. Create your favorite chart layout—a specific type with customized axes, colors, and so on. The second tool near the right top corner of the chart may be very helpful to apply a nice style.

2. While in the chart, use a right-click and select *Save As Template*.

3. Store your template in the default *Templates* folder as an *.crtx* file. It is best to always store your templates there.

You apply the new template as follows:

1. On the *Insert* tab, click the *Recommended Charts* button.

2. Choose the *All Charts* tab, select *Templates* in the left panel, and choose the template of your liking.

3. If desired, you can make your new chart template your default chart (see above).

Figure 3.26 offers an added attraction: pictures as a part of a template. Here's how you proceed:

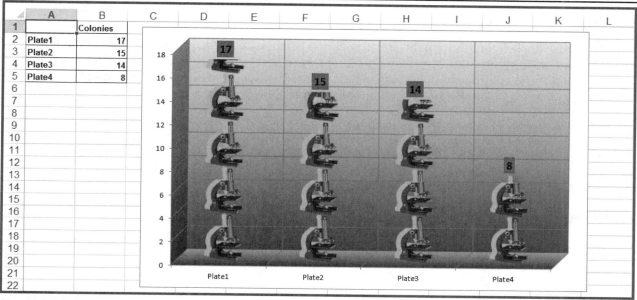

Figure 3.26

1. Create a *Column* chart.

2. Right-click the series, select *Format Data Series*, and choose *Fill & Line*: ⊙ *Picture or Texture fill* | click the *File* button.

3. Locate the file *Micro.wmf* (in your current folder).

4. Choose *Stack* (or *Scale* to 3 units).

5. In the *Apply To* box, choose *Front*.

Chapter 26: Axis Scales

The *value* axis usually requires more attention than the *category* axis. You need to decide on the maximum and minimum values, the value steps, the format, and the gridlines. It is detailed work that will pay off in the end when the graph conveys better information. And, of course, you can save your graph settings in a template or make them part of your default graph (refer to Chapter 25).

To work on any axis, you do one of the following:

- Right-click it and choose *Format Axis*.

- Click the *Axes* button on the *Layout* tab.

You manage gridlines in one of two ways:

- By right-clicking the axis and then choosing *Add Major Gridlines* and/or *Add Minor Gridlines*.

- By clicking the *Gridlines* button on the *Layout* tab.

The *category* axis kicks in automatically, even when there are categories at different levels. Sometimes there are so many details, though, that the category axis does not do a good job. In such cases, you may have to manually decrease the font size, decrease the gap between columns, and/or change the *Alignment* with a *Custom angle*.

The value axis, on the other hand, usually requires more attention. The most common procedure on value axes is setting ranges and steps in the *Format Axis* dialog box, which involves the following:

- To change axis dimensions, you click *Fixed* and then set *Min*, *Max*, *Major Unit*, and *Minor Unit*.

- The *Minor Unit* setting does not kick in until you set its tick mark type (*Axis Options | Tick Marks*).

- Sometimes you can solve a cramped space problem by displaying units in thousands or other large units (*Axis Options | Display Units*).

Figure 3.27 shows a relatively complicated problem. Getting from the left graph to the right graph takes a few extra steps:

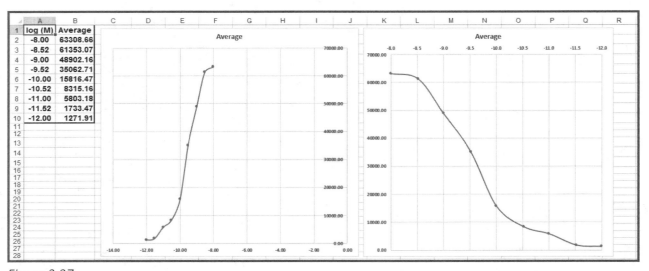

Figure 3.27

1. Select the horizontal axis and set *Axis Labels* to *High*.

2. Select *Axis Options*: ☑ *Values in Reverse Order*.

3. Select *Tick Marks*: *Label Position | High*.

4. Move the Y-axis to the left: *Axis Labels | High*.

5. For the top axis, select *Add Major Gridlines*, and set *Max* to -8.

6. Set *Minimum* to -12, *Maximum* to -8, and *Major Units* to 0.5.

Figure 3.28 shows two different *XY* graphs based on the same data source—the relationship between weight and oxygen consumption of several species. The one on the left has a clustering of values near the origin of the graph. You could have used two broken axes because one value is way out in the top-right corner. But in this case, it is probably much better to make both axes logarithmic—by right-clicking the axis, choosing *Format Axis*, and then ☑ *Logarithmic Axis*. (Part 4 discusses this issue in more detail.) In order to create the appropriate labels you need some extra steps: *Format Data Labels | Label Options | ☑ Value from Cells | Select Range: A2:A15 |* and then unmark the other options. When things get crowded, it is sometimes wise to choose *Data Callout*; you may still have to move individual labels over by hand.

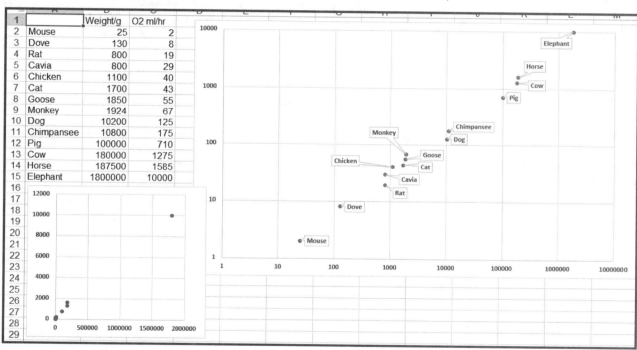

Figure 3.28

Figure 3.29 shows a *Radar* chart of the daily cycle in body temperature. You could give the 37 degrees marker in this chart extra emphasis as follows:

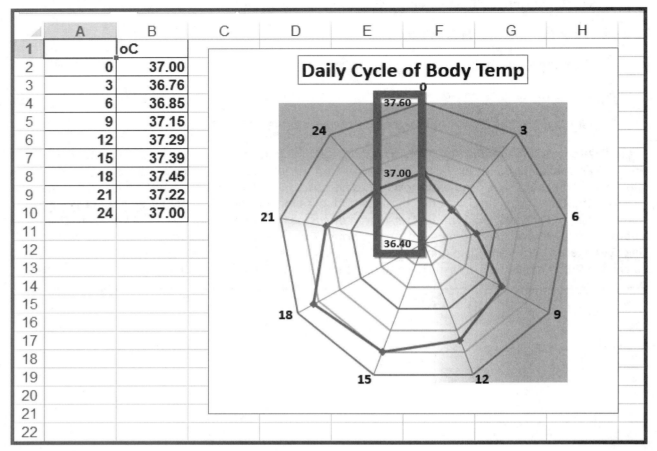

Figure 3.29

1. Make it a major gridline (different from the rest) by adjusting four *Format Axis Options*:

   ◦ Set *Minimum* to 36.4.

   ◦ Set *Maximum* to 37.6.

   ◦ Set *Major Unit* to 0.6.

   ◦ Set *Minor Unit* to 0.2.

2. Add major and minor gridlines by using the *Layout* menu and clicking the *Gridlines* option.

3. Give the major gridlines a more pronounced line color and style.

Figure 3.30 tackles another axis issue. In this example, column B is based on the FREQUENCY function. Because this function requires numeric values in column A as a top bin value, you cannot gather from the horizontal axis what the boundaries are for each bin if the *categories* are based on column A. Because the category axis does not properly describe the bin, you would like "20 to 25" instead of 20. Here's what you do:

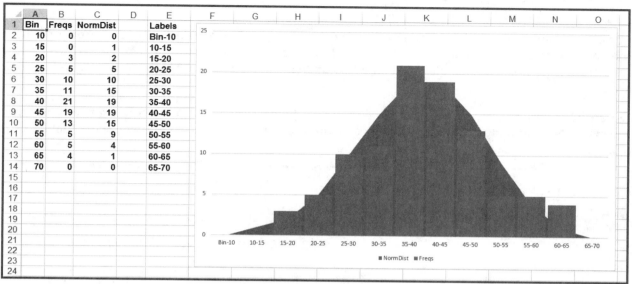

	A	B	C	D	E
1	Bin	Freqs	NormDist		Labels
2	10	0	0		Bin-10
3	15	0	1		10-15
4	20	3	2		15-20
5	25	5	5		20-25
6	30	10	10		25-30
7	35	11	15		30-35
8	40	21	19		35-40
9	45	19	19		40-45
10	50	13	15		45-50
11	55	5	9		50-55
12	60	5	4		55-60
13	65	4	1		60-65
14	70	0	0		65-70

Figure 3.30

1. Create an extra column (in E) and type the following formula in E2: =A1 & "−" & A2. (Or you could use the CONCATENATE function instead, as described in Chapter 15.)

2. Use the *Select Data* dialog box to change the *category* labels (right panel) from column A to column E.

Chapter 27: More Axes

You are not limited to having only two axes in a chart or graph. First of all, each axis can have a *secondary axis*, in cases when you are dealing with two sets of values of different magnitude; in addition, you can create a third axis on its own.

Let's first examine the problem of having values at the extreme ends of a scale. Because Excel does not have a broken axis option, you found a way in Chapter 24 to solve this problem by using two charts with adjusted axis scales. Another good—and perhaps better—solution might be to give the high (or the low) values their own axis.

Figure 3.31 shows a case you worked on in Chapter 24. But this time, instead of creating two charts, you work with one chart and add an extra axis. *Day0*, in this example, has extravagantly high values that deserve their own secondary axis. This is what you do:

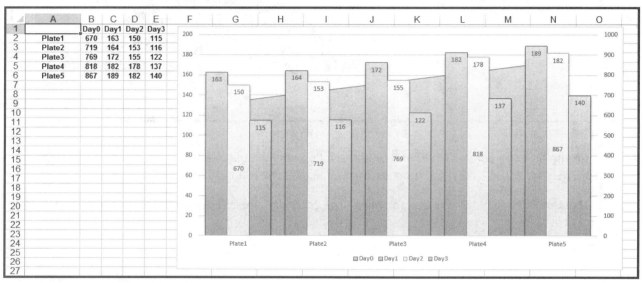

Figure 3.31

1. Right-click the high series of *Day0* | *Format Data Series* | ⊙ *Secondary Axis*.

2. Change the chart type of this *Data Series* to *Line* or *Area*.

3. Add axis titles if you like—either by selecting *Add Chart Element* on the *Layout* tab or by clicking the first button in the right top corner of your chart.

4. Connect each series with the proper axis by using one of the following methods: Give each series and its axis the same font color.

   ◦ Use axis labels.

   ◦ Use arrow shapes by selecting *Insert*, *Shapes*.

Figure 3.32_shows a case that deals with very low values before a certain treatment and very high values after. This calls for a broken axis, but this time you create one by implementing a secondary axis. Here's how you do it:

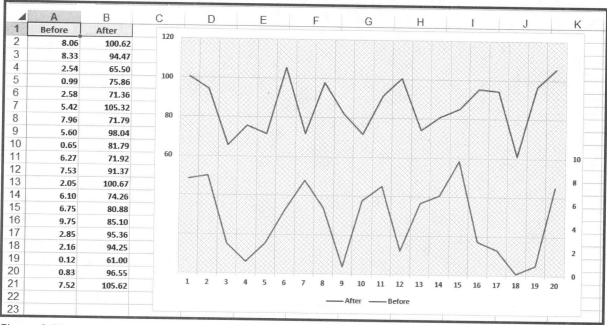

	A	B
1	**Before**	**After**
2	8.06	100.62
3	8.33	94.47
4	2.54	65.50
5	0.99	75.86
6	2.58	71.36
7	5.42	105.32
8	7.96	71.79
9	5.60	98.04
10	0.65	81.79
11	6.27	71.92
12	7.53	91.37
13	2.05	100.67
14	6.10	74.26
15	6.75	80.88
16	9.75	85.10
17	2.85	95.36
18	2.16	94.25
19	0.12	61.00
20	0.83	96.55
21	7.52	105.62
22		
23		

Figure 3.32

1. Connect the low series of values to a *secondary* axis.

2. The trick is now to come up with the proper minimum and maximum settings for each axis:

   ◦ Set the *secondary* axis from 0 to 20.

   ◦ On the left axis, hide values below 60 with a *Custom Number* format as follows: `[>=60]0;;;`. Hit the *Add* button.

   ◦ On the right axis, hide values over 10 with a *Custom Number* format as follows: `[<=10]0;;;`. Hit the *Add* button.

Figure 3.33 shows a case that deals with extremely high and low values in both dimensions, clustered in the left-lower and top-right corner of the graph shown on the left. This example calls for two secondary axes in the other graph shown to the right. Although the procedure to do so is a little different this time, using secondary axes may be a good solution for displaying extremely disparate readings in the same graph (instead of using multiple graphs). Here's how you do it:

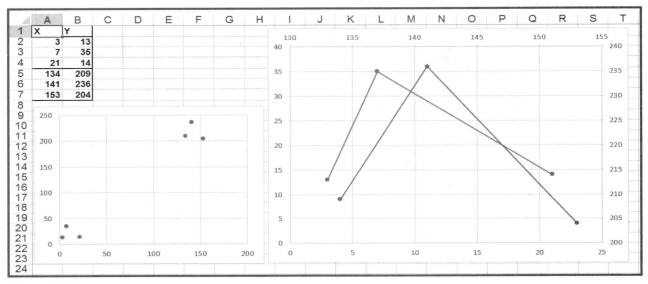

Figure 3.33

1. Create **two** series of values for your *XY* graph: A2:B4 for the low end and A5:B7 for the high end.

2. Once you have created a secondary axis for the second, high series of values, then (but only then!) the *Axis* option under *Add Chart Elements* offers you the option of making a *Secondary Horizontal Axis*.

3. Now one and the same graph can display low values on both primary axes and high values on both secondary axes.

In addition to creating secondary axes, you can also create a third axis on its own. A graph with a third axis is also called a *3D* chart. But not every 3D chart has a third axis. Most 3D charts have only a 3D appearance. Remember those beautiful 3D *Pie* charts? They look 3D, but they don't have any axis at all. And then there are those great-looking 3D *Column*, *Area*, and *Surface* charts. But even if a chart seems to have a third axis, that axis is often merely a glorified legend.

Figure 3.34 plots the probability (according to the Student's *t*-distribution; see Chapter 46) against the *t*-value and the sample size. It is a *Surface* type chart—which is basically a subset of the *Line* type. Doesn't it look like you have three value axes here? Yes, it does, but two of them are *category* axes. There is only one value axis here—the vertical one; the other two constitute category axes that happen to have equal intervals. Consequently, the third axis is just a glorified *legend*.

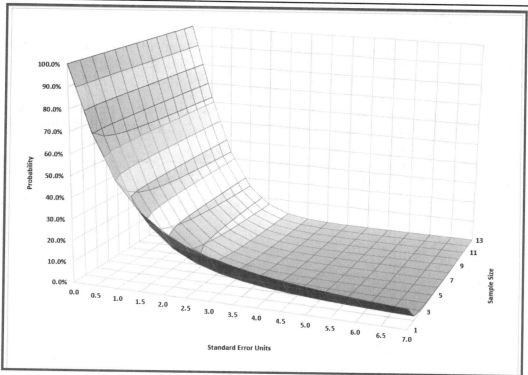

Figure 3.34

So the question is: Does Excel let you add a third value axis? Not really. But it lets you get close by using a *Bubble* graph, which is basically an *XY* graph with a third dimension. The *Bubble* type can handle X, Y, and Z values at the same time. Let us see how.

Figure 3.35 plots the number of colonies grown under different conditions of pH and nutrient level. The graph does have something like a third value axis. It is a graph of the *Bubble* type. Notice that its *Data Source* has X-values, Y-values, and Z-values (the *Bubble Size*)—in other words, the size of the bubbles represents the Z-values. It's not really an elegant solution, but it is the closest Excel can come to a "real" 3D graph with three numeric dimensions.

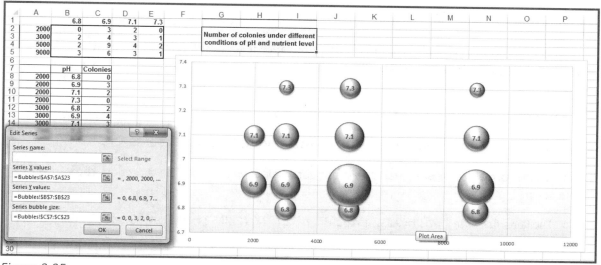

Figure 3.35

Note

When you create the graph shown in Figure 3.35 on your own, you may have to stretch the vertical axis so the bubbles get more spread out without covering each other.

Chapter 28: Error Bars

One of the main reasons for adding bars to a scientific graph is to display the size of the standard deviation or standard error. That's why they are often called *error bars*. Creating *error bars* is easy, but coming up with the right structure for the graph itself can be a challenge. Let's look at the reasons.

Figure 3.36 displays two different ways of using *error bars*. Both charts show the mean monthly temperature for two different locations, Boston and San Diego, plus for Boston the standard deviation around the mean through *error bars*. Yet they are different:

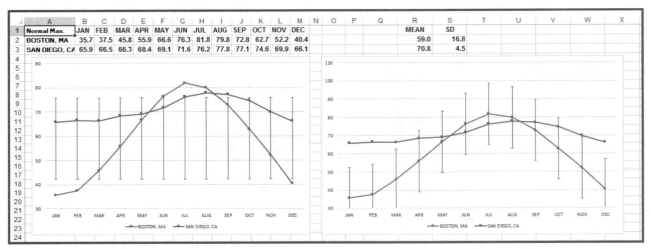

	A	B	C	D	E	F	G	H	I	J	K	L	M	N	O	P	Q	R	S	T	U	V	W	X
1	Normal Max.	JAN	FEB	MAR	APR	MAY	JUN	JUL	AUG	SEP	OCT	NOV	DEC					MEAN	SD					
2	BOSTON, MA	35.7	37.5	45.8	55.9	66.6	76.3	81.8	79.8	72.8	62.7	52.2	40.4					59.0	16.8					
3	SAN DIEGO, CA	65.9	66.5	66.3	68.4	69.1	71.6	76.2	77.8	77.1	74.6	69.9	66.1					70.8	4.5					

Figure 3.36

- Using the chart on the left makes more sense if you want to show whether each actual temperature is within one times the standard deviation. Creating this chart is simple:

    1. Select Boston's *Data Series*.

    2. *Design* tab | *Add Chart Elements* | *Error Bars* | ⊙ *Standard Deviation*.

    3. If you want something other than standard deviation (Excel's default), change it.

    4. Do the formatting through the *Format* section or by right-clicking the error bar.

- The chart on the right is really rather confusing because it suggests that the standard deviation range is specific for each temperature. You would create the chart on the right manually, based on results from calculations in column S:

    1. Select Boston's *Data Series*.

    2. *Design* tab | *Add Chart Elements* | *Error Bars* | *More Error Bar Options*.

    3. In the *Format Error Bars* dialog that appears, select ⊙ *Both* for the direction, then select ⊙ *Custom*.

    4. Hit *Specify Value* | *Positive*: S2 | *Negative*: S2 | *OK*. (Cell S2 has a calculated standard deviation.)

It is hard to tell which chart is best. It depends. The left one is best when you want to see which values are in- or outside a certain range. The right one is best to show whether or which individual values have the same variability. In the above case, it is obvious that the standard deviation in the chart on the right should not move up or down with the temperature moving up or down. However, the technique applied to this chart might be better or even necessary for other occasions—as we will see next.

Figure 3.37 shows two charts: The chart on the right shows the standard deviation range for each individual strain. The chart on the left was created automatically and doesn't really make sense in this situation. So here's how you create the chart on the right:

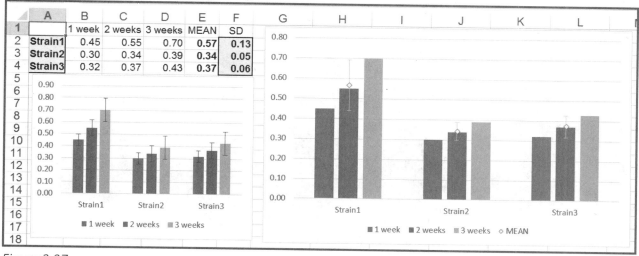

Figure 3.37

1. Start a *Column* graph based on the range A1:E4 only.

2. If you want to display the standard deviation range for each individual strain, select *Switch Row/Column*.

3. Change the mean Data Series into a *Line* graph, with ⊙ *No Line*, and the marker formatted to your liking.

4. Add custom *error bars* to the mean like we discussed earlier.

5. Specify the custom error bar values by setting the *Positive* and *Negative Error* value to F2:F4.

Note

If you hadn't created your own mean and standard deviation calculations, a click on *error bars* would have given you the graph to the left, which is actually the same result as if you had based it on the mean of column B, the mean of C, and the mean of column D.

Figure 3.38 shows a summary of repeated measurements on certain plates. You can only make these error bars manually:

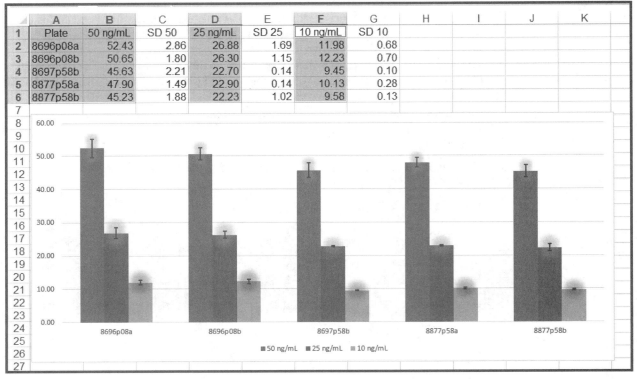

	A	B	C	D	E	F	G	H	I	J	K
1	Plate	50 ng/mL	SD 50	25 ng/mL	SD 25	10 ng/mL	SD 10				
2	8696p08a	52.43	2.86	26.88	1.69	11.98	0.68				
3	8696p08b	50.65	1.80	26.30	1.15	12.23	0.70				
4	8697p58b	45.63	2.21	22.70	0.14	9.45	0.10				
5	8877p58a	47.90	1.49	22.90	0.14	10.13	0.28				
6	8877p58b	45.23	1.88	22.23	1.02	9.58	0.13				

Figure 3.38

1. Insert a *Column* graph based on the ranges A1:B6, D1:D6, and E1:E6.

2. Select the first *Data Series* | *Error Bars* | *Custom +/-*: C2:C6.

3. To get some special effects: *Format Error Bars* | *Line Weight*: 1.5 | set *Glow Presets*. You can also add a label with the standard error value.

4. Do something similar for each other *Data Series*.

Chapter 29: More Bars

You can use the bars that Excel calls *error bars* for many more purposes than just indicating statistical error ranges. You can also apply them to anything that needs to be offset against certain values, such as residuals, percentiles, and drop lines.

Figure 3.39 plots the relationship between the hemoglobin percentage and the erythrocytes count in a *Scatter* graph. Column C predicts or estimates the red blood cell count, as if there were a linear relationship between the count and the hemoglobin percentage. (Part 4 talks about this further.) This calculation is done with the multi-cell array function TREND (which you use by selecting multiple cells and then pressing *Ctrl+Shift+Enter*; see Chapters 14 and 17). Column D calculates how far off the predictions are—that is, the *residuals*—using the formula =B2−C2 (that is, observed minus predicted, or reversed).

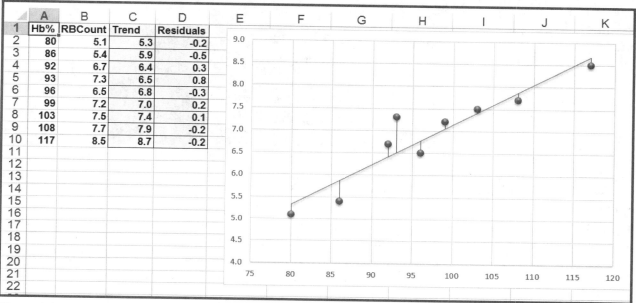

Figure 3.39

Now you can add the residuals to the graph by using error bars:

1. Select the trend series in the graph (which is the straight line), add *Error Bars* from the *Layout* menu, and then choose *More Error Bar Options*.

2. Choose ⊙ *Plus* (only), ⊙ *No Cap*, then ⊙ *Custom*.

3. Click on *Specify Value*: D2:D10 is the range for both positive and negative values, and click *OK*.

4. Click the horizontal bars (which you do not need) and then press *Delete*.

Note

Instead of taking steps 1–2, you could choose the series RB-Count instead (the scattered dots in the graph) and then select ⊙ *Minus* (only). The rest would be the same

Figure 3.40 uses *Drop Lines*. Excel 2013 does offer them, but only in *Line* and *Area* charts. This is how you create them: *Design* tab | *Add Chart Elements* | *Lines* | *Drop Lines*. However, if you want an *XY* graph instead, you need to create them manually—as *Error Bars*, that is. We will do so in one of the upcoming exercises.

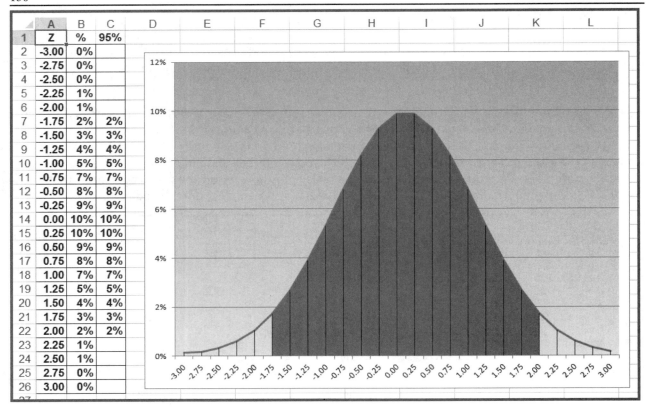

Figure 3.40

Figure 3.41 plots the median per strain plus a range between the 25th and 75th percentiles. You create these error bars as percentile bars by using intermediate calculations, as follows:

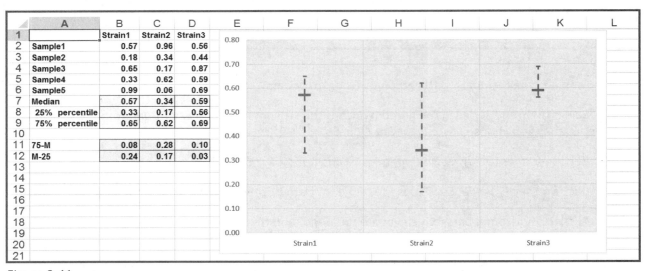

Figure 3.41

1. Calculate the values in B7:D9. The formulas would be as follows:

   ○ In B7: =MEDIAN(B2:B6).

   ○ In B8: =PERCENTILE(B2:B6,0.25).

   ○ In B9: =PERCENTILE(B2:B6,0.75).

2. Create the following intermediate calculations in B11:D12:

∘ The difference between the 75th percentile and the median is for the plus section of the *error bars*.

∘ The difference between the median and the 25th percentile is for the minus section of the *error bars*.

3. Create a *Line* chart based on B1:D1 and B7:D7. Change settings to ⊙ *No Line*, and to a pronounced marker.

4. Add *error bars* according to the instructions under #2.

Figure 3.42 simulates a population pyramid and works with a *Stacked Bar* chart—and many formulas:

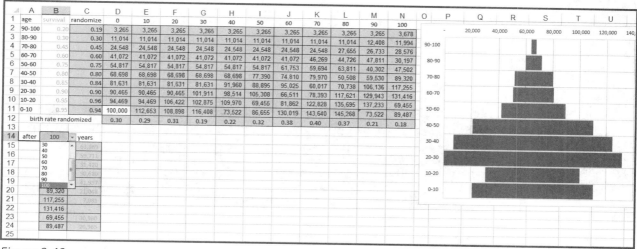

Figure 3.42

5. To mark and protect the formulas, you could use *Conditional Formatting* for all cells on the sheet: =ISFORMULA(A1).

6. Column C randomizes the survival rates of column B. In C2: =B2+((1-2*RAND())/100).

7. Row 12 randomizes birth rates. In D12:N12: =RANDBETWEEN(10,40)/100.

8. Cell D11 has a fixed population size of 100,000 (until you change it).

9. In D2: =D3*$C3, and copied down to D10.

10. In E11: =SUM(D$2:D$9)*D$12, and copied to the right to N11.

11. In E2: =D3*$C3, and copied all the way to N10.

12. In B16: =HLOOKUP($B$15,$D$1:$N$11,ROW(A2),0), and copied down to B25.

13. In C16: =MAX($B$16:$B$25)-B16)/2, and copied down to C25. These values create the empty space to the left of each bar.

14. The *stacked bar* chart is based on two *Series* of values: C15:C24 and B15:B24. Make the first *Series* a *bar* section without fill colors or border lines.

Note

Because of the random functions on this sheet, which are volatile, each time you press *Shift+F9*, the sheet recalculates and the population pyramid adjusts accordingly. When you press only the key *F9*, the sheet will also recalculate, but besides all other sheets in this workbook will.

Chapter 30: Line Markers

You can outfit charts and graphs with extra lines or markers in order to demarcate specific sections, locate means, designate quality control limits, and so on. These line markers can dramatically enhance the functionality of your plots. When you know how to create them, you can make them work to your benefit.

Figure 3.43 includes a dynamic marker for the mean of all the readings. The "secret" series behind this *Area* chart is located in column C. Because this chart is of the *Area* and *Column* type, you need a mean value for each *category*, so each cell carries the same formula =AVERAGE($B$2:$B$21). That's the price you pay. But it is clear; you could never receive this result with errors bars.

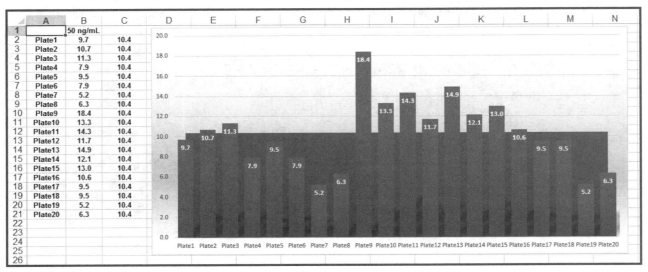

Figure 3.43

The graph in Figure 3.44, on the other hand, is not of the *Line* type but of the *XY* type. Because you are not dealing with *categories* here, you need pairs of coordinates. Remember that *XY* graphs work with paired values. You should therefore create a mini-table with a new series of coordinates for the lowest and highest X-value paired with the mean of all Y-values. Here's how:

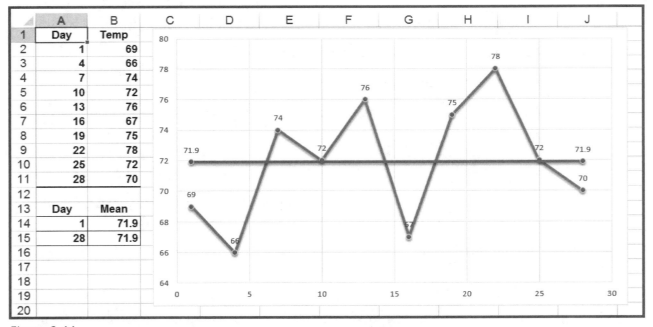

Figure 3.44

132

1. In A14, use the formula =MIN(A2:A11).

2. In A15, use the formula =MAX(A2:A11).

3. In B14 and B15, use the formula =AVERAGE($B$2:$B$11).

4. Add a new *Data Series* to the graph, with X-values from A14:A15 and Y-values from B14:B15.

Figure 3.45 shows an example of quality control: Let us assume that samples should be within the range of three times the standard error. The *standard error* is the *standard deviation* (E2) divided by the square root of the sample size (E3). This is calculated in cell E4: =3*(E2/SQRT(E3)). (More on this in Part 5.)

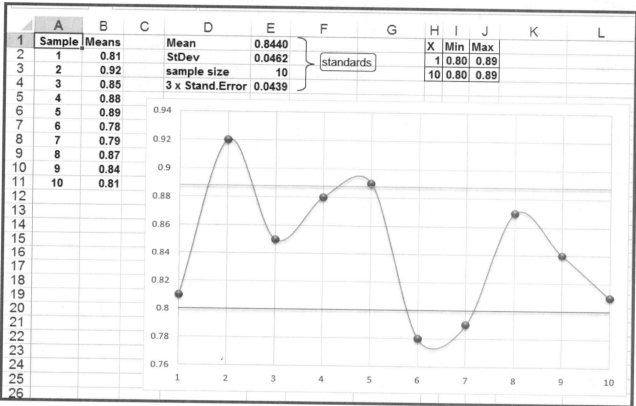

Figure 3.45

The graph can be a *Line* chart or an *XY* graph, but the line markers are implemented differently for these two types:

- If this would have been a *Line* chart, you would need two extra columns:

   1. In one column: the mean minus three times the standard error.

   2. In another column: the mean plus three times the standard error.

- Because this is an *XY* graph, you need a mini-table of coordinates:

   1. Place in columns I and J the coordinates—for instance, in cell I1: =$E$1-$E$4.

   2. Create the Min *Series* from H2:H3 and I2:I3.

   3. Create the Max *Series* from H2:H3 and J2:J3.

Figure 3.46 offers one more example of playing with extra columns in a *Line* graph. It shows a rather unusual situation: One of the units of measurement works with a tiny subscale. Because there is already a *secondary* axis, you need to find another solution. For example, you could use an extra series of "hidden" X- and Y-values. Here's how:

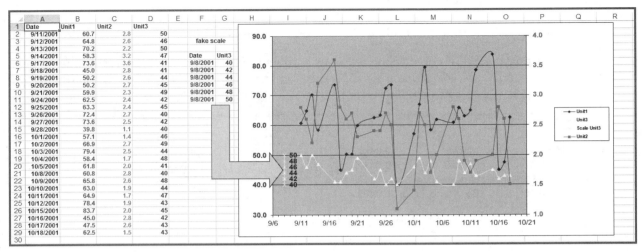

Figure 3.46

1. Hide a fake scale in columns F and G.

2. You can place the scale units at any position on the *category* axis. I chose a (date) value on the X-axis smaller than the lowest value in column A—for instance, 9/8/2001.

3. Add the new *Data Series* to the *XY* graph by using X-values from F6:F11 and Y-values from G6:G11.

Chapter 31: Interpolation

Interpolation is a process of estimating a missing value by using existing, observed values. For example, in a graph, you might want to mark a specific point on the curve that has not been measured; so it has to be interpolated. The graph must be of the *XY* type because interpolation works with values in between—and such values do not exist in charts carrying a *category* axis.

Figure 3.47 shows how interpolation can be done in the *Data Source* and in the graph.

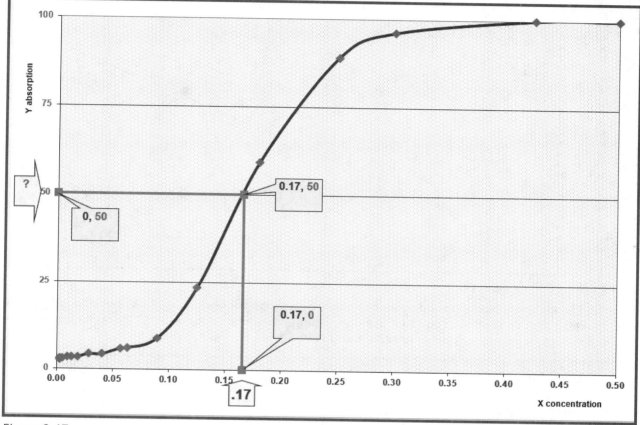

Figure 3.47

- The dots lined up along the curve are observed pairs of values. An X-value of 0.17 was never observed, so you must use interpolation to find its corresponding Y-value—in this case, 50.

- To calculate this Y-value, we need the TREND function somewhere on the sheet

- You have a choice as to what you want marked in the graph:

  - One pair of coordinates: 0.17 and 50

  - Three pairs of coordinates: 0.17,50 and 0,50 and 0.17,0

Figure 3.48 uses only one pair of coordinates. The thick interpolated marker on the linear *Trendline* (at position 74 and 52) is based on the pair of coordinates shown in cells H2 (74) and I2 (52). Cell I2 (Y) is regulated by cell H2 (X) through a formula based on a linear trend: *Y=1.286*X-43.11*. Cell H2, in turn, is regulated by a *control* to its left (which runs from 70 to 110). Part 4 discusses how this formula is found and how to implement a control like this. For now only this: You need to add the two coordinates from H2 and I2 to the graph as a new *Data Series*. Moving the *control* makes the interpolated marker move along the linear *Trendline*.

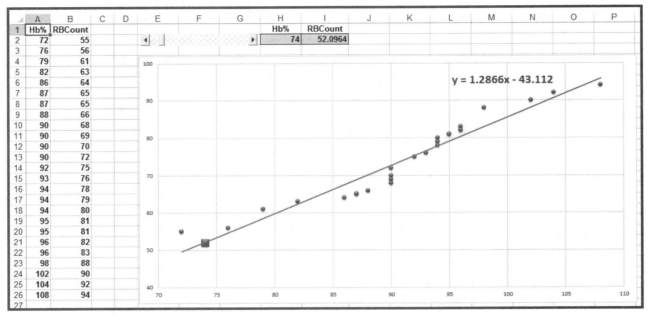

Figure 3.48

Figure 3.49 uses three pairs of coordinates to mark the mean of the X- and of the Y-values. If you want the line markers to touch the axis, you must use the minimum and maximum value of the axes (and not the lowest and highest value in the list of observations). Here's how it works:

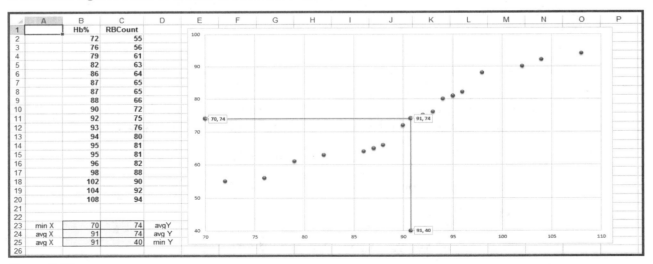

Figure 3.49

1. Calculate the three sets of coordinates in B23:C25, and add them as a new *Data Series* to the *XY* graph, with X-values from B23:B25 and Y-values from C23:C25.

2. If you want a connecting line between the new coordinates, change their chart type to *Scatter with Straight Lines*; otherwise, you get a strangely curved line.

3. If desired, add data labels to the insert.

Figure 3.50 shows another instance of three pairs of coordinates for interpolation. The curve shows the increasing speed of a falling ball. Thanks to the help of a "classic" physics formula, we know the speed in cell B4: =$B$3*(A4^2). Say that you want to interpolate what the speed would be at 4.5 seconds. To find out, you need again a mini-table of three pairs of coordinates in A11:B13. Here's how you do it:

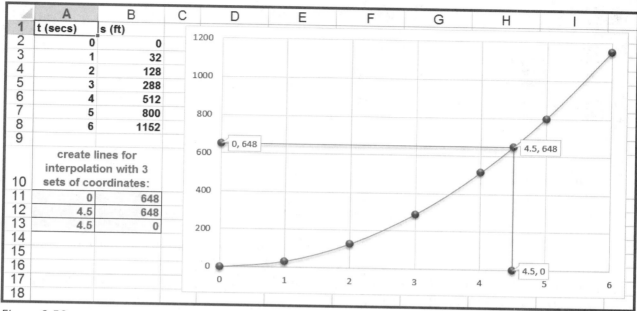

Figure 3.50

1. Ensure that A12 is the only independent cell. In this case, enter 4.5.

2. Base cell B12 on A12 by using the formula =$B$3*(A12^2).

3. Set A11 to 0 (the origin of the X-axis), A13 to =A12, B11 to =B12, and B13 to 0 (the origin of Y-axis).

4. Add this new *Data Series* to the *XY* graph and change its type to *Scatter with Straight Lines and Markers*.

Figure 3.51 applies extrapolation as well as interpolation to data about the world population, but this time without your knowing the formula behind the curve. So you have to somehow estimate the interpolated values:

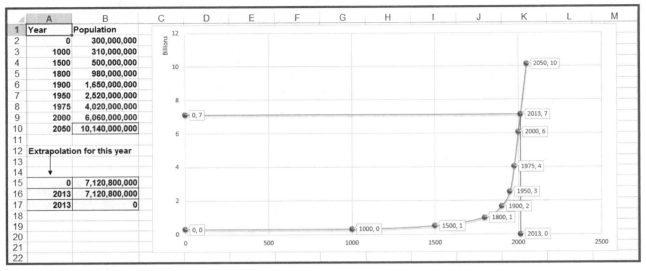

Figure 3.51

1. To predict the world population in 2050 (cell A10), apply the TREND function in cell B10 to the two closest observations (1975 and 2000): =TREND(B8:B9,A8:A9,A10).

2. Add 2050 and its estimated population size (6.1 billion) to the graph, either by expanding the *Series* range or by using the *Data Source*.

3. Create a mini-table in A15:B17, starting in A16 with =YEAR(TODAY()).

4. Enter the formula =TREND(B8:B9,A8:A9,A16) in cell B16. Apparently, you use extrapolation here based on the two latest observations rather than interpolation based on the latest observation and an already extrapolated value.

5. Finish the other cells in the mini-table and add the interpolated coordinates to the graph with straight lines.

Chapter 32: Graph Formulas

Excel is a formula program, so it's not surprising that its graphs use formulas as well. Not only do they plot what comes out of formulas, they also use formulas in the background—and you can make them behave differently by using formulas. When you know how to manipulate formulas, the sky is the limit.

You may have never noticed it, but when you select a specific *Series* in a chart or graph, the *formula bar* displays its formula. Its syntax (which is not available through f_x, by the way) is SERIES (*label, categories, values, order*). When you click in the *formula bar* and press *F9*, you see the formula perform. Then you have a choice: Either press *Esc* to get the formula back or press *Enter* to keep these static values (but then the graph is detached from the data source and can no longer update).

Thanks to formulas, you can also make graphs automatically expand when the data source expands. You do this in two steps:

- First, you create a *Name* that refers to a dynamic range. This can be done with the OFFSET function or the INDEX function (both functions were already discussed in part 1 and 2):

  ○ The syntax of the OFFSET function is OFFSET (*start, row-offset, col-off-set, #rows, #cols*). The range A1:A10, for instance, would be =OFFSET (A1, 0, 0, 10). Usually the number 10 here would be replaced with a COUNT function or so. The last argument is typically not used.

  ○ The syntax of the INDEX function is INDEX (*array, row#, col#*). The range A1:A10, for instance, would be =A1 : INDEX (A:A, 10). Usually the number 10 here would be replaced with a COUNT function or so.

- Second, to have a graph work with dynamic *names*, you use the SERIES function, which has the syntax SERIES (*label, categories, values, order*). Usually the second and third argument are replaced with a dynamic *name,* so when the named range becomes shorter or longer, the graph adjusts to that changed range.

Figure 3.52 shows a dynamic graph that expands when more temperature readings are added to the data set. You follow these steps to create such an effect:

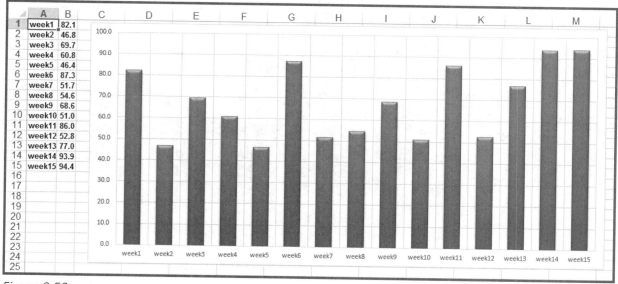

Figure 3.52

1. Use the *Name Manager* to give the range A1:A15 the dynamic name *Weeks*.

2. In the *Refers To* box, enter `=OFFSET($A$1,0,0,COUNTA($A:$A))`. Be careful with `COUNT` and `COUNTA`; the first one only counts cells containing numbers, and would not count labels or so.

3. Use the *Name Manager* again to give the range B1:B15 the dynamic name *Temps*.

4. In the *Refers To* box, enter `=OFFSET($B$1,0,0,COUNT($B:$B))`.

5. Use the new dynamic names in the `SERIES` function:

    ◦ Highlight A1:A15 in the formula bar and replace it with the name *Weeks*.

    ◦ Highlight B1:B15 in the formula bar and replace it with the name *Temps*.

Caution

Because of the random functions on this sheet, which are volatile, each time you press *Shift+F9*, the sheet recalculates and the population pyramid adjusts accordingly. When you press only the key *F9*, the sheet will also recalculate, but besides all other sheets in this workbook will.

1. Press *Enter*, and the sheet references are replaced by book references because these *names* function at the book level. The end result is `=SERIES(,'BookName.xlsx'!Weeks,'BookName.xlsx'!Temps,1)`.

2. Watch how the ranges get properly highlighted. But this time, they are dynamic and can automatically adjust, so when you add new entries to the table, or delete some, the graph nicely responds.

You saw Figure 3.53 already in Chapter 23. This time, the chart should adjust to changes in D1 as well. Here's how you make that happen:

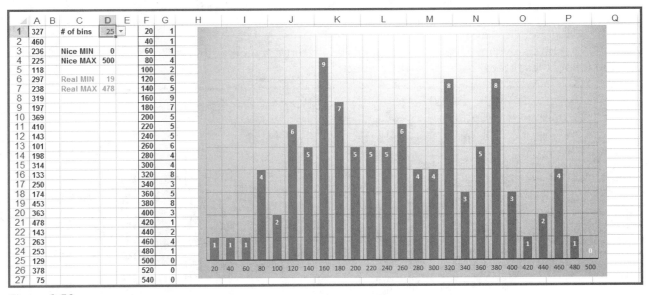

Figure 3.53

1. Assign the name *Bins* to column F: `=OFFSET(DynBins!$F$1,0,0,DynBins!$D$1)`.

2. Assign the name *Freqs* to column G: `=OFFSET(DynBins!$G$1,0,0,DynBins!$D$1)`.

3. Replace the ranges (not their sheet names!) with the range *names* in the graph's `SERIES` formula.

4. Press *Enter*, and the formula should look like this:
`=SERIES(,'BookName.xlsx'!Bins,'BookName.xlsx'!Freqs,1)`.

Figure 3.54 has something else going on: In this example, pH readings greater than or equal to 7.1 get flagged. You discovered in Chapter 11 that sheets use *conditional formatting*. But charts do not! So what's the secret to the chart in this figure? You add an extra column for a new *Data Series*:

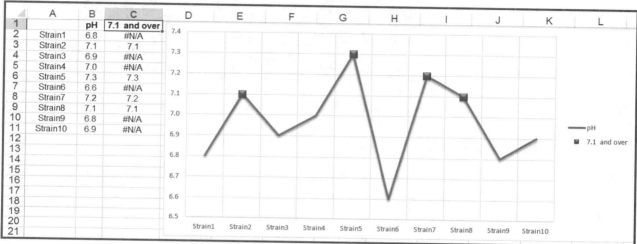

Figure 3.54

1. Cell C1 contains a real number, but the number has a Custom format: *0.0" and over"* (see Chapter 15 for more on how to do this). If this were not a real number, you could never use comparison operators such as > and <. Now we can create formulas that single out values above the value featuring in cell C1.

2. In cell C2, enter the formula `=IF(B2>=$C$1,B2,NA())`, which does not show values below 7.1 (in cell C1). You used the function `NA` earlier (refer to Chapter 22); it does not show up in a graph.

3. Add column C as a new *Data Series* and fix its format (with no line but some kind of a marker).

4. When you change cell C1, the markers will adjust.

Figure 3.55 shows a similar example: It flags all temperatures above the mean. Again, you need another column for this, so you follow steps 1–3 from the Figure 3.54 example. This time, however, you encounter another problem: The two series may not overlap.

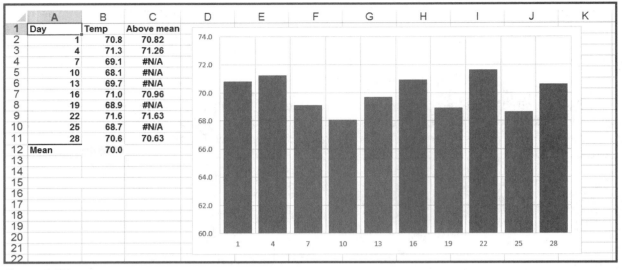

Figure 3.55

1. You therefore need to change their overlap: *Format Data Series | Series Options | Overlap*: 100%.

2. By coincidence, the second series might be hidden behind the first series. If it is, you change 1 to 2 in the last argument of the SERIES formula (or change the series order through the *Data Source*, with the arrow up or down button).

3. All temperatures were created randomly with this formula: =70+(2−4*RAND()). So each time you hit *F9*, the temperatures as well as the chart will change.

Excel may not have all the tools needed for graphic representations of your scientific data, but it does have an impressive array—and you can do the rest. This part of the book tried to give you a number of examples and hints to help you get your creativity going when it comes to graphs.

Part 3 Exercises

You can download all the files used in this book from www.genesispc.com/Science2013.htm, where you can find each file in its original version (to work on) and in its finished version (to check your solutions).

1. Types of Charts

    1.1. Create a *Line* chart based on A3:B14.

    1.2. Create an *XY* graph based on A3:B14.

    1.3. Because of the connecting lines, notice how the sorting order in the data source is critical.

    1.4. Add axis titles, gridlines, and data labels.

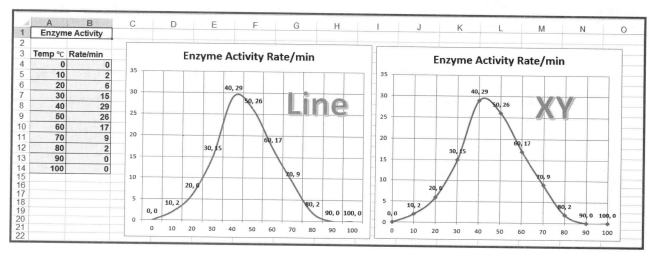

2. Types of Charts

2.1. Create a *Line* chart based only on columns C and E.

2.2. Change the type from *Line* to *XY*, and do the necessary axis work.

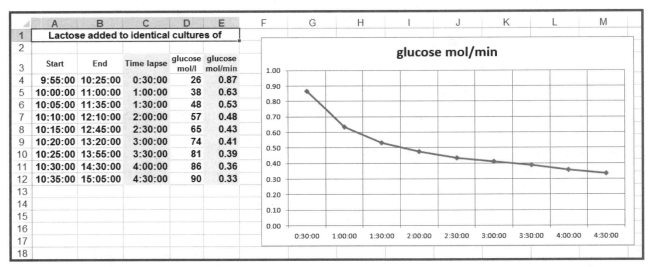

3. Types of Charts

3.1. Determine the chart type of the left chart and create it.

3.2. Determine the chart type of the right chart and create it.

3.3. Which one is best when?

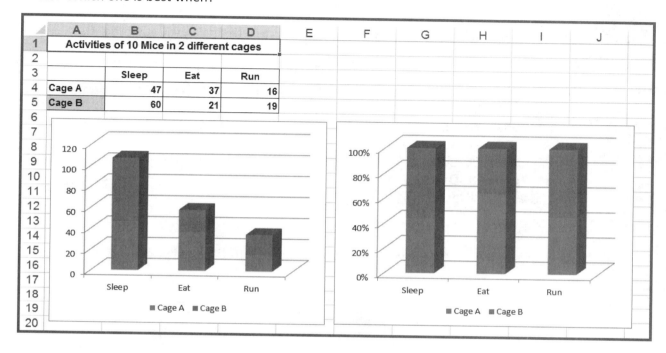

4. Data Source

4.1. Create a *Column* graph for this database.

4.2. Remove columns C and E from the *Data Source*.

4.3. Hide the details in the table.

4.4. Remove the grand standard deviation from the *Data Source*—whatever way you prefer.

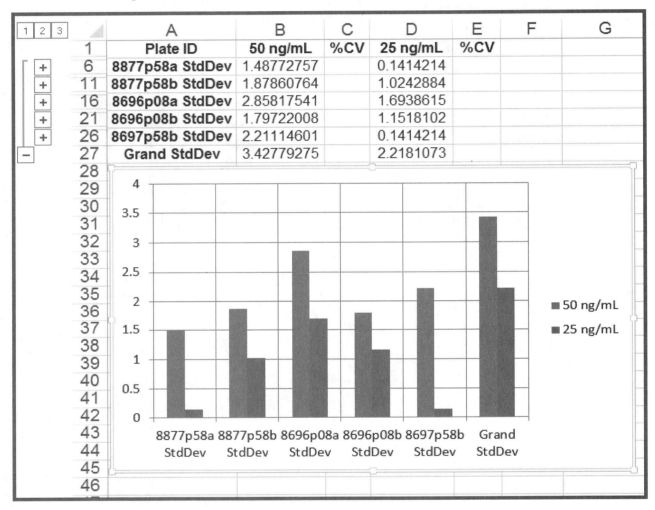

5. Data Source

5.1. Create a *Column* chart for the data source to the left.

5.2. Fix the trouble that occurs.

5.3. Create a *Column* chart for the data set to the right, and fix the column gaps.

5.4. Add the frequencies for a second time as an *Area* chart.

5.5. Why does this second chart cause no trouble?

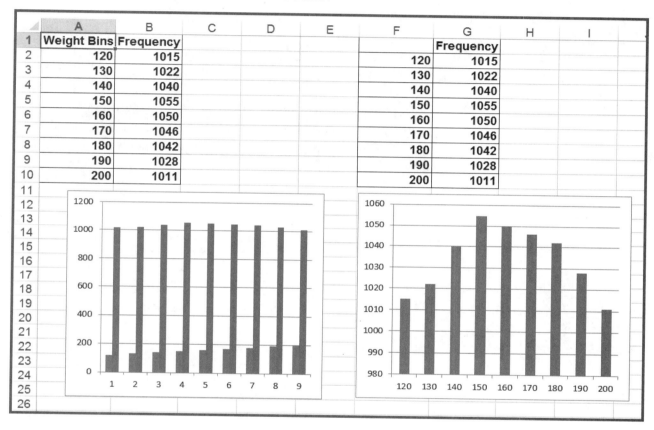

6. Combining Types

6.1. Create a Column chart and use *Switch Row/Column*.

6.2. Calculate the mean for each strain (in row 9).

6.3. Add the means to the chart and fix the format as shown.

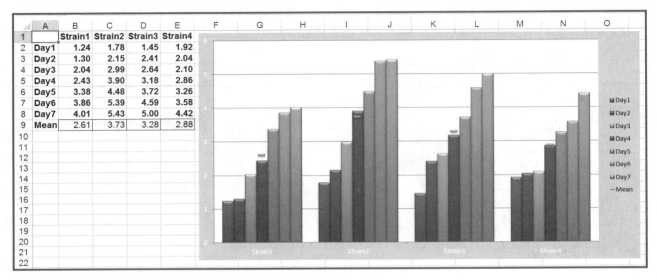

	Strain1	Strain2	Strain3	Strain4
Day1	1.24	1.78	1.45	1.92
Day2	1.30	2.15	2.41	2.04
Day3	2.04	2.99	2.64	2.10
Day4	2.43	3.90	3.18	2.86
Day5	3.38	4.48	3.72	3.26
Day6	3.86	5.39	4.59	3.58
Day7	4.01	5.43	5.00	4.42
Mean	2.61	3.73	3.28	2.88

7. Combining Types

7.1. Create a *Column* chart for this database.

7.2. Change the *Data Series* of column C into an *Area* chart.

7.3. Adjust the gap between the columns.

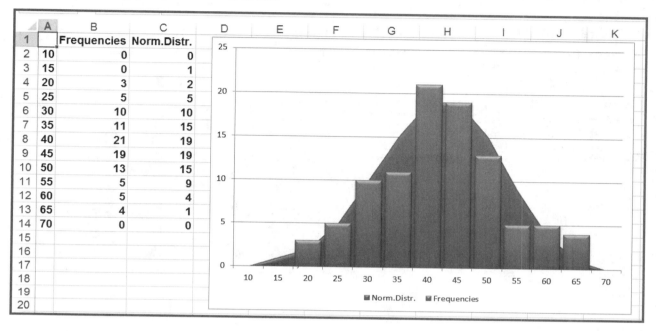

	A	B	C
1		Frequencies	Norm.Distr.
2	10	0	0
3	15	0	1
4	20	3	2
5	25	5	5
6	30	10	10
7	35	11	15
8	40	21	19
9	45	19	19
10	50	13	15
11	55	5	9
12	60	5	4
13	65	4	1
14	70	0	0

8. Axis Scales

8.1. Create an empty *chart sheet*.

8.2. Move the chart located below the data source into the empty *chart sheet*.

8.3. Create another chart with the same format and move that one also into the *chart sheet*.

8.4. Create the effect of a broken axis by changing the Y-axis scales.

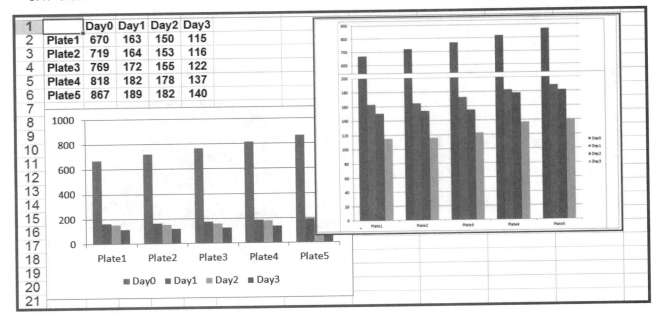

	Day0	Day1	Day2	Day3
Plate1	670	163	150	115
Plate2	719	164	153	116
Plate3	769	172	155	122
Plate4	818	182	178	137
Plate5	867	189	182	140

9. More Axes

9.1. Calculate the cumulative totals in column D.

9.2. Add the cumulative totals to the chart.

9.3. Assign a secondary axis.

9.4. Change the *Series Order*, if necessary, and/or create transparency.

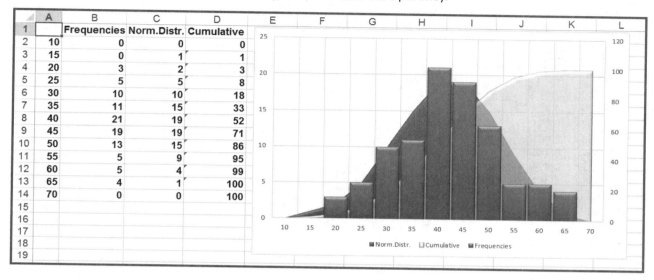

	A	B	C	D
1		Frequencies	Norm.Distr.	Cumulative
2	10	0	0	0
3	15	0	1	1
4	20	3	2	3
5	25	5	5	8
6	30	10	10	18
7	35	11	15	33
8	40	21	19	52
9	45	19	19	71
10	50	13	15	86
11	55	5	9	95
12	60	5	4	99
13	65	4	1	100
14	70	0	0	100

10. More Axes

10.1. Create an *XY* graph based on the data on the left: the relationship between age, near point, and focal power.

10.2. Assign a secondary axis to one of the two curves.

10.3. Adjust axis scales.

10.4. Add a label to each axis.

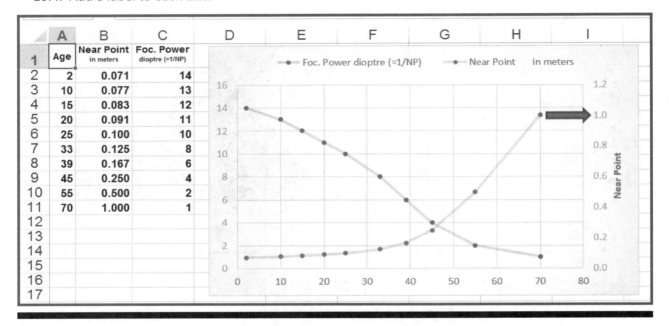

	A	B	C
	Age	Near Point in meters	Foc. Power dioptre (=1/NP)
2	2	0.071	14
3	10	0.077	13
4	15	0.083	12
5	20	0.091	11
6	25	0.100	10
7	33	0.125	8
8	39	0.167	6
9	45	0.250	4
10	55	0.500	2
11	70	1.000	1

11. Error Bars

11.1. Add the standard deviation for *Strain1* as *errors bars* to the column of *Strain1*.

11.2. Add to the chart the mean for each week (based on row 5).

11.3. Display in the chart the standard deviation for each week (based on row 6).

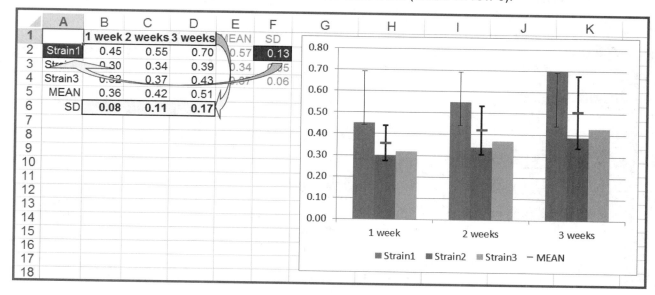

12. Error Bars

12.1. Use the bottom summary (based on the top data) for this *Bar* graph.

12.2. Display the mean cholesterol values (row 15) per ethnic group.

12.3. Add the standard error values (row 18) as *error bars*.

12.4. Add manually text boxes to the error bars, linked to the values in row 18.

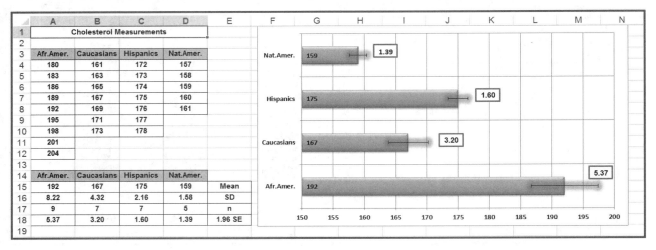

13. More Bars

13.1. Add the vertical drop lines as error bars: ⊙ *Minus* | *Custom*: B10 (only negative, the length of the longest line).

13.2. Do something similar for the horizontal drop lines: ⊙ *Minus* | *Custom*: A10 (only negative, the length of the longest line).

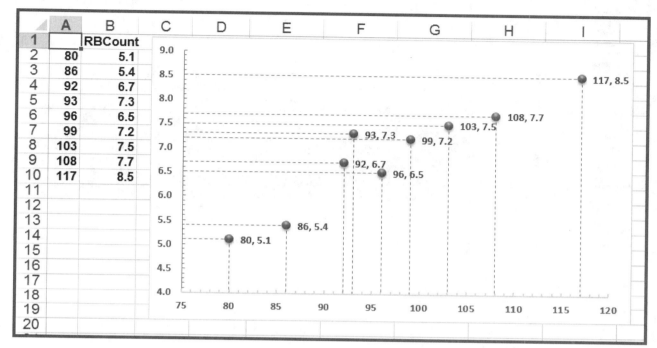

14. Line Markers

14.1. Create 25th percentile calculations in column C and make them show up as a *Line* or *Area* chart.

14.2. Create 75th percentile calculations in column D and make them show up as a *Line* or *Area* chart.

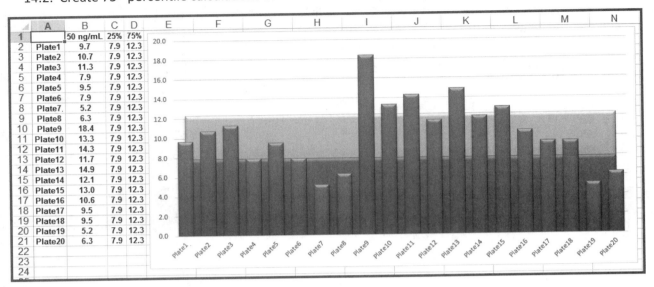

	A	B	C	D
1		50 ng/mL	25%	75%
2	Plate1	9.7	7.9	12.3
3	Plate2	10.7	7.9	12.3
4	Plate3	11.3	7.9	12.3
5	Plate4	7.9	7.9	12.3
6	Plate5	9.5	7.9	12.3
7	Plate6	7.9	7.9	12.3
8	Plate7	5.2	7.9	12.3
9	Plate8	6.3	7.9	12.3
10	Plate9	18.4	7.9	12.3
11	Plate10	13.3	7.9	12.3
12	Plate11	14.3	7.9	12.3
13	Plate12	11.7	7.9	12.3
14	Plate13	14.9	7.9	12.3
15	Plate14	12.1	7.9	12.3
16	Plate15	13.0	7.9	12.3
17	Plate16	10.6	7.9	12.3
18	Plate17	9.5	7.9	12.3
19	Plate18	9.5	7.9	12.3
20	Plate19	5.2	7.9	12.3
21	Plate20	6.3	7.9	12.3
22				
23				
24				

15. Line Markers

15.1. This is an *XY* graph with *fixed* maxima and minima on the scales.

15.2. Determine the coordinates to draw the vertical median line.

15.3. Determine the coordinates to draw the horizontal median line.

15.4. Add both median lines to the graph.

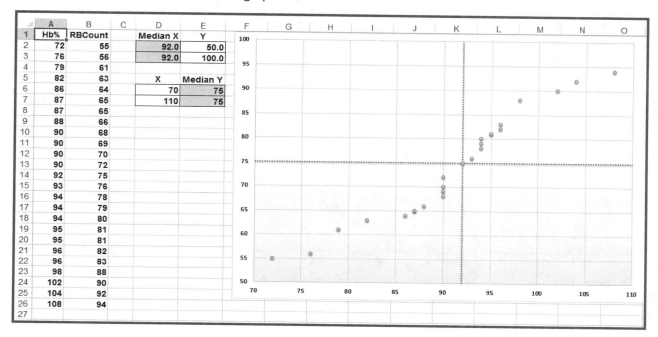

	A	B	C	D	E
1	Hb%	RBCount		Median X	Y
2	72	55		92.0	50.0
3	76	56		92.0	100.0
4	79	61			
5	82	63		X	Median Y
6	86	64		70	75
7	87	65		110	75
8	87	65			
9	88	66			
10	90	68			
11	90	69			
12	90	70			
13	90	72			
14	92	75			
15	93	76			
16	94	78			
17	94	79			
18	94	80			
19	95	81			
20	95	81			
21	96	82			
22	96	83			
23	98	88			
24	102	90			
25	104	92			
26	108	94			
27					

16. Interpolation

16.1. Create the coordinates (D13:E15) for an insert to mark *pKa* for acetic acid.

16.2. Create the coordinates (D19:E20 and D23:E24) to mark the range where acetic acid buffers best—which is *pKa±1*.

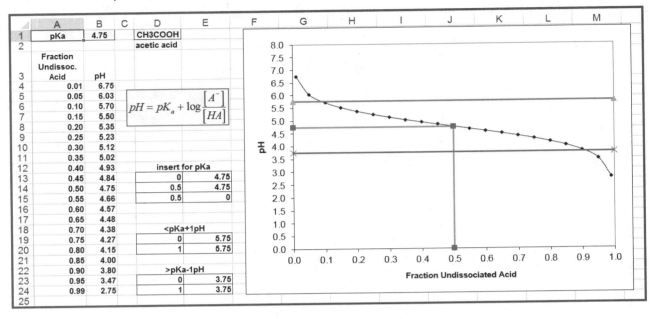

17. Interpolation

17.1. Create the insert for the top scroll-bar *control* by using the proper coordinates in cells E8:F10.

17.2. Create the insert for the bottom scroll-bar *control* by using the proper coordinates in cells E20:F22.

17.3. Test the outcome with the controls.

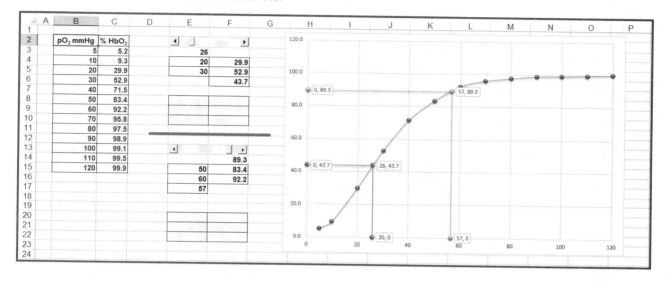

18. Graph Formulas

18.1. Create the dynamic name *Weeks* for A1:A16 by using the `OFFSET` function and starting with the week mentioned in E1.

18.2. Create the dynamic name *Temps* for B1:B16 by using the `INDEX` function and starting with the week mentioned in E1.

18.3. Replace the `SERIES` references in the chart with the new *names*.

18.4. Make sure changes in E1 work correctly.

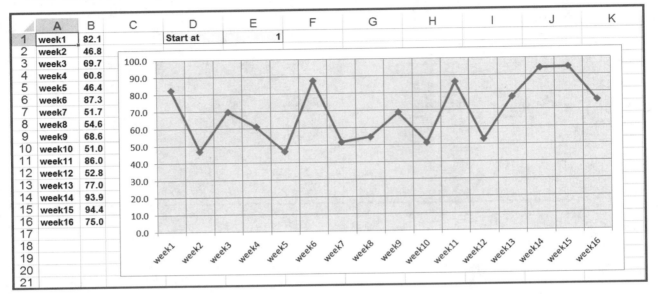

Part 4: Regression and Curve Fitting

Chapter 33: Linear Regression

Regression analysis is the process of making predictions of some variable, based on the relationship between this *dependent factor* and an *independent factor* (or set of factors). It is a scientist's task to find a model or an equation to make such predictions possible.

Single linear regression assumes a linear relationship between two factors: a dependent factor (y) and an independent factor (x). By using the linear equation $y=a_1x+a_0$, you can derive, estimate, determine, or predict the dependent factor (y) from the independent factor (x). Independent factors are also called *explanatory* or *predictor* variables.

Figure 4.1 explains a bit of the terminology used in connection with linear regression. Let's assume that there is a linear relationship between hemoglobin percentage and the erythrocyte count in human blood. You determine what the independent factor is and plot that variable on the X-axis. The linear equation $y=a_1x+a_0$ uses a slope (a_1) and an intercept (a_0). Thanks to this model, you can predict, determine, or estimate y based on x.

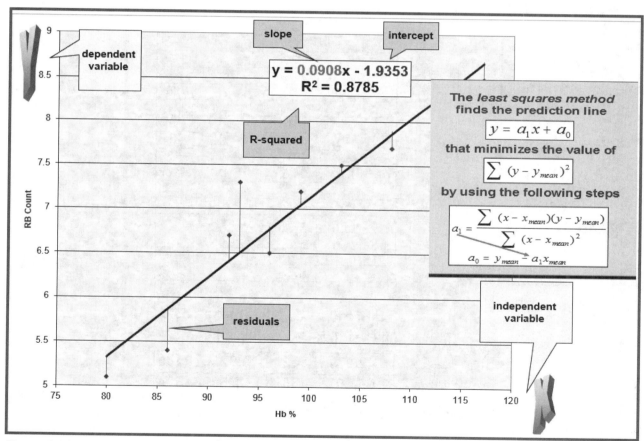

Figure 4.1

The actual, observed values are usually clustered around the linear regression line. R^2 (pronounced *R squared*) is a "measure of scatter" around the regression line; it ranges from 0 to 1. It is sometimes referred to as *RSQ* or r^2. The closer R^2 comes to 1, the better values coincide with the regression line, so the better you can estimate or predict. The differences between the observed values and the predicted values are called *residuals*. The linear regression line is calculated in such a way that the sum of all residuals is 0 (so they have "evened each other out"). The residuals are basically the unexplained parts of the regression analysis—the "leftovers."

If you want to know more about what is going on in the background, you need to realize that for each point in the graph (or for each data pair in the data set), Excel calculates the following sums of squares (*SS*):

- The squared difference between the estimated y-value and the observed y-value. The sum of these squared differences is called the *residual sum of squares*, SS_{resid} (which is the unexplained part of the regression).

- The total sum of squares, SS_{total}, which is the sum of the squared differences between the observed y-values and the mean of the y-values.

- The regression sum of squares, SS_{regr}, or the explained part of the regression: $SS_{regr} = SS_{total} - SS_{resid}$.

- *RSQ*, R^2 or r^2, measures how well the equation explains the relationship among the variables: $R^2 = SS_{regr}/SS_{total}$.

The graph in Figure 4.2 plots the relationship between the G-C% of different DNA samples and the thermal denaturation, T_m, of the double helix. What the independent factor stands for is up to you. If you want to determine, predict, or estimate T_m by using G-C%, then G-C% would be the independent factor (x), whereas T_m would be the dependent factor (y). But the reverse is possible too.

	A	B	C	D
1			%G-C Pairs	T_m in °C
2	A plot of the		24%	79
3	G-C % of 15		98%	110
4	different		55%	94
5			80%	106
6	DNA		27%	83
7	samples		9%	73
8	against the		87%	108
9	thermal		13%	75
10			94%	109
11	denaturatio		72%	99
12	n of the		36%	84
13	double helix		79%	103
14			18%	76
15	(T_m)		45%	90
16			62%	97
17				
18			determine T_m by using %G-C	determine %G-C by using T_m
19		Slope (a₁)	42.97705652	0.023070486
20		Intercept (a₀)	69.50755456	-1.59904624
21		R-squared	0.991501581	0.991501581
22				
23		X	50%	95
24		Y	90.99608282	0.59264993
25				

Figure 4.2

To perform regression analysis on this set of data, we need to gather some important information:

1. Name the C2:C16 range *GC* and the D2:D16 range *Tm*. (Refer to Chapter 4.)

2. Use the SLOPE function in cell C19: =SLOPE(Tm,GC).

3. Use the INTERCEPT function in cell C20: =INTERCEPT(Tm,GC).

4. Use the RSQ function in cell C21: =RSQ(Tm,GC).

5. Predict, determine, or estimate in cell C24 what T_m would be if you had a DNA sample containing 50% G-C bonds: =C19*C23+C20.

6. Predict or estimate G-C% based on T_m in cell D24: =D19*D23+D20.

<u>Note</u>

Notice that *RSQ* is and should be the same after step 6 as after step 5.

Figure 4.3 presents graphically what you have done so far mathematically. To get these regression lines and their equations to show up in a graph, you follow these steps:

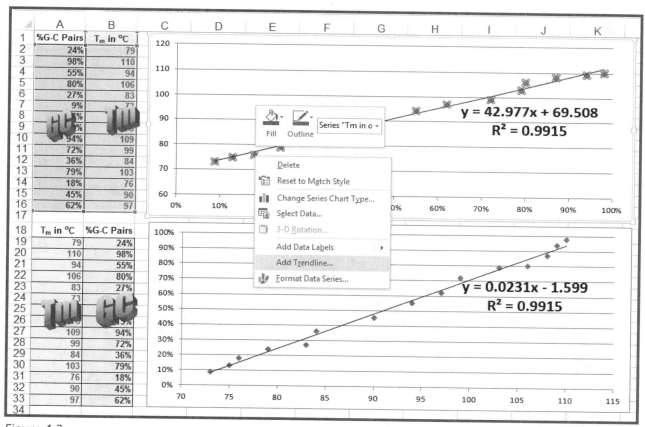

Figure 4.3

1. Right-click the series of data points in the top *XY* graph and select *Add Trendline*.

Note

Excel uses the term *trendline* rather than *regression line*.

2. By default, Excel always goes for a linear regression line—which is okay here. Make sure you also include *RSQ* and the equation by marking those two options at the bottom of the dialog box.

3. Notice that slope, intercept, and *RSQ* are identical to the ones you calculated earlier by using functions. All observed values are very close to the predicted or estimated regression line—that's why *RSQ* is so high.

4. Repeat steps 1, 2 and 3 for the reversed situation in the second graph where the x-axis and y-axis have been interchanged. Because Excel only creates regression lines for values on the x-axis, you must switch the axes.

5. Notice that both slope and intercept are different this time, but *RSQ* has not changed.

If you want both regression lines in the same *XY* graph, you must create the second one manually. In the graph shown in Figure 4.4, the *RSQ* was manually lowered; otherwise, both lines would have practically coincided. *RSQ* is basically a measure of the angle between both regression lines. If the angle were 90 degrees, *RSQ* would be 0, and the observation points would be scattered all over the graph.

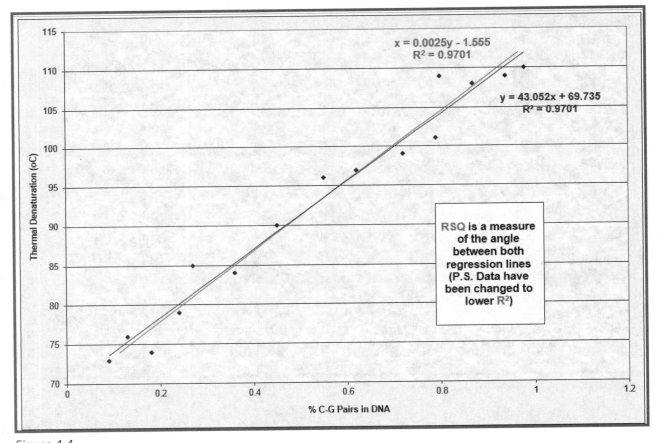

Figure 4.4

Figure 4.5 shows another way of making predictions or estimates: by using the function TREND. Based on observed x-values and y-values, TREND calculates a series of expected or estimated y-values, assuming a linear regression. The advantage of using TREND is that you can calculate the residuals as well—that is, the difference between observed and expected (or reversed, but this book consistently sticks to the first option).

Another advantage of using TREND is the possibility of predicting non-observed values. But if you want to use it in that way, you need its third argument. Let us find out what TREND can do for us:

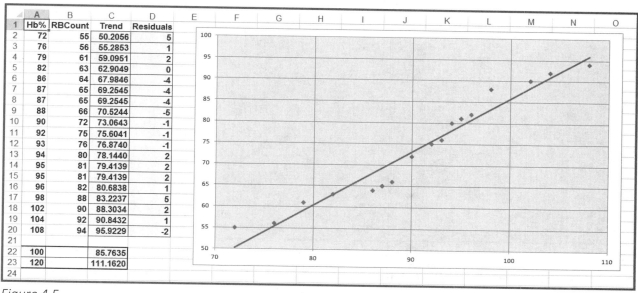

Figure 4.5

1. Select all cells C2:C20 and apply the formula =TREND(B2:B20,A2:A20).

2. Press *Ctrl+Shift+Enter*, for this is an array function (see also Chapter 17).

Note

The "manual" regression line (based on the TREND formula results) is exactly identical to the linear *Trendline* Excel creates after a right-click on the series of observed data points.

3. Calculate in column D the residuals by entering =B2-C2 in cell D2. Notice that the sum of residuals is—as you would expect—zero. (You can watch the sum on your status bar at the bottom of your screen while the values in column D are selected.)

4. To predict non-observed values, use TREND again, this time with its third argument. The values for the argument *New_x's* determine what the x-values should be in this case (e.g. 100 and 120 in A22:A23). So enter the following formula in C22:C23: =TREND(B2:B20,A2:A20,A22:A23).

Caution

The first value in the TREND formula of step 4 is based on interpolation; the second one is based on extrapolation (see also Chapter 31). Extrapolation is always potentially dangerous; for example, a 120% hemoglobin content could possibly be lethal!

Note

You can do extrapolation graphically by using Excel's *trendline*. All you need to do is indicate a forward (or backward) step in the *trendline*'s dialog box—in this case, 12 periods forward. However, the advantage of using TREND is that you can calculate the residuals as well.

Figure 4.6 shows a graph in which you want to predict the erythrocyte count for a specific hemoglobin percentage (regulated by a scroll-bar *control*). Let's use this example to compare three different methods of interpolation:

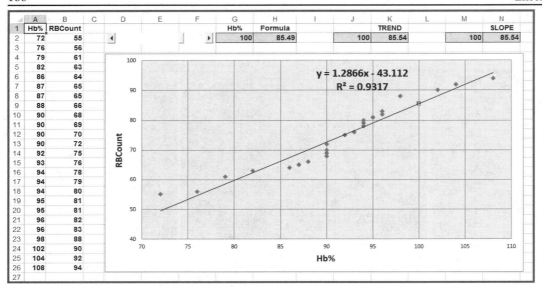

Figure 4.6

- **Using an equation:** In cell H2, enter `=1.286*G2-43.11` (taken from the equation that comes with the *Trendline*).

- **Using TREND:** In cell K2, enter `=TREND(B2:B26,A2:A26,J2)`.

- **Using a combination of SLOPE and INTERCEPT:** In cell N2, enter `=SLOPE(B2:B26,A2:A26)*M2+INTERCEPT(B2:B26,A2:A26)`.

Only the first cell (H2) differs from the two other cells because it is based on an equation that has been rounded and is therefore less precise than the others.

Figure 4.7 plots the pulmonary function *FVC* (forced vital capacity), per liter, against the age of participants in this study. Although the *RSQ* is not bad here (0.96), you see many "ups and downs"—even for people of the same age. Why? In general, there are three possible explanations:

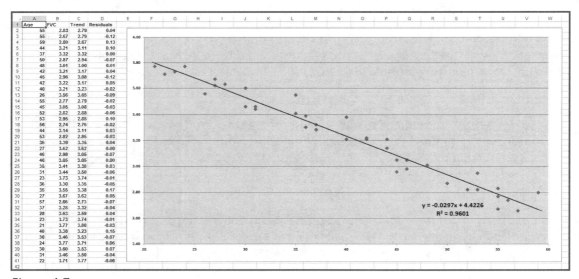

Figure 4.7

- You always deal with errors, inaccuracy, randomness, and just "noise" as part of any measuring procedure; let's disregard such factors here.

- There may be additional variables involved; we'll discuss this issue in Chapter 39.

- The relationship is not really linear; we'll discuss this next in Chapter 34.

Chapter 34: Nonlinear Regression

Many, or perhaps most, relationships between paired sets of data are not of the linear type. The most common alternatives are logarithmic, exponential, power, and polynomial. This chapter describes the characteristics of these various relationships.

The most flexible alternative to a linear relationship is a polynomial regression line. This type can grow into an nth degree curve, which makes this type flexible—but also increasingly unmanageable, as you will see. Polynomial curves essentially change direction—from up to down, or from down to up:

- $y = a_2 x^2 + a_1 x + a_0$: This is a polynomial curve of the second order. This quadratic curve changes direction once; its pattern is concave downward (u-shaped) when slope a_2 is negative, and it is concave upward (n-shaped) when a_2 is positive.

- $y = a_3 x^3 + a_2 x^2 + a_1 x + a_0$: This is a polynomial curve of the third order and is also called *cubic*. The cubic or third-degree curve changes direction twice; it is ~-shaped.

- $y = a_4 x^4 + a_3 x^3 + a_2 x_2 + a_1 x + a_0$: This is a polynomial curve of the fourth order. The fourth-degree curve changes direction three times; it is w- or m-shaped.

- $y = a_n x^n + ... + a_1 x + a_0$: This is an nth degree curve—that is, of the nth order. The nth degree curve changes direction $n-1$ times.

Figure 4.8 shows a linear regression line with a decent *RSQ*, but it is not the best regression model. I am sure your scientific gut feelings tell you there must be a better connection. The following are two possible improvements:

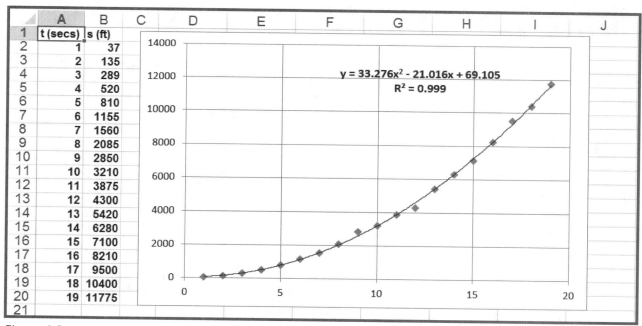

Figure 4.8

- You can add a new line by right-clicking the series and selecting *Add Trendline*.

- You can replace the current line by right-clicking the line and selecting *Format Trendline*.

A polynomial regression line of the second order seems to fit better and makes *RSQ* go up. Yes, this is a trial-and-error method, but it is good enough for now. (You will do better in Chapter 35.)

Figure 4.9 shows the fraction of un-dissociated acetic acid as a function of the pH. Trial and error has suggested a polynomial regression line of the fifth order! As you can see, you can often force your data into a polynomial regression line by adding more and more slopes. The result is often awkward. You could often get the same result with a much simpler formula. We will discuss that later.

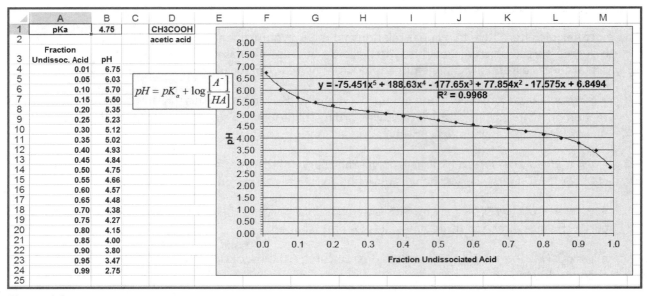

Figure 4.9

Note

Could you use TREND—which is for linear regression predictions—also for polynomial situations? You sure can. The shortest formula for a polynomial situation of the fifth degree would be: =TREND(-known_y's, known_x's ^ {1,2,3,4,5}), followed by *Ctrl+Shift+Enter*. The third argument creates five arrays, each one raised to a different power.

Figure 4.10 shows the increase of population size after each generation. It is definitely a case in which a linear regression line would not fit. You may get far with a polynomial line, but your intuition probably tells you to go for an exponential regression line. Shortly, we will discuss the equation, slope, and intercept of an exponential regression line. For now, remember that an exponential curve is the upper part of a hyperbola—always located above the x-axis: It goes up toward infinity when its exponent is positive; it goes down asymptotically toward 0 when its exponent is negative.

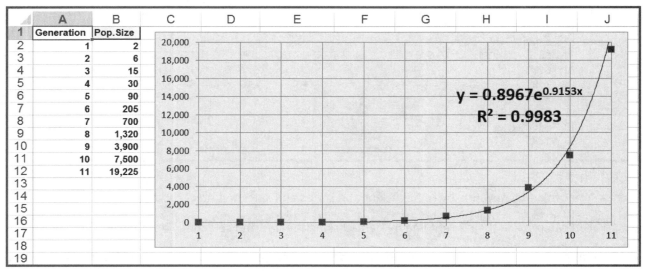

Figure 4.10

Figure 4.11 shows a similar case—this time for the metabolic rate of breaking down lactose into D-glucose and D-galactose. Again, you could get far with a high-degree polynomial version (the most curved one). But it probably makes more sense to go for a power regression line—although that brings down *RSQ* a little. Don't forget that you have just a few observations here, so observation errors and randomness have a more prominent impact.

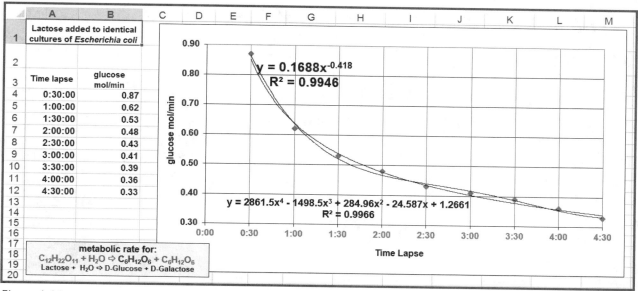

Figure4.11

Figure 4.12 shows the facilitated uptake of glucose by erythrocytes. A polynomial regression line would be quite a stretch in this situation. It probably makes much more sense to try a logarithmic regression line. But even that latter fit is not great because you seem to be dealing here with a sigmoid curve (also called logistic or s-shaped), which you'll learn more about in Chapter 36.

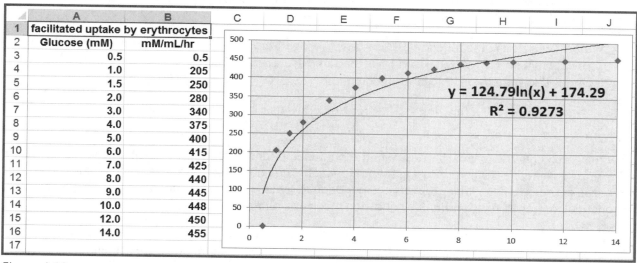

Figure 4.12

Figure 4.13 provides an overview of the formulas behind the curves we've looked at so far. Excel offers the following functions for use in this context:

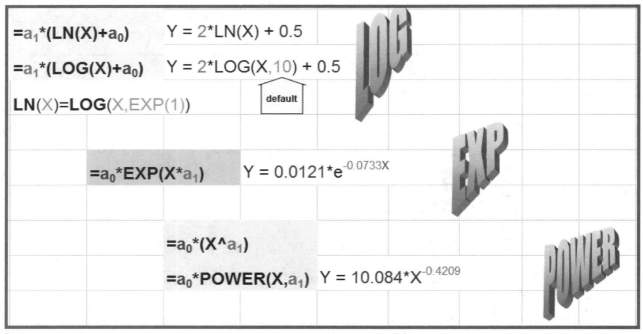

Figure 4.13

- **LN(x):** the function LN returns the natural logarithm of x. Natural logarithms are based on the constant e (that is, 2.71828182845904).

- **EXP(x):** the function EXP returns e raised to the power of x. The constant e equals 2.71828182845904, the base of the natural logarithm. The natural logarithm of e raised to the power of 3 would be =LN(EXP(3)).

- **LOG(x,base):** the function LOG returns the logarithm of x to the base you specify; the base is 10 by default. So =LOG(x,EXP(1)) is the same as =LN(x). There is also a function called LOG10; it always takes the base-10 logarithm of a number.

- **POWER(x,n):** The function POWER returns x raised to the power of n and is equivalent to $x\hat{}n$ in Excel.

Now that you know the formulas, you are better equipped to understand what is behind each curve. At any time, you can "linearize" values by using the LN function. The question is, of course, which values need to be linearized in order to get a linear regression line. Depending on whether you are dealing with a logarithmic, exponential, or power relationship, this question receives a different answer:

- **Logarithmic:** Figure 4.14 represents a logarithmic case. At any time, you can "linearize" a logarithmic curve by linearizing the x-values (in column A) via the LN function used in column C. The top graph uses the original values from column A on its x-axis. The bottom graph, on the other hand, uses the linearized values of column C on its x-axis instead. Notice the linear regression line in the bottom graph versus the logarithmic regression line in the top graph. The logarithmic equation (in the upper graph) has the same slope and intercept as the linear equation (in the lower graph).

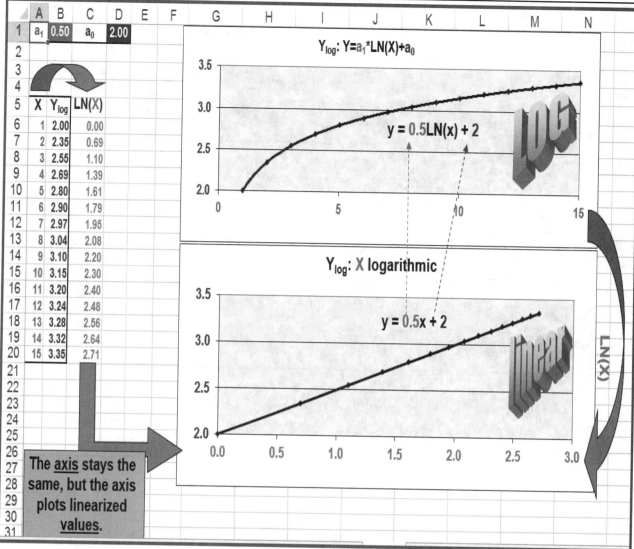

Figure 4.14

- **Exponential:** Figure 4.15 has an exponential curve in its top graph. In order to linearize an exponential curve, you must apply the `LN` function to the y-values (in column B)—which has been done in column C. The bottom graph uses the linearized values from column C on its y-axis. Notice how the slope and intercept match again between the exponential and linear versions of regression, provided that you "unlinearize" the linearized slope first by using the function `EXP`: `EXP(0.6931) = 2`.

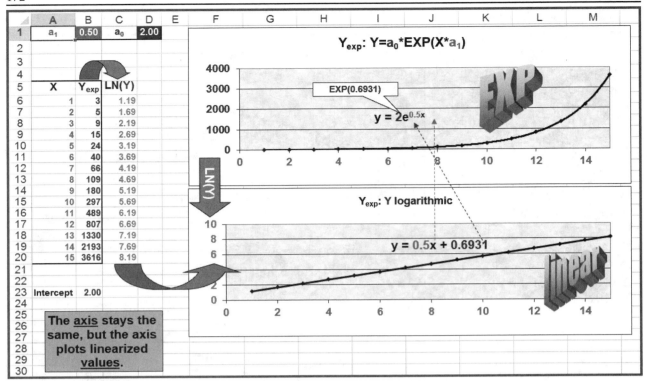

Figure 4.15

- **Power:** Figure 4.16 shows a power curve in its top graph. In order to linearize a power curve, you must apply the LN function to both x-values and y-values. In this case, you find linearized values also on both axes of the bottom graph.

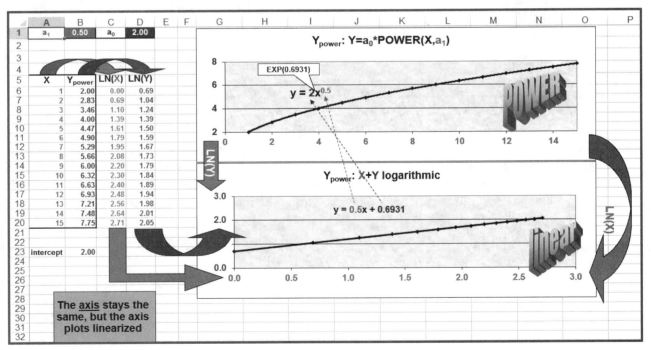

Figure 4.16

Remember that LN(X) is the same as LOG(X, EXP(1)). So instead of linearizing values, you could instead linearize the axis by making its scale logarithmic, as is shown in Figure 4.17. Be aware that the graphs to the right use the regular values—not the linearized ones—so each regression line is of the same type as the one used by its partner graph to the left. To put it differently: What you linearized here is the axis, not the values. Instead of using linearized values, you created a logarithmic scale for a specific axis:

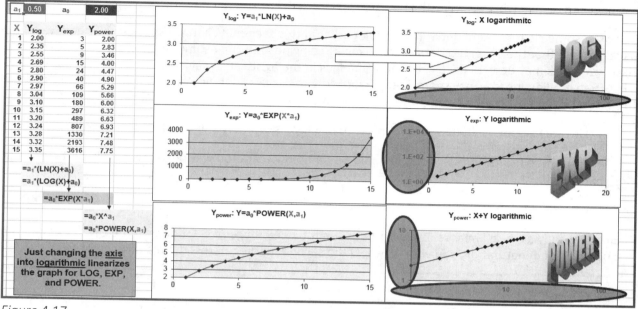

Figure 4.17

- A logarithmic curve needs the x-axis to be logarithmic.

- An exponential curve needs the y-axis to be logarithmic.

- A power curve needs both axes to be logarithmic.

Note

Linearizing is a way of transforming data so they serve better your specific needs. There are other kinds of transformations, which will be the subject of Chapter 55.

Chapter 35: Curve Fitting

Finding the proper regression curve in a methodical way is called *curve fitting*. Curve fitting is the process of trying to find the model or equation that best represents the sample data. So far, you have used intuition and trial-and-error to do this—and that may very often work. But there is also a more methodical way of finding a model and testing whether it fits the data.

You used some clear cases of linear regression earlier in this section. When we speak of a "clear" case, we usually mean that the observed dots seem to nicely coincide with the estimated or predicted linear curve. However, looks may be very deceiving. Mere changes in the axis scales may change our impressions drastically. Even nonlinear cases may seem linear if you work the scales a bit. So you need additional tools to test the assumed regression model. You have two tools available:

- **The *RSQ* value:** As discussed earlier, improving *RSQ* is basically still a matter of trial-and-error.

- **The residuals method:** Residuals should be randomly scattered without showing any particular pattern.

Let's now study this latter method more in detail.

Figure 4.18 shows a nice linear relationship between the percentage of G-C bonds in the DNA helix and the temperature of denaturation. You want to apply the second method here—the residuals test:

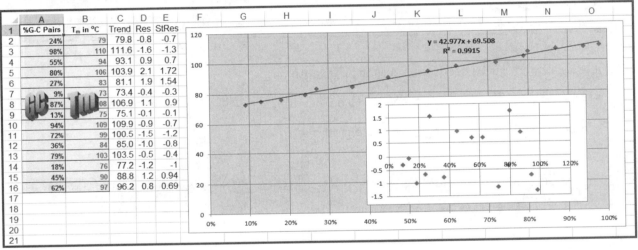

Figure 4.18

1. To find the residuals, calculate in column C what the predicted/estimated y-values would be if the linear model were correct: `=TREND(B2:B16,A2:A16)`. (The function `TREND` is based on linearity.)

2. In column D, calculate the residuals: `Yobserved - Ypredicted` (or reversed).

Note

y-predicted is also called *y-expected* or *y-estimated*.

3. Plot x-values versus the residuals in an *XY* graph (the result is shown in the insert in Figure 4.18). If you are really dealing with a linear relationship, the residuals should be randomly distributed above and below the x-axis—and they are in this case!

4. Ideally, go one step further and calculate the *standardized* version of residuals: *residual / SD*$_{residuals}$, by placing in cell E2 the formula `=D2/STDEV($D$2:$D$16)`.

Note

Notice that all the dots of the standardized residuals nicely occur in the range between -2 and +2. If there are a few standardized residuals beyond +3 or -3, they are usually called *outliers*; you may want to check whether those extreme values are reliable or find out what else is going on. We will discuss this issue more in detail in Chapter 49.

The bottom line of the residuals test is that the pattern of residuals should be random:

- There shouldn't be any visible pattern.

- Most residual values should be clustered around the zero line.

- The farther you get from zero, the fewer of them should occur.

- 95% of them are expected to lie between -2 and +2.

In other words, if the residuals are not randomly distributed above and below the x-axis—but show a distinctive pattern instead—you are not dealing with linear regression and therefore need another, nonlinear model.

As you have seen, to determine whether the regression line is linear, you calculate the trend, determine the residuals, plot the residuals against their y-values, and calculate standardized residuals, if needed.

Figure 4.19 shows a case in which you definitely should use the residuals method of curve fitting:

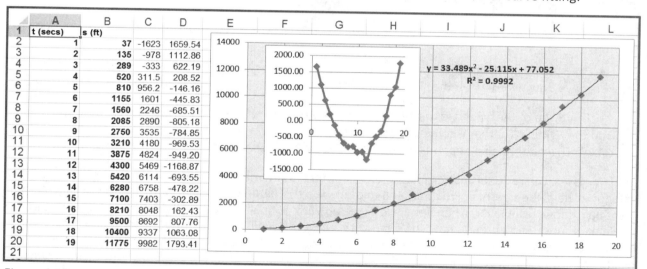

Figure 4.19

1. Use TREND in column C.

2. Calculate residuals in column D: =B-C.

3. Plot the residuals against the y-values (see the insert in Figure 4.19). The pattern of the residuals is far from randomly scattered. It looks more like a parabola. So we do not even need to calculate the standardized residuals.

A parabola is a curve type that is symmetric on both sides of a vertical axis, running parallel with the y-axis. When the pattern of residuals comes close to being a parabola, you should at least consider using a polynomial type of regression.

Each of the four main nonlinear regression types shows its own distinctive pattern of residuals. How do they differ, then, in their residuals patterns? Figure 4.20 systematizes their differences:

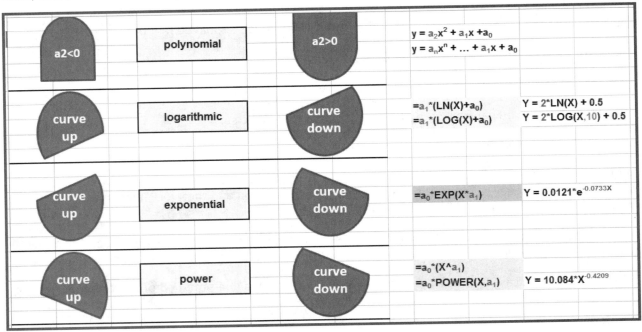

Figure 4.20

- Only the polynomial type has a symmetrical, vertical residuals pattern—a parabola. This pattern is concave downward when the slope, a_2, is negative, and it is concave upward when a_2 is positive.

- The three other types are not symmetrical, and their central axis is not parallel to the y-axis. How do they differ? There are some general tendencies in their residuals pattern, as summarized in Figure 4.20. This pattern also depends on whether the original curve went upward or downward.

In many cases, the residuals pattern based on linear regression may not clearly fit into one of the particular categories described here. So you may still end up with trial-and-error by checking whether the *RSQ* value went up or down. However, when you have come up with a "final" model, you should not forget to test this nonlinear model—no matter what type it is—with a new residuals test, but this time based on the nonlinear model. You should check your nonlinear model by using its new regression equation and then plotting the residuals pattern again. The residuals pattern should be randomly scattered, without showing any distinctive pattern. If the pattern is not randomly scattered, you have to keep revising your latest model until you come up with one that does have a random pattern in its residuals test.

Figure 4.21 presents a case in which several nonlinear models would qualify—even a linear model. (One of the reasons is the small number of observations.) In cases like these, you could create residual patterns for each model you are considering, and then compare those patterns with each other. Another way of testing your models is linearizing the axes (either one or both) and watching for a more or less straight line. Again, that is basically eye-balling.

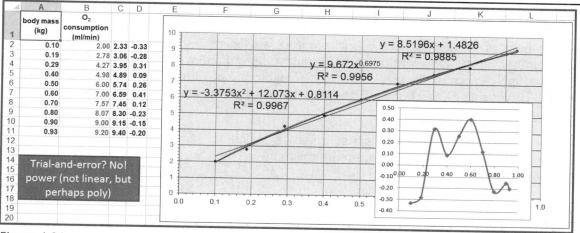

Figure 4.21

There is also a less time-consuming alternative available in Excel: the *Analysis Toolpak*, which has a tool for regression analysis that calculates all the related statistics plus a series of plots, including a residuals plot. Based on this information, you can decide whether linear regression is an acceptable model or has to be replaced by a nonlinear model.

The *Analysis Toolpak* comes standard with Excel as an add-in, but it is not automatically active. In order to activate it, you need to install the add-in:

1. Click the *File* tab.

2. Choose *Options* (way down).

3. Select *Add-Ins*.

4. Under *Manage*, select *Excel Add-Ins*.

5. Click *Go*.

Once the *Analysis Toolpak* is active, it is available through the *Data* tab (way to the right). You can use it for several purposes, including regression analysis.

Figure 4.22 shows a residuals plot, based on linear regression, of the data from Figure 4.21. It shows a rather distinctive pattern, so you should reject the linear model and test the residuals pattern after choosing alternative models. Unfortunately, the *Analysis Toolpak* cannot do the latter part for you—that's still a manual task.

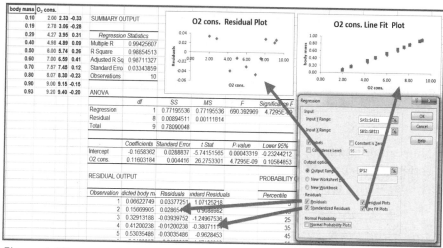

Figure 4.22

Chapter 36: Sigmoid Curves

Many regression curves used in research (especially in the life sciences) are S-shaped; they are also called *sigmoid*, *sigmoidal*, or *logistic* curves. None of the nonlinear types discussed so far covers these cases (although a high-level polynomial model may come close sometimes, but with an awkward equation). Unfortunately sigmoid curves require much more work than the common nonlinear curves—especially so since Excel does not support them directly.

A general characteristic of a sigmoid curve is that, in the beginning, the curve grows exponentially, but its growth gets increasingly inhibited up to an asymptotic saturation point. So, in general, a sigmoid curve has two important landmarks or markers:

- **The inflection point:** This is where a concave upward curve (with a positive slope) changes into a concave downward curve (with a negative slope); this point is also called the *saddle*.

- **The saturation point:** This is the maximum value and is approached asymptotically.

Figure 4.23 offers a typical example of a sigmoid curve: It has an inflection point (at $N=100$) and a saturation point (at $N=200$). The formula shows that the rate of increase depends on the relationship between the value reached (N) and the value of the saturation point (*Max*). Closer to *Max*, N/Max comes closer to 1, so $(1 - N/Max)$ comes closer to 0 and thus reduces the rate more and more. This is why column C in in this graph initially goes up and then gradually slows down. But to get the formula behind column D, you need mathematical tools such as differentiation and integration. Integration would make the distance between the x-values infinitely small.

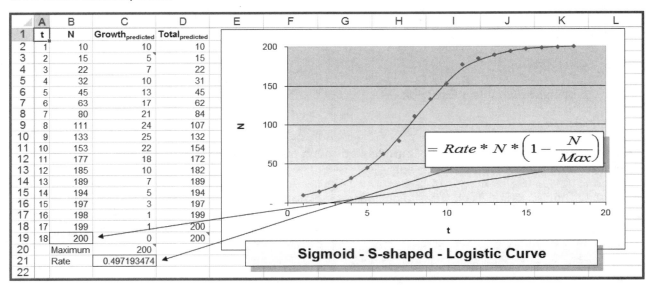

Figure 4.23

Many scientists don't feel comfortable with this kind of math, especially not with integration. Excel can help you with the math, but it does not do the math for you. So next we'll look at some more friendly alternatives. If you know how to integrate painlessly and feel comfortable doing it, go ahead and skip the rest of this chapter. Otherwise, you might discover an alternative way of dealing with sigmoid curves. Here are two suggestions:

- Figure 4.24 shows a simple, but rather primitive, solution. You locate the inflection point (by estimating visually) and split the series of data points into two sections—each one with its own polynomial curve. This solution is very unsatisfying because you need two different equations to predict a single regression line.

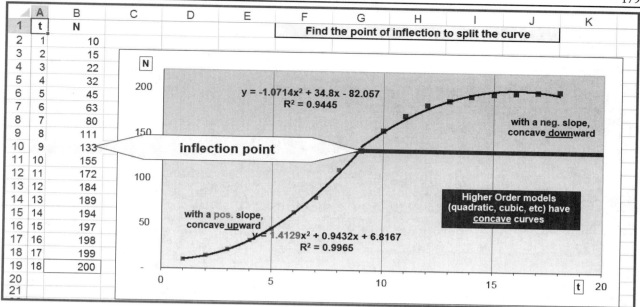

Figure 4.24

Figure 4.25 offers a more sophisticated approach (without requiring the use of integration). The formula on the left creates a sigmoid curve; however, it returns values between 0 and 1—that is, between 0% and 100%). So you could transform it into the formula on the right by including the inflection point (*IP*) and the saturation point (*SP*).

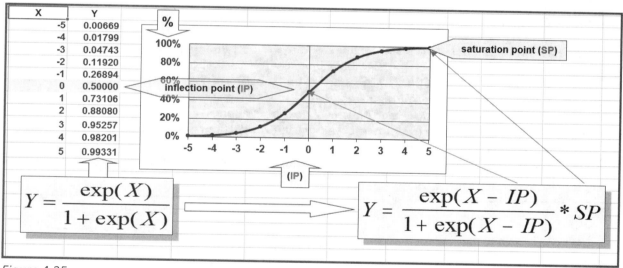

Figure 4.25

For the rest of this chapter, you will use the second approach, with an improved formula. Figure 4.26 shows the addition of a slope (a_1) to the equation. Now three variables in the equation help you regulate the sigmoid curve:

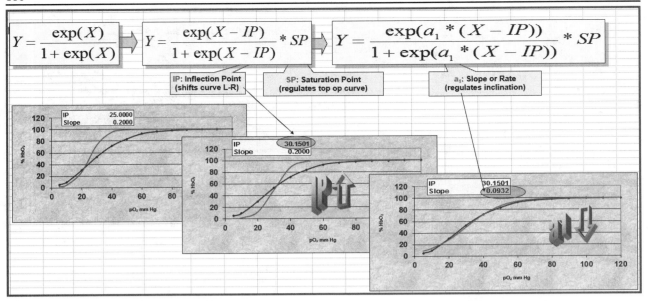

Figure 4.26

- *SP* determines the asymptotic top of the curve.

- *IP* allows you to shift the curve to the left or to the right.

- a_1 determines the steepness of the curve.

- For cases where the curve does not start at 0, you may want to add another factor.

Figure 4.27 has two scroll-bar *controls* to change settings for *IP* and *slope* independently (see Chapter 42). Moving the *controls* makes the sigmoid curve change in response, which in turn affects the sum of the squared residuals in cell D21. The sum of the squared residuals should be as low as possible: `=SUM(D3:D20)`. The first *control* regulates *IP* and thus moves the curve to the left or to the right. The second *control* regulates the *slope* and thus changes the steepness of the curve. Using trial-and-error on the controls, I have come up with the settings *IP=7.5388* and *slope=0.5032*. Perhaps you can do better! When you have proper settings for slope, *IP*, and *SP*, you can apply the equation to column C in order to create a sigmoid regression line—without using integration! Cell C3 has this formula in it: `=EXP($G$12*(A3-$G$10))/(1+EXP($G$12*(A3-$G$10)))*$B$20`.

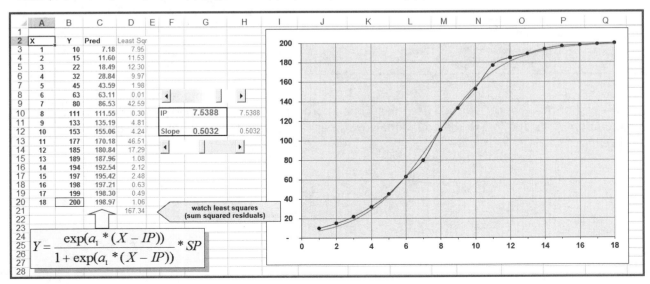

Figure 4.27

Note

As to the sum of the squared residuals in cell D21, you have a choice (without using intermediate residual calculations):

- A regular Excel function: `=SUMXMY2(C5:C21,D5:D21)`.

- A single-cell array formula: `=SUM(((C5:C21)-(D5:D21))^2)` (followed by *Ctrl+Shift+Enter*).

Figure 4.28 shows an example of what is usually called *EC50* determination. The *EC50* is the concentration of a drug that gives half-maximal response—the 50% effective concentration. Is this an *EC50* or an *IC50* issue? That difference is a semantic matter. *EC* is the effective concentration—an up-hill dose-response curve that plots an increased response. *IC* is an inhibitory concentration—a down-hill dose-response curve that plots an inhibitory response.

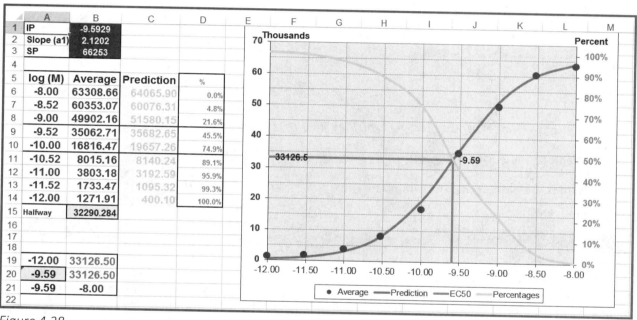

Figure 4.28

Since you are dealing here with a sigmoid curve relationship, you could use our previous sigmoid formula in column C—which creates the upward curve over the observation points in the graph. Here is how you do all of this:

1. Start your predictions in cell C6:
   `=EXP($B$2*(A6-$B$1))/(1+EXP($B$2*(A6-$B$1)))*$B$3`.

2. Start in D6 the calculation of percentages:
   `=1-(B6-MIN($B$6:$B$14))/(MAX($B$6:$B$14)-MIN($B$6:$B$14))`. This creates the downward curve, associated with the secondary Y-axis

3. Locate in cell B15 the 50% point: `=B14+(B6-B14)/2`. (You could have used the functions MIN and MAX instead.)

4. Use the TREND function in A20: `=TREND(A9:A10,B9:B10,B15)`.

5. Cell B20 makes a sigmoidal prediction again:
   `=EXP($B$2*(A20-$B$1))/(1+EXP($B$2*(A20-$B$1)))*$B$3`.

After you finish the three sets of coordinates in A19:B21, the graph shows the corresponding insert for *EC50*.

The values in B1:B3 could be based on trial-and-error, but were actually found by using another method, which we discuss in Chapter 41.

Figure 4.29 shows you that there are more ways of creating sigmoid curves than the simple formula we used so far. Here are three possible formulas:

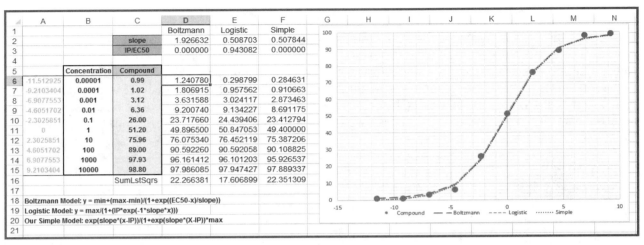

Figure 4.29

- The simple model used so far: $y = exp(slope*(x-IP))/(1+exp(slope*(X-IP))*max$.

- The Boltzmann Model: $y = min+(max-min)/(1+exp((EC50-x)/slope))$.

- A three-parameter Logistic Model: $y = max/(1+(IP*exp(-1*slope*x)))$.

Note

When the curve starts above or below 0, we may also need a factor to shift values up or down.

Since the concentrations recorded in column B have a logarithmic pattern, you have a choice: either make the X-axis logarithmic or take the LN function of the concentrations in column A. I decided to do the latter, by placing in cell A6: =LN(B6), and then using that value in the three formulas, instead of the B6 value. The columns D:F show that using different formulas leads to slightly different values. To show each curve individually in the graph, you just temporarily hide one or two of the column D:F.

Chapter 37: Predictability

Regression analysis is aimed at predictability. But predictability is a very ambiguous concept. It covers two very different issues:

- How close can you get in your predictions, estimations, or expectations as far as a particular sample is concerned? *RSQ* is a good measure of that closeness, so we found out. It measures how well you can predict in a particular sample. This is a matter of correlation—*RSQ* (or r^2) is the squared correlation coefficient (*r*) that measures the proportion of the variance in y attributable to the variance in x. Go for high correlations! (See Chapter 38 for more information on correlation.)

- But there is another dimension to predictability: How well can you replicate the results you have found so far? In other words, how well can you predict in the population from which this particular sample comes based on the data of your sample? This is a matter of probability; the more probable the results, the more randomness has interfered. Go for low probabilities!

This chapter tackles the latter question, which takes us deeper into statistics (in preparation of Part 5). The fact that you have found a linear regression line in your data—even with a "reasonable" *RSQ* value—doesn't mean you have hit on a "real" connection. A high *RSQ* means only that a relatively high proportion of y-variance can be credited to x-variance. But variance can be a random effect—as it usually is. The more cases you have, the more unlikely it is that both variances correlate by chance—but the possibility is still there. The problem is that *RSQ* may be strong in the particular sample under investigation, but this doesn't mean that the sample is highly representative for the entire population. Would you get similar results if you were to test other samples of the same size? As they say, "Results may vary."

Figure 4.30 offers an assessment as to how repeatable the linear relationship between *HbA1C* readings and glucose levels in humans would be—given the fact that only 15 pairs of observations are available:

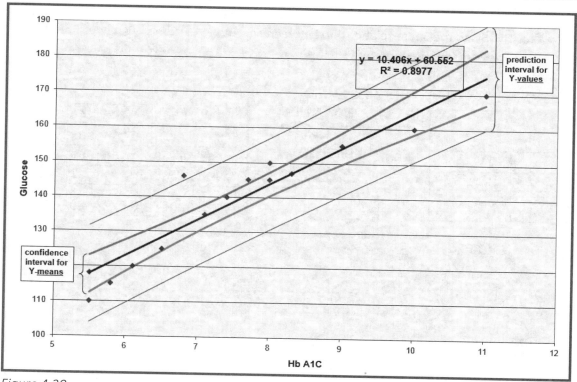

Figure 4.30

- **The outer boundaries mark the 95% prediction interval** (it is about individual observations and their values)**:** 95% of the y-values to be found for a certain x-value will be within this interval range around the linear regression line. The chance for an individual observation of falling outside this range is less than 5%.

- **The inner boundaries mark the 95% confidence interval** (it is about repeated observations and their means)**:** 95% of the y-means to be found for a certain x-value will be within this interval range around the linear regression line. The chance for an observed mean of falling outside this range is less than 5%.

It is obvious that single observation values have a wider range of variance than mean observation values that each represent an average of several individual observations, called replicates. When a certain value is just outside the prediction interval, it is acceptable—but unlikely, because it has a less than 5% chance of occurring—if it is based on a single observation. But if it were the mean of multiple observations, it would be extremely unlikely, unless it were inside the confidence interval. As to whether we are dealing with an outlier here will be further discussed in Chapter 49.

Had you increased the number of cases in your sample, both interval ranges would get narrower and narrower. So although the results may vary, they will vary less and less so. Larger samples tend to be more reliable!

How do you calculate these intervals? Unfortunately, many calculations have to be performed! This chapter does not go into all the details, but one of the tools you need is the function `LINEST`, one of the multi-cell array functions mentioned in Chapter 37. `LINEST` returns several statistical values for linear regression lines, and it does so in the following order:

- Both slope and intercept
- The standard error (*SE*) of both
- *RSQ* and the *SE* of y-values
- *F* and *df* (which are explained in Part 5)
- Two *sums of squares*

Figure 4.31 applies `LINEST` to the linear relationship between age and *FVC*. Here's what you should do:

	A	B	C	D	E	F	G
1	Linest			EXPLAINED: Sum of Squared Measurements or squared SDs. The function is called DEVSQ.			
2	a_1	a_0				-0.0270667	4.4904444
3	SE a_1	SE a_0				0.0027159	0.1141538
4	R^2	SE y				0.934162	0.1051862
5	F	df				99.321588	7
6	$SS_{regression}$	$SS_{residuals}$				1.0989067	0.0774489
7				Unexplained regression			
8	Age M	$FVCM_{obs}$					
9	60	2.8					
10	55	3.0					
11	50	3.1		R^2	0.934162007		
12	45	3.3					
13	40	3.5					
14	35	3.7					
15	30	3.6					
16	25	3.9					
17	20	3.8					
18							

Figure 4.31

1. Select multiple cells at once, F2:G6.

2. Call `LINEST` and supply its arguments: `=LINEST(B9:B17,A9:A17,1,1)`.

3. Make sure the last argument is set to `1` or `TRUE`; otherwise, you won't get the rows 4–6.

4. Press *Ctrl+Shift+Enter*. Notice that the slope is negative (-0.027) and `RSQ` is reasonably high (0.93).

5. Sometimes, you want only one or two of these statistics; at other times, all of them. To get only one, nest `LINEST` inside `INDEX`. For *RSQ* (in row 3 of column 1), the formula would be `=INDEX-(LINEST(B9:B17,A9:A17,1,1),3,1)`.

Let's consider again the confidence intervals for means based on replicates, this time in Figure 4.32. The sheet has a `LINEST` calculation in the cells G20:H24, and it has the output of the *Analysis Toolpak* with its *regression tool* in the columns K:S. What is the difference between the `LINEST` results and the *Analysis Toolpak* results? The latter ones may be more detailed and faster, but they are "dead." Changing data later on does not affect those results anymore, unless you run the *Toolpak* again. But their advantage is that they display more information—including some probabilities in O15:O16. These probabilities are very low, so there is a good chance that you would get similar results if you tested more samples of the same size (and the same population, of course). Let's leave it at that for now. (You learn more about probabilities in Part 5.)

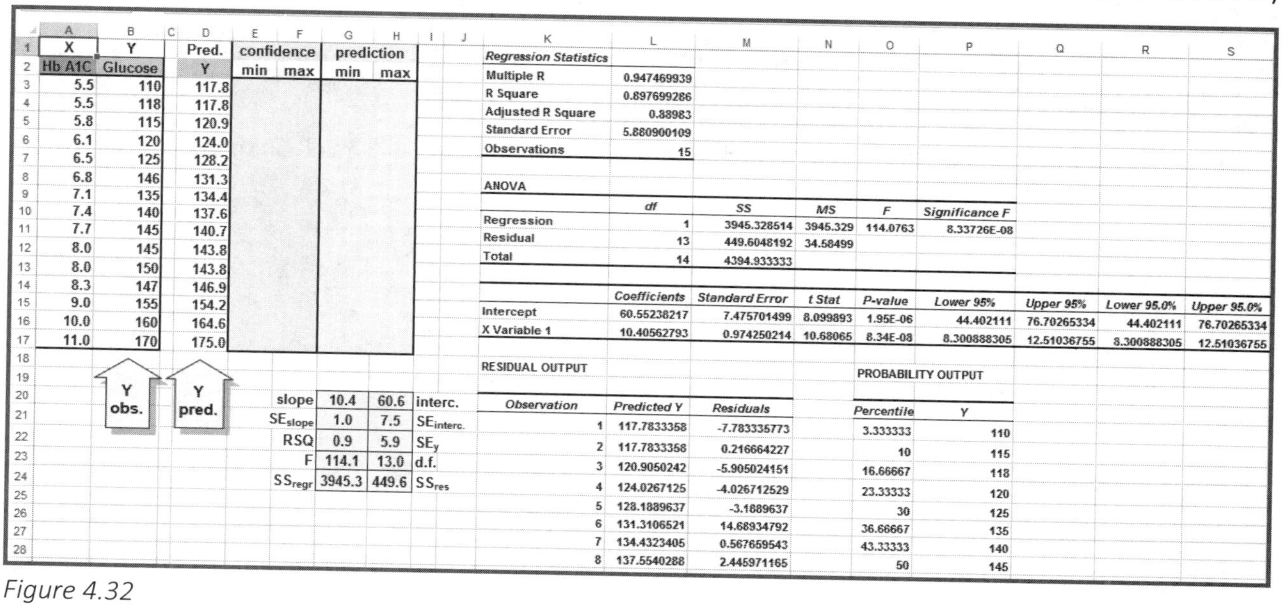

X	Y	Pred.	confidence		prediction	
Hb A1C	Glucose	Y	min	max	min	max
5.5	110	117.8				
5.5	118	117.8				
5.8	115	120.9				
6.1	120	124.0				
6.5	125	128.2				
6.8	146	131.3				
7.1	135	134.4				
7.4	140	137.6				
7.7	145	140.7				
8.0	145	143.8				
8.0	150	143.8				
8.3	147	146.9				
9.0	155	154.2				
10.0	160	164.6				
11.0	170	175.0				

slope	10.4	60.6	interc.
SE_{slope}	1.0	7.5	$SE_{interc.}$
RSQ	0.9	5.9	SE_y
F	114.1	13.0	d.f.
SS_{regr}	3945.3	449.6	SS_{res}

Regression Statistics	
Multiple R	0.947469939
R Square	0.897699286
Adjusted R Square	0.88983
Standard Error	5.880900109
Observations	15

ANOVA

	df	*SS*	*MS*	*F*	*Significance F*
Regression	1	3945.328514	3945.329	114.0763	8.33726E-08
Residual	13	449.6048192	34.58499		
Total	14	4394.933333			

	Coefficients	*Standard Error*	*t Stat*	*P-value*	*Lower 95%*	*Upper 95%*	*Lower 95.0%*	*Upper 95.0%*
Intercept	60.55238217	7.475701499	8.099893	1.95E-06	44.402111	76.70265334	44.402111	76.70265334
X Variable 1	10.40562793	0.974250214	10.68065	8.34E-08	8.300888305	12.51036755	8.300888305	12.51036755

RESIDUAL OUTPUT

Observation	*Predicted Y*	*Residuals*
1	117.7833358	-7.783335773
2	117.7833358	0.216664227
3	120.9050242	-5.905024151
4	124.0267125	-4.026712529
5	128.1889637	-3.1889637
6	131.3106521	14.68934792
7	134.4323405	0.567659543
8	137.5540288	2.445971165

PROBABILITY OUTPUT

Percentile	*Y*
3.333333	110
10	115
16.66667	118
23.33333	120
30	125
36.66667	135
43.33333	140
50	145

Figure 4.32

Even all the information so far is not enough to get the final results for confidence intervals. Figure 4.33 shows a few more intermediate steps, which are not discussed here. All this is old-fashioned manual work. After you have implemented the calculations in columns E:H, you can create the graph we used already in Figure 4.30. Notice the difference between the confidence interval calculations in E:F and the prediction interval calculations in G:H.

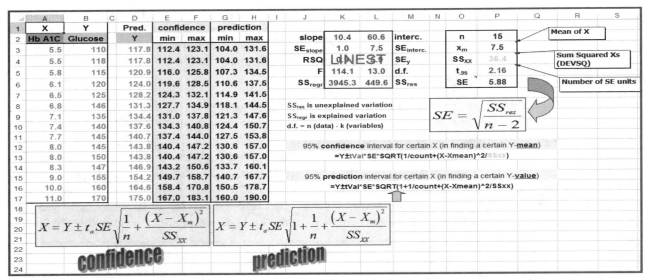

Figure 4.33

The information discussed in this chapter is highly statistical in nature. We will dwell on this issue much more intensely in the Part 5.

Chapter 38: Correlation

The correlation coefficient (r) is the ratio of the explained variation to the unexplained variation. The better x-variations explain y-variations, the smaller the unexplained variation is, which makes r come closer to ±1 (closer to a positive or negative correlation). Its squared version is RSQ (r^2 or R^2). Excel has two different functions you can use to determine the correlation coefficient: CORREL and PEARSON. Both of these functions use the same math, so you can just take your pick.

Figure 4.34 takes us back to an earlier example: the relationship between a person's age and their *FVC*, in liters (see Chapter 33). You assume that variations in age determine variations in *FVC*, but there is some unexplained variation here—for instance, three 55-year-olds have different *FVC* readings. Where does this unexplained variation come from? There are three theoretical answers:

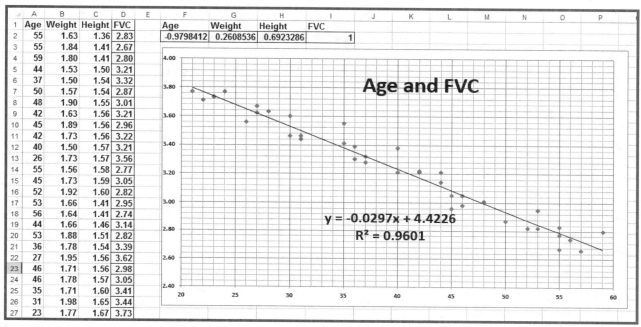

Figure 4.34

- There is always inaccuracy and randomness in the observations. Let's skip this possibility for now.

- The linear model is incorrect, as discussed in Chapter 34.

- Additional factors are involved. This is the main topic in this chapter.

Let's think about the possibility that other independent variables, such as weight and height, affect variation in *FVC*. This idea suggests some kind of multiple regression. So far, we have only discussed single regression—with only one independent factor affecting the dependent factor. Because there may be many factors of potential impact, you need a tool to assess their individual effects—and that tool is the correlation coefficient. One of the reasons for using r is the fact that you can test the usefulness of independent variables in a pilot study first. You don't need to spend money on variables that have no impact! Here's how you calculate r for each of three independent factors in relationship to the dependent factor, *FVC*:

1. Select F2:I2.

2. Call CORREL or PEARSON and provide the proper arguments. In cell F2, you could enter =CORREL(A2:A41,$D$2:$D$41), and then use *Ctr+Enter* (not *Ctr+Shift+Enter*, because this

is not an array function). Alternatives would be =PEARSON(A2:A41,$D$2:$D$41), or even =SQRT(RSQ(A2:A41,$D$2:$D$41)).

3. The order of diminishing impact appears to be age (-0.98), height (0.69), and then weight (0.26). (Later we will discuss whether weight has enough impact to even be included in a multiple regression formula.)

Figure 4.35 shows a similar case: Someone studied the impact of five different independent factors on the dependent factor systolic blood pressure. You can test the individual impact of each factor on the dependent variable by calculating correlations.

	A	B	C	D	E	F	G
1	Systolic	Exercise	Drink	Smoke	Weight	Age	Parents
2	153	0	4	1	215	47	0
3	141	5	2	1	207	46	0
4	137	5	2	0	190	36	0
5	135	0	2	0	214	44	2
6	133	3	3	0	237	45	2
7	131	10	2	0	179	45	0
8	146	5	3	1	217	53	0
9	140	5	4	1	196	56	2
10	145	5	4	1	232	56	2
11	142	2	2	1	202	53	1
12	130	10	2	0	196	42	1
13	146	5	3	1	216	48	1
14	155	0	7	1	199	63	2
15	133	3	3	0	203	39	1
16	137	5	3	0	218	61	2
17	141	0	4	1	207	53	2
18	141	5	3	1	194	54	1
19	147	0	4	1	221	47	0
20	144	3	1	1	209	57	0
21	132	10	2	0	177	54	0
22	115	15	0	0	185	46	0
23	151	3	6	1	229	53	2
24	139	5	3	0	207	61	2

Number of hours spent per week

Number of ounces consumed per week

0, does not smoke
1, does smoke

0, no parent high
1, one parent high
2, both parents high

Systolic	Exercise	Drink	Smoke	Weight	Age	Parents
1	-0.84	0.83	0.73	0.57	0.30	0.09

Systolic Blood Pressure based on 6 independent variables.

	Systolic	Exercise	Drink	Smoke	Weight	Age	Parents
Systolic	1						
Exercise	-0.836581709	1					
Drink	0.829274117	-0.680184287	1				
Smoke	0.731552949	-0.521731473	0.60270981	1			
Weight	0.569287662	-0.521582991	0.511679721	0.400077472	1		
Age	0.29854725	-0.181147043	0.273633194	0.295671653	0.082984335	1	
Parents	0.089917572	-0.18279872	0.333820476	-0.014932027	0.170745497	0.22439132	1

Figure 4.35

There is another reason why it is prudent to assess the correlation between factors: A very high correlation (beyond ±0.7) between the independent variables themselves can cause trouble, because they share their contribution to determining the dependent variable. This phenomenon is called *colinearity*. You test for *colinearity* as follows:

1. In cells I8:O8, you perform a correlation test for each independent factor in relation to the dependent factor systolic blood pressure. The formula in cell I8 is: =PEARSON($A$2:$A$51,A2:A51). The order of impact turns out to be exercise, drink, smoke, weight, age, and finally parents.

2. Test for *colinearity* by using the *Correlation* option of the *Analysis Toolpak* in cells I16:P23. The section K18:P23 shows us that there is no correlation beyond 0.7 or -0.7 between the independent variables, so *colinearity* does not seem to interfere here.

Note

An alternative way of testing for *colinearity* involves the use of range *names* in combination with the function INDIRECT (see Chapters 4 and 13). The advantage of doing things this way is that these results would update, whereas the *Analysis Toolpak* delivers only static results. The formula in J17 could be: =CORREL(INDIRECT($I17),INDIRECT(J$16)).

Figure 4.36 requires a different treatment. You need to determine whether there is a correlation between the number of drinks per week and the diastolic blood pressure. Unfortunately, the correlation coefficient can only be used when the observations are normally distributed. But here you find most observations clustered in the left-lower corner of the graph. In other words, the correlation coefficient, as found here with CORREL or PEARSON in cell B13, is not reliable. So you need a *distribution-free* test (see Chapter 53). In this case, you can apply the Spearman's rank test first, by using the function RANK.AVG. Here's how it works:

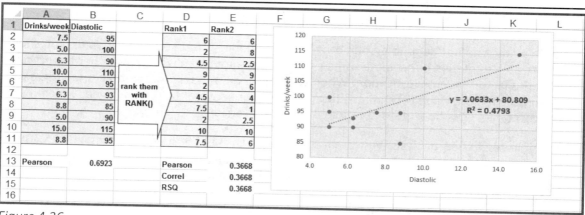

Figure 4.36

1. Create ranks in columns D and E by entering the formula `=RANK.AVG(A2,$A$2:$A$11,1)` in cell D2. The last argument creates averages when there are ties.

2. Now that you have "ranked" values, you can apply the functions `PEARSON` in cell E13, `CORREL` in cell E14, and `RSQ` in cell E15.

Notice that the spuriously high initial assessment has gone down dramatically, from 0.69 to 0.37.

Figure 4.37 deals with the correlation between fat consumption and heart disease. Notice that, based on an exponential *trendline*, RSQ is not impressive at all: 0.14 (so the correlation, r, is actually $\sqrt{0.14} = 0.37$). However, the physician Ancel Keys once declared a strong *RSQ* between the two: 0.96 (which equates to a correlation of 0.98). How come? Keys had carefully selected the data he used to have his hypothesis confirmed. You can see the data he had selected by changing cell B3 from 0 to 1 (this cell regulates through formulas in columns E and F what to display in the graph; refer to Chapter 32). Had he made a different selection of data, Keys would actually have gotten an equally high, but this time negative correlation of 0.98. You can simulate this by choosing 2 in the dropdown box of cell B3.

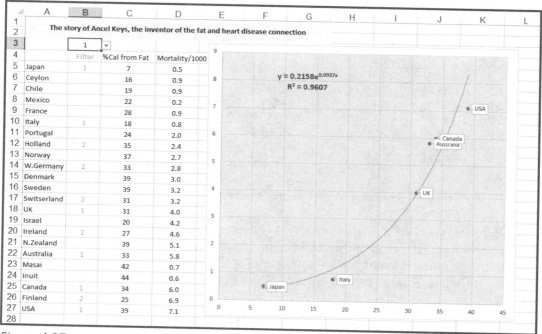

Figure 4.37

What is the lesson to learn? Not only did Keys use biased data but he also forgot to factor in the existence of another variable—for instance, the consumption of sugar. This is called a *confounding* factor or hidden variable. Always be on the lookout for those.

Chapter 39: Multiple Regression: Linear Estimates

Most variables in science do not depend on one other single variable, but on several variables. You should therefore be more able to predict or estimate some particular factor if you have several other factors available that impact the factor under investigation. When you decide on multiple (or multifactorial) regression analysis, you can usually go for linear estimates because there are several factors involved, which makes linearity more acceptable. (This book does not discuss nonlinear versions.)

To perform multiple regression analysis, you use $\texttt{LINEST}$, which has the following syntax: $\texttt{LINEST(-Known\_y's,Known\_x's,Const,Stats)}$. It can handle multiple independent factors in its second argument. The formula for multiple regression has a *slope* for each factor (also called a *coefficient*) plus an *intercept*, with the following syntax: $a_n x_n + \ldots + a_2 x_2 + a_1 x_1 + a_0$. So when $\texttt{LINEST}$ displays the slopes and standard errors, it does so in this syntactical order: $a_n x_n + \ldots + a_2 x_2 + a_1 x_1 + a_0$ (that is, the last factor first). When the last argument is set to $\texttt{TRUE}$, $\texttt{LINEST}$ also returns additional statistics, such as *RSQ* and standard errors for each coefficient.

$\texttt{LINEST}$ is used in Figure 4.38. The top-left section shows what $\texttt{LINEST}$ returns when dealing with up to *n* multiple factors. This case shows only three independent factors in addition to the dependent factor *FVC* (so $\texttt{LINEST}$ needs 4 columns to display its results). In cells F13:I17, you use the formula =LINEST(D9:D17,A9:C17,TRUE,TRUE), followed by *Ctrl+Shift+Enter*). Notice how $\texttt{LINEST}$ handles multiple factors (A:C) at the same time in its second argument. Be aware that the slopes (or coefficients) appear in reversed order, starting at factor *n*. The standard errors for each factor appear in the next row down, in the same order. And then there are some additional statistics in the other rows.

	A	B	C	D	E	F	G	H	I
1	The order of regression statistics (4th argument set to *True*)								
2	a_n	a_{n-1}	...	a_2	a_1	a_0			
3	SE a_n	SE a_{n-1}	...	SE a_2	SE a_1	SE a_0			
4	R^2	SE y							
5	F	df							
6	$SS_{regression}$	$SS_{residuals}$							
7									
8	Age M	Height M	Weight M	FVCM$_{obs}$					
9	60	164.0	60.6	2.8					
10	55	165.0	52.0	3.0					
11	50	167.6	55.8	3.1					
12	45	168.0	60.9	3.3		weight	height	age	intercept
13	40	169.0	57.1	3.5		-0.00903166	0.06738713	-0.01018955	-7.07722632
14	35	172.0	59.0	3.7		0.010849	0.05417439	0.01379816	9.61428952
15	30	171.0	55.5	3.6		0.95240303	0.10582151	#N/A	#N/A
16	25	173.0	52.0	3.9		33.3495709	5	#N/A	#N/A
17	20	174.0	60.6	3.8		1.1203646	0.05599096	#N/A	#N/A
18									

Figure 4.38

Figure 4.39 applies multiple regression to a case you studied in Chapter 38. You have six independent factors here in addition to the dependent factor systolic blood pressure. Some independent factors may not score high for correlation with the dependent factor, but let's still use all of them in the multiple regression model. (You'll learn more on this issue later.) Here's how you create Figure 4.39:

	Systolic	Exercise	Drink	Smoke	Weight	Age	Parents		SBP
2	153	0	4	1	215	47	0		150.0
3	141	5	2	1	207	46	0		140.2
4	137	5	2	0	190	36	0		134.4
5	135	0	2	0	214	44	2		138.0
6	133	3	3	0	237	45	2		138.5
7	131	10	2	0	179	45	0		130.1
8	146	5	3	1	217	53	0		143.7
9	140	5	4	1	196	56	2		142.0
10	145	5	4	1	232	56	2		143.7
11	142	2	2	1	202	53	1		142.0
12	130	10	2	0	196	42	1		128.9
13	146	5	3	1	216	48	1		141.4
14	155	0	7	1	199	63	2		154.5
15	133	3	3	0	203	39	1		137.9
16	137	5	3	0	218	61	2		137.6
17	141	0	4	1	207	53	2		147.0
18	141	5	3	1	194	54	1		141.1
19	147	0	4	1	221	47	0		150.3
20	144	3	1	1	209	57	0		141.3
21	132	10	2	0	177	54	0		131.0
22	115	15	0	0	185	46	0		121.1
23	151	3	6	1	229	53	2		149.6
24	139	5	3	0	207	61	2		137.0
25	126	10	1	0	214	53	1		128.8

Correlations (K2:Q2):

Systolic	Exercise	Drink	Smoke	Weight	Age	Parents
1	-0.84	0.83	0.73	0.57	0.30	0.09

LINEST results (K9:Q13):

Parents	Age	Weight	Smoke	Drink	Exercise	
-1.66	0.12	0.05	3.83	2.24	-0.97	121.52
0.62	0.08	0.04	1.21	0.44	0.16	9.06
0.90	3.11	#N/A	#N/A	#N/A	#N/A	#N/A
62.70	43.00	#N/A	#N/A	#N/A	#N/A	#N/A
3629.61	414.87	#N/A	#N/A	#N/A	#N/A	#N/A

Correlation matrix (K17:R24):

	Systolic	Exercise	Drink	Smoke	Weight	Age	Parents
Systolic	1						
Exercise	-0.836581709	1					
Drink	0.829274117	-0.680184287	1				
Smoke	0.731552949	-0.521731473	0.60270981	1			
Weight	0.569287662	-0.521582991	0.511679721	0.400077472	1		
Age	0.29854725	-0.181147043	0.273633194	0.295671653	0.082984335	1	
Parents	0.089917572	-0.16279872	0.333820476	-0.014932027	0.170746497	0.22439132	1

Figure 4.39

1. Use cells K2:Q2 to calculate the correlations between the independent factors and the dependent factor. In K2, enter =PEARSON($A$2:$A$51,A2:A51).

2. Use cells K9:Q13 to return LINEST results: =LINEST(A2:A51,B2:G51,1,1). The factor smoking seems to have the highest coefficient. Coefficients that are very close to zero are basically useless. (You'll learn more on this issue later.)

3. The section K17:R24 (created with the *Analysis Toolpak*) shows that there is no *colinearity* interfering, so predict or estimate systolic blood pressure in column I, using either of these methods:

  ◦ Use the coefficients from LINEST:
  =$K$9*G2+$L$9*F2+$M$9*E2+$N$9*D2+$O$9*C2+$P$9*B2+$Q$9 (in I2).

  ◦ Use the TREND function: =TREND(A2:A51,B2:G51). Yes, TREND also works for multiple independent factors.

This example uses all the factors shown in columns B:G, which is not always a good practice. It is often difficult to decide which factors to use. Here are some general rules:

• Eliminate the factors that have a very low *correlation* with the dependent factor.

• Eliminate the independent factors that have near-to-zero *coefficients*.

• Eliminate one of the two independent factors that show *colinearity*.

Next, let's look at one more rule.

Figure 4.40 shows that when you eliminate factors step by step (the poorest-correlated one first), your prediction/estimation power (*RSQ*) goes down—or, reversed, it does go up when you add more factors. But don't get fooled by *RSQ*: It will always go up or down when you add or eliminate additional factors. Every extra factor helps, of course. That's why you need an *adjusted RSQ, RSQ_{adj}*, as shown in the formula in the left-lower corner of Figure 4.40. Column M uses this formula. The *adjusted RSQ* takes into account how many values are in the model already; it considers the number of cases (*n*) plus the number of variables (*df+1*). Adding another variable may counteract the effect of its added values. Notice in column M that adding variables does not always increase *RSQ_{adj}*. Its value actually goes down, for instance, after you add the factors weight and age.

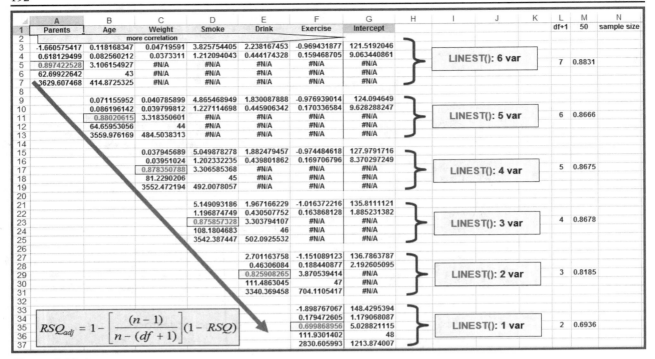

Figure 4.40

Once again, you could do much of this work by using the *Analysis Toolpak*, as shown in Figure 4.41. Its regression tool gives you an overview with some extra information:

	A	B	C	D	E	F	G	H	I	J	K	L	M	N	O	P	Q
1	SS$_{regression}$	explained variation									153	0	4	1	215	47	0
2	SS$_{residuals}$	unexplained variation									141	5	2	1	207	46	0
3	SS$_{total}$	expl. + unexpl. variation									137	5	2	0	190	36	0
4	RSQ	expl.var / total var									135	0	2	0	214	44	2
5											133	3	3	0	237	45	2
6	RSQ	measures the **strength** of the relationship									131	10	2	0	179	45	0
7	P	measures the **probability** of random correlation									146	5	3	1	217	53	0
8											140	5	4	1	196	56	2
9	RSQ	% of variation in Y explained by variations in X															

Some important tests:

- Look for high correlations
- Go for adjusted RSQ values
- Eliminate co-linearity
- Eliminate zero coefficients
- Go for low probabilities
- Check residuals plots

	A	B
11	*Regression Statistics*	
12	Multiple R	0.947323877
13	R Square	0.897422528
14	Adjusted R Square	0.883109393
15	Standard Error	3.106154927
16	Observations	50
17	ANOVA	

		df	SS	MS	F	Significance F
18		df	SS	MS	F	Significance F
19	Regression	6	3629.6075	604.9346	62.6992	0.00000000
20	Residual	43	414.8725	9.6482		
21	Total	49	4044.4800			

P-value measures the probability of randomness.

		Coefficients	Standard Error	t Stat	P-value	Lower 95%	Upper 95%	Lower 95.0%	Upper 95.0%
23		Coefficients	Standard Error	t Stat	P-value	Lower 95%	Upper 95%	Lower 95.0%	Upper 95.0%
24	Intercept	121.52	9.06	13.4076	0.0000	103.2410	139.7974	103.2410	139.7974
25	Exercise	-0.97	0.16	-6.0791	0.0000	-1.2910	-0.6478	-1.2910	-0.6478
26	Drink	2.24	0.44	5.0389	0.0000	1.3424	3.1339	1.3424	3.1339
27	Smoke	3.83	1.21	3.1563	0.0029	1.3813	6.2702	1.3813	6.2702
28	Weight	0.05	0.04	1.2643	0.2129	-0.0281	0.1225	-0.0281	0.1225
29	Age	0.12	0.08	1.4313	0.1596	-0.0483	0.2847	-0.0483	0.2847
30	Parents	-1.66	0.62	-2.6865	0.0102	-2.9072	-0.4140	-2.9072	-0.4140

	K	L	M	N	O	P	Q
27	139	5	2	0	224	45	1
28	150	0	6	1	229	56	1
29	133	10	2	0	215	50	0
30	138	5	2	0	207	50	1
31	132	7	2	0	196	45	2
32	148	2	5	1	200	52	2
33	145	5	4	1	228	53	1

32 | SBP = -0.97*Exerc (± 0.16) + 2.24*Drink (± 0.44) + ... + 121.52 (± 9.06)

Figure 4.41

- It automatically calculates not only *RSQ* but also the *adjusted RSQ*.

- It also shows the probability for each *coefficient*. Remember that a high probability indicates a great deal of randomness. A low probability means that testing another sample of the same size would not greatly sway the results. Notice that the two factors with a relatively high probability (weight and age) are the very same ones that didn't improve the value of RSQ_{adj}.

You now have two ways of testing multiple regression: Either add the factors with the lowest probabilities one by one or eliminate the factors with the highest probabilities first.

To summarize, there are some good tests for multiple regression. You should use them together and combine them with common sense. Here are the rules in a nutshell:

- Look for high correlations.

- Go for *adjusted RSQ* values.

- Avoid *colinearity*.

- Eliminate near-to-zero *coefficients*.

- Go for low probabilities.

- Check the residual plots for random scatter.

There is one more issue that needs attention: the *interaction* between factors. For example, in Figure 4.42, we assume that bone growth depends on Ca and P intake, yet *RSQ* is rather poor, so the prediction is poor. Why? There is interaction between these independent factors: More Ca-intake inhibits P-intake, and reverse. What is the solution? You add another "factor" and base it on the *interaction* of the two original factors: *Ca * P*. Here's how:

	A	B	C	D	E	F	G	H	I	J	K
1	**Bone growth**	**Ca**	**P**	prediction		**Bone growth**	**Ca**	**P**	**Interaction**	prediction	
2	22.5	3.4	1.6	27.6		22.5	3.4	1.6	5.4	22.9	22.913828
3	22.7	3.4	1.5	27.5		22.7	3.4	1.5	5.1	22.4	
4	33.4	3.5	3.5	28.2		33.4	3.5	3.5	12.3	32.4	
5	33.3	3.3	3.7	28.6		33.3	3.3	3.7	12.2	34.2	
6	25.5	7.4	1.6	21.1		25.5	7.4	1.6	11.8	25.5	
7	26.0	7.5	1.5	20.9		26.0	7.5	1.5	11.3	26.0	
8	17.2	7.4	3.7	22.0		17.2	7.4	3.7	27.4	17.1	
9	16.9	7.5	3.6	21.8		16.9	7.5	3.6	27.0	17.1	
10											
11	0.43	-1.62	32.39			-2.30	12.97	4.32	-0.04		
12	2.10	1.08	8.22			0.12	0.72	0.34	2.00		
13	0.32		#N/A			0.99	0.74	#N/A	#N/A		
14	1.16	5.00	#N/A			169.32	4.00	#N/A	#N/A		
15	87.89	190.02	#N/A			275.74	2.17	#N/A	#N/A		
16											
17	Y = 0.43P * -1.62Ca + 32.39					Y = -2.3Ca*P + 12.97P + 4.32Ca - 0.04					
18											

Ca * P

(⇩ P, Ca ⇧;
⇧ P, Ca ⇩)

Figure 4.42

1. In cell I2, enter `=G2*H2`.

2. In F11:I15, enter `=LINEST(F2:F9,G2:I9,1,1)`. Notice that *RSQ* goes up dramatically—from a low of 0.32 to a high of 0.99.

3. Make your prediction in column J in one of the following ways:

   ◦ Use TREND: `=TREND(F2:F9,G2:I9)`.

   ◦ Use coefficients: `=$F$11*I2+$G$11*H2+$H$11*G2+$I$11`.

4. In Column K, calculate the residuals between observations and predictions. Check whether the sum of the residuals is 0. In addition, you could test with a residuals plot.

Chapter 40: Reiterations and Matrixes

One of the many tasks scientists have to perform in their work is solving complex equations. One possible way of solving equations is to have a computer go through a series of iterations (trials and errors) until it finds the correct solution. When the cell containing the equation is itself part of the equation, we speak of *circular reference*.

The two marked cells in Figure 4.43 (cells D2 and D5) have a *circular reference* problem. They display either the highest value from column B or their own value—whichever is the highest. So they have some kind of memory stored inside them. A formula that refers to its own results causes a *circular reference*; Excel usually rejects this because very often those formulas were created by mistake. But there are times when you want to create them intentionally. Here's how you would go about it:

	A	B	C	D
1	Sample1	1.28		Highest ever
2	Sample2	1.18		1.97
3	Sample3	1.49		
4	Sample4	1.21		Highest mean
5	Sample5	1.27		1.57
6	Sample6	1.43		
7	Sample7	1.89		
8	Sample8	1.53		
9	Sample9	1.72		
10	Sample10	1.96		
11	Sample11	1.91		
12	Sample12	1.77		
13	Sample13	1.29		
14	Sample14	1.79		
15	Sample15	1.09		
16	Sample16	1.95		
17	Sample17	1.97		
18	Sample18	1.53		
19	Sample19	1.58		
20	Sample20	1.46		
21				

Figure 4.43

1. Enter the following formula in cell D2: =MAX(B:B,D2). (Notice the reference to D2 in D2's formula.)

2. Make the formula final. Excel gives you a *circular reference* warning. Click *Cancel*.

3. Excel does not perform the calculation until you go to *File*, *Options*, and enter the *Formulas* section, where you can enable ☑ *Iterative Calculation*. By default, Excel performs a maximum of 1,000 iterations.

4. Click *OK*. The calculation in cell D2 works and from now on always shows the highest value.

5. Enter another "problematic" formula for the highest mean in cell D5: =MAX(AVERAGE(B:B),D5). When you close this file and open it again, you won't be alerted until you turn *iterations* off again.

Figure 4.44 presents a similar situation. Column A holds 100 random numbers. In column D and E, you would like to create 10 equal bins between the minimum value (in D1) and maximum value (in D10). Column F shows the frequencies at this point. Here's what you do:

	A	B	C	D	E	F
1	0.028		min	0.005	0.005	1
2	0.757			0.117	0.117	13
3	0.240			0.229	0.228	11
4	0.243			0.339	0.338	9
5	0.005			0.448	0.448	13
6	0.670			0.558	0.558	12
7	0.500			0.667	0.667	10
8	0.546			0.776	0.776	7
9	0.406			0.885	0.885	10
10	0.884		max	0.994	0.994	14
11	0.596					
12	0.400					
13	0.905					
14	0.346					
15	0.559					

Figure 4.44

1. Enter the following formula in cell D2: =AVERAGE(D1:D3). This formula contains *circular reference*. Copy the formula down to D9.

2. Enter the following formula in cell E2: =AVERAGE(E1,E3). This formula does **not** contain a *circular reference*. Copy the formula down to E9.

3. Calculate in column F the frequencies for the bins in column D or column E.

4. Each time you hit *F9* (or *Shift+F9*), the entire sheet recalculates with iterations.

Results may differ between column D and E, but the formula with *circular reference* is more accurate.

Iterations are a great tool for *simulations*, as Figure 4.45 illustrates. Here you create a certain quantity (specified in row 1) of unique random numbers between 0 and N (specified in row 2). To do so follow these steps:

	A	B	C	D	E	
1	# of ##	5	10	15	20	
2	Up to	10	15	20	25	
3		4	4	5	4	
4		8	5	18	22	
5		1	1	16	1	
6		6	6	9	6	
7		11	8	6	19	
8			7	19	2	
9			11	8	25	
10			15	10	7	
11			13	4	16	
12			2	1	9	
13				12	14	
14				14	18	
15				3	23	
16				20	12	
17				11	17	
18					8	
19					11	
20					10	
21						
22						

Figure 4.45

1. Select range B3:E21 and apply *Conditional Formatting*: =ROW(A1)<=B$1.

2. In that same range, starting in B3, you place a formula that creates a random number between 1 and 10 (B2), but only applies it if the number does not exist yet in B3:B21. Here is that formula for cell B3: =IF(COUNTIF(B$3:B$21,B3)=1,B3,RANDBETWEEN(1,B$2)). Notice the *circular reference* again.

3. To make sure there are no numbers in the cells past the 5th row, 10th row, etc., you nest the previous IF function inside the following IF formula: =IF(ROW(B1)<=B$1, IF(…),""). This formula is for the entire range B3:E21.

4. If you decide to change values in row 1 and/or 2, you must copy the cell in B3 all the way again in order to get a recalculation, for *F9* won't do this for you.

Figure 4.46 shows another kind of *simulation* based on *iterations*. Say that you want to simulate what happens in between a few points (marked at the four corners of A4:E8 and in the center). This calls for a *gradient*. Gradients are very common in science—gradients of temperatures, of altitudes, of pressure, of concentrations, of allele frequencies in populations, and so on. A *Surface* type of graph may help us visualize the situation. Follow these steps:

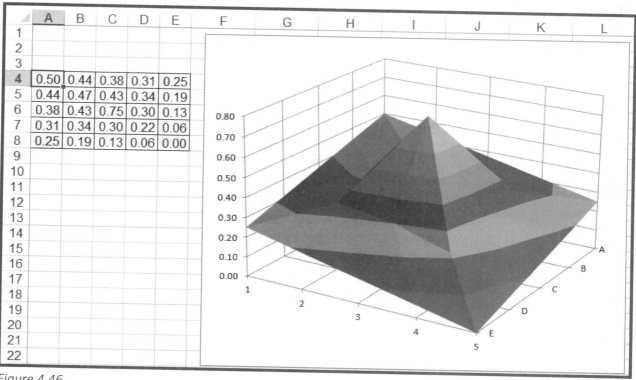

Figure 4.46

1. First you fill in the four boundary areas. Start with B4:D4 and enter the following formula in cell B4: =AVERAGE (A4:C4). (There is a *circular reference* again.)

2. Then you do something similar for the three other boundary areas—B8:D8, A5:A7, and E5:E7.

3. Finally, you fill the areas in between (except the center cell in this case). For B5, you enter =AVERAGE (A4:C6).

Note

Make sure 1,000 iterations are enough for Excel to reach a stable matrix, so you press *F9* until stability sets in. The finer the grid or matrix system, the longer it takes to get final results.

You can sometimes use *matrixes* to solve equations. For example, Figure 4.47 has three equations with three unknown x-values:

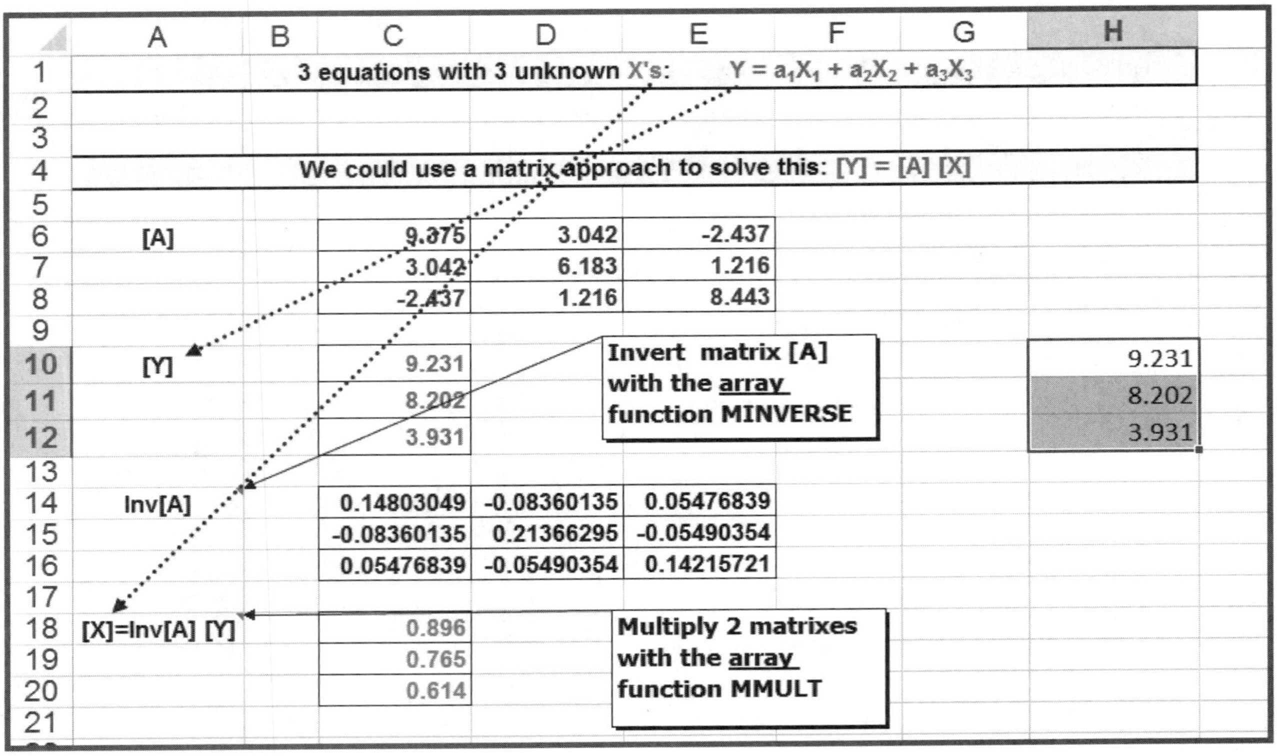

Figure 4.47

- Each equation uses three different coefficients for *A*, as shown in matrix *[A]*.

- The three equations should equate to the y-values shown in matrix *[Y]*.

- You need to determine what the x-values must be to solve the equations.

Here's what you do (similar to what we discussed in Chapter 17):

1. Invert matrix *[A]* by using the multi-cell array function MINVERSE in cells C14:E16:
=MINVERSE(C6:E8).

2. Multiply the matrix *Inv[A]* with the matrix *[Y]* by using the array function MMULT in cells C18:C20:
=MMULT(C14:E16,C10:C12).

3. You could have eliminated rows 14-16 by using a nested function instead:
=MMULT(MINVERSE(C6:E8),C10:C12).

Thanks to this multiplication, the cells C18:C20 contain the three x-values that you were looking for to solve three equations with three unknown x-values. The three x-values you have found make the three equations, based on the *A* values specified in the first matrix, equate to the y-values specified in the second matrix. To test the outcome in a cell like H10, use this formula: =C6*$C$18+D6*$C$19+E6*$C$20. The result should be exactly the same as the value in cell C10—9.231.

Note

Once you are done with the file used in this chapter, you may want to turn *Iterations* off in Excel.

Chapter 41: Solving Equations

In Chapter 40, you solved some mathematical problems manually. Fortunately, Excel has also two dedicated solving tools to offer: *Goal Seek* and *Solver*. *Goal Seek* is for simple situations, whereas *Solver* is for more complicated mathematical problems. Both use iterative processes.

You can use Figure 4.48 to explore both of Excel's solving tools. Notice that the dark gray cells on the sheet contain formulas; the formulas are displayed in the lighter gray cells above them.

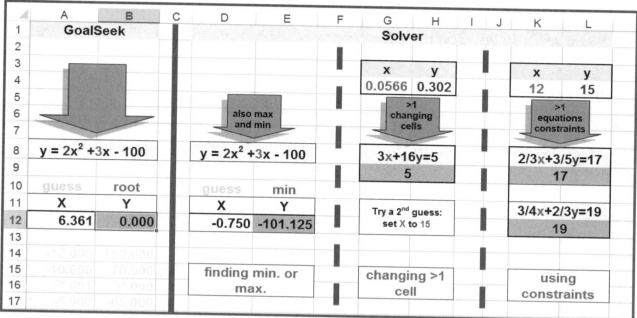

Figure 4.48

Let's start with *Goal Seek*, the simpler of the two solving tools. To open it, you go to the *Data* tab and select *What-If Analysis*, then *Goal Seek*. Say that you want to find the root of the quadratic equation shown in row 8—in other words, you want to solve for which x-value the equation equates to 0. *Goal Seek* can find the answer, but you must observe a few rules:

- The *Set* cell must contain a formula.

- The *Changing* cell must contain a value that has been used in the previous formula.

When you apply *Goal Seek* to the problem just described, it uses the initial value for x (in A2: 20) as a starting point and goes through a series of iterations to come up with a solution: x is 6.361.

When you look at the graph behind the equation in Figure 4.49, you can see why *Goal Seek* comes up with 6.4 (and not -7.8). It searches in the direction that comes closer to a solution. A good starter for -7.8 would be anything down from -1 (so definitely not 0). Very often, *Goal Seek* finds the solution you are looking for, but if you have a wrong starter or ask for the impossible (for example, when does y equal -120?), it does not give the correct solution. And then there are certain questions *Goal Seek* could never solve, such as: What is the lowest y-value? That's where *Goal Seek* has reached it limits, and *Solver* comes to the rescue because *Solver* can also find maximum and minimum values.

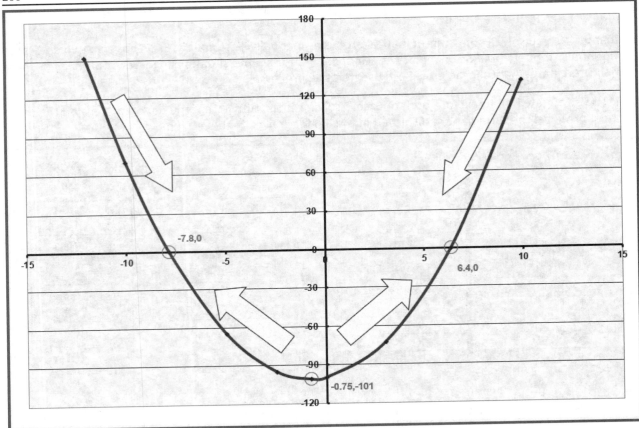

Figure 4.49

Solver is not installed by default. If you haven't already done so, you need to activate this add-by clicking the *File* tab and selecting *Options* plus *Add-Ins*. Once *Solver* has been activated, it is available from the *Data* tab in the *Analysis* section way to the right. (If *Solver* had already been added but does not show up on the ribbon, deactivate it and then activate it again.)

When using *Solver*, you need to follow these rules:

- The *Target* cell is always a formula—but only a single formula. (This is the same as in *Goal Seek*.)

- Besides *Value*, there are two more options: *Min* and *Max*. (This is not like *Goal Seek*.)

- Unlike in *Goal Seek*, *Solver*'s *Changing* cells can consist of more than one cell. (The *Guess* button finds all the value cells the formula is based on, which is sometimes what you want.)

- Unlike *Goal Seek*, *Solver* accepts *constraints*.

- When *Solver* finds a solution, you can either keep or reject the solution.

The same Figure 4.48, which we referred to earlier, also shows how you can apply *Solver* to some common kinds of mathematical problems. For example, in columns D:E, you can use *Solver* to find the minimum value of the equation $y = 2x^2 + 3x - 100$:

1. Set the *Target* cell E12 to ⊙ *Min*.

2. Set D12 as the *Changing* cell or click the *Guess* button. Once you click *OK*, *Solver* finds the following solution: x=-0.75 and y=-101.125.

3. To see if there are more solutions, try other starting values.

In columns G:H, you can set the equation *3x+16y* to a specific value (say, 5) by changing more than one value cell (both x in G4 and y in H4). You cannot do this with *Goal Seek*, but here's how it works with *Solver*:

1. Set the *Target* cell G9 to ⊙ *Value Of*: 5.

2. Set G4:H4 as the *Changing* cells or click the *Guess* button. Solver finds x=0.0566 and y=0.302 as one of the many solutions.

You can also use *Solver* to solve several equations at the same time, as is done in columns K:L. Because *Solver* can only handle one equation in its *Target* cell, you must treat the other equation(s) as *constraints*. Here's what you do:

1. Set the *Target* cell K9 to ⊙ *Value Of*: 17.

2. Set K4:L4 as the *Changing* cells or click the *Guess* button.

3. Add a *constraint* to set the second equation to 19. Solver finds this solution based on the starting settings: x=12 and y=15.

Figure 4.50 looks like another candidate for *Solver*. It shows a sigmoid-like equation (as discussed in Chapter 36) based on an estimated *slope* (in cell B2) and *IP* (in cell B1). You may be able to improve the estimated *slope* and *IP* by applying *Solver* to either the sum of residuals (in cell C23) or the sum of the least squares (in cell C24). Here's what you do:

	A	B	C	D	E	F	G	H
1	IP	7.5000						
2	Slope	0.5000						
3								
4	**X**	**Y**	**Predict**					
5	1	10	7.47				0	
6	2	15	12.02			0	IP	7.4421
7	3	22	19.07			232.91	Slope	0.5252
8	4	32	29.61					
9	5	45	44.54				Min	
10	6	63	64.16			20.41	IP	7.5388
11	7	80	87.56			167.34	Slope	0.5032
12	8	111	112.44					
13	9	133	135.84				Both	
14	10	153	155.46			0	IP	7.4336
15	11	177	170.39			204.53	Slope	0.5038
16	12	185	180.93					
17	13	189	187.98					
18	14	194	192.53					
19	15	197	195.40					
20	16	198	197.19					
21	17	199	198.28					
22	18	200	198.96					
23	**Sum Residuals**		13.17					
24	**Least Squares**		172.80					
25								

Figure 4.50

1. In cell C23, enter the following array formula for the sum of residuals: `=SUM((B5:B22) - (C5:C22))`.

2. In cell C24, enter the following array formula for the sum of the least squares: `=SUM(((B5:B22) - (C5:C22))^2)`. You could instead use Excel's function `SUMXMY2`.

3. Try *Solver* in three different ways:

    ◦ **Set C23 to 0**: *Solver* finds 7.4421 for *IP* and 0.5252 for *slope*. (*Cancel* the solution.)

    ◦ **Set C24 to *Min***: *Solver* finds 7.5388 and 0.5032. (*Cancel* the solution.)

    ◦ **Set C24 to *Min* and add a *constraint* of 0 for C23**: *Solver* finds 7.4336 and 0.5038.

If you click the *Options* button in *Solver*'s dialog box, you find several intricate options. One of them is the precision with which you want *Solver* to work. You can test these options on your own.

Chapter 42: What-If Controls

Besides using Excel tools, such as *Goal Seek* and *Solver*, you can solve equations by using *controls* that allow you to regulate values used in formulas. *Controls* are great tools for *what-if analysis*. Although they're a form of trial-and-error, *controls* can be great for simulations because they beautifully imitate the impact of certain changes. However, *controls* may not always be the ideal tools for finding the very best settings; *Solver* is better at that.

Let's consider Figure 4.51 as a starting point. To create a scroll-bar *control* for interpolation like the one placed over the cells D2:F2, you follow these steps:

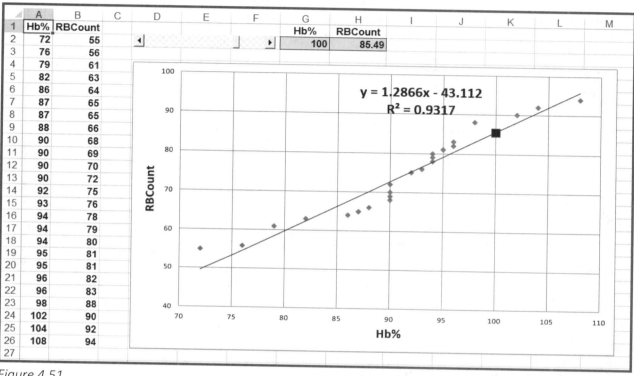

Figure 4.51

1. In cell H2, enter the linear regression formula shown in the graph: *=1.286*G2-43.11*. When the value in G2 changes, the values in H2 will change accordingly. Now we will use a scroll-bar *control* to regulate the value in G2 – and thus indirectly in H2.

2. To create the *control* itself, activate the *Design* mode on the *Developer* tab (way to the right). If the *Developer* tab is not available, click the *File* tab and select *Options, Customize Ribbon*, and check ☑ *Developer*. From now on, you can insert controls on your sheets—for instance, a scroll-bar—from the *Insert* button in the *Controls* section, by using the second listing (called *Active X Controls*) of the drop-down box.

3. After you draw the *control*—say, over cells B2:F2—click on *Properties* in the *Controls* section, and then set at least these properties:

    ◦ *Min*: 72.

    ◦ *Max*: 102.

    ◦ *Linked Cell*: G2. You must manually type this address; do not select the cell.

○ **SmallChange** and **LargeChange**: Set these properties to integer values—for instance, 1. The *SmallChange* kicks in when you click at either end of the scroll-bar; the *LargeChange* kicks in when you click next to the ends.

4. Turn **off** *Design* Mode; otherwise, you continue to work on the scroll-bar object, which is just floating on the sheet. Notice how the slider of the scrollbar jumped to the 100 position of cell G2.

5. When you are back on the sheet, make the values in cells G2 and H2 go up and down through the control, and watch the line marker in the graph "walk" along the linear regression line.

Because *controls* can use only integers, the minimum change is always 1. This could be a problem in a case like the one shown in Figure 4.52, where cell F17 requires decimals. Situations like these force you to store a *control*'s integer in an intermediate cell and then use a division formula in the real target cell. Here's how you do that:

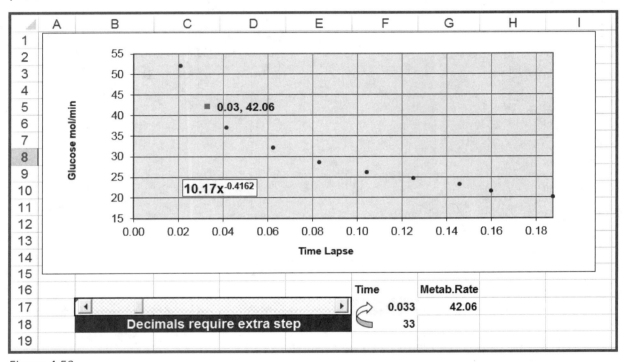

Figure 4.52

1. Place a scroll-bar on the sheet—for instance, over cells B17:E17.

2. Link the scrollbar to cell F18 through the *LinkedCell* property.

3. Set *Min* to 20 and *Max* to 180.

4. Stop the *Design Mode* by clicking on its button.

5. Enter the following formula in cell F17: `=F18/1000`.

6. Hide the intermediate cell by either using a white font or placing it behind the control.

In Figure 4.53, we regulate a sine wave with a scroll-bar for the frequency and a spin-button for the amplitude of the wave. (The rest of the sheet you can figure out yourself.) Here's how you make those controls:

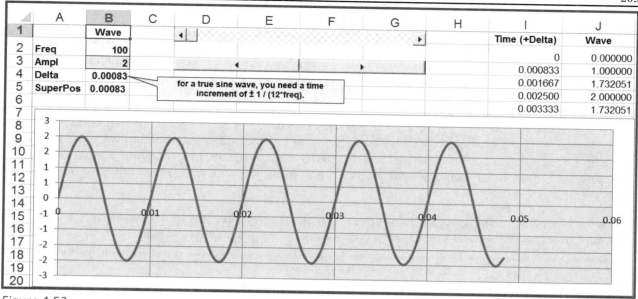

Figure 4.53

1. Place a scroll-bar on the sheet—for instance, over cells D1:G1. Set its properties: *LinkedCell* = B2 | *Min* = 100 | *Max* = 2000 | *SmallChange* = 10 | *LargeChange*= 100.

2. Next draw over the cells D3:G3 a spin-button running from 1 to 10 and linked to cell B3.

3. To test these two controls, you need to turn *Design Mode* **off** first.

Chapter 43: Syntax of Functions

Although Excel provides numerous built-in functions, you may sometimes need to construct your own user-defined functions (*UDF*) for the particular time-consuming calculations you perform regularly. This Excel feature opens up a world of unlimited power.

All the functions you have encountered so far **return** something—usually a number—but other types of return values are possible as well; but even numbers can be of different types. For numbers, you have a choice between *long* and *integer* (both have no decimals, but they differ in maximum value) and between *single* and *double* (both accept decimals, but they differ in their maximum precision). *Variant* is the most comprehensive type; it can hold any of the other types, but it requires with more computer memory and slows the processing speed.

Figure 4.54 lists the most important data types returned by common Excel functions. Most functions have *arguments*—that is, information that the functions work on. Here are some examples:

	A	B	C	D	E	F	G	H	I	J
1	Function	returns				type	size	remarks	range	
2	INT()	*Integer*				**Integer**	2 bytes		± 3,2767	
3	ROW()	*Long*				**Long**	4 bytes		± 2,147,483,647	
4	SQRT()	*Double*				**Single**	4 bytes	Precision up to 7 decimals/digits	± 1.4E-50 - 3.4E43	
5	NOW()	Date								
6	AND()	Boolean				**Double**	8 bytes	Precision up to 15 decimals/digits	± 4.9E-337 – 1.7E321	
7	UPPER()	*String* of capitalized text								
8						**Date**	8 bytes		1/1/100 – 12/31/9999	
9						**Boolean**	2 bytes		1 (on) and 0 (off)	
10			Variant:			**String**	?		Variable length	
11			the most comprehensive							
12			one (but costly)			**Variant**	16 bytes		Any of the above	
13										
14										

Figure 4.54

- SQRT has one argument—the number whose square root you want.

- COUNTIF has two arguments—the range in which to count and the criteria that define when to count.

- IF has three arguments—the criteria plus what to do when TRUE and what to do when FALSE.

Some arguments are optional; in the function's dialog box, they show up as non-bold:

- TREND and LINEST, for instance, have two optional arguments at the end; when you don't specify them, a default setting kicks in.

- IF has two optional arguments, but if you leave them blank, the function returns either *TRUE* or *FALSE*.

- SUMIF has the syntax SUMIF(*range, criteria, sum_range*), with the last argument being optional; however, the last argument is not optional when *range* and *criteria* are non-numeric.

Excel provides numerous functions. However, in some situations, Excel does not offer a function that meets your exact needs. For example, Excel has a function to calculate the square root of a number, SQRT, but it has no function to calculate the cube root. In this situation, you can create a function of your own.

You create functions in *Visual Basic* or *VBA*. VBA stands for *Visual Basic for Applications*; in this case, the application is Excel. This chapter does not delve into *VBA* programming; it shows just the tip of the iceberg, and it describes only how to create **functions** in *VBA*.

Note

Here's how you use *VBA* to create a user-defined function (*UDF*) in Excel:

1. Click the *Visual Basic* button on the *Developer* tab. If the *Developer* tab is not available, you must implement it (refer to Chapter 42).

2. When you are in *Visual Basic*, select *Insert, Module*. If you see several projects open in the left panel, just ignore them and double-click the project *Functions.xlsm*.

3. On the new *Module* sheet that appears, enter the following:

    ◦ Start a function by typing the word `Function`. (Be sure to spell it correctly.)

    ◦ Assign the name `CubeRoot` to the function. (Note that a function name cannot have a space in it.)

    ◦ Type an opening parenthesis: `(`.

    ◦ Type a creative name, such as the word `number`, for an argument.

    ◦ Specify the type of the argument: `As Double`. (A list pops up when you type the `d` or `do` of `Double`). Double-click on *Double* or click on it followed by the *Tab* key.

    ◦ Type a closing parenthesis: `)`.

    ◦ Specify the type that the function returns: `As Double`.

    ◦ Altogether, you have typed
    `Function CubeRoot(number As Double) As Double`. Press *Enter*, and *VBA* encapsulates the function.

4. Inside the function, type what the function should achieve:
    `CubeRoot = number ^ (1 / 3)`.

Warning

This is probably not the function you have been dreaming of for years, but it is a good example of what is possible. Now you need to test your new user-defined function in Excel.

This is what you do:

1. The new function should now feature in the regular listing of functions under f_x, where you can find it in both the categories *All* and *User-Defined*. (By not fully capitalizing the function name, you can distinguish your own creations from Excel's functions.)

2. Type on a new sheet in cell A1 the number 4. Let us find in cell B1 the cube root of this number by using our new function: `=CubeRoot(A1)`. And the result should be 1.587 (or more decimals).

The new function seems to work fine, but it doesn't provide user-friendly information until you do the following:

1. In Excel, click the *Macros* button on the *Developer* tab.

2. Because a function is not a macro, it is not listed under *Macros*, so just type its name in the top box: `CubeRoot`.

3. Click the *Options* button.

4. Type a description or an explanation and click *OK*.

5. Close the *Macros* box (but do not click *Run* because this is not a macro). Now, when you open the function box, your UDF should look a bit more professional. Adding a real *Help* feature, though, is beyond the scope of this book.

Note

For those who prefer to just type a formula or function in a cell, there is still some kind of help available when using user-defined functions: Start typing the function name and hit *Ctrl+Shift+A* after the opening parenthesis in order to get the names of the arguments. (*Ctrl+A* will just open the function dialog box.)

The new function you have created here is rather limited because it only calculates cube roots. Here's how you create a function for any kind of root:

1. Start a new function in *VBA*—this time, with two arguments:
`Function AnyRoot(`*number* `As Double,` *root* `As Integer) As Double`.

2. Press *Enter*, and *VBA* encapsulates the function

3. Inside the function, type `AnyRoot = number ^ (1 / root)`.

4. Test the new function in Excel. Figure 4.55 shows how both new functions can be used in Excel.

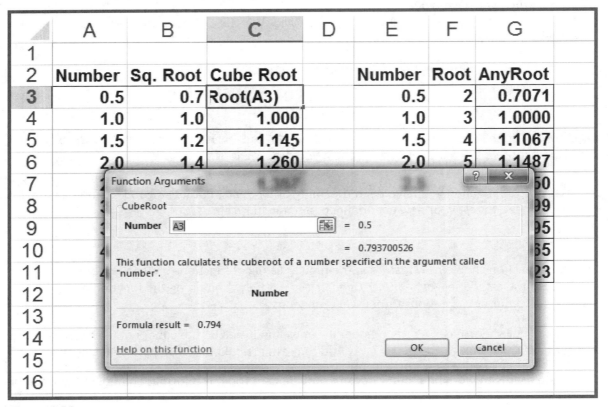

Figure 4.55

Now you're ready to create a function that is a more realistic and useful function—one that calculates the standard error, as Excel does not provide a function for this. Most scientists calculate the standard error manually: = SD / √n. In VBA, it goes like this:

1. Go back to *Visual Basic* if it is still open, or open it from the *Developer* tab.

2. Type after all previous functions:
`Function StError(SD As Double, size As Double) As Double.`

3. Inside the function, type `StError = SD / AnyRoot(size,2).`

Note

Notice that here you use the function `AnyRoot` that you created earlier. If you want to use `Sqr(-size)` instead, be aware that the *VBA* version is `SQR`, whereas Excel uses `SQRT`. Of course, you could also divide the standard deviation by (`size ^ (1 / 2)`).

If you do use your *AnyRoot* function, specify the second argument because it is not optional until you do make it optional. To do so, add to the second argument the word `Option-al` and set it to 2 (thus making it the default value). This is what the first line looks like now:
`Function AnyRoot(number As Double, Optional root As Integer = 2) As Double.`

Note

Optional arguments should always be the last ones in the list of arguments. Consequently, using `AnyRoot` anywhere in Excel does not always require a second argument now. If you don't specify the second argument, the function assumes that you want the square root. In `StError`, for instance, you could use this line: `StError = SD / AnyRoot(size)`. But the original line is still acceptable as well: `StError = SD / AnyRoot(size,2)`.

Figure 4.56 shows how you can apply the user-defined function `StError` in a regular spreadsheet. Cell B2 holds the following formula: `=StError($A2,B$1)`. Part 4 discusses the statistical implications of this. For now, just know that increasing the sample size reduces the standard error for a given standard deviation.

SD \ Size	5	10	15	20	25	30	35	40	45	50
1.0	0.4472	0.3162	0.2582	0.2236	0.2000	0.1826	0.1690	0.1581	0.1491	0.1414
1.5	0.6708	0.4743	0.3873	0.3354	0.3000	0.2739	0.2535	0.2372	0.2236	0.2121
2.0	0.8944	0.6325	0.5164	0.4472	0.4000	0.3651	0.3381	0.3162	0.2981	0.2828
2.5	1.1180	0.7906	0.6455	0.5590	0.5000	0.4564	0.4226	0.3953	0.3727	0.3536
3.0	1.3416	0.9487	0.7746	0.6708	0.6000	0.5477	0.5071	0.4743	0.4472	0.4243
3.5	1.5652	1.1068	0.9037	0.7826	0.7000	0.6390	0.5916	0.5534	0.5217	0.4950
4.0	1.7889	1.2649	1.0328	0.8944	0.8000	0.7303	0.6761	0.6325	0.5963	0.5657
4.5	2.0125	1.4230	1.1619	1.0062	0.9000	0.8216	0.7606	0.7115	0.6708	0.6364
5.0	2.2361	1.5811	1.2910	1.1180	1.0000	0.9129	0.8452	0.7906	0.7454	0.7071
5.5	2.4597	1.7393	1.4201	1.2298	1.1000	1.0042	0.9297	0.8696	0.8199	0.7778
6.0	2.6833	1.8974	1.5492	1.3416	1.2000	1.0954	1.0142	0.9487	0.8944	0.8485
6.5	2.9069	2.0555	1.6783	1.4534	1.3000	1.1867	1.0987	1.0277	0.9690	0.9192
7.0	3.1305	2.2136	1.8074	1.5652	1.4000	1.2780	1.1832	1.1068	1.0435	0.9899
7.5	3.3541	2.3717	1.9365	1.6771	1.5000	1.3693	1.2677	1.1859	1.1180	1.0607
8.0	3.5777	2.5298	2.0656	1.7889	1.6000	1.4606	1.3522	1.2649	1.1926	1.1314
8.5	3.8013	2.6879	2.1947	1.9007	1.7000	1.5519	1.4368	1.3440	1.2671	1.2021
9.0	4.0249	2.8460	2.3238	2.0125	1.8000	1.6432	1.5213	1.4230	1.3416	1.2728
9.5	4.2485	3.0042	2.4529	2.1243	1.9000	1.7345	1.6058	1.5021	1.4162	1.3435
10.0	4.4721	3.1623	2.5820	2.2361	2.0000	1.8257	1.6903	1.5811	1.4907	1.4142

Figure 4.56

Figure 4.57 shows the *VBA* code for all the functions you have created so far. It is clear that you could create also user-defined functions for polynomial formulas of the second order, or for sigmoidal curves, or anything you want or need. The sky is the limit.

```
Function CubeRoot(number As Double) As Double
    CubeRoot = number ^ (1 / 3)
End Function


Function AnyRoot(number As Double, Optional root As Integer = 2) As Double
    AnyRoot = number ^ (1 / root)
End Function


Function StError(SD As Double, size As Double) As Double
    StError = SD / AnyRoot(size)
End Function


Function Poly2(slope1 As Double, slope2 As Double, intcpt As Double, X As Double) As Double
    Poly2 = slope1 * X ^ 2 + slope2 * X + intcpt
End Function


Function Sigmoid(X As Double, slope As Double, IP As Double, SP As Double) As Double
    Sigmoid = Exp(slope * (X - IP)) / (1 + Exp(slope * (X - IP))) * SP
End Function
```

Figure 4.57

Note

Regular Excel functions recalculate whenever you change any cell on the spreadsheet. You can have your user-defined function do the same, by adding the following new line, right under the `Function` statement: `Application.Volatile`.

There is one more issue we need to address. When you close an Excel file containing *VBA* code, you must save it as a *Macro-enabled* file with the *.xlsm* extension (otherwise you lose the *VBA* code). When you open the file later on, you receive a security warning that says "Macros have been enabled." (They are not really macros, of course, but there is *VBA* code in the file.) If you don't enable the VBA code by clicking the *Enable* button next to it, you won't be able to recalculate or apply the new functions. The existing calculations remain, but you cannot reapply them.

If you don't want to be notified each time that there is *VBA* code in the file you are using, you can store the file in what is called a "trusted location." Here are the steps to do so:

1. Go to *File | Options | Trust Center*.

2. Click the button *Trust Center Settings*.

3. Make sure you are in the section *Trusted Locations* (left panel).

4. Click the button *Add New Location*, so you can indicate which folders or subfolders you want to be considered trusted. Any file stored in a trusted location will no longer generate a security warning.

When you close a file in which you made custom functions and open another file, you won't find your custom functions because they are stored in the original file only. You can solve this problem in two different ways. The first way is using a *VBAproject* called *FUNCRES.XLAM*. This solution may not always be possible, but if it is, do the following:

1. Open *Visual Basic* (again).

2. Locate the *Solution Explorer* in the left panel of the *VBA* screen; it shows one or more *VBAProjects*, including their modules. If that panel is missing, click the *Project Explorer* button on the toolbar.

3. If you see the project *FUNCRES.XLAM*, open it with a double-click.

4. Select *Insert*, then *Module*.

5. Double-click the original module (in the left panel) that you have worked on before and copy its entire function code.

6. Paste the code into the new module.

You can now use all functions in any `.xlsx` file on your machine.

Another solution to the problem of having no access to custom functions outside the file you created them in would be to create a *Personal Macro Workbook* by recording a fake macro first. Here's how:

1. Click the *Record Macro* button on the *Developer* tab.

2. Accept the macro name that is already there.

3. Indicate to store the macro in the *Personal Macro Workbook* and click *OK*.

4. Record anything—for example, the action *Ctrl+Home*.

5. Stop recording by again clicking the button that was before named *Record Macro*. Now there is a new section in the left panel of your *VBA* screen, and it includes a module that contains your recorded macro.

6. Replace the macro code with a copy of your function code.

Any Excel file on your machine has access to the *Personal Macro Workbook*, including its customized function(s). This *VBAProject* is called *PERSONAL.XLSB* and stands for *Personal Macro Workbook*.

Chapter 44: Worksheet Functions

When you create functions on your own, you can also base them on preexisting Excel worksheet functions. You don't want to keep reinventing the wheel, so you can use existing Excel functions in your own user-defined functions in order to get exactly the functionality you need.

Figure 4.58 uses a customized function that works with cell *ranges* to incorporate existing Excel functions that use cell ranges as well. The function here works with the preexisting function AVERAGE. It calculates the difference between the mean of two sets of values—for instance, before and after a certain treatment. Here's how you create such a function:

◢	A	B	C	
1		**Before**	**After**	
2	**Patient1**	213.4	200.1	
3	**Patient2**	225.0	216.4	
4	**Patient3**	217.0	195.6	
5	**Patient4**	183.7	175.0	
6	**Patient5**	197.2	202.3	
7	**Patient6**	223.6	214.8	
8	**Patient7**	224.2	215.7	
9	**Patient8**	215.2	200.7	
10	**Patient9**	202.4	211.7	
11	**Patient10**	217.7	216.1	
12	**Patient11**	221.0	208.5	
13	**Patient12**	219.9	188.4	
14	**Patient13**	205.4	211.4	
15	**Patient14**	195.1	180.9	
16	**Patient15**	218.0	184.1	
17	**Patient16**	207.6	202.3	
18				
19	**Mean Change**		**-10.15**	
20				

Figure 4.58

1. To declare variables as being of the *Range* type, enter the following line: `Function Mean-Change(Before As Range, After As Range) As Double`.

2. Inside this function, you want to find the difference between the mean of the *After* range and the mean of the *Before* range. So type inside the function skeleton this line:
`MeanChange = WorksheetFunction.Average(After) - WorksheetFunction.Average(Before)`.

Note

When you type a dot after the word *WorksheetFunction*, you get a list of all the functions Excel provides, including *Average*.

3. Switch back to Excel. The function `MeanChange` should now work correctly in cell C19: `=MeanChange(B2:B17,C2:C17)`.

Note

In Chapter 18, you got the same result by using a single-cell array formula. However, creating a customized function makes more sense if you do this kind of calculation frequently.

Figure 4.59 presents a similar case. In Chapter 43, you created a function for the standard error, based on a standard deviation and a count. This time, you create one that uses the original list of readings—which is a cell range—instead of using intermediate calculations in E1:E2. Here's what you do:

	A	B	C	D	E	
1	abc	1.71		SD	0.28	
2	abc	1.11		Count	18	
3	abc	1.84		SE	0.07	
4	abc	1.24				
5	abc	1.94		SE	0.07	
6	klm	1.97				
7	klm	1.18				
8	klm	1.54				
9	klm	1.69				
10	klm	1.76				
11	mno	1.50				
12	mno	1.78				
13	mno	1.78				
14	mno	1.40				
15	xyz	1.97				
16	xyz	1.29				
17	xyz	1.80				
18	xyz	1.45				
19						

Figure 4.59

1. On the first line, enter `Function SERange(Series As Range) As Double`.

2. Inside this function, type the three existing Excel functions `STDEV`, `SQRT`, and `COUNT` so that the second line looks like this: `SERange = WorksheetFunction.StDev_S(Series) / Sqr(WorksheetFunction.Count(Series))`.

Note

In Chapter 18, you got the same result by using a single-cell array formula. However, creating a customized function makes more sense if you do this kind of calculation frequently.

3. In Excel, use the new function in cell E5: `=SERange(B1:B18)`. The advantage of using this function is that you don't have to do the calculations in the cells E1 and E2 first.

Figure 4.60 shows an *EC50* or *IC50* situation again. This time, you want to calculate the *EC50* or *IC50* value based on the "halfway" y-value. All the steps we did before in Chapter 36, we combine and implement in a user-defined function. Follow these steps:

	A	B	C	D	E	F	G	H
1	log (M)	Average		X	Y		Concentration	Compound
2	-8.00	63308.66		1	10		0.00001	0.99
3	-8.52	60353.07		2	15		0.0001	1.02
4	-9.00	49902.16		3	22		0.001	3.12
5	-9.52	35062.71		4	32		0.01	6.36
6	-10.00	16816.47		5	45		0.1	26.00
7	-10.52	8015.16		6	63		1	51.20
8	-11.00	3803.18		7	80		10	75.96
9	-11.52	1733.47		8	111		100	89.00
10	-12.00	1271.91		9	133		1000	97.93
11				10	153		10000	98.80
12	EC/IC	Half Y		11	177			
13	-9.59	32290.28		12	185		EC/IC	Half Y
14				13	189		0.95	49.90
15				14	194			
16				15	197			
17				16	198			
18				17	199			
19				18	200			
20								
21				EC/IC	Half Y			
22				7.81	105			
23								

Figure 4.60

1. On the first line, enter `Function ECIC(X As Range, Y As Range, Y50 As Range) As Variant`. You need to return a *Variant* because the function is ultimately going to return a TREND calculation, which is an array function and therefore needs to return an array, even if the array has only one element in this case. A *Variant* type can do so.

2. On the second line, you declare some temporary variables by using the *Dim* keyword: `Dim Row1 As Integer, Row2 As Integer, Asc As Integer, X1 As String, Y1 As String`.

3. Because you are going to use the MATCH function, you need to know whether the values are in an ascending or descending order. A possible way of checking this for the y-values is comparing the first

cell in the range with the second cell by using the following line:
`If Y.Cells(1, 1) < Y.Cells(2, 1) Then Asc = 1 Else Asc = -1`.

4. Next you use the function `MATCH` to determine in which row the observed value preceding the "halfway" y-value is located: `Row1 = WorksheetFunction.Match(Y50, Y, Asc)`.

5. Now you know in which row the next observed value is located: `Row2 = WorksheetFunction.Match(Y50, Y, Asc) + 1`. You could have also typed: `Row2 = Row1 + 1`.

6. You store in the string variable *Y1* the range address of these two cells together (something like "B5:B6"):
`Y1 = Y.Cells(Row1, 1).Address & ":" & Y.Cells(Row2, 1).Address`.

7. Do something similar for the two corresponding cells in range
X: `X1 = X.Cells(Row1, 1).Address & ":" & X.Cells(Row2, 1).Address`.

8. Finally use the `TREND` function to calculate what the *EC50* or *IC50* value would be and return this value: `ECIC = WorksheetFunction.Trend(Range(X1), Range(Y1), Y50)`.

9. Use the new function in the cells A13, D22, and G14.

Figure 4.61 shows all the *VBA* code created in this chapter. If you don't fully understand what is going on in the background, don't worry about it; all you need to know for now is that *VBA* is a very powerful tool that you can use to customize your Excel experience.

```
Function MeanChange(Before As Range, After As Range) As Double
    MeanChange = WorksheetFunction.Average(After) - WorksheetFunction.Average(Before)
End Function


Function SERange(Series As Range) As Double
    SERange = WorksheetFunction.StDev(Series) / Sqr(WorksheetFunction.Count(Series))
End Function


Function ECIC(X As Range, Y As Range, Y50 As Range) As Variant 'TREND returns Variant
    Dim Row1 As Integer, Row2 As Integer, Asc As Integer, X1 As String, Y1 As String
    If Y.Cells(1, 1) < Y.Cells(2, 1) Then Asc = 1 Else Asc = -1 '1 for asc. and -1 for desc
    Row1 = WorksheetFunction.Match(Y50, Y, Asc)
    Row2 = WorksheetFunction.Match(Y50, Y, Asc) + 1
    X1 = X.Cells(Row1, 1).Address & ":" & X.Cells(Row2, 1).Address
    Y1 = Y.Cells(Row1, 1).Address & ":" & Y.Cells(Row2, 1).Address
    ECIC = WorksheetFunction.Trend(Range(X1), Range(Y1), Y50)
End Function
```

Figure 4.61

Note

To delve more deeply into VBA, see the CD-ROM *Excel 2013 VBA* from MrExcel's *Visual Learning Series*: www.mrexcel.com/excel2013vbatraining.html.

Part 4 Exercises

You can download all the files used in this book from www.genesispc.com/Science2013.htm, where you can find each file in its original version (to work on) and in its finished version (to check your solutions).

1. Linear Regression

1.1. Create an "automatic" linear *Trendline* in the graph, including its regression formula and *RSQ* value.

1.2. Create a linear regression line manually by using column C.

1.3. Extrapolate a 20% mutation rate (B16) on the linear regression line by using the TREND function in cell A16.

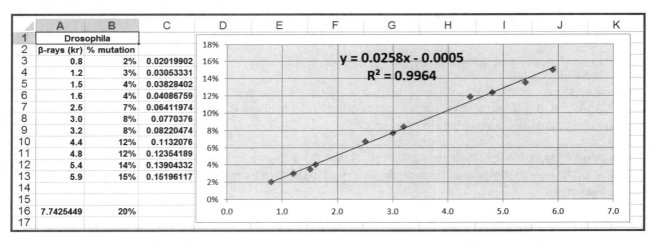

	A	B	C
1	Drosophila		
2	β-rays (kr)	% mutation	
3	0.8	2%	0.02019902
4	1.2	3%	0.03053331
5	1.5	4%	0.03828402
6	1.6	4%	0.04086759
7	2.5	7%	0.06411974
8	3.0	8%	0.0770376
9	3.2	8%	0.08220474
10	4.4	12%	0.1132076
11	4.8	12%	0.12354189
12	5.4	14%	0.13904332
13	5.9	15%	0.15196117
14			
15			
16	7.7425449	20%	
17			

y = 0.0258x - 0.0005
$R^2 = 0.9964$

2. Nonlinear Regression

2.1 For each graph shown here, make the proper axis or axes logarithmic.

2.2 Add the proper regression line to each graph.

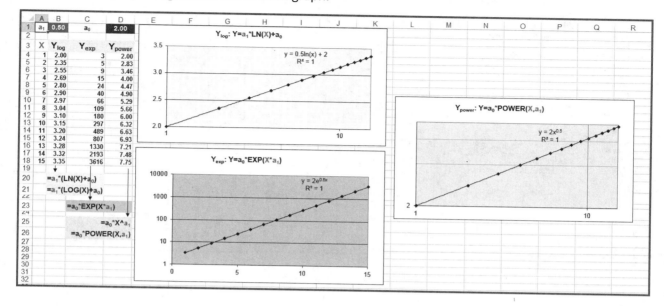

3. Nonlinear Regression

3.1. Create a graph that looks like the one shown here.

3.2. Apply the correct type of regression line.

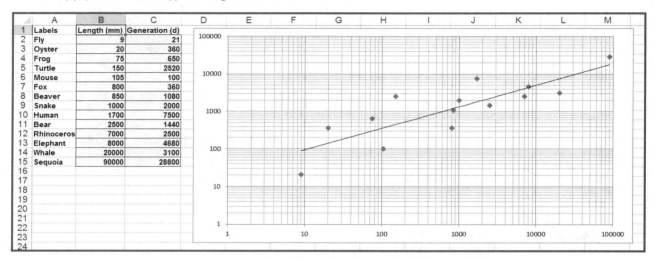

	A	B	C
1	Labels	Length (mm)	Generation (d)
2	Fly	9	21
3	Oyster	20	360
4	Frog	75	650
5	Turtle	150	2520
6	Mouse	105	100
7	Fox	800	360
8	Beaver	850	1080
9	Snake	1000	2000
10	Human	1700	7500
11	Bear	2500	1440
12	Rhinoceros	7000	2500
13	Elephant	8000	4680
14	Whale	20000	3100
15	Sequoia	90000	28800

4. Curve Fitting

4.1. Use the function TREND in column C.

4.2. Create a residuals plot as shown in the insert, based on column D.

4.3. Standardize the residuals in column E.

4.4. Decide on the proper regression line for the original curve.

4.5. Apply a final curve-fitting test.

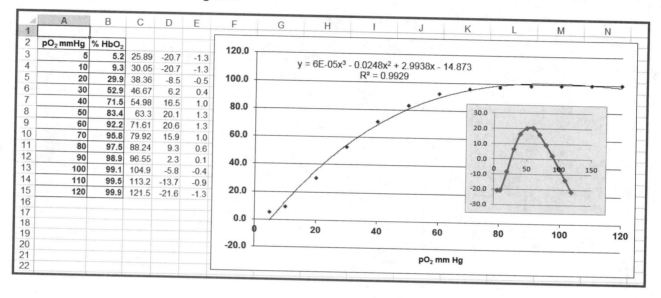

	A	B	C	D	E
1					
2	pO_2 mmHg	% HbO_2			
3	5	5.2	25.89	-20.7	-1.3
4	10	9.3	30.05	-20.7	-1.3
5	20	29.9	38.36	-8.5	-0.5
6	30	52.9	46.67	6.2	0.4
7	40	71.5	54.98	16.5	1.0
8	50	83.4	63.3	20.1	1.3
9	60	92.2	71.61	20.6	1.3
10	70	95.8	79.92	15.9	1.0
11	80	97.5	88.24	9.3	0.6
12	90	98.9	96.55	2.3	0.1
13	100	99.1	104.9	-5.8	-0.4
14	110	99.5	113.2	-13.7	-0.9
15	120	99.9	121.5	-21.6	-1.3

$y = 6E\text{-}05x^3 - 0.0248x^2 + 2.9938x - 14.873$

$R^2 = 0.9929$

pO_2 mm Hg

5. Sigmoid Curves

5.1. In column C, predict or estimate the percentage of hemoglobin oxygenation based on partial oxygen pressure if the relationship is of the sigmoid type.

5.2. Add the sigmoid regression curve to the graph.

5.3. Do the necessary curve fitting work.

5.4. Are there any outliers here?

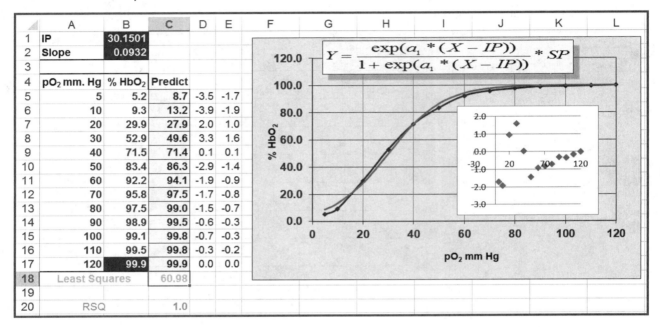

6. Linear Estimates

6.1. Calculate correlations in H2:K2.

6.2. Find the multiple regression statistics in H6:K10.

6.3. Predict or estimate FVC in column F by using *coefficients*.

6.4. Predict or estimate FVC in column G by using the TREND function.

6.5. Add a linear regression line to the graph.

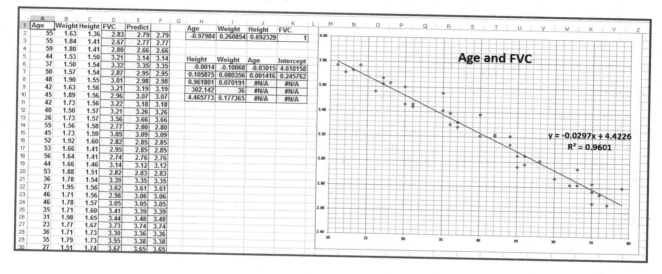

7. Linear Estimates

7.1. Calculate correlations in H2:K2.

7.2. Find the multiple regression statistics in H6:K10.

7.3. Predict or estimate FVC in column F by using *coefficients*.

7.4. Predict or estimate FVC in column G by using the TREND function.

7.5. Add a linear regression line to the graph.

	A	B	C	D	E	F	G	H	I	J	K	L	M	N	O
1	Clearance mL/min	Weight	Age	Serum Creatinine mg/dL			SUMMARY OUTPUT								
2	206.49	170	36	1.07	218.58										
3	257.79	172	57	0.81	252.46		Regression Statistics								
4	311.36	178	24	0.93	321.23		Multiple R	0.96119274							
5	283.94	181	44	0.81	306.65		R Square	0.92389148							
6	463.83	184	37	0.58	420.44		Adjusted R Square	0.90313461							
7	433.02	148	26	0.58	405.94		Standard Error	26.9745083							
8	307.42	169	32	0.83	320.99		Observations	15							
9	401.69	135	29	0.53	397.27										
10	153.85	130	52	0.93	164.92		ANOVA								
11	293.05	165	28	0.94	286.61			df	SS	MS	F	Significance F			
12	222.17	186	35	1.21	190.87		Regression	3	97159.9905	32386.6635	44.5101578	1.923E-06			
13	314.42	175	33	0.78	345.03		Residual	11	8003.86509	727.624099					
14	192.16	152	67	0.89	162.36		Total	14	105163.856						
15	310.61	184	71	0.55	322.65										
16	287.92	159	41	0.71	323.74			Coefficients	tandard Erro	t Stat	P-value	Lower 95%	Upper 95%	Lower 95.0%	Upper 95.0%
17							Intercept	504.441067	73.0375947	6.90659474	2.5652E-05	343.686405	665.195729	343.686405	665.195729
18		Clearance mL	Weight	Age	Creatinine mg/d		Weight	1.38368972	0.41537466	3.33118476	0.00669717	0.46945627	2.29792318	0.46945627	2.29792318
19	Clearance	1					Age	-3.210651	0.4944423	-6.4934796	4.4674E-05	-4.2989112	-2.1223908	-4.2989112	-2.1223908
20	Weight	0.10763	1				Serum Creatinine	-378.97841	37.5198118	-10.100755	6.6877E-07	-461.55896	-296.39786	-461.55896	-296.39786
21	Age	-0.45245	0.01668	1											
22	Serum Cre	-0.75227	0.19266	-0.0999423	1										
23															
24							RESIDUAL OUTPUT								
25															
26							Observation	d Clearance	Residuals	ndard Residuals					
27							1	218.577981	-12.086808	-0.5055053					
28							2	252.456077	5.33130324	0.22297056					

8. Reiterations

8.1. Activate iterations in this workbook.

8.2. Fill in the entire table, keeping A4, A10, D7, G4, and G10 fixed but calculating the gradient values in between.

8.3. Check whether all values have been stabilized.

8.4. Change some key values.

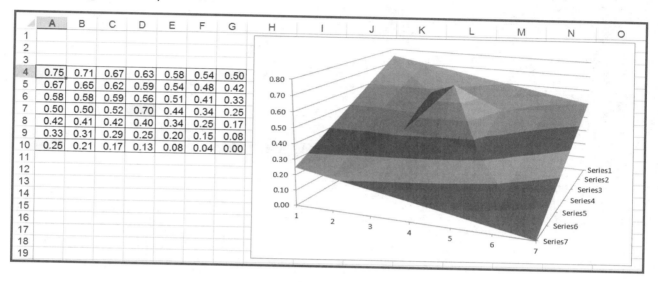

	A	B	C	D	E	F	G
4	0.75	0.71	0.67	0.63	0.58	0.54	0.50
5	0.67	0.65	0.62	0.59	0.54	0.48	0.42
6	0.58	0.58	0.59	0.56	0.51	0.41	0.33
7	0.50	0.50	0.52	0.70	0.44	0.34	0.25
8	0.42	0.41	0.42	0.40	0.34	0.25	0.17
9	0.33	0.31	0.29	0.25	0.20	0.15	0.08
10	0.25	0.21	0.17	0.13	0.08	0.04	0.00

9. Solving Tools

9.1. Use *Solver* to solve three equations with three unknown x-values (in A4:A6) by setting H4:H6 to the values in G4:G6.

9.2. Use *Solver* again, but this time minimize the sum of the squared residuals in cell I15.

9.3. In both cases, ensure that the three unknown x-values are the same as the ones found with the matrix system in cells I24:I26.

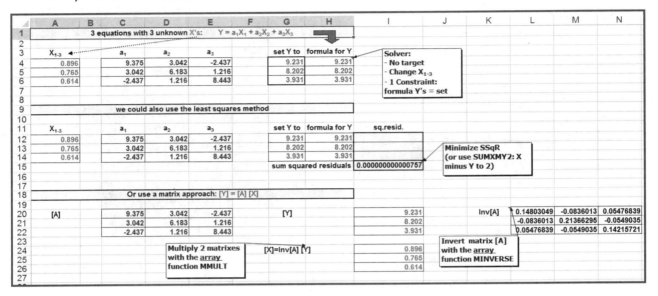

10. Solving Tools

10.1. Use *Goal Seek* on cell B11 by changing the guess value in B5.

10.2. Use *Solver* on cell C11. (The formulas in B11 and C11 are identical.)

10.3. Which one comes the closest?

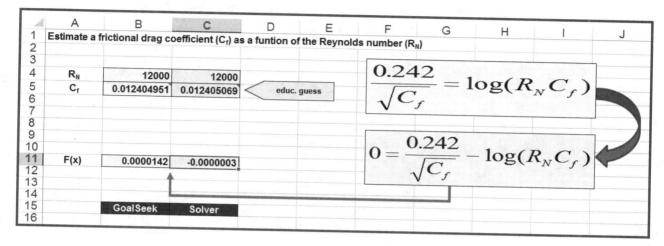

11. What-if Controls

11.1. Create a scroll-bar *control* that regulates *IP* (used in the formula of column C) with a precision of two decimals.

11.2. Create another scroll-bar *control* that regulates the *slope* with a precision of two decimals.

11.3. In the cells H10 and H12 are the best values for *IP* and *slope*. Test them with *Solver*.

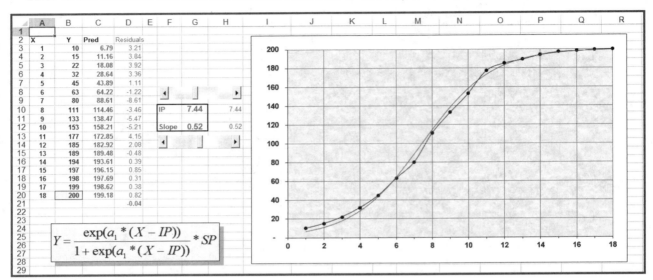

$$Y = \frac{\exp(a_1 * (X - IP))}{1 + \exp(a_1 * (X - IP))} * SP$$

12. Syntax of Functions

12.1. Create a user-defined function (*UDF*) that returns a *Variant*. It calculates the offspring of *y* organisms (in B1) after *x* generations (B5:B9), with a growth rate of *z* per generation (C4:G4).

12.2. Add some explanation to the user-defined function.

12.3. Use the new function in the range C5:G9.

	A	B	C	D	E	F	G
1	Initial	2		How much food do we need to keep the offspring of 2 rabbits alive?			
2							
3							
4		Rate	2	2.2	2.4	2.6	2.8
5	Generations	5	64	103	159	238	344
6		10	2,048	5,312	12,681	28,233	59,239
7		15	65,536	273,760	1,009,715	3,354,519	10,195,311
8		20	2,097,152	14,108,590	80,399,774	398,562,978	1,754,650,492
9		25	67,108,864	727,104,808	6,401,931,729	47,354,766,002	301,981,806,790
10							
11							
12							
13							
14			PopGrowth = iStart * (dRate ^ iGens)				
15							
16							
17						return a Variant	

13. Syntax of Functions

13.1. Create a user-defined function that calculates the minimum sample size based on a certain mean and SD plus a requested margin of error. Use the formula shown.

13.2. Make the variable 1.96 *optional* and *default*; it stands for a confidence level of 95% but should be adjustable.

13.3. Apply the new function to E2:J2, E5:J5, and E8:J8.

	A	B	C	D	E	F	G	H	I	J
1	Mean	4.15		Margin	0.05	0.1	0.15	0.2	0.25	0.3
2	SD	0.32		Size	157	39	17	10	6	4
3										
4	Mean	6.80		Margin	0.01	0.02	0.03	0.04	0.05	0.06
5	SD	0.05		Size	96	24	11	6	4	3
6										
7	Mean	175.00		Margin	5	10	15	20	25	30
8	SD	25		Size	96	24	11	6	4	3
9										
10										

$$n = \left(\frac{1.96}{margin / \mu} \right)^2 \left(\frac{SD}{\mu} \right)^2$$

14. Worksheet Functions

14.1. Create a user-defined function that calculates the mean but skips error values. Do this by using existing Excel functions such as AVERAGE and IFERROR.

14.2. Use the new function in cell E20.

14.3. Use a single-cell array formula as well to compare the outcome.

	A	B	C	D	E
1					SD
2	abc	1.71	1.46	1.25	0.23
3	abc	1.11	1.90	1.85	0.44
4	abc	1.84	1.46	1.57	0.20
5	abc				#DIV/0!
6	abc	1.94	1.82	1.18	0.41
7	klm	1.97	1.34	1.99	0.37
8	klm	1.18	1.47	1.38	0.15
9	klm	1.54		1.39	0.11
10	klm	1.69	1.28	1.34	0.22
11	klm			1.86	#DIV/0!
12	mno	1.50	1.07	1.47	0.24
13	mno	1.78	1.72	1.22	0.31
14	mno	1.78	1.76	1.46	0.18
15	mno	1.40	1.74	1.94	0.27
16	xyz	1.97	1.03	1.91	0.53
17	xyz	1.29	1.33	1.14	0.10
18	xyz	1.80	1.66	1.89	0.12
19	xyz	1.45	1.30	1.17	0.14
20		Mean			1.44
21					

Part 5: Statistical Analysis

Chapter 45: Why Statistics?

Because scientists usually work with samples taken from huge populations, they need to deal with the fact that samples are never exact replicas of the population they come from or represent. In order to assess how much this fact may impact results, you need statistics. This chapter doesn't provide a crash course on statistics, but you'll learn the basics of how to use Excel in your statistical work.

Figure 5.1 illustrates what happens in sampling. Let's pretend you want to study the "infinite population" of random numbers between 0 and 10 by taking 20 different samples with size 10. Each row represents one of those 20 samples. You calculate in column L for each sample the mean of all 10 random numbers drawn from the population. The columns B:K recalculate each time you hit *F9* or *Shift+F9*, because they use volatile functions—either =INT(RAND()*11) or RANDBETWEEN(0,10).

sample	each sample holds 10 random numbers between 0 and 10										mean
1	6	4	2	10	3	3	10	0	5	1	4.4
2	7	4	10	7	5	6	4	8	7	4	6.2
3	4	4	7	1	6	8	7	8	6	0	5.1
4	2	6	2	7	10	6	10	1	6	9	5.9
5	1	2	10	9	10	4	1	5	9	3	5.4
6	3	5	5	1	9	6	10	5	9	2	5.5
7	9	3	6	10	7	1	1	5	10	2	5.4
8	5	1	2	8	0	9	10	6	0	4	4.5
9	8	7	7	2	8	0	5	7	6	4	5.4
10	7	1	5	6	9	9	2	7	10	6	6.2
11	4	8	2	4	5	0	9	10	6	1	4.9
12	6	5	8	6	3	2	0	3	9	9	5.1
13	7	2	9	10	5	7	10	3	5	3	6.1
14	4	6	6	5	10	7	5	9	10	5	6.7
15	6	7	1	2	6	4	9	6	10	9	6.0
16	1	3	4	3	9	10	8	5	3	10	5.6
17	8	6	1	9	5	7	10	1	1	9	5.7
18	2	6	1	10	7	5	9	7	7	8	6.2
19	4	0	6	5	7	8	1	9	1	9	5.0
20	0	10	9	8	3	3	1	0	6	0	4.0
					mean of 20 sample means						5.5

each sample holds 10 random numbers between 0 and 10

Figure 5.1

Notice that those means may vary quite a bit; the extreme low and high ones are displayed in a different font (which is done with *Conditional Formatting*). What you try to simulate here is drawing new samples from the same population—and yet the mean found in the sample keeps changing. That's what happens in research! As they say, "Results may vary." However, there is one value that doesn't change as widely: the mean of all these 20 means, featured in cell L22. Whereas the individual means may reach 3 or 7 rather easily, it is unlikely that the *mean of means* ends up outside the range of 4.5 to 5.5. A sample's mean is often symbolized as $\bar{x}$, x_m, or *m*. The mean of means is usually symbolized as μ_m.

Note

Excel uses the function AVERAGE to calculate the mean. In science and statistics, it is more common to speak of *mean* than of *average*. Let us follow that custom.

Figure 5.2 shows another aspect of this phenomenon. To create a spreadsheet like this, you first create a frequency table of individual means (on the right); then, you plot those frequencies in a graph (in the center). The vertical line in the graph represents the current *mean of the means*; it is the mean of all 20 sample means combined. The range of the mean of the means is rather narrow. The curve representing the frequency of means usually has some kind of a bell shape. A common technique in research is to find the range of means based on the mean of a particular sample.

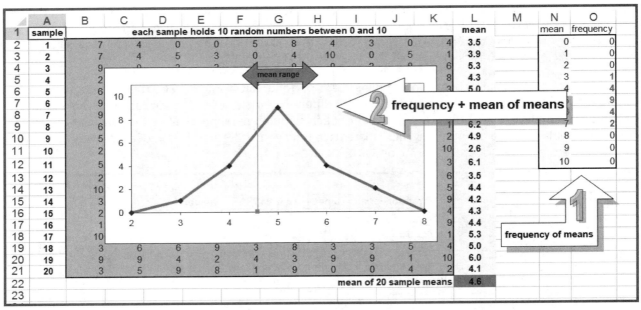

Figure 5.2

Figure 5.3 brings us closer to the central issue. It shows two frequency distributions: The one on the left is for frequencies of values (as found in sample 5, for instance); it is called a *sample distribution*. The distribution on the right is for frequencies of means (all samples taken together), and it is called a *sampling distribution*. Basically, research is about the graph on the left, and statistics is about the graph on the right.

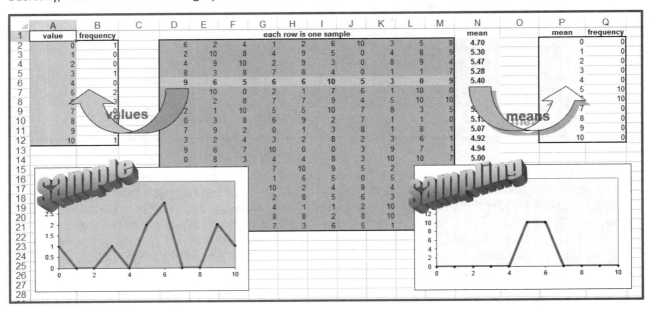

Figure 5.3

Figure 5.4 shows another key concept in this context—the standard deviation (SD); the standard deviation is a measure of how widely values are dispersed from their mean. Figure 5.4 calculates the standard deviation twice (in row 14): The left one is the SD of observations (in the *sample* distribution); the right one is the SD of means (in the *sampling* distribution). How are these two SD's related? The SD of means is always smaller than the SD of observations; the SD of means decreases with increasing sample size.

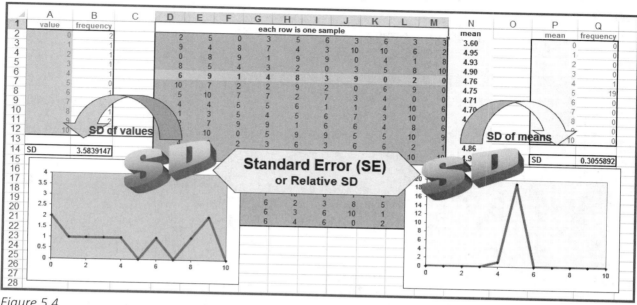

Figure 5.4

Because research is basically about the left part of this screen, you often do not know about the mean of the means and the standard deviation of the means to the right. All you have on hand are the mean and SD as found in the sample to the left. So you have to obtain an **estimate** of the SD of the means based on the SD of the observations. You do this by calculating the standard error (SE), also called the *relative SD*. The formula for the SE is: $SE = SD / \sqrt{n}$. As you can gather from this formula, the SE decreases when the sample size increases.

Note

There is a battle of "n versus n-1." Some divide by the square root of n, others by the square root of n-1. Why? They call the first one "biased," as it is always off, in the long term, by a very small amount from its target value, so they "tweak" it by subtracting 1. Take your pick; in this book I go for √n.

Figure 5.5 shows the normal distribution, which is at the heart of statistics. The normal distribution is a *sampling* distribution of means. The mean of means is located at 0 on the x-axis. The units plotted on this axis are *units of SE*. The *SE units* on the horizontal axis are called *unit free*—that means they don't change when the units of measurement change. It doesn't matter whether you are dealing with degrees Celsius or Fahrenheit or with ounces or kilograms—these *SE units* are *unit free*.

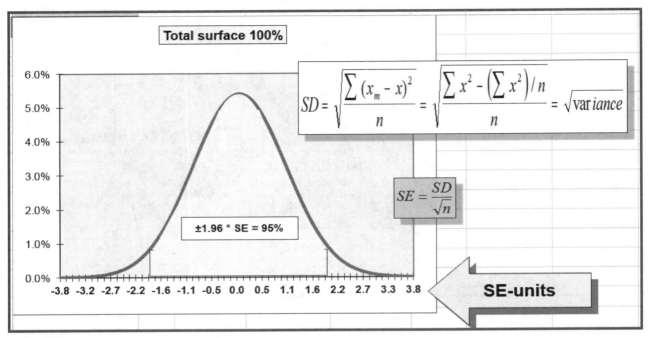

Figure 5.5

Means that are more than 1.96 *SE units* away from the mean of means are extremely rare—with actually only 5% of the means occurring in those two outer ranges. (They can run from -4 to +4, but even a wider range is possible, because the curve is asymptotic on both sides.) The other 95% of means are located in the center range (between -1.96 and 1.96). The *units of SE* around the mean of means determine how much of the curve's surface has been covered: 70% for ±1 *SE*; 90% for ±1.65 *SE*; 95% for ±1.96 *SE*; and 97.5% for ±2.25 *SE*. You'll learn more on this later.

Imagine that a population has a mean of 15 (whether °C, ng/ml, mol, or whatever), whereas a sample of 16 cases has a mean of 14 and a *SD* of 2. How many *SE units* are these two means apart from each other? The answer is *(15-14)/SE = (15-14)/(SD/√16) = 0.5 SE units*. This is actually very close to the population mean. ⸱

Chapter 46: Types of Distributions

The *normal* distribution is only one of the several types of *sampling* distributions used in statistics. This chapter discusses the main distributions, their characteristics, and when to use each one. Distributions are *sampling* distributions that are meant to help us evaluate *sample* distributions.

The *normal* distribution has two versions, as Figure 5.6 demonstrates: the noncumulative version (to the left) and the cumulative version (to the right). The cumulative graph shows that the area to the left of 0 in the noncumulative graph covers 50% of all cases. It also shows that a mean being +2 *SE units* away from the *mean of means* covers up to 97.5% of all cases. As mentioned earlier, the x-axis features *units of SE*. These are "universal" units that can be applied to means of any magnitude (pH, °C, ng/ml, mol, volts, and so on). In case of a *normal* distribution, these units are called *Z-values*. They can be positive or negative because the normal distribution is symmetrical.

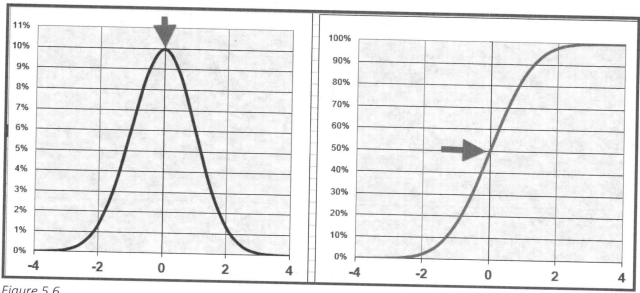

Figure 5.6

But there are additional types of distributions. For example, Figure 5.7 shows the *t*-distribution, the *Chi-squared* distribution, the *binomial* distribution, and the *F*-distribution. There are a few more distributions, but these are the ones discussed in this part of the book. The four curves shown in Figure 5.7 are all non-symmetrical, so the x-axis has only positive *SE-units* (unlike the normal bell-shaped curve), and they happen to be of the cumulative type, so the vertical axis has a scale up to either 50% or 100%. And again, the x-axis has *units of SE*. The y-axis shows their *probabilities* of occurring.

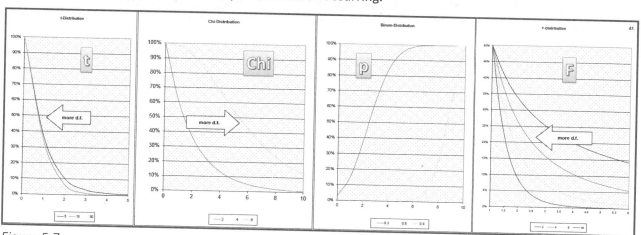

Figure 5.7

The *units of SE* have been named after the distributions they come with:

- *Z*-values are for means.

- *t*-values are also for means.

- *Chi*-values are for frequencies.

- *p*-values are for proportions.

- *F*-values are for variances.

How do you use Excel functions to calculate the values on these axes? Figure 5.8 offers an overview:

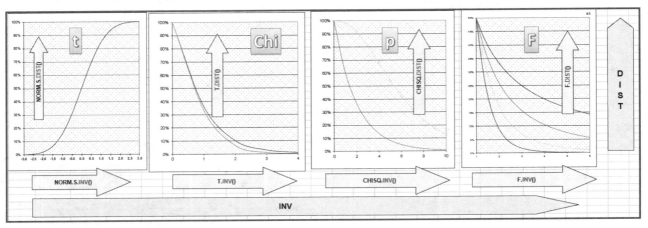

Figure 5.8

- The x-axis holds the *units of SE* (*Z*-values, *t*-values, and so on). To calculate *SE* values, Excel uses functions whose names end with `INV`. The function `NORM.S.INV`, for instance, would find the *Z*-value for a certain probability, and `T.INV` would find the *t*-value for that probability.

- The y-axis plots the *probabilities* with which those values occur (usually either noncumulative, or cumulative). To calculate probabilities, Excel uses functions whose names end with `DIST`. `NORM.S.DIST`, for instance, would find the probability of a certain *Z*-value.

<u>Note</u>

The dot inside a function name was introduced with Excel version 2010. If you want to be able to use these functions in older versions, go for the dot-less name. Otherwise I would recommend you use the newer names—also because they offer sometimes more and better options.

Let's look at the *normal* distribution first. As you can see in Figure 5.9, *normal* distributions work with two different DIST functions: NORM.DIST and NORM.S.DIST. Both of these functions are designed to find probabilities:

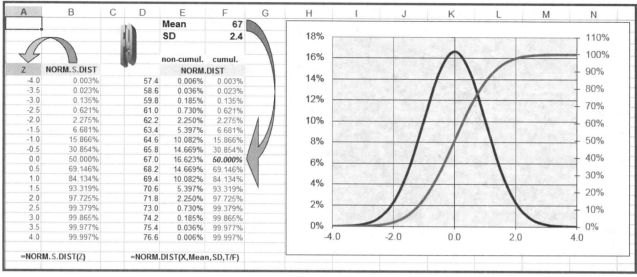

Figure 5.9

- **NORM.S.DIST:** This function is *Z*-related, for it uses *Z* to find its probability (see column B). Cell B6 uses it: =NORM.S.DIST(A6). The function NORM.S.DIST returns 50% for a *Z*-value of 0 because it is cumulative and symmetrical.

- **NORM.DIST:** This function (without .S.) is **not** *Z*-related; it uses a specific mean (of any magnitude) to find its probability. In addition, NORM.DIST has two versions:

  ◦ Cumulative version (in column F); cell F6: =NORM.DIST(D6,Mean,SD,TRUE). The cumulative version of NORM.DIST returns 50% for the mean used in cell F1.

  ◦ Noncumulative version (in column E); cell E6: =NORM.DIST(D6,Mean,SD,FALSE). The noncumulative version of NORM.DIST could never return 50%; the last argument makes it noncumulative.

<u>Note</u>

When you hit *F9* in the file of figure 5.9, the mean and *SD* in cells F1 and F2 change (they are volatile). The only columns that will change also are the columns D and E. The rest should stay the same.

Figure 5.10 shows the use of two INV functions for *normal* distributions. Here is how they work:

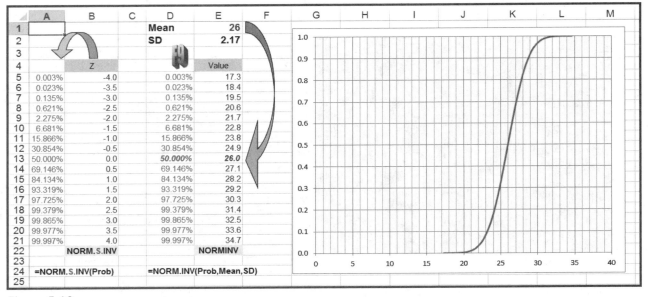

Figure 5.10

- **NORM.S.INV:** This function is *Z*-related again and cumulative: It finds the *Z*-value for a certain probability. Cell B5 uses it: =NORM.S.INV(A5). There is, for instance, a 6.68% probability that *Z*-values would be farther than 1.5 *SE-units* to the left of the mean.

- **NORM.INV:** This function (without .S.) is not *Z*-related and is cumulative: It finds a value on either side of the population mean (E1) at a certain probability level. A 50% probability comes with the mean featured in cell E1. There is, for instance, a 6.68% chance of finding a mean of 22.8 or lower in a sample taken from a population with a mean of 27. Cell C5 uses this function: =NORM.INV(D5,Mean,SD).

Figure 5.11 shows another type of sampling distribution. The so-called *Student's t*-distribution works with *t*-values instead of *Z*-values. Both graphs on the right are based on the T.DIST function: They are both cumulative but not always symmetrical—in other words, *t*-values (unlike *Z*-values) are usually only positive (unless you use the function T.INV). The difference between the two graphs is that the top one has a y-axis up to 100%, the lower one up to 50%.

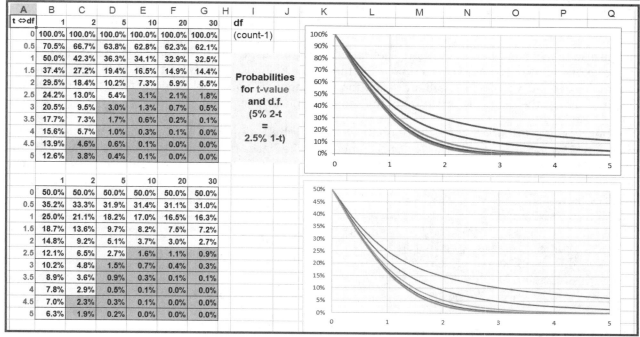

Figure 5.11

The reason for this difference is that `T.DIST` comes in three different versions, as is shown in Figure 5.12:

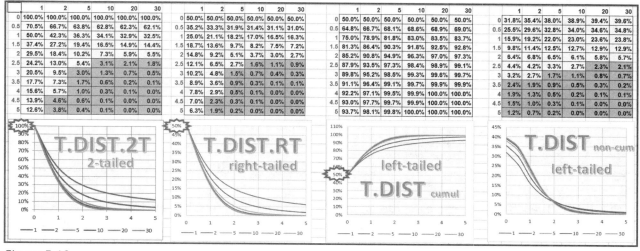

Figure 5.12

- `T.DIST.2T` returns the *two*-tailed *t*-distribution.

- `T.DIST.RT` returns the *right*-tailed *t*-distribution.

- `T.DIST` returns the *left*-tailed *t*-distribution (this one has an argument for cumulative or noncumulative; the noncumulative `T.DIST` comes closest to the right half of a bell distribution based on NORM.DIST).

Another major difference from the *normal* distribution is that the *t*-distribution takes into account the **size** of the sample; it does this by using *degrees of freedom*—which is the sample size minus 1 ($df = n - 1$). When the sample size increases, the *t*-curve becomes steeper, and high *t*-values become more unlikely. To put it differently, the x-axis of *t*-values extends farther to the right when the samples become smaller; it stretches like chewing gum.

The top table on the left in Figure 5.11 is based on a series of *t*-values (in column A) and a series of *degrees of freedom* (in row 1). The intersection uses `T.DIST.2T`, with cell B2 set to `=T.DIST.2T($A2,B$1)`.

The bottom table on the left does the same, but uses `T.DIST.RT`, with cell B15 set to `=T.DIST.RT($A15,B$14)`. Notice that 5% two-tailed is the same as 2.5% one-tailed (more on this later).

Notice also that higher *t*-values are more likely in smaller samples. When the sample size comes closer to 30, the scale of *t*-values becomes shorter; above 30, the *t*-scale is almost identical to the *Z*-scale. In other words, in samples over 30, you can use either distribution, but under 30, you should use the *t*-distribution because it acknowledges the relatively small size of the sample (which *Z* plainly ignores).

Another type of distribution, the *F*-distribution, which is plotted in Figure 5.13, is used for *variances*, instead of means. The variance is the average of the squared differences from the mean, whereas the *SD* is the square root of *variance*. The *F*-value (or *F*-ratio) compares the variances of two data sets: the larger variance divided by the smaller variance. *F* works with **two** *degrees of freedom*—the one that comes with the larger variance first.

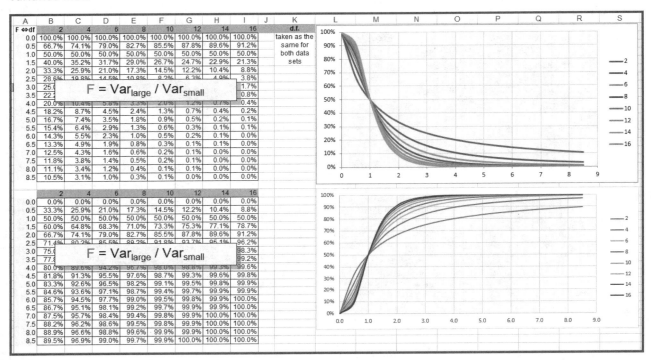

Figure 5.13

Both tables to the left use the same *degrees of freedom* for both data sets, but the top table uses F.DIST.RT, whereas the bottom one uses F.DIST. So the formula in cell B2 is `=F.DIST.RT($A2,B$1,B$1)` —which is the right-tailed version. The formula in B22 uses the left-tailed version: `=F.DIST($A22,B$1,B$1,TRUE)` — the last argument makes it cumulative.

Figure 5.14 shows another type of distribution: the *Chi-squared* distribution (*Chi-squared*, or χ^2). This is the perfect distribution for frequencies. With this distribution type, the *degrees of freedom* are related to the number of bins, or categories, you have used. There are two versions again: `CHISQ.DIST` for left-tailed situations (bottom table and graph) and `CHISQ.DIST.RT` for right-tailed ones (top table and graph). The formula in cell B2 is `=CHISQ.DIST.RT($A2,B$1).`, and in cell B22 `=CHISQ.DIST($A22,B$1,TRUE)`. Notice that more bins make higher *Chi*-values more likely—the opposite of what you see for a *t*-distribution.

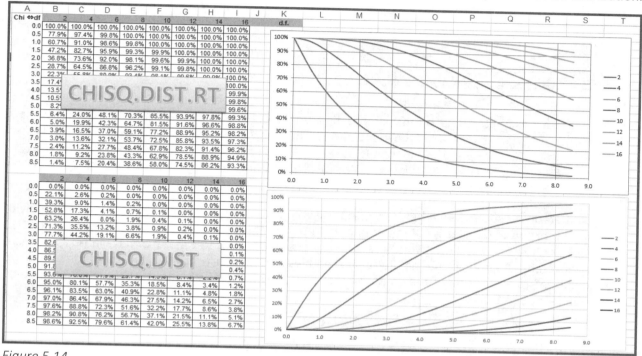

Figure 5.14

Figure 5.15 shows a fourth kind of distribution: the *binomial* distribution. Binomial distributions deal with *proportions*, such as the proportion of finding one of two. The classic example is head/tails, but anything dual or binary qualifies for a *binomial* distribution: yes/no, success/failure, sick/healthy, defect/non-defect, immunized/nonimmunized, male/female, increased/decreased, or even true/false.

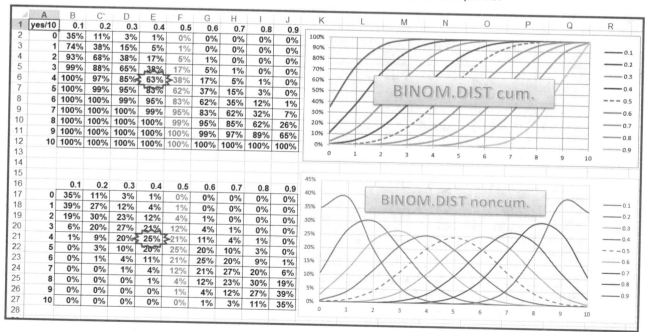

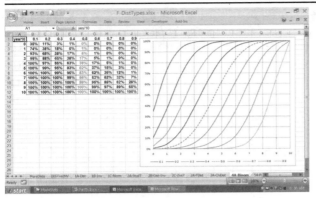

Figure 5.15

Let's consider an example: How often will you find **up to** 4 females in a sample of 10 individuals if the *proportion* of females is 0.4 in the population? The answer is 63%, as cell E6 shows: =BINOM. DIST($A6,$A$12,E$1,1). The function BINOM.DIST has four arguments: *number_s* (4), *trials* (10), *probability* (0.4), *cumulative* (1 or TRUE). The *proportion* of success (or yes) is *p*, whereas the *proportion* of failure (or no) is *(1-p)*.

A slightly different questions would be: How often will you find **exactly** 4 females in a sample of 10 individuals if the *proportion* of females is 0.4 in the population? The answer is 25%, as cell E21 shows: =BINOM. DIST($A21,$A$12,E$1,) —in which case the last argument is set to FALSE or left blank. The noncumulative version has a curve in the middle that resembles a normal distribution. But the other curves are more "squeezed" to either side of the graph. For "extremely squeezed" situations, there is an alternative: the *Poisson* distribution.

Note

This part of the book uses the word *probability* only for what DIST functions return, and it uses the term *proportion* (*p*) for the probability of "success." Some scientists, especially in the medical field, use *p* also for probabilities.

The left part of Figure 5.16 shows calculations for a *Poisson* distribution—noncumulative in column B and cumulative in column C. This type of distribution is for very rare occasions: low proportions (*p*) among numerous cases (*N*). The general rule is *Np<5*. (*Np* is also called the *mean*.) Notice how the results for the *Poisson* (on the left) and *binomial* (on the right) distributions come pretty close to each other. Cell B4 has the formula =BINOM.DIST($F4,$E$6,$E$9,0). Cell G4 has =BINOM.DIST($F4,$E$6,$E$9,0).

	A	B	C	D	E	F	G	H	I
1		POISSON					BINOMIAL		
2									
3		cumulative	non-cumul.				2%		
4	0	30.1%	30.1%		(should be >50)	0	29.8%	29.8%	
5	1	36.1%	66.3%		sample size	1	36.4%	66.2%	
6	2	21.7%	87.9%		60	2	21.9%	88.1%	
7	3	8.7%	96.6%			3	8.7%	96.8%	
8	4	2.6%	99.2%		% affected	4	2.5%	99.3%	
9	5	0.6%	99.8%		2%	5	0.6%	99.9%	
10	6	0.1%	100.0%			6	0.1%	100.0%	
11	7	0.0%	100.0%		Np=lambda=mean	7	0.0%	100.0%	
12	8	0.0%	100.0%		1.2	8	0.0%	100.0%	
13	9	0.0%	100.0%		(should be <5)	9	0.0%	100.0%	
14	10	0.0%	100.0%			10	0.0%	100.0%	
15									

Figure 5.16

Poisson distributions deal with the probability of rare events—but under two conditions: their occurrences are independent of each other; their probability is proportional to the length of the time interval. In science, *Poisson* distributions are used for situations such as the number of defects in production, the number of electrons emitted by a heated cathode, the number of mutations occurring in bacteria over time, and the number of atoms disintegrating per second in radioactive materials.

Figure 5.17 shows a typical example of a *Poisson* distribution. For each generation, you expect two mutations to occur in a large population of microorganisms. POISSON.DIST has three arguments: x (that is, the number of events), `mean`, and `cumulative`. In cell B2, the formula is =POISSON.DIST(B$1,$A$1*$A2,0). It may look strange that the total number of mutations (in column L) decreases after each generation, but don't forget that the table shows only up to nine mutations.

	A	B	C	D	E	F	G	H	I	J	K	L
1	2/generation	0	1	2	3	4	5	6	7	8	9	mutations
2	1	14%	27%	27%	18%	9%	4%	1%	0%	0%	0%	100%
3	2	2%	7%	15%	20%	20%	16%	10%	6%	3%	1%	99%
4	3	0%	1%	4%	9%	13%	16%	16%	14%	10%	7%	92%
5	4	0%	0%	1%	3%	6%	9%	12%	14%	14%	12%	72%
6	5	0%	0%	0%	1%	2%	4%	6%	9%	11%	13%	46%
7	6	0%	0%	0%	0%	1%	1%	3%	4%	7%	9%	24%
8	7	0%	0%	0%	0%	0%	0%	1%	2%	3%	5%	11%
9	8	0%	0%	0%	0%	0%	0%	0%	1%	1%	2%	4%
10	9	0%	0%	0%	0%	0%	0%	0%	0%	0%	1%	2%
11	10	0%	0%	0%	0%	0%	0%	0%	0%	0%	0%	0%
12	generations											

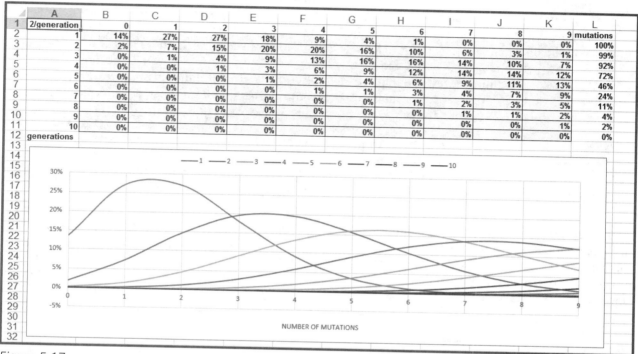

Figure 5.17

In the following chapters, you'll learn more about these five types of distributions:

- The *normal* distribution for *means* (with sample sizes over 30)

- The *t*-distribution for *means* of any sample size

- The *Chi-squared* distribution for *frequencies*

- The *binomial* (and *Poisson*) distribution for *proportions*

- The *F*-distribution for *variances.*

Chapter 47: Simulating Distributions

It is possible to simulate the types of distributions discussed in Chapter 46 and then show them on an Excel spreadsheet. You might want to do so, for example, to study their characteristics or to compare an empirical sample distribution with an ideal sampling distribution. You can make such *simulations* from the option *Data Analysis* on the *Data* tab. If that option is not available, you must install the *Analysis Toolpak* first as an add-in (see Chapter 35). Through the *Data Analysis* option, you can activate the option *Random Number Generation*.

Note

> When talking about random number generation, you may ask the question: How random are Excel's *random* numbers? Most random numbers used in computer programs are *pseudo-random*, which means they are generated in a predictable fashion using a mathematical formula. (Don't forget that the first 10,000 digits of π look random from the point of view of any tests concerning the existence of patterns, yet you know they are completely determined.) This is fine for many purposes, but it may not be random in the way you might expect. Pseudo-random number generators (*PRNGs*) are algorithms that can automatically create long runs of numbers with good random properties but eventually the sequence repeats (or the memory usage grows without bound).
>
> The string of values generated by such algorithms is generally determined by a fixed number called a *seed*. One of the most common pseudo-random-number-generators is the linear congruential generator, which uses the recurrence $X_{n+1} = (aX_n + b) \bmod m$ to generate its random numbers. The maximum number of numbers the formula can produce is the modulus, *m*.

Figure 5.18 shows the simulation of a *uniform* distribution type. The random number generator was instructed to generate 100 random numbers between 0 and 10 with a *uniform* distribution, so all numbers have an equal chance to occur. The frequency distribution in column D shows that this is more or less the case. Had you generated many more numbers, the results would be even more equally distributed. Be aware that the random numbers in column A are hard-coded, and not formulas, so you need to run the *Toolpak* again.

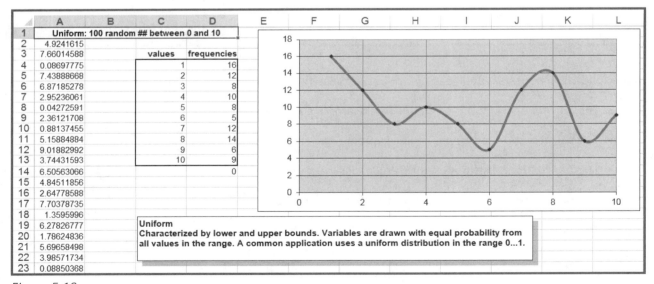

Figure 5.18

Note

> The dialog box also allows you to enter a *Random Seed*. If you leave this option empty, Excel uses its own pre-set seeds. Otherwise, enter an optional value from which to generate random numbers. You can reuse this value later to produce the same set of random numbers.

Figure 5.19 does something similar, but this time with formulas. Although column A was still done with the *Toolpak*, the rest was done with formulas. This is what you do:

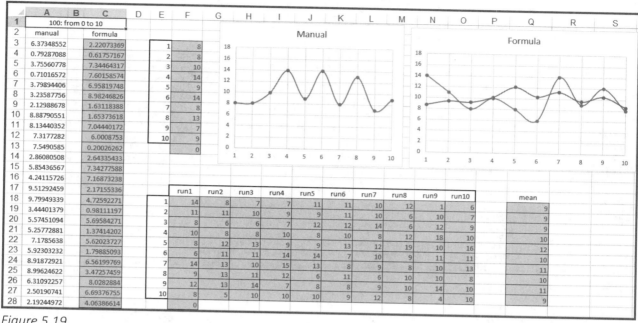

Figure 5.19

1. Place in cell C3 the formula =RAND()*10, and copy this formula down to A100. Once you put in a formula, the cell gets marked through *Conditional Formatting* applied to the entire sheet: =ISFORMULA(A1).

2. Calculate in F1:F13 the frequencies of the *Toolpak* results in column A. The left graph shows the results.

3. Calculate in F18:F28 the frequencies of the random numbers in column C. The right graph shows the results.

4. Since we generated only 100 numbers, we would get better results if we ran the first run at least 10 more times. We could easily do so with a *Data Table*, which we discussed earlier in Chapter 3. So take the following steps:

   ◦ Select F17:O27.

   ◦ Use *Data | What-if Analysis | Data Table*.

   ◦ Set the row input to an empty cell outside the table (e.g. E17) and leave the column input blank, for the column has already formulas.

   ◦ Hit *OK* and average the results in column Q.

   ◦ Each time you hit *F9* or *Shift+F9,* the first run is repeated nine more times, which is 10 x 100 = 1,000 random numbers. The graph on the right shows *run1* and the means of 10 runs.

Figure 5.20 shows a *normal* distribution created by the *Random Number Generator* based on the following settings: 100 numbers with a mean of 10 and *SD* of 0.5 (and no *seed*). After you calculate the frequencies, you get a simulated *normal* distribution in the graph to the right. But again, the results are "dead."

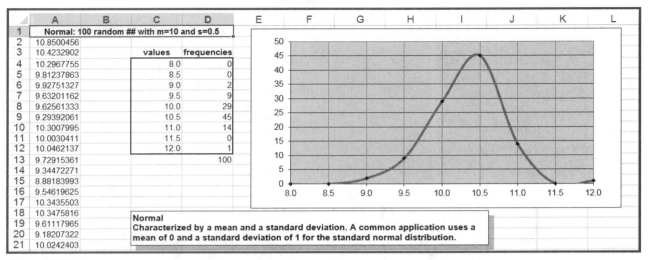

Figure 5.20

<u>Note</u>

The file you are working on in this chapter contains many *Data Tables*. Each time you change any value on any sheet, all the tables will recalculate, which may take some time. To prevent this from happening change some settings: *File | Options | Formulas | ⊙ Automatic except for data tables* (or choose ⊙ *Manual*, and then use *Shift+F9* to only recalculate the sheet you are on, or *F9* to recalculate the entire file).

Figure 5.21 does the previous simulation with formulas in column C and their results plotted in the right graph: 10 random numbers with a mean of 10 and *SD* of 3. (Column A and the left graph have *Toolpak* results.) The formula in C3 is =NORMINV(RAND(),10,3). Calculate the frequencies in F18:F28 again, and create a *Data Table* for 10 runs. The curve that always comes closest to a *normal* distribution is the one based on 10 runs.

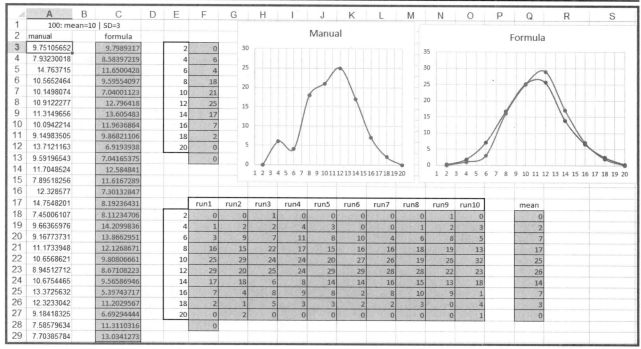

Figure 5.21

Figure 5.22 simulates a *discrete* distribution representing a situation where certain values occur with specific probabilities based on table C5:D8. An example would be multiple alleles of a gene, with each allele having its own frequency in a population. First you need to make a table of values and their probabilities. The table must contain two ranges: range C4:C13 for values and range D4:D13 for probabilities associated with the values in that row; the sum of the probabilities must be 1. Excel's *Random Number Generator* takes care of the rest, so you can create a frequency table and plot the results. The graph shows that the expected and generated values are not too far apart from each other, as long as you have a good size sample.

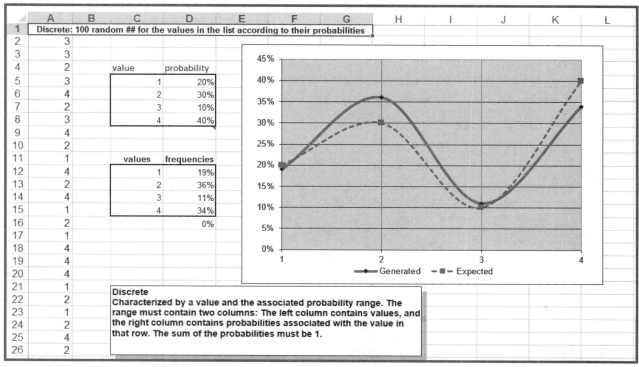

Figure 5.22

Figure 5.23 simulates another *discrete* distribution, but this time with the help of formulas. To generate discretely distributed random numbers, we must generate a random percentage and take the value that comes with it from the probabilities table in F2:G5 by using the function VLOOKUP. However, VLOOKUP can only look in the first column of the lookup table and it always looks for a previous value in an ascending order. So we need a column before F, with a formula that creates cumulative percentage totals running from 0% to 60% in this case. Here are all the steps together:

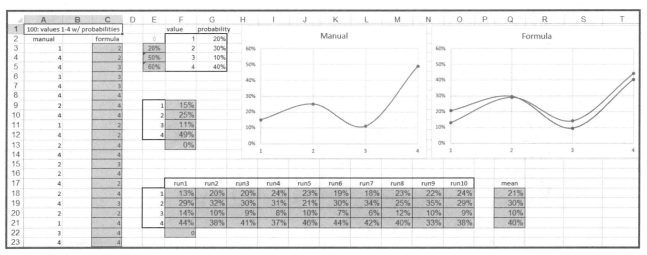

Figure 5.23

1. Place in cell E3 =SUM($G$2:G2), and copy down to E5. (The 0% in E2 covers everything from 0% to 20%.)

2. Place in cell C3 =VLOOKUP(RAND(),$E$2:$G$5,2,1), and copy down to C102.

3. Calculate in F9:F13 the frequencies of the *Toolpak* results in column A. The left graphs plots them.

4. Calculate in F18:F22 the frequencies of the formula results in column C and execute nine more runs with a *Data Table*.

Figure 5.24 simulates a *binomial* distribution. In this case, it is based on 100 random numbers with *p=0.5* and 10 trials. The curve happens to look like a normal distribution because *p* equals 0.5 in this case. The curve would get more squeezed to the left or right if *p* were closer to 0 or 1.

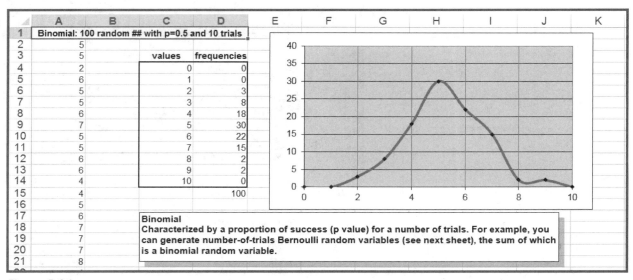

Figure 5.24

Figure 5.25 uses formulas to simulate another *binomial* distribution, based on 23 trials and a *p*-value specified in cell F1. The formula in cell C3 is =BINOM.INV(23,$F$1,RAND()). The rest is the same as you did in previous simulation cases. When you lower the *p*-value, the curve shifts to the left.

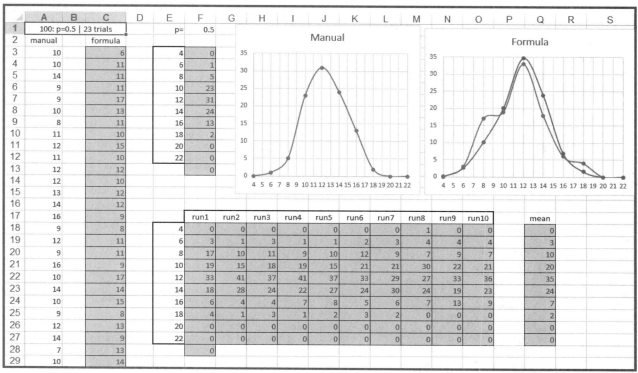

Figure 5.25

Figure 5.26 shows a *Poisson* distribution generated by the *Toolpak*. In this case, the distribution shows a pattern of the number of events that occur per unit of time given the fact that they have on average 3 occurrences per time unit.

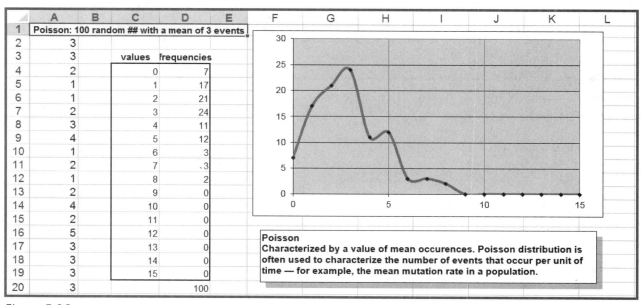

Figure 5.26

Figure 5.27 uses formulas to generate a *Poisson* distribution again—100 numbers with 3 events per unit of time. Because there is only a `BINOM.DIST` function, but no `BINOM.INV` function, you must use in column C the function `VLOOKUP` to find values in the table E19:G27. Here are the formulas:

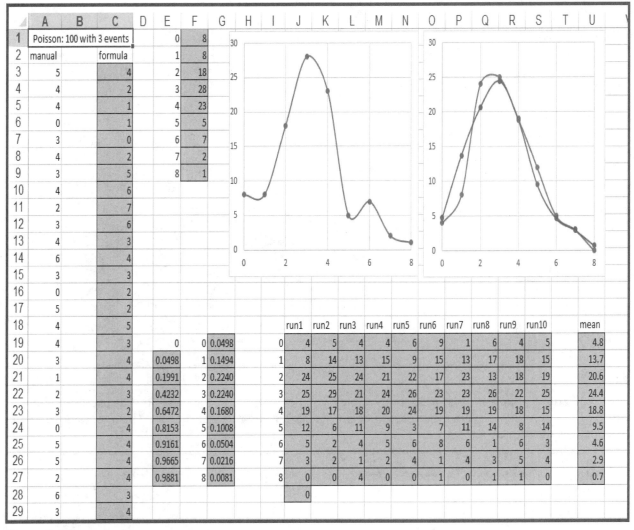

Figure 5.27

1. In C3: `=VLOOKUP(RAND(),$E$19:$G$27,2,TRUE)`.

2. In E20: `=SUM($G$19:G19)`.

3. In G19: `=POISSON.DIST(F19,3,FALSE)`.

4. The rest you can do on your own.

Figure 5.28 deals with a *lognormal* distribution. As there is no *Toolpak* version for this type of distribution, you need to create one with formulas. Here are the formulas:

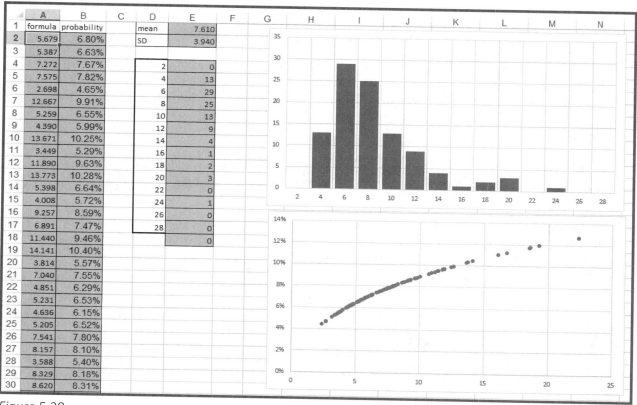

Figure 5.28

1. Place in column A: `=LOGNORM.INV(RAND(),2,0.5)`.

2. Calculate in E4:E18 the frequencies of the numbers in column A. The top graph plots these results.

3. Place in column B: `=LOGNORM.DIST(A2,$E$1,$E$2,TRUE)`. These probabilities are for the bottom graph.

This chapter uses *simulations* quite a bit. If you would like to explore how simulations can do great work for you in many areas of interest—from physics to genetics, from finances to Monte Carlo simulations—go for my book *Excel Simulations* (www.mrexcel.com). It has almost 100 different simulations for various areas of interest.

Let's examine the *normal* distribution in greater depth by using Figure 5.29:

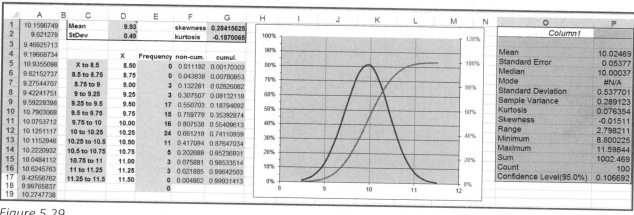

Figure 5.29

1. Create, in column A, 100 random numbers according to a *normal* distribution, with a mean of 10 and a *SD* of 0.5: `=NORM.INV(RAND(),10,0.5)`.

2. Calculate the actual mean of these numbers in cell D1 and the *SD* in cell D2. The randomness of 100 cases makes the mean and *SD* slightly deviate from the targets set in your formula.

3. Use the function `SKEW` in cell G2. Positive *skewness* indicates an asymmetric distribution with values bunched up on the low end of the scale and a tail extending toward more positive values; negative *skewness* indicates an asymmetric distribution with values bunched up on the high end of the scale and a tail extending toward more negative values.

Note

At what point is a distribution too much skewed? A rough estimate of the standard error of `SKEW` (*SES*) is `SQRT(6/N)`. So more than 2x *SES* is considered significantly skewed.

4. Use the function `KURT` in cell G2 to characterize the relative *peakedness* or flatness (that is, *kurtosis*) of a distribution compared with the *normal* distribution. Ideal *normal* distributions produce a *kurtosis* statistic of about 0. As the *kurtosis* statistic departs further from 0, a positive value indicates a taller distribution, and a negative value a flatter distribution.

Note

When is a distribution too flat or too peaked? A rough estimate of the standard error of `KURT` (*SEK*) is `SQRT(24/N)`. So more than 2x *SEK* is considered significantly flattened or peaked. When is a distribution too flat or too peaked? A rough estimate of the standard error of `KURT` (*SEK*) is `SQRT(24/N)`. So more than 2x *SEK* is considered significantly flattened or peaked.

5. Create the frequency bins in column D and the frequency for each bin in column E.

6. Use `NORM.DIST` in columns F:G. (The sum of the probabilities in column F may be greater than 1, because the bins are too gross.)

7. Instead of taking the above steps, if you want a quick overview of your main statistics, you can use the *Analysis Toolpak*'s *Descriptive Statistics* option. You must specify in the dialog box that you want ☑ *Summary Statistics*. The output in O1:P17 should be the same as in the formulas D1:D2 and G1:G2, but when column A recalculates, the *Toolpak* figures become outdated, unless you apply the tool again.

Note

In addition to the *Mean* (the sum of values divided by the count), the *Toolpak* also features a *Median* (the value in the middle of a sorted data set) and a *Mode* (the most frequently occurring value in a data set). The statistic most sensitive to skewed data is the *Mean*. In case of a positive *skewness*, these statistics have the following relationship: *Mode* < *Median* < *Mean*.

Chapter 48: Sampling Techniques

The validity of research depends on good samples. Good samples must have the proper size in order to be representative. In addition, good samples need items that had an equal chance to be chosen. In so-called *biased* samples, some items are more likely to be chosen than others—and that's not make for good research. Unfortunately, the mind's eye is not a good guide in selecting items for a sample. You need the unbiased verdict of a mathematical tool.

Scientists have many sampling tools available. The simplest one is the RAND function, as illustrated in Figure 5.30. Here's how you can use it:

	A	B	C	D	E	F	G
1	Biased Samples: Some more likely to be chosen than others						
2							
3	Top 5	Plate ID	Analyst		25%	Plate ID	Analyst
4	0.9635	8877p58b	bdo			8696p08a	ksm
5	0.9182	8877p58b	tkm			8696p08a	ksm
6	0.8744	8697p58b	tjk			8696p08a	gmv
7	0.8217	8697p58b	tjk		+	8696p08a	gmv
8	0.7938	8697p58b	tkm			8696p08b	bdo
9	0.7108	8877p58b	tkm			8696p08b	bdo
10	0.7034	8696p08b	ksm			8696p08b	ksm
11	0.6750	8877p58a	gmv			8696p08b	ksm
12	0.6725	8696p08a	gmv		+	8697p58b	tjk
13	0.5101	8697p58b	tkm			8697p58b	tjk
14	0.4543	8696p08b	bdo			8697p58b	tkm
15	0.3745	8877p58b	bdo			8697p58b	tkm
16	0.2768	8696p08b	bdo			8877p58a	gmv
17	0.2615	8696p08a	ksm			8877p58a	gmv
18	0.1797	8877p58a	tjk		+	8877p58a	tjk
19	0.1795	8696p08a	ksm			8877p58a	tjk
20	0.1460	8696p08b	ksm		+	8877p58b	tkm
21	0.0823	8877p58a	gmv			8877p58b	tkm
22	0.0440	8696p08a	gmv			8877p58b	bdo
23	0.0118	8877p58a	tjk			8877p58b	bdo
24							

Figure 5.30

1. In column A, apply the function RAND.

2. Change the formula results into values: *Copy | Paste Special | ⊙ Values*.

3. Sort the values by random number.

4. Select the first *n* items for your sample. (Later in this chapter, we'll discuss what the magnitude of *n* should be.)

5. If you want a certain percentage of cases (see cell E3), and you want even this percentage to be randomly fluctuating, you can use RAND again but this time nested inside an IF function, as is done in cell E4: =IF(RAND()<$E$3,"+",""). Each time you press *F9* (or *Shift+F9*), you get a different sample of cases of varying sizes.

The *Analysis Toolpak* has also a simple sampling tool, as Figure 5.31 demonstrates. An ideal sampling technique puts a chosen item back into the population so it can be chosen again; in science, however, this is not a common practice. Figure 5.31 shows the use of the sampling tool that comes with the *Analysis Toolpak*.

	A	B	C	D	E	F	G
1	1		Using the Sampling tool in the Analysis Toolpak				
2	92						
3	6		Col A: 100 unique numbers between 1 and 100				
4	63						
5	61		sample of 20		one more of 20		periodic (5)
6	38		64		19		61
7	93		27		49		75
8	39		34		100		76
9	12		72		64		56
10	75		74		99		52
11	45		20		36		57
12	33		16		43		21
13	68		94		93		65
14	69		35		29		32
15	76		81		42		83
16	51		1		72		74
17	95		2		77		17
18	43		40		76		30
19	90		19		70		50
20	56		32		87		13
21	88		40		5		37
22	73		81		44		18
23	27		38		9		41
24	94		22		77		86
25	52		36		89		48
26	81						

Figure 5.31

- Column C has the result of choosing ⊙ *Random* for a sample of 20. Notice that there happens to be a duplicate set in the outcome—but you may not have this.

- Another draw of 20 items in column E happens to include another set of duplicates—at least in this example.

- Choosing the option ⊙ *Periodic* in column G eliminates duplicates if the original list doesn't have any. But the original list should not have some hidden periodic pattern.

Figure 5.32 shows another sampling tool, called *weighted sampling*. Items would have different chances to be included in a sample by giving them each a "weight" (column C). In column D, you could give them a "bar code" according to a table placed to the right in I3:J6. The main secret of this tool is located in column A, where you give each place a cumulative "weight," so plate 2 (in A4) is *0+4*, plate 3 is *0+4+2*, and so on. The second secret is 10 VLOOKUP formulas located in column F for 10 "weighted" items. Here are the steps:

	A	B	C	D	E	F	G	H	I	J
1					10 weighted plate numbers					
2	cumul.	plate#	weight	bar		sample of 10	weighted			
3	0	203	1	+		209	++++		1	+
4	1	204	4	++++		214	+		2	++
5	5	205	2	++		204	++++		3	+++
6	7	206	1	+		215	++++		4	++++
7	8	207	1	+		203	+			
8	9	208	1	+		213	+			
9	10	209	4	++++		225	++			
10	14	210	3	+++		224	++++			
11	17	212	1	+		219	+			
12	18	213	1	+		210	+++			
13	19	214	1	+						
14	20	215	4	++++						
15	24	216	2	++						
16	26	217	1	+						
17	27	218	1	+						
18	28	219	1	+						
19	29	224	4	++++						
20	33	225	2	++						
21	35	228	1	+						
22	36	240	1	+						
23										

Figure 5.32

1. In cell A4, enter the formula =A3+C3, and copy the formula down to cell A23.

2. In cell D3: =VLOOKUP(C3,$I$3:$J$6,2,0), and copy down.

3. In cell F3: =VLOOKUP($A$23*RAND(), $A$3:$B$22, 2). The function RAND takes a random number between 0 (in cell A3) and 37 (in cell A23). The second plate, for instance, has four times more chances (from 1 to 5) to be selected than the first plate (from 0 to 1).

4. The last step, in column G, is purely for cosmetic reasons—to show or prove that plates with a higher rank tend to be chosen more often. Hitting *F9* will demonstrate it.

A second important sampling rule says that the *sample* must have a proper size to be representative for the *population*. One of the considerations is this: The larger the *SD* is in proportion to the *mean*, the larger the sample should be (which is in the last part in the formula). Another consideration is this: The closer you want to stay to the mean (called the *margin* in this case), the larger the sample should be (which is in the first part in the formula). This technique and its formula are shown in Figure 5.33:

	A	B	C	D	E	F	G	H	I	J
1										
2		Z or t				margin/mean				
3			1.96	0.01	0.02	0.05	0.1	0.25		
4			0.1	384	96	15	4	1		
5			0.2	1537	384	61	15	2		
6			0.3	3457	864	138	35	6		
7			0.4	6147	1537	246	61	10		
8			0.5	9604	2401	384	96	15		
9		SD/mean	0.6	13830	3457	553	138	22		
10			0.7	18824	4706	753	188	30		
11			0.8	24586	6147	983	246	39		
12			0.9	31117	7779	1245	311	50		
13			1	38416	9604	1537	384	61		
14			2	153664	38416	6147	1537	246		
15			3	345744	86436	13830	3457	553		
16										
17										
18										
19		SD	0.32	0.0771084						
20		Mean	4.15							
21		Margin	0.11	0.026506						
22		Z or t	1.96							
23										
24		Size		32.510731						
25										

$$n = \left(\frac{1.96}{margin\,/\,\mu} \right)^2 \left(\frac{SD}{\mu} \right)^2$$

Figure 5.33

1. In cell D4, enter the formula =$C4^2*($C$3/D$3)^2. After you apply the formula, you find out what the minimum sample size should be under the given conditions.

2. In the section below the table, apply parts of the formula as follows:

   ◦ Cell D19: =C19/C20

   ◦ Cell D21: =C21/C20

   ◦ Cell D24: =D19^2*(C22/D21)^2

These results say that you need a sample size of at least 33 to have 95% confidence of finding a mean between 4.04 (*4.15-0.11*) and 4.26 (*4.15+0.11*).

Figure 5.34 tests how often you detect defects in samples of different sizes from batches with different sizes.

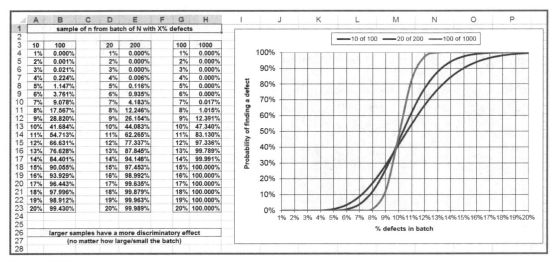

Figure 5.34

- Cell B4 holds the following formula: `=1-BINOM.DIST($A$3,$B$3,A4,1)`. To determine the chances of finding defects, you must use `1-BINOM.DIST` because the chance of rejecting the batch is 1 minus the chance of accepting the batch. There is a similar formula in cells B4 and H4.

- Now we can find out, for instance, what the chance would be of detecting a defect in a sample of 10 from a batch of 100 that has 7% defects. The answer is: a chance of 9% (cell B10).

- Based on the data, we can conclude that larger samples have a more discriminatory effect.

- Apparently the ratio of sample-size to batch-size doesn't matter at all. Only sample size matters.

Figure 5.35 shows all this in action. By moving the scroll-bar *control* located above the table, you can see the effect of increasing sample sizes:

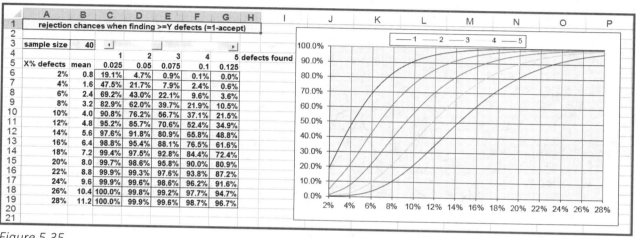

Figure 5.35

- Because the size of the batch doesn't matter, this example uses only the size of the sample (in cell B3).

- Because you use the `POISSON.DIST` function in this example, you also need the mean, which is *Np*, so you enter `=A6*$B$3` in column B.

- The formula in cell C6 is `=1-POISSON.DIST(C$4,$B6,1)`.

- This example calculates the chances of rejecting a batch when greater than or equal to y defects are found. There is, for instance, a 62% chance (cell D9) of rejecting a sample of 40 with 2 defects taken from a batch with 8% defects.

- By moving the control, you can see the effect of changing sample sizes.

Chapter 49: Test Conditions and Outliers

When should you use which sampling distribution? We have discussed some general considerations—such as using the *binomial* distribution for *proportions*. However, most distributions are subject to some extra conditions. The most frequent condition is that a sample—and thus the population it is taken from—must be normally distributed. And this is not always the case, as you most likely realize.

Figure 5.36 shows with a few plots what can go "wrong" with a bell-shaped distribution:

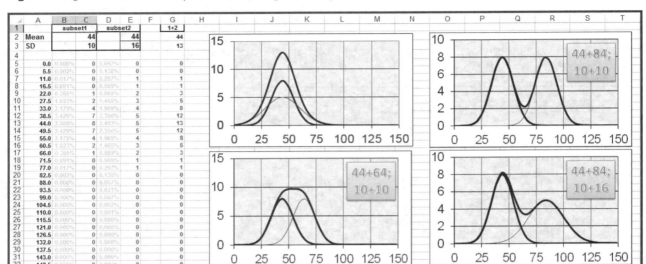

Figure 5.36

- The top curve on the left has the nice bell-shape of a *normal* distribution, but is actually based on two subsets—which could be a subset of males and a subset of females, for instance—each of which has its own bell shape. The two subsets have the same mean (44) but different variances (10 and 16), so the total curve looks and is normally distributed.

- In the bottom curve on the left, the two subsets have a different mean (44 and 64) but the same variance (10). As a result, the total curve looks and is normally distributed again.

- If the means of the subsets were farther apart, though, the curve would become *bimodal*. (A *mode* is a peak in a curve.) This is the case with the top graph on the right; it has the same variances (10) but very different means (44 and 84).

- If the variances of the subsets were different as well (10 and 16), that would definitely affect the *skewness* of the curve. The lower curve on the right is an example of this situation. In other words, the means of the samples taken from this population would not vary equally to either side of the mean of the population.

For "abnormal" situations like the last two, you could not use the *normal* sampling distribution to test the sample for issues such as estimating, significance, and confidence—so Z-values or t-values become useless, or at least unreliable. In Figure 5.37 we have a similar problem. It is based on a *Poisson* distribution; cell B3 has the following formula: =POISSON($A3,B$2,0). Curves like these are usually not normally distributed, so we cannot test them as if it were a *normal* distribution.

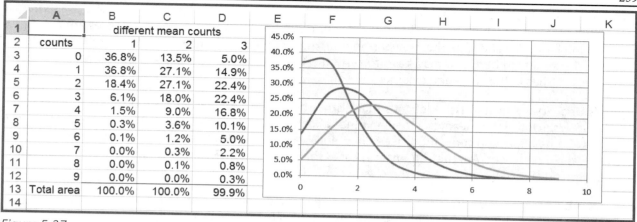

counts	different mean counts		
	1	2	3
0	36.8%	13.5%	5.0%
1	36.8%	27.1%	14.9%
2	18.4%	27.1%	22.4%
3	6.1%	18.0%	22.4%
4	1.5%	9.0%	16.8%
5	0.3%	3.6%	10.1%
6	0.1%	1.2%	5.0%
7	0.0%	0.3%	2.2%
8	0.0%	0.1%	0.8%
9	0.0%	0.0%	0.3%
Total area	100.0%	100.0%	99.9%

Figure 5.37

Apparently, statistical testing comes with certain conditions. Figure 5.38 provides an overview of some conditions.

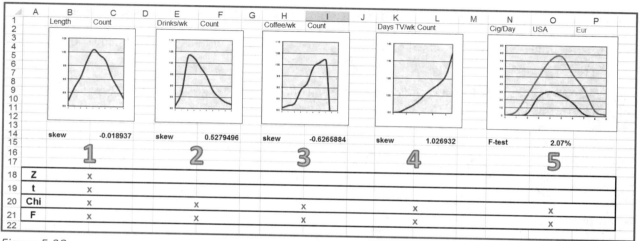

Figure 5.38

- Cases 2 through 4 are heavily skewed (row 14), whereas case 5 has two very different variances, or *SD*s.

- The *Z*-test and the *t*-test (rows 18 and 19) can be used only when the samples or populations are not too skewed and do not vary too much in their variances (case 1).

- An added condition for *Z* versus *t* is that *Z* can only be used for samples greater than 30, as mentioned earlier.

- The *Chi-squared* test does not have these extra conditions and can be applied even in the absence of a normally distributed sample and/or population, but it has another, minor requirement, which is discussed in Chapter 54.

- Although the *p*-distribution applies only to *binomial* situations, sometimes the *binomial* sampling distribution can be a solution that works where the previous distributions have failed. See Chapter 53.

You end up with the following series of alternatives: When a *Z*-value is not possible because the sample is too small, a *t*-value may be feasible. When that is out of the question because the variances are too different, you can try an *F*-value. If all the previous ones are unacceptable because the sample and/or population is not normally distributed, you may have to reshuffle the data and try *p* and/or *Chi*. You will learn more about these issues in the chapters to come.

There is one closely related issue left. Normal distributions can easily be affected by the presence of so-called *outliers*. (Unlike the mean, the median is not affected by *outliers* and *skewness*.) Besides, *outliers* can have quite some impact on curve fitting (see Chapters 35 and 37) and statistical analysis. So you need to spot them and diagnose them. Are they anomalous cases that you should discard? Are they erroneous measurements that you should ignore? Or are they just a random but very improbably outcome?

Outliers are defined as numeric values in any random data set that have an unusually high deviation from either the statistical mean or the median value. The reasons for such a deviation can be very diverse:

- *Outliers* can occur by chance in any distribution. Especially when dealing with large samples, we should expect a small number of *outliers*.

- Sometimes, *outliers* are indicative of measurement errors. If so, measure again or discard them.

- Sometimes, they are an indication that we are indeed dealing with a heavy-tailed distribution, in which case *Z*- and *t*-values become questionable.

Figure 5.39 shows three different techniques of locating *outliers*. In this case, column E spotted two *outliers*, column M three, and column K only one. In general, the third technique is the most cautious one. Here is what each one does:

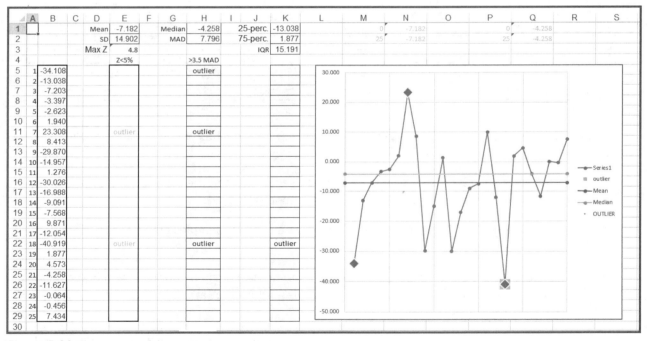

Figure 5.39

- The first, rather simple, method is based on *Z*-values (provided you have more than 30 cases). When the *Z*-value of an observation point has a probability under 5% or 2.5%, you could consider that observation an *outlier*. However, you should not use *Z* itself but rather its probability, for *Z* can never get larger than $(N-1)/\sqrt{N}$.

- A more robust statistical technique is based on the *Median Absolute Deviation* (*MAD*). Any number in a data set exceeding 3.5 times *MAD* is considered an *outlier*.

- In the 1970s, the famous statistician John Tukey came up with a more formal definition. He called any observation value an *outlier* if it is smaller than the first quartile (cell K1) minus 1.5 times the *IQR* (cell K3), or larger than the third quartile (cell K2) plus 1.5 times the *IQR*. The *Inter-Quartile Range, IQR,* is the width of the interval that contains the middle half of the data.

Figure 5.39 shows how all this can be done:

1. Place in cell B5: `=NORMINV(RAND(),30,15)*(1-2*RAND())`. This formula will randomly create *outliers* every once in a while. Copy the formula down.

2. Place in cell E5: `=IF(NORM.S.DIST(ABS(B5-$E$1)/$E$2,FALSE)<0.05,"outli-er","")`. Copy the formula down.

3. Calculate *MAD* in cell H2: `=MEDIAN(ABS(MEDIAN(B5:B29)-B5:B29))`. This is an array formula, so you must use *Ctrl+Shift+Enter*.

4. Place in cell H5: `=IF(ABS(H$1-B5)>(3.5*H$2), "outlier", "")`. Copy the formula down.

5. Calculate *IQR* in cell K3: `=AVERAGE($B$5:$B$29)+(1.5*(K2-K1))`.

6. Enter in cell K5: `=IF(OR(B5>($K$2+1.5*$K$3),B5<($K$1-1.5*$K$3)),"outli-er","")`. Copy the formula down.

7. Place in cell N5: `=IF(H5="OUTLIER",B5,NA())`. Copy the formula down. This formula marks *outliers* in the graph for the second technique (see Chapter 32).

8. Place in cell O5: `=IF(K5="outlier",B5,NA())`. Copy the formula down. This formula marks *outliers* in the graph for the third technique.

Locating an *outlier* is one thing, but what to do with it is a completely different ball game:

- The value is interesting. You may have discovered a polymorphism in a gene, or a new clinical syndrome or so.

- The value is a mistake—a reading error or a faulty data entry.

- The distribution is not *normal*, but perhaps a *lognormal* distribution with a heavy tail, or another type of distribution.

- The value may simply be the tail of a *normal* distribution. If you define *alpha* to be 5%, then you'll mistakenly identify an *outlier* in 5% of the samples you test.

Now that you know the basics of some sampling distributions and their limitations, you should be ready to estimate error margins based on samples (see Chapters 50 and 51) and test for significance based on samples (see Chapters 52 to 54).

Chapter 50: Estimating Means

Finding a specific mean in a sample does not imply that other samples taken from the same population will have the same mean—nor will the population. Remember the slogan "Results may vary"? In other words, the mean found in the sample stands for a much wider range of means. A scientist must estimate the margins around the mean found in a specific sample. These margins are often called the "margins of error."

Say that in a normally distributed sample, you have measured a mean of 4.15 (pH, °C, ng/ml, mol, or whatever). Now you need to estimate which range of means you should/could expect in other samples taken from that same population. Let's go for 95% of the *normal* curve, so the *mean*$_{exp}$ ranges from a minimum value (at 1.96 * *SE* to the left of *mean*$_{obs}$) to a maximum value (at 1.96 * *SE* to the right of *mean*$_{obs}$). The distance to the left and the right of the observed mean is called a *confidence limit*, *confidence margin*, or *margin of error*. Figure 5.40 depicts this scenario for a normal distribution based on a *Z*-test. So you end up with a statement like this: The mean is 4.15±0.11, or something like that.

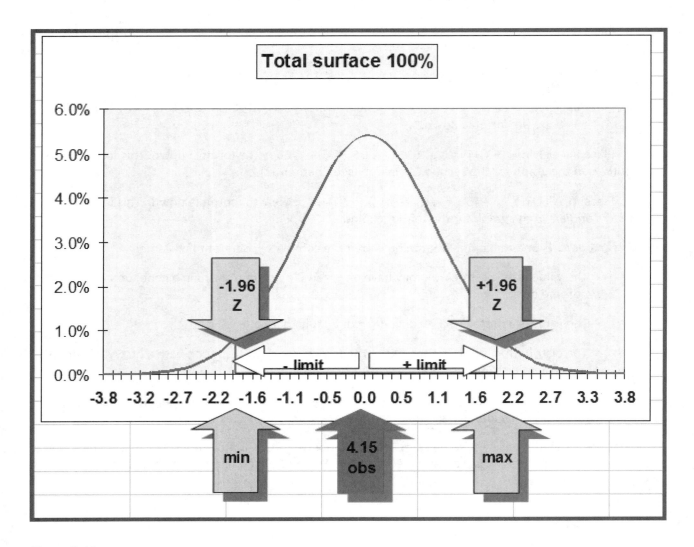

Figure 5.40

The 95% area under the curve that you usually choose represents the area you want to be covered. So you can say that you have 95% confidence that the mean will be found inside the stated range. The area under the curve to the left of the minimum value amounts to 2.5% (or half of the area outside the 95% confidence range). The area under the curve to the right of the maximum value amounts also to 2.5% (or half of the area outside the 95% confidence range). Because you are checking the lower range as well as the upper range, you are dealing with a *two*-tailed situation:

- The cumulative probability of -1.96 Z (at the left tail) is 2.5%.

- The probability of +1.96 Z (at the right tail) is 97.5% because you are dealing with cumulative probabilities.

Be aware, though, that the situation is a bit different for the t-distribution because that distribution is typically not symmetrical (so there are usually no negative t-values). You therefore need to treat t-values differently, as Figure 5.41 shows you:

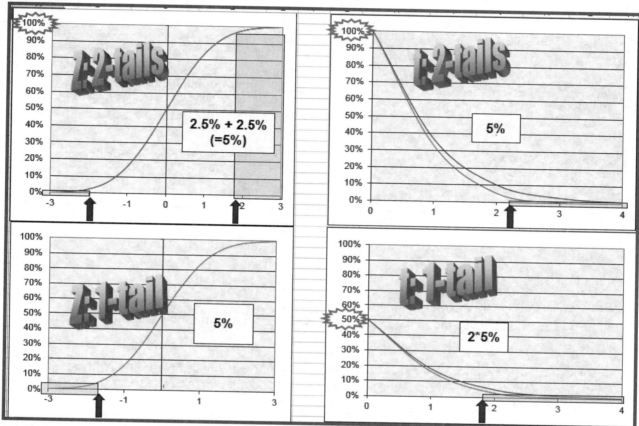

Figure 5.41

- In a two-tailed test, you would choose 5%.

- In a one-tailed test, you would choose 2.5%.

Figure 5.42 shows an example of estimating the margin (of error) around the mean—with either *Z*-values or *t*-values. The first situation is as follows: In a sample of 35 cases, you have measured a mean of 4.15 and a *SD* of 0.32. But, again, "results may vary." In other words, you shouldn't come up with a single value but with a range of values when talking about the mean. What are the lowest mean and the highest mean you could encounter with 95% confidence? In order to find out, you need the *Z*-value that comes with 2.5%, plus the *SE* of this sample mean. Here's how you find it:

	A	B	C	D	E	F	G	H	I	J	K	L	M	N
1											confidence limit			confidence intervals
2														
3		SAMPLES						Confidence					Mean	
4	Feature	Mean	SD	Count		Level	2-tails	1-tail	Z or t	StErr	Margin	Min	Max	
5														
6														
7		size over 30							Z	use *Normal* Distribution				
8	Weight	4.15	0.32	35		95%	5%	2.5%	-1.96	0.05	0.11	4.04	4.26	
9							Confidence uses 5%+SD:				0.11	4.04	4.26	
10														
11														
12		size under 30							t	use t-table: *t*-Distribution				
13	Weight	4.15	0.32	10		95%	5%	2.5%	2.26	0.10	0.23	3.92	4.38	
14							Confidence uses 5%+SD:				0.23	3.92	4.38	
15														

Figure 5.42

1. In cell I8, calculate the *Z*-value that comes with 2.5%: `=NORM.S.INV(H8)`.

2. In cell J8, find the standard error: `=C8/SQRT(D8)`.

3. In cell K8, calculate the *margin* (of error) or *confidence limit* on either side of the mean: `=ABS(I8)*J8`. You use the function `ABS` because it does not matter now whether *Z* is positive or negative.

4. In cell L8, use the formula `=B8-K8` to find the *lowest* mean you expect to find (with 95% confidence) in another sample of the same size and the same population. And use the formula `=B8+K8` in cell M8 to find the *highest* mean.

5. If you find this margin of 0.11 too wide, either reduce the level of confidence (which is not wise to do!) or increase the size of the sample (which costs you or your employer more time and money!). You can determine what the proper sample size would be—if you want to reduce the margin to 0.05, for instance—by using *Goal Seek* (see Chapter 41).

6. If you find the above steps too involved, you can use the function `CONFIDENCE.NORM` instead. However, this function works a bit differently:

   ○ It uses one tail (so 5% instead of 2.5%).

   ○ It calls for the *SD* instead of the *SE*; it does the required calculation for you!

   ○ The formula in cell K9 would be `=CONFIDENCE.NORM(G8,C8,D8)`.

Next let's tackle the same sample again, but this time based on a smaller sample size (10 vs. 35). Because of the small sample size (under 30), you cannot use *Z*-values but only *t*-values. You could do all the statistical work manually, as follows:

1. Find the *t*-value in cell I13: `=T.INV.2T(G13,D13-1)`. Because `T.INV.2T` uses two tails, you must look for the *t*-value that comes with the 5% area outside the confidence area of 95%. Had you

used the one-tailed version, $\mathtt{T.INV}$, based on 2.5%, you would have gotten the same result, but this time negative: -2.26.

2. Use the same formulas in J13:M13 as in the previous scenario (J8:M8).

3. If you prefer a quicker way, use $\mathtt{CONFIDENCE.T}$ instead. Enter in cell K14: $\mathtt{=CONFI\text{-}DENCE.T(G13,C13,D13)}$. Again, it uses one tail (so 5% instead of 2.5%) and it calls for the *SD*, not the *SE*.

Obviously, the margins are quite different for the first sample and the second sample because *t*-distributions are more cautious when the sample size becomes smaller. Smaller samples are more susceptible to random effects. The *t*-distribution would give you results similar to the *Z*-distribution if you increased the sample size to 35, as in the first sample. Just try it out on your spreadsheet.

It is common policy to use a 5% error range, as explained in Chapter 52. However, you or your organization may decide for some reason to change this number someday or in certain cases. If so, you have to change all your formulas and/or cell entries. So it might be prudent to use a *name* that represents the current standard of 5%. To do this, follow these steps:

1. On the *Formulas* tab, select *Name Manager*.

2. Click the *New* button and type its new *Name*: $\mathtt{signific}$ (or whatever name you want).

3. Set *Refers To* to $\mathtt{=0.05}$.

4. Instead of typing 5% in your formulas, use the *name* $\mathtt{signific}$ (or whatever name you chose) from now on. When you change what the *name* refers to, all cells using that *name* will automatically apply the new value.

You could use this method in Figure 5.43.

	A	B	C	D	E	F	G	H	I	J	K	L	M
1	Hb A1C	Glucose				Mean	SD	Count	5%?	t	SE	Margin	Min	Max
2	5.5	110		Hb A1C	7.513	1.6133	15	0.05	2.1448	0.4165	0.8934	6.620	8.407
3	5.5	118		Glucose	138.73	17.718	15	0.05	2.1448	4.5747	9.8118	128.921	148.545
4	5.8	115											
5	6.1	120											
6	6.5	125											
7	6.8	146											
8	7.1	135											
9	7.4	140											
10	7.7	145											
11	8.0	145											
12	8.0	150											
13	8.3	147											
14	9.0	155											
15	10.0	160											
16	11.0	170											
17													

Figure 5.43

1. Place in the cells H2 and H3: $\mathtt{=signific}$.

2. Place in cell I2: $\mathtt{=T.INV.2T(H2,G2\text{-}1)}$. Copy to I3.

3. Place in cell J2: $\mathtt{=F2/SQRT(G2)}$. Copy to J3.

4. Place in cell K2: $\mathtt{=J2*I2}$. Copy to K3.

5. Place in cell L2: $\mathtt{=E2\text{-}K2}$. And do something similar for the remaining cells.

Chapter 37 discusses a regression graph like the one depicted in Figure 5.44. This chapter doesn't go through all the details again, but now that you've learned more about statistics, it might be easier to understand what's happening in this graph. The regression line is based on sample information, but samples represent a range of possible values that fluctuate per sample. *RSQ* may be strong in this particular sample, but it is an altogether different issue whether this sample is representative for future samples taken from the same population. Therefore, you also want to find a *margin of error* based on 95% confidence. Because the CONFIDENCE function cannot achieve this, you need to do manual work again—which is even more involved than what you did earlier in this chapter. After finishing all necessary calculations, you end up with two different intervals:

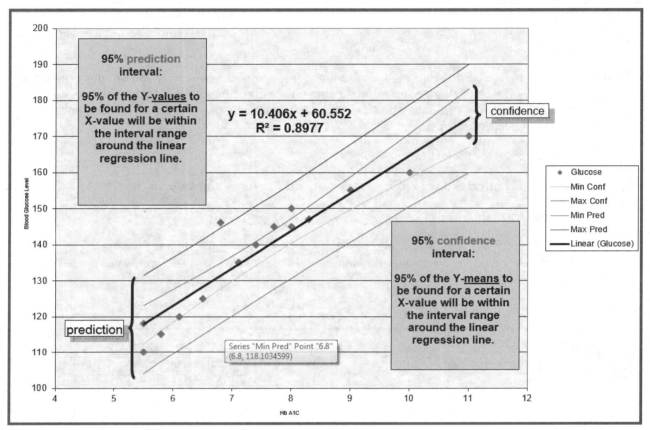

Figure 5.44

- The outer range is the 95% *prediction* interval for individual observations. For each x-value, 95% of the individual y-values is to be expected within this range, if each y-value represents a single observation.

- The inner range is the 95% *confidence* interval for averaged observations. For each x-value, 95% of the mean y-values is to be expected within this range, if each y-value represents the mean of a series of replicates.

Chapter 51: Estimating Proportions

When finding a specific *binomial* proportion, *p*, in a sample, you realize now that you should expect a wider range when taking other samples from the same population. Although those proportions don't completely follow a *normal* distribution pattern, they do come close.

Before going into confidence limits and intervals for proportions, you should review the basics of proportions by using Figure 5.45. `BINOM.DIST` has the following syntax: `BINOM.DIST(Yes,Trials,pYes,F/T)`. Here's what it means

	A	B	C	D	E	F	G	H	I	J
1	**Trait**	**Yes**	**No**	**Total**	**p$_{yes}$**		**Trials**	**Find Yes**	**Exactly**	**Up to**
2	**Defect**	**24**	76	**100**	0.24		**10**	**10**	**0.00%**	**100.00%**
3										
4	**Male**	**45**	55	**100**	0.45		**10**	**6**	**15.96%**	**89.80%**
5										
6	**Immune**	**165**	35	**200**	0.83		**10**	**3**	**0.03%**	**0.04%**
7										

Figure 5.45

- If you find 24 defects (*Yes*) in a sample of 100 items, the proportion of "yes," or "success," is 0.24, or 24% (cell E2).

- If you take 10 *trials* from this batch (with 24% defects), what is the chance of finding 10 defects? `BINOM.DIST` tells the following:

  ○ The chance of finding *exactly* 10 defects is almost 0%: `=BINOM.DIST($H2,$G2,$E2,0)`

  ○ The chance of finding *up to* 10 defects is 100%—cumulative: `=BINOM.DIST($H2,$G2,$E2,1)`

- You can do something similar for the other cases.

Now you are ready to get back to estimating 95% confidence intervals in Figure 5.46. Be aware that *SE* is calculated differently for *binomial* distributions: `=SQRT(p*(1-p)/n)`. Here's how you estimate the 95% confidence intervals:

	A	B	C	D	E	F	G	H	I	J	K	L	M	N
1														
2											confidence limit			
3													confidence intervals	
4														
5			**Yes**	No	**Size**	**p$_{yes}$**		**Level**	**Error**	**2-tails**	**Z**	**StError**	**Margin**	**Min P$_{yes}$**	**Max P$_{yes}$**
6	**Defect**	**11**	89	**100**	0.11		95%	5%	2.5%	-1.96	0.03	0.06	0.05	0.17
7														
8	**Male**	**45**	55	**100**	0.45		95%	5%	2.5%	-1.96	0.05	0.10	0.35	0.55
9														
10	**Immune**	**165**	35	**200**	0.83		95%	5%	2.5%	-1.96	0.03	0.05	0.77	0.88
11														
12														
13														
14														
15														

Standard Error is an estimate of the StDev of the means in the sampling distribution based on the StDev in the sample distribution. For probabilities: =Sqrt(p(1-p)) / Sqrt(n). OR: =Sqrt(p*(1-p)/n)*

Figure 5.46

1. Determine the value of Z (or of t if the sample is small) for a 2.5% two-tailed error margin in cell J6: =NORM.S.INV(I6).

2. Determine the standard error in cell K6: =SQRT(E6*(1-E6)/D6).

3. Determine the margin of error, *Z*SE*, using =ABS(J6*K6).

4. Determine the confidence limits or confidence intervals like you did before.

In the last case scenario (row 10), you have 95% confidence of finding between 77% and 88% immunized cases in samples of size 200.

Figure 5.47 is about a slightly different situation. Instead of calculating boundary **percentages** (as is done in column B with POISSON.DIST and in column C with BINOM.DIST), you may want a minimum and maximum border **value** for, let's say, the 5% and 95% level (making for a confidence interval of 90%). If you were told that certain test plates usually have 5 colonies per plate, you could find out which minimum and maximum count to expect:

	A	B	C	D	E	F	G	H	I
1	mean count	5			On average 5 counts per plate (5/100)				
2	0	0.7%	0.6%						
3	1	3.4%	3.1%						
4	2	8.4%	8.1%		BINOM.INV			SE-Units	
5	3	14.0%	14.0%						
6	4	17.5%	17.8%		mean	5%		mean	5%
7	5	17.5%	18.0%		trials	100		trials	100
8	6	14.6%	15.0%		interval	90%		interval	90%
9	7	10.4%	10.6%		min	2.00		SE	0.021794
10	8	6.5%	6.5%		max	9.00		t	1.660391
11	9	3.6%	3.5%					min	1.381261
12	10	1.8%	1.7%					max	8.618739
13	11	0.8%	0.7%						
14	12	0.3%	0.3%						
15	13	0.1%	0.1%						
16	14	0.0%	0.0%						
17	15	0.0%	0.0%						
18	16	0.0%	0.0%						
19	17	0.0%	0.0%						
20	18	0.0%	0.0%						
21	19	0.0%	0.0%						
22	20	0.0%	0.0%						
23									

Figure 5.47

1. In cell F9, enter =BINOM.INV($I$7,$I$6,(1-$I$8)/2).

2. In cell F10, enter =BINOM.INV($I$7,$I$6,$I$8+(1-$I$8)/2).

The results tell you that you can expect between 2 and 9 colonies in 90 out of 100 plates; the remaining 10 plates may be outside this range. Had you done this as you did before (with *SE* and *Z* or *t*), you would have gotten slightly different results in I11:I12. Part of the explanation is that the left calculation works with (rounded) values, whereas the right calculation works with percentages.

Figure 5.48 uses scroll-bar *controls* that regulate the size of the sample (in B1), the confidence level (in B2), and the number of sick cases (in G1) that were found in the sample. The section on the left calculates the minimum and maximum number of sick cases (at a given confidence level) for different proportions of sick cases in the population (column A). The section on the right calculates the probability of finding sick cases in these samples up to the number chosen in cells G1—again for different proportions in the population (column F). Here is how it can be done:

	A	B	C	D	E	F	G	H	I	J
1	Sample Size	105 ◄ ⌐			►	Sick Cases	15 ◄⌐			►
2	Confidence	95% ◄		⌐	►					
3										
4	sick in popul.	Min sick of 105	Max sick of 105			sick in popul.	Prob. of finding up to 15 cases			
5	5%	2	9			5%	0.01%			
6	10%	6	16			10%	5.81%			
7	15%	10	22			15%	51.44%			
8	20%	14	28			20%	91.40%			
9	25%	19	34			25%	99.45%			
10	30%	24	39			30%	99.99%			
11	35%	29	45			35%	100.00%			
12	40%	34	50			40%	100.00%			
13	45%	39	56			45%	100.00%			
14	50%	44	61			50%	100.00%			
15	55%	49	66			55%	100.00%			
16										

Figure 5.48

- In cell B5: `=BINOM.INV($B$1,$A5,1-$B$2)`.

- In cell C5: `=BINOM.INV($B$1,$A5,$B$2)`.

- In cell G5: `=IFERROR(1-BINOM.DIST(G$1,$B$1,$F5,TRUE),"")`.

Chapter 52: Significant Means

When you find a mean outside the range or margin you had expected for samples from a specific population, you may wonder whether that mean is really coming from the same population—or perhaps some treatment made it no longer representative for the population it came from. This is considered to be an issue of testing for *significance*—which is the topic of this chapter.

What does testing for *significance* entail? Say that you had expected a mean of 33 but in fact observed or measured a mean of 35.3. Is this difference significant? In other words, is this difference likely to be the mere result of random sampling? Or is the actual difference (measured in *SE-units* as *Z*- or *t*-values) beyond the critical difference that you take as a borderline case for being random? If the latter is the case, you would consider this sample to be from a different population, which usually means that some specific treatment affected the sample and had a significant impact.

When dealing with testing for *significance*, the term *hypothesis* comes into play:

- The *null* hypothesis states that the difference between observed and expected is the outcome of randomness: "Results may vary."

- The *alternative* hypothesis states that the difference is caused by a real difference in the underlying sample (caused by the factor under investigation).

There are two possible outcomes in testing for *significance*:

- When the **actual** *Z*- or *t*-value is less than the **critical** *Z*- or *t*-value, the *null* hypothesis is accepted. Conclusion: The difference is (very) likely a matter of randomness.

- When the **actual** *Z*- or *t*-value is greater than the **critical** *Z*- or *t*-value, the *alternative* hypothesis is accepted. Conclusion: The difference is most likely caused by the factor under investigation.

Where are the critical *Z*- and *t*-values located? Usually you place them at the border(s) where 95% of the potential means are covered. So 5% is left out in the critical area—which is 2.5% to the left and 2.5% to the right of the margin of error on a symmetrical curve. Figure 5.49 shows the critical values:

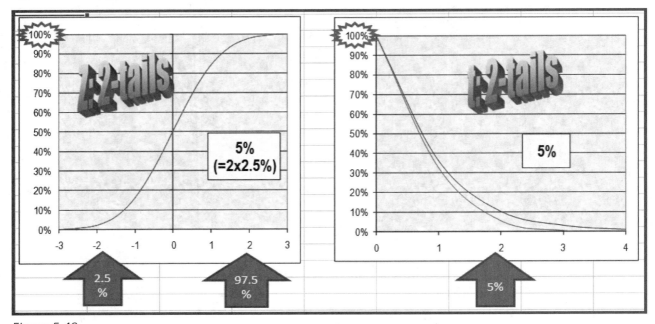

Figure 5.49

- At 2.5% and 97.5% for *Z*-values, provided you test for both tails, with 95% confidence

- At 5% if you test for *t*-values in a two-tailed test

• At 2.5% if you test for *t*-values in a one-tailed test

The area outside the 95% range is called the *significance area*; it is beyond the critical Z- or *t*-values. Why this magic 95% versus 5%? It is basically a strategic decision. You say it is so unlikely that values found in the *significance area* can be attributed to mere randomness. But what is "so unlikely"? Why decide on 5% and not on 10% or 2.5%?

Let's find out why by examining Figure 5.50. In a significance range of 5% (2.5% + 2.5% two-tailed), you accept the *alternative* hypothesis, but you take a 5% chance of rejecting a true *null* hypothesis; in other words, the difference between observed and expected could still be random. This value is also called an *alpha error*. The concave curve shows the (*alpha*) chances of accepting a true hypothesis at a 2.5% significance level. Notice that the chances of accepting a true *null* hypothesis dramatically decline when you get farther away from the center.

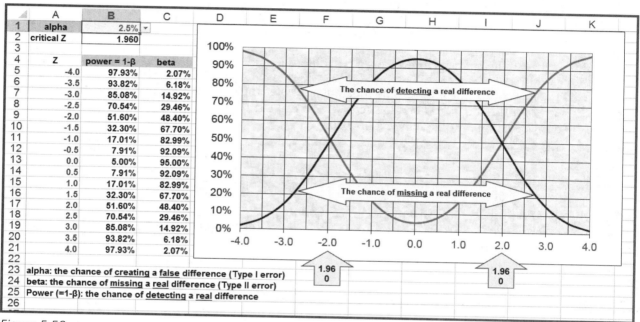

Figure 5.50

Whereas *alpha* designates the error chance of rejecting a true *null* hypothesis, there is also a *beta* chance—alpha's mirror image. *Beta* designates the error chance of accepting a false *null* hypothesis. The convex curve plots *beta* errors for 2.5% *alpha* error settings.

So you have a dilemma here: A smaller risk of rejecting a true null hypothesis results in a larger risk of not recognizing the null hypothesis as false. In other words, you have to make a compromise: A small value of *alpha* is certainly desirable, but making it too small may result in a *beta* so large that you seldom recognize a false null hypothesis. That's why most scientists have settled on a 5% (*alpha*) error chance for two-tailed testing; it is the point where the two curves cross each other.

Since the sample is not the entire population, we always take a chance of making an error. The *null* hypothesis claims that an observed difference is not real (but a random result), whereas the *alternative* hypothesis claims that the difference is actually real (and not fake). Consequently, we can make two types of errors:

• *Alpha* (α) is the chance of making a *Type I error* by creating a false difference. At an *alpha* level of 1%, for instance, we would go for the *alternative* hypothesis by claiming a real difference, but there is still a 1% chance of creating a fake difference.

• *Beta* (β) is the chance of making a *Type II error* by missing a real difference. This happens when we go for the *null* hypothesis by claiming there is no difference, but we still run the risk of missing a very real difference.

How can we reduce our chances of making these errors? To reduce the chance of a *Type I error*, we could reduce the value of *alpha* – but by doing so, we would also increase the chance of making a *Type II error*. To reduce the chance of making a *Type II error*, we could take larger samples – but by doing so, we would also increase the chance of a *Type I error*. So we are stuck in the middle: Choose a large sample size and a small α level (<0.05).

So let us take a different approach. Instead of looking at the chances of *missing* a real difference, we could look at the chances of *detecting* a real difference. Instead of looking at the weakness of a hypothesis test, we could look at the *power* of a hypothesis test. The *power* of a hypothesis test is "one minus the probability of making a Type II error": $1 - \beta$.

So we end up with three different concepts:

- *Alpha*: the chance of creating a false difference (*Type I error*)

- *Beta*: the chance of missing a real difference (*Type II error*)

- *Power* (=1-β): the chance of detecting a real difference.

In Figure 5.51, you want to test whether the mean of a set of sample measurements (in column A) is significantly different from the mean you had expected (31 in cell E5). The *null* hypothesis states that the difference is a random outcome. Here's what you do:

	A	B	C	D	E	F
1	**Measurements**		**Null Hypothesis: Observed = Expected**			
2	30.3			**Skewed?**	0.2150918	**no**
3	34.7					
4	40.0			**Observed**	**Expected**	
5	36.1		**mean**	35.3	31	
6	41.3		**SD**	4.24		
7	34.5		**n**	7		
8	30.5		**level of probability**	5%	use name	
9			**stderror**	1.60		
10			**actual t-value**	2.71		
11			**critical t-value**	2.45		
12		made				
13		for	**"p"**	3.50%	2-tailed	
14		growth	**actual t-value**	2.71		
15						
16			**Random or Significant?**	**Significant**		
17			**Rand/Sign/Highly Sign.**	**Significant**		
18						

Figure 5.51

1. Before applying a Z- or t-test, check whether the distribution is more or less normally distributed by using SKEW in cell E2. This is one of the conditions for using either a Z- or t-test (see Chapter 49).

2. Test this value versus *SES*—SQRT (*6/N*) —in cell F2:
`=IF(E2>2*SQRT(6/COUNT(A:A)),"yes","no")`.

3. Calculate the mean, *SD*, and count of all measurements in D5:D7.

4. If you want, assign a *name* for the 5% significance level and use it in cell D8 (see Chapter 50).

5. Calculate the *SE* in cell D9.

6. Calculate the *actual* t-value in D10: `=ABS(D5−E5)/D9`. Because t-values are *SE-units*, you must divide the actual distance between the observed and expected value by the *SE*.

7. Find the *critical* t-value in D11: `=T.INV.2T(D8,D7−1)`. You need t-values, because Z-values would be too optimistic, given a sample size below 30.

8. If you rather want to know what the probability is of finding a mean that is 2.71 *SE-units* (cell D10) away from what was expected (cell E5), use `T.DIST.2T` and find in D13 that there is a 3.5% chance.

Note

Especially in medical literature, this probability is often called *p*, but this book reserves *p* for *binomial* proportions.

9. As a test, use cell D14 to find the actual t-value back, but now based on *p*:
`=T.INV.2T(D13,D7−1)`.

10. Enter the following in cell D16: `=IF(D10<D11,"Random","Significant")`.

11. For a three-tiered verdict, use a nested IF function: `=IF(D10<D11,"Random",IF(D10<T.INV.2T(D8/2,D7−1),"Significant","Highly Significant"))`. (Chapter 5 describes how to create a nested formula.)

Had you expected a mean of 30 (instead of 31) in cell E5, the second verdict would become highly significant.

Figure 5.52 shows a similar case in which you test whether a weight-loss pill actually works. This time, you check whether the difference before and after administering the pill is significantly different from a zero weight loss—which is the *null* hypothesis here. A similar situation would be the comparison between a group that received the weight-loss pill and a group that received a placebo. This is what you do:

	A	B	C	D	E	F	G	H	I	J	K
1	Before	After	Bef-Aft		Null Hypothesis: weight loss is random						
2	219.0	211.0	8.0		skewness	-0.36	-0.25	-0.03			
3	215.0	209.0	6.0								
4	194.0	191.0	3.0			2-tail		1-tail			
5	222.0	211.0	11.0		mean of diff.	7.13		7.13			
6	217.0	220.0	-3.0		stdev of diff.	7.35		7.35			
7	204.0	200.0	4.0		n	16		16.00			
8	192.0	175.0	17.0		level of probability	5%		10%			
9	180.0	178.0	2.0		stderror	1.84		1.84			
10	223.0	224.0	-1.0		actual t-value	3.88		3.88			
11	219.0	202.0	17.0		critical t-value	2.13		1.75			
12	187.0	169.0	18.0		random or significant	significant		significant			
13	205.0	193.0	12.0								
14	213.0	200.0	13.0		Pill causes >7 pounds weight loss?						
15	193.0	198.0	-5.0								
16	190.0	179.0	11.0		actual diff - claimed diff.	0.13					
17	222.0	221.0	1.0		actual t-value	0.07					
18					claim justified?	NO					
19											
20	estimating				min. loss on average	3.21					
21					max. loss on average	11.04					
22											

Had you used T.INV (based on 5%) instead of T.INV.2T (based on 10%), you would get the same value (1.75) but negative (-1.75).

because the observed difference has sampling errors

Figure 5.52

1. In cell C2, type =A2-B2. Do not use ABS, because differences can even each other out.

2. Check for *skewness* in F2:H2. In F3, enter:
=IF(ABS(H$2)<(2*SQRT(6/$F$7)),"no","yes"), and copy to H3. It turns out you can continue with a *t*-test.

3. Calculate the basic statistics on the differences in F5:H12. You could use two different tests:

   ◦ Testing at *two* tails is proper when you are testing for any significant weight change—increase or decrease (*t* at 5%).

   ◦ Testing at *one* tail is appropriate when testing for a significant weight loss only (*t* at 10%). In cell H11, you have a choice: Using T.INV (based on 5%) gives you the same result, 1.75, as T.INV.2T (based on 10%) but this time negative (-1.75).

Apparently, the pill causes a significant weight loss—both in the one-tailed test and the two-tailed test.

Can you claim that the pill causes a weight loss of at least 5 pounds on average? No, such a claim is not justified; the mean 7.13 was just a sample value, but "results may vary" in the next sample. You therefore need to find the 95% *confidence margin* of this sample mean (see Chapter 50). Cell F20 finds the minimum weight loss (3.21 pounds) based on a 95% confidence: =F5-(F9*F11). All you could claim with 95% confidence is that the pill causes an average weight loss of at least 3 pounds. Anything higher is not statistically sound.

If you don't like all the in-between calculations you've had to do so far, you can use the function T.TEST, which nicely combines many tedious calculations. T.TEST does all the work for you, but it returns a probability (or *p* for some). But there is more good news. Not only does T.TEST do all the work for you internally, you can also use it for more complicated situations, thanks to its last argument. The last argument allows you to specify the type of test: two paired samples (#1), two samples with equal variances (#2), or two samples with unequal variances (#3).

This last argument is especially helpful when you are not dealing with paired samples, as Figure 5.53 demonstrates. Using the manual calculations in this unpaired case would be very cumbersome because you would have to deal with *pooled* standard deviations and what comes with it. T.TEST eliminates all this work, but you must decide whether you are dealing with equal or unequal variances. You can do this with the help of F.TEST, which is used in cell E17: =F.TEST(A:A,B:B). Because the combination of these two variances turns out to be very likely (61%), you may decide on an equal-variance (#2) test in E16: =T.TEST(A:A,B:B,2,2). In this case, the *null* hypothesis wins, with a high 99% probability. The conclusion is that the effect of a specific treatment on the sample in column A cannot be substantiated.

	A	B	C	D	E	F	G
1	**Treated**	**Non-treated**		**Null Hypothesis: Difference is random**			
2	**1.11**	0.97					
3	**3.77**	4.33			**Treated**	**Non-treated**	
4	**5.94**	5.35		**mean**	**3.17**	**3.15**	
5	**2.90**	2.30		**SD**	**1.90**	**1.56**	
6	**1.04**	1.19		**SSD (sum of squared SDs)**	**18.01**	**16.97**	
7	**4.23**	3.88		**n**	**6**	**8**	
8		3.12		**d.f.**	**12**		
9		4.09		**level of probability**	**5%**		**sqrt((SSD1 + SSD2)/df)**
10				**POOLED SD**	**1.71**		
11				**actual t-value**	**0.01**		
12				**critical t-value**			
13				**verdict**			
14							
15		=(ABS(X1-X2)/PooledSD)*SQRT((n1*n2)/(n1+n2))					
16							
17					**TTEST**	**99.047%**	
18					**FTEST**	**61.059%**	

Figure 5.53

There is more good news. You could have also done the previous analysis with the *Analysis Toolpak*, if you are willing to accept hard-coded values. Figure 5.54 is based on the same data as Figure 5.53, but this time it includes the *Toolpak* option *t-Test: Two-Sample Assuming Equal Variances*. Notice that the results coincide nicely with your own calculations—but they are hard-coded, of course.

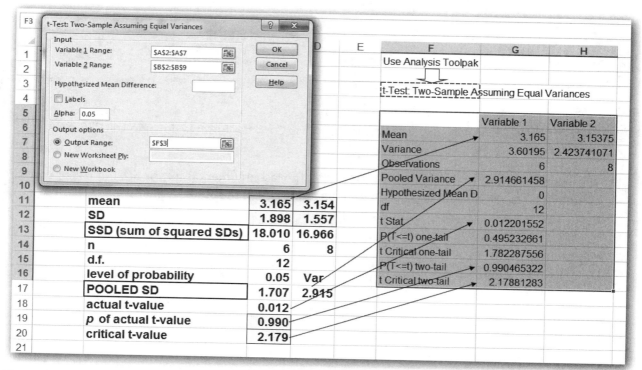

Figure 5.54

One more function we should discuss, Z.TEST, because it works differently than T.TEST, F.TEST, and CHISQ.TEST. It returns the one-tailed probability that the mean of sample data is greater than the mean expected based on population data or data gathered before a certain treatment. It calculates the likelihood of getting a higher sample mean by chance compared with the mean of a population or of a comparable sample.

Figure 5.55 has an example of this. It shows the mean and *SD* of the population (or a before-treatment sample) in the cells F4 and G4. Column B repeats this mean so it shows up as a line in the graph. Column C creates sample data on the fly (test with *F9*), so the cells H4 and I4 can calculate the sample mean and *SD*. Column D repeats this mean for it to show up as another line in the graph. Cell I5 applies the Z.TEST function. If it returns a very low probability—presumably below 5%—we may assume that the sample mean is significantly higher than the other mean. Here are the steps:

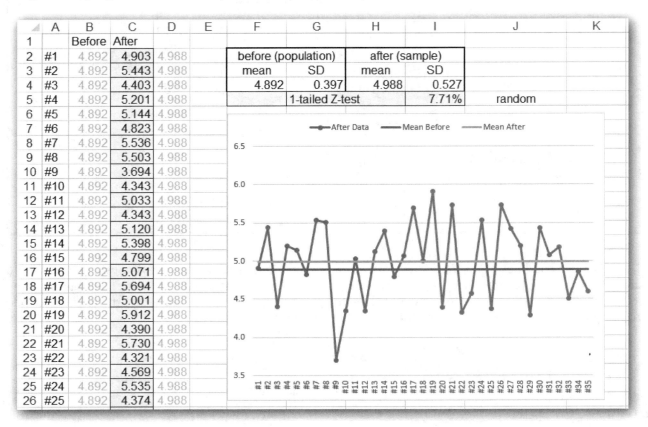

Figure 5.55

1. In cell C2, enter =NORM.INV(RAND(),5,0.5). Copy the formula down to cell C36. *Shift+F9* recalculates.

2. In cell I5, enter =Z.TEST(C2:C36,F4,G4). The last argument is for the *SD*, but it is optional. If you do not have a *SD* for the population, the function will use the *SD* of the sample.

3. Cell J5 makes a verdict: =IF(I5<0.05,"significantly higher","random").

Chapter 53: Significant Proportions

What you did for means in the previous chapter you can also do for *proportions*. When finding a proportion different from an expected proportion, you want to test whether the proportion found is significantly different from the proportion expected.

Figure 5.56 helps explain this concept. You perform three different tests—a one-tailed test at the lower end, a one-tailed test at the higher end, and a two-tailed test:

Occurrence	Yes	No	Count	p_{yes}	Alternative Hypo		pNull	95% cumul. pSign	Min.L.	Verdict
Anthrax	16	44	60	0.27	vaccine lowers p		50%	5%	24	Significant

Diet	Yes	No	Count	p_{yes}	Alternative Hypo		Null: p	95% cumul. pSign	Max.R.	Verdict
Caffeine	29	21	50	0.58	caffeine raises p		50%	95%	31	Random

Gender	Yes	No	Count	p_{yes}	Alternative Hypo		Null: p	pSign	Min+Max	Verdict
Female	35	45	80	0.44	gender has an impact					
					fewer females	$<p_{null}$	50%	2.5%	31	Random
					more females	$>p_{null}$	50%	97.5%	49	

Figure 5.56

- In a sample of 60 vaccinated cases, you found 16 anthrax infections ("yes," or "success") versus 44 non-infected cases—so p=27%:

  ○ The *null* hypothesis claims no effect from vaccination, so p=50% in cell I4. It claims that 27% is a random deviation from 50%, due to sample size.

  ○ The *alternative* hypothesis claims that vaccination has a *lowering* effect. Therefore, you need to test only at one tail—the lower tail (p<5%). It claims that 27% is significantly below 50%.

  ○ You can use `BINOM.INV` to test the *null* hypothesis: 60 trials with a proportion of 50% at the lower end's *significance* level (one-tail: 5%). In cell K4, you enter `=BINOM.INV(D4,I4,0.05)`.

  ○ Because 16 cases is below the 5% level of 24 cases (if random), the verdict is: significant. Cell L4 contains the formula: `=IF(B4<K4,"Significant","Random")`.

- In the second case, you test whether drinking caffeine increases the proportion of high systolic blood pressure:

  ○ You test the *null* hypothesis (p=50%) at one tail, but this time at the high end: >95%.

  ○ In cell K9, you type `=BINOM.INV(D9,I9,J9)`.

  ○ The verdict is: `=IF(B9<K9,"Random","Significant")`. Apparently, there is no significant effect.

- In the third case, you test whether gender has any impact on the proportion of diabetics (up or down):

  - The test is *two*-tailed; with 2.5% in cell J4 and 97.5% in cell J5.

  - In cell K15, you check the lower tail: =BINOM.INV($D$14,I15,J15).

  - In cell K16, you test for the upper tail: =BINOM.INV($D$14,I16,J16).

  - The verdict requires a nested AND function:
  =IF(AND(B14>K15,B14<K16),"Random","Significant").

Figure 5.57 examines how many defects you can accept at the most in samples of 10, 20, and so on before you reject the whole batch if that batch is supposed to have 1%, 1.5%, and so on defects. Here's how it works:

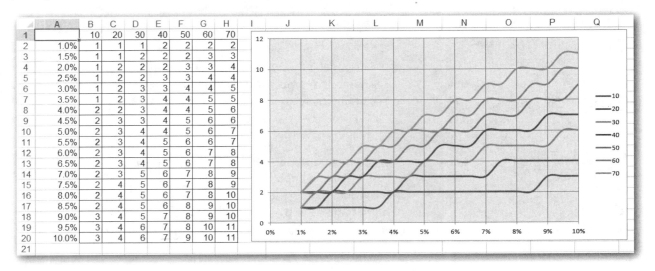

Figure 5.57

- Cell B2 holds the formula =BINOM.INV(B$1,$A2,95%).

- By setting the last argument to 95%, you take a 5% risk of rejecting a batch that should not have been rejected.

- Each curve seems jagged; the reason is that BINOM.INV rounds to numbers of the integer type.

Figure 5.58 shows that a *binomial* situation can often also be solved with the tests we discussed in the previous chapter. The columns A and B simulate a binomial situation by using 0s and 1s (for yes/no, true/false, success/failure, and so on). You test whether the values in A differ significantly from the values in B, or reversed. You can do so by using three different methods, each one with the same outcome:

	A	B	C	D	E	F
1	0	0		mean	0.371	0.457
2	0	1		Count	35	35
3	0	0		SD	0.490	0.505
4	1	0		SE	0.084	0.087
5	0	0				
6	0	1		act. T-value	1.019	0.989
7	0	0		crit. T-value	2.032	2.032
8	0	1		verdict	random	random
9	1	1				
10	0	0		t-test		0.236944
11	0	1		verdict		random
12	0	1				
13	1	0		count zeros	22	19
14	1	0		proport. zeros	0.629	0.543
15	1	0		lower tail	13	16
16	1	1		upper tail	25	27
17	0	0		verdict	random	random
18	1	1				
19	0	0				
20	0	1		Sh+F9		
21	0	1				
22	0	0				

Figure 5.58

- Comparing actual *t*-values with critical *t*-values (or *Z*-values for that matter for large enough samples) in E6:F8.

- Using the T.TEST function for probabilities in F10:F11.

- Using binomial functions such as BINOM.INV in E13:F17.

Because the yes-no values in the columns A and B are based on volatile functions, each recalculation creates two new samples that you can compare with each other as to their difference. Here are the step to take:

1. Enter in the cells A1 and B1 this formula: =IF(RAND()<0.5, 0,1). Copy the formula 35 rows down.

2. Calculate the *actual* t-value in cells E6 and F6: =ABS(E1-F1)/E4.

3. Calculate the *critical* t-value at the 95% level in cells E7 and F7: =T.INV.2T(0.05,E2-1).

4. Apply T.TEST to cell F10: =T.TEST(A1:A35,B1:B35,1,2).

5. To count the number of 0s, use =COUNTIF(A1:A35,0) in E13 and =COUNTIF(B1:B35,0) in F13.

6. Calculate the proportion of 0's in E14 and F14 with =E13/E2 and =F13/F2.

7. The minimum number of 0s at the 2.5% level would be =BINOM.INV(E2,F14,0.025) in cell E15 and =BINOM.INV($F$2,$E$14,0.025) in F15.

8. The maximum number of 0s at the 97.5% level would be =BINOM.INV(E2,F14,0.975) in cell E16 and =BINOM.INV($F$2,$E$14,0.975) in cell F16.

9. Implement the verdicts in the marked cells with IF functions. Only the last two require also the AND function.

Using the *F9* key will typically lead to identical verdicts for all three methods, although there may occasionally be a slight difference caused by rounding.

Chapter 54: Significant Frequencies

Researchers often have to deal with *frequencies* instead of means and binomial proportions because they have their cases categorized in bins. The *Chi-squared* distribution allows you to compare observed frequencies with expected frequencies. The *Chi-squared* distribution works with qualitative variables—with data based on category counts rather than measurements.

Chi-tests are usually based on tables with a two-way structure. Each cell in a two-way table contains counts. However, the *Chi*-test has one important condition: Each cell count must be at least 5. Could you use percentages instead? No, because percentages disregard sample size. For instance, "80 out of 100" is statistically better than "8 out of 10"—but in either case, the percentage would be the same, 80%.

The basic idea behind a *Chi*-test is that the observed frequencies have to be tested against the expected frequencies. In other words, you need to create a copy of the observed frequencies table and replace them with expectations. How do you do this?

Figure 5.59 shows a situation in which the *Chi*-test is an appropriate choice. You test the effect of a certain pill on the recurrence of estrogen-fed tumors versus the effect of placebos, and you end up with four categories and their frequency counts. Because of the *frequencies*, the *Chi*-test is called for. The table of observed frequencies (A3:D6) has total calculations in the end row and column. The table of expected frequencies (A11:D14) is an exact replica of the table above it, except for the observed frequencies (B12:C13). The observed frequencies have to be replaced by calculated, expected frequencies. Here's how you handle it:

	A	B	C	D	E	F	G	H
1	**Observed frequencies:**					**Null Hypothesis: Independence**		
2						CHITEST ⇨ "p"	0.1012%	
3	estrogen-fed tumors	**Recur**	**Stop**	**TOTAL**		5.0%	significant	
4	**Letrozole**	75	2425	2500		1.0%	highly	
5	**Placebo**	120	2380	2500				
6	**TOTAL**	195	4805	5000		critical CHI-value	3.8415	
7						actual CHI-value	10.8061	
8						CHI-probability	0.1012%	
9	**Expected frequencies (if indep.):**							
10								
11	estrogen-fed tumors	**Recur**	**Stop**	**TOTAL**		$$\chi^2 = \sum \left[\frac{(f_{obs} - f_{exp})^2}{f_{exp}} \right]$$		
12	**Letrozole**	97.5	2403	2500				
13	**Placebo**	97.5	2403	2500				
14	**TOTAL**	195	4805	5000				
15						**Degrees of Freedom:**		
16	Letrozole/Recurrence					**(#rows - 1) * (#cols - 1)**		
17	=Subtotal$_{Letr}$ * Subtotal$_{Recur}$ / Total							

Figure 5.59

1. In the first cell (B12), add a proportional value based on a *null* hypothesis of independence: `=SubtotalRow1 * SubtotalColumn1 / Total`. If you do this with the proper relative/absolute settings, you can fill the range B12:C13 by using a single formula: `=$D4*B$6/$D$6`.

2. Apply the function `CHISQ.TEST` in cell G2: `=CHISQ.TEST(B4:C5,B12:C13)`. It quickly does all the tedious work for you. Like all other `TEST` functions, `CHISQ.TEST` returns the probabil-

ity of the difference being random. Apparently, this combination of observed and expected frequencies is very unlikely (only 0.1%). In other words, the effect of the pill is highly significant.

3. In G3, enter =IF(G2<F3,"significant","random"). In G4, enter =IF(G2<F4, "highly","not highly").

4. When you work with CHISQ.INV.RT, you also need to know the *degrees of freedom*. They are calculated this way: *(#rows - 1) * (#cols - 1)*. So calculate the *critical Chi*-value in cell G6 with the formula =CHISQ.INV.RT(signific,1). The *actual Chi*-value in G7 is: =CHISQ.INV.RT(G2,1). The *actual Chi*-value (10.81) is far beyond the *critical Chi*-value (3.84) and is, therefore, highly significant.

5. And CHISQ.DIST.RT would/should come up in G8 with the same probability as CHISQ.TEST: =CHISQ.DIST.RT(G7,1).

Caution

Unlike most other sampling distributions, the *Chi-squared* distribution curve becomes steeper when the *degrees of freedom* decrease. The larger and finer the matrix system, the more *degrees of freedom* you have and therefore the slower the curve's decline.

You can also use the *Chi-squared* distribution for cases in which you want to test law-like predictions for frequencies, as shown in Figure 5.60. Let's consider Mendel's law of independent segregation as an example. Two genes, each with two alleles (*A/a* plus *B/b*), are assumed to have independent segregation or no linkage—and this assumption acts here as the *null* hypothesis. Here's what you do:

▲	A	B	C	D	E	F	G
1	Observed frequencies:					Hypothesis of Independence	
2						CHITEST	0.82%
3	AaBb x aabb	Bb	bb	TOTAL		5.0%	significant
4	Aa	15	21	36		1.0%	highly
5	aa	20	32	52			
6	TOTAL	35	53	88		critical CHI-value	3.841
7						actual CHI-value	7.000
8	Expected frequencies (no linkage):					CHI-probability	0.82%
9							
10	AaBb x aabb	Bb 50%	bb 50%	TOTAL			
11	Aa 50%	22	22	44			
12	aa 50%	22	22	44			
13	TOTAL	44	44	88			
14							

Figure 5.60

1. Calculate the expected frequencies in B11:C12 according to Mendel's second law: ½ * ½ * total.

2. Use CHISQ.TEST in G2: =CHISQ.TEST(B4:C5,B11:C12).

3. Enter the verdict in G3: =IF(G2<F3,"significant","random"). The outcome is highly significant.

4. The rest speaks for itself.

Let's again consider the case used in Figure 5.59: Say that someone realized that there is one more independent factor involved in the effect of the tested pill on the recurrence of estrogen-fed tumors. The overlooked fact is that some of these women also received radiation and some didn't—which is a *confounding factor*. Confounding factors can have quite an impact on the verdict. Let's find out what the impact is with the help of Figure 5.61:

	A	B	C	D	E	F	G	H	I
1		Observed frequencies:						Null Hypothesis: Independence	
2								CHITEST ⇒ "p"	1.331%
3	estrogen-fed tumors	No radiation		Plus radiation				5.0%	significant
4		Recur	Stop	Recur	Stop	TOTAL		1.0%	not highly
5	Letrozole	70	400	5	2025	2500			
6	Placebo	111	368	5	2000	2484			
7	TOTAL	181	768	10	4025	4984			
8									
9									
10		Expected frequencies (if indep.):							
11									
12	estrogen-fed tumors	No radiation		Plus radiation					
13		Recur	Stop	Recur	Stop	TOTAL			
14	Letrozole	90.79	385.2	5.016	2019	2500			
15	Placebo	90.21	382.8	4.984	2006	2484			
16	TOTAL	181	768	10	4025	4984			
17									

$$\chi^2 = \sum \left[\frac{(f_{obs} - f_{exp})^2}{f_{exp}} \right]$$

Degrees of Freedom:
(#rows - 1) * (#cols - 1)

Figure 5.61

1. Calculate the expected frequencies again in the second table.

2. Create your verdict in cell I3 at the 5% level and in cell I4 at the 1% level.

3. If you want to work with CHISQ.INV.RT, etc., set the *degrees of freedom* as follows:
((2-1) rows * (4-1) columns) = 3.

The (random) probability of this combination of observed and expected values went up from 0.1% to 1.3%. It is still a significant result, but it is not so impressive any more. The bottom line is that you need to always be on the lookout for *confounding* factors.

Chapter 55: More on Chi-Squared Testing and Box-Cox Power

The *Chi-squared* sampling distribution is great for frequencies, but in that capacity, it may also be a good alternative for situations in which other types of distributions fail. This chapter examines cases in which *Chi*-values can come to your aid. You will also discover that skewed values can be transformed with *Box-Cox* power.

Chapter 49 discusses the fact that some sampling distributions have specific conditions on their applicability. If the variable under investigation has unequal variances or is not normally distributed, you may not be able to use *Z*, *t*, or *F*. Fortunately, the *Chi-squared* distribution is less demanding—it requires only a minimum cell count of five.

Figure 5.62 demonstrates a situation in which you have measured cholesterol levels among several ethnic groups. Here's how you determine whether you can use *Z* and *t* distributions:

	A	B	C	D	E
1	Cholesterol Measurements				
2	Afr.Amer.	Caucasians	Hispanics	Nat.Amer.	
3	179	160	171	130	
4	183	163	173	152	
5	186	165	174	159	
6	189	167	175	160	
7	192	169	176	161	
8	195	171	177	162	
9	198	173	178		
10	201				
11	204				
12					
13	-0.0760	-0.1806	-0.3673	-2.0471	skew
14	no	no	no	yes	significant
15					
16	F.TEST	Afr.Amer.	Caucasians	Hispanics	Nat.Amer.
17	Afr.Amer.		0.1539	0.0069	0.3250
18	Caucasians			0.1458	0.0318
19	Hispanics				0.0011
20	Nat.Amer.				
21					

Figure 5.62

1. Use `SKEW` in cell A13: `=SKEW(A3:A11)`. Copy the formula all the way to cell D13.

2. To find out if any of these values is significant, use in cell A14: `=IF(ABS(A13)>(2*SQRT(6/COUNT(A3:A11)))‚"yes"‚"no")`. Copy all the way to cell D14 and find out that at least one sample is significantly skewed

3. Use `F.TEST` in C17:E19. You find out that some probabilities are extremely low, which means unequal variances are highly likely.

Based on these results, Z and t values would not be reliable for this project. An additional problem is that you would need Z or t values for A-versus-B, A-versus-C, A-versus-D, B-versus-C, B-versus-D, and C-versus-D. Because each Z or t value would have a 5% error chance, the collective error chance would be quite large.

Figure 5.63 may offer a way out of this dilemma. You cannot use T.TEST here for three reasons: You would need six tests combined, most subgroups are skewed (A25:D25), and some subgroups vary significantly (M2:O4). The alternative is a Chi-test, which has only one condition: Each cell must hold at least five elements. The problem is, however, that you may have to reshuffle the data: You need categories instead, and for each category, you need frequencies (observed vs. expected). Here are three possible ways of doing this:

	A	B	C	D	E	F	G	H	I	J	K	L	M	N	O
1	Afr.Am.	Cauc.	Hisp.	Nat.Am.		Ethnicity	X	SD	n			Afr.Am.	Cauc.	Hisp.	Nat.Am.
2	169	172	168	191		Afr.Amer.	190.64	14.30	22		Afr.Am.		0.34157	0.52175	0.16323
3	168	163	173	193		Caucasians	176.61	11.82	22		Cauc.			0.75452	0.02089
4	169	191	174	195		Hispanics	179.22	13.18	22		Hisp.				0.04401
5	193	167	165	146		Nat.Amer.	166.95	19.51	22		Nat.Am.				
6	196	169	176	161											
7	189	171	191	171			>180	16	8	5	5	34			
8	209	173	178	175										2.302%	
9	195	169	167	176				8.5	8.5	8.5	8.5	34			
10	207	168	173	173											
11	201	169	174	172		low	180	6	14	17	17	54			
12	204	167	199	199		high	250	16	8	5	5	34			
13	180	191	194	158				22	22	22	22	88			
14	207	192	197	140											
15	186	201	210	165		low	180	13.5	13.5	13.5	13.5	54		0.142%	
16	189	169	169	151		high	250	8.5	8.5	8.5	8.5	34			
17	199	171	176	142				22	22	22	22	88			
18	203	195	177	164											
19	188	181	165	168		low	170	5	9	7	12	33			
20	201	169	169	156		moderate	190	5	7	10	5	27			
21	204	171	176	135		high	210	12	6	5	5	28			
22	168	195	177	197				22	22	22	22	88			
23	169	181	165	145											
24						low	170	8.25	8.25	8.25	8.25	33		10.222%	
25	-0.541	0.85	1.25	0.1514		moderate	190	6.75	6.75	6.75	6.75	27			
26	no	no	yes	no		high	210	7	7	7	7	28			
27								22	22	22	22	88			
28															

Figure 5.63

1. Create just one category for high cholesterol levels (for instance, >180). In cell H7, use the formula =COUNTIF(A2:A23,$G$7). Copy the formula all the way to cell K7. In L7 is the total.

2. Determine the expected frequencies based on a *null* hypothesis by typing =34/4 in cell H9, or using the formula =$L$7/COUNT($H$7:$K$7). Copy all the way to cell K9.

3. Use =CHISQ.TEST(H7:K7,H9:K9) in cell N8. This tells you that the probability of finding these frequencies together is very low (2.3%). In other words, the *alternative* hypothesis kicks in: The racial difference of high cholesterol counts in this sample is significant. Needless to say, any changes

in the category's border (cell G7) would affect the outcome of the *Chi*-test. Make sure, though, that each cell still holds at least five elements.

4. In the second table, expand the number of categories—and therefore, the number of *degrees of freedom*. Select the cells H11:H12, and enter this array formula: =FREQUEN–CY(A2:A23,$G$11:$G$12). Copy the formula of these two cells to the right.

5. Use cell H15 to find the expected count if the results were random: =$L11*H$13/$L$13. Copy the formula one row down and three columns to the right.

6. Enter in cell N14 =CHISQ.TEST(H11:K12,H15:K16).

7. In the third table, use three categories, calculate their frequencies, determine their expected frequencies (according to a *null* hypothesis), and apply the *Chi*-test again.

Creating a finer matrix with more cells usually means that randomness can play a larger role, so the probability of the difference may go up. It is not a good policy, however, to adjust the number of categories to your needs. You should set up your categories ahead of time so you don't manipulate them afterward in order to force a favorable verdict.

There is another way of dealing with non-normal distributions by applying a so-called *transformation*. Figure 5.64 shows an example of this technique. The values in column A have a *lognormal* distribution and are significantly skewed as is shown in the top graph (based on the frequency table C2:D12) and in the table at the bottom (cells A28 and A29). But after a *transformation* in column F, they are no longer skewed (cells F28 and F29), and more normally distributed (based on the frequency table C17:D24). Here is how the work is done:

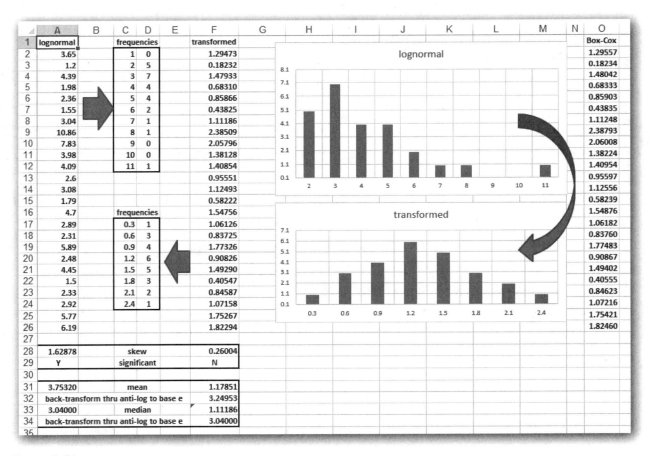

Figure 5.64

1. The *transformation* in cell F2 you can do by returning the natural logarithm of your numbers: =LN(A2). Copy this formula all the way down.

2. Make sure in the cells F28 and F29 that the transformed numbers are no longer significantly skewed.

3. Obviously, the new *mean* in F31 has to be "back-transformed" in F32 through *anti-log* to the base *e* of a natural logarithm: =EXP(F31).

4. Do the same for the new *median* in F33. Again, the median is less prone to change than the mean.

Note

Transformations are quite common. *Lambda* (λ) indicates the power to which all data should be raised in order to transform them:

- For λ=1: no transformation.

- For λ=2: raises all values to the power of 2.

- For λ=0.5: takes the square root of all values.

- For λ=0.33: takes the cube root of all values.

- For λ=0.0001: takes the logarithm of all values.

- For λ=-1: takes the reciprocal inverse (very small becomes very large, and reversed).

- For λ=-0.5: takes the reciprocal square root of all values.

The statisticians George Box and David Cox developed a formula and a procedure to identify the exponent—*lambda* or λ—to which all data should be raised in order to transform the data into a "normal" shape. This is their basic formula: $(y^{\lambda-1})/\lambda$. You could test this formula in column O, for instance, so cell O2 would have the following formula: =(A2^0.001-1)/0.001. Notice how the results in column O closely match the values in column F.

Figure 5.65 explains the use of a *Box-Cox transformation* for the significantly skewed data shown in column A. You have a problem, though. When you want to apply its basic formula, you do not know how to determine λ for this specific situation. Trial-and-error is obviously not a good option. Here are the steps to do better:

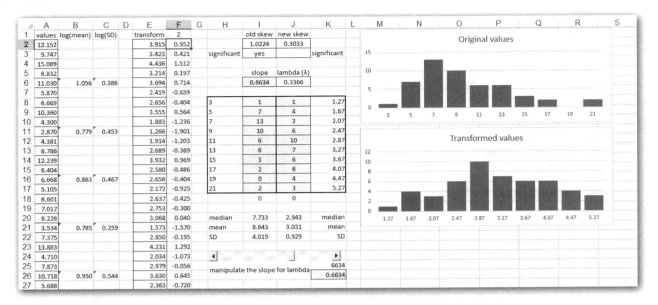

Figure 5.65

1. Split your series of values in at least 10 parts (in this case, 2-6, 7-11, etc.).

2. Calculate for each section the logarithm of the mean—for instance, in B6: `=LOG(AVERAGE(A2:A6))`.

3. Calculate also the logarithm of the standard deviation—for instance, in C6: `=LOG(STDEV.S(A2:A6))`.

4. Copy B6:C6 all the way down.

5. Calculate the slope of columns B and C in cell I6: `=SLOPE(C6:C51,B6:B51)`.

6. Estimate *lambda* (λ) in J6 based on the slope in I6: `=1-I6`. (Later, you will replace I6 with K26). You have come up with an estimate of 0.3366.

7. Now you can use this value of *lambda* (λ) in column E for a *Box-Cox transformation*. Hence enter in E2: `=(A2^$J$6-1)/$J$6`.

8. Calculate their frequencies in J8:J17 based on rounded bins in K8:K17: `=FREQUENCY(E2:E51,K8:K17)`. Notice the "transformed" graph.

9. To check things one step further, add a *Z*-test to cell F2: `=STANDARDIZE(E2,$J$21,$J$22)`. The sum of all values in column F should be zero.

10. To test how important the value of *lambda* is, use the scroll-bar *control* to manually change λ. It regulates cell K25, so place in K26 `=K25/10000`, and in J6 `=1-K26` (instead of I6). The best value is 0.3366.

Once you have transformed your data into values with a *normal* distribution, you can estimate *confidence intervals* for means and perform *significance* tests with regular tests such as Z-test and *t*-test—like you did in earlier chapters. Do not forget to "back-transform" your results.

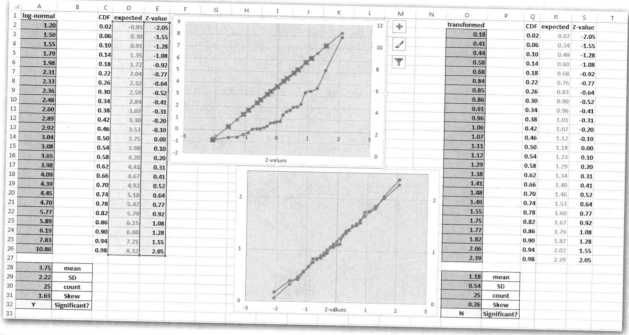

Figure 5.66

Figure 5.66 shows how you can test whether a set of data is normally distributed. We used the same data as in Figure 5.65: The log-normal data were sorted in column A, whereas the transformed data were sorted in column O. The normality-test works as follows:

1. Calculate the *Cumulative Distribution Factor* (CDF). In cell C2: `=1/(2*$A$30)`, and in cell Q2: `=1/(2*O30)`. In cell C3: `=C2+2/(2*$A$30)`, and copy this formula down. In cell Q3: `=Q2+2/(2*$O$30)`, and copy this formula down. So these two columns run from almost 0 to almost 1 (100%), but you must make sure that the data set is sorted.

2. Now calculate the expected values if this were a normal distribution. In cell D2: `=NORM.INV(C2,$A$28,$A$29)`, and copy down. In cell R2: `=NORM.INV(Q2,$O$28,$O$29)`, and copy down.

3. Finally, calculate the corresponding z-values. In cell E2: `=NORM.S.INV(C2)`, and copy down. In cell S2: `=NORM.S.INV(Q2)`, and copy down.

4. Now we can plot the z-values versus the expected values, which should be a straight line in the graph. Next we plot the z-values versus the observed values. The latter plot should nicely "hug" the straight line if we are dealing with a normally distributed set of data, as is the case in the lower graph, based on the transformed data.

Chapter 56: Analysis of Variance

When two or more samples have a *normal* distribution but differ in their variances, you have another option left: the so-called *Analysis of Variance* (also called *ANOVA*). With this test, the difference among sample variances is used to estimate the population's variance, depending on the number of factors and the number of samples you have available from the population under investigation. *ANOVA* compares samples and uses *F*-values that determine the ratio between the larger variance and the smaller variance, so we can test them for significance.

Let's work with the *F*-test in Figure 5.67 before tackling the *ANOVA* tool. This sheet shows how two measuring methods have produced a set of differences in precision. Do these methods vary significantly as to their precision? Here's how you figure it out:

	A	B	C	D	E	F	G	H
1	**Test1**	**Test2**		**Comparing variances (SD²) instead of means**				
2	1.11	0.97		**F is the ratio between large and small variance**				
3	3.77	4.33						
4	5.94	5.35		SD1	1.90			
5	2.90	2.30		SD2	1.56			
6	1.04	1.19	actual F	Var1	3.60	=VAR(A:A)		
7	4.23	3.88		Var2	2.42	=VAR(B:B)		
8		3.12		F: Ratio L/S	1.49	degree of diversity for 2 data sets		
9		4.09				F = Var_large / Var_small		
10								
11			critical F	F.DIST	28%	1-tailed (x2)	d.f.LargeVar	d.f.SmallVar
12				F.INV.RT 0.05	3.97	Random	d.f.LargeVar	d.f.SmallVar
13								
14	d.f. = 5	d.f. = 7		F.TEST	61%	2-tailed		
15								
16		this is a good test to find out whether the variances "really" differ						
17								

Figure 5.67

1. In cell E8, enter the *actual F*-value: =E6/E7.

2. In cell E11, calculate the probability of such an *F*-value: =F.DIST(E8,COUNT(A:A) – 1,COUNT(B:B)-1,FALSE). The first *degree of freedom* is for the larger variance. (Be aware that F.DIST is left-tailed, whereas F.DIST.RT is right-tailed.)

3. In cell E12, calculate the *critical F*-Value: =F.INV.RT(5%,COUNT(A:A) – 1,COUNT(B:B)-1). (Be aware that F.INV.RT is right-tailed, whereas F.INV is left-tailed.)

4. In cell F12, enter a verdict: =IF(E8<E12,"Random","Signif."). Because the actual *F*-value (E8) is less than the critical *F*-value (E12), the difference in precision of these two measuring methods is random and not significant.

5. Use the F.TEST function in cell E14: =F.TEST(A2:A7,B2:B9). This function is always two-tailed. Because F.DIST is one-tailed, its result in cell E11 is only half the result of F.TEST (which is two-tailed) in cell E14.

Often you deal with two or more samples that vary too much in variance, so you cannot use your regular testing tools, but need another tool—either a *Chi*-test or *ANOVA*. Because *ANOVA* is an elaborate process, this chapter only discusses the *Anova* tool from the *Analysis Toolpak*.

Let's take Figure 5.68 as an example. The question is, could the three samples in columns A:C be analyzed with a *t*-test? Yes, they could (provided their variances do not differ significantly). However, such a test would require three tests (A-versus-B, A-versus-C, and B-versus-C). Because each test has a 5% error chance, the total error chance would be *1-(1-0.05)^3 = 14%*. An *F*-test, on the other hand, requires only one test: variance of the sample means versus the variance of all items.

	A	B	C	D	E	F	G	H	I	J	K	L	M	N	O	P	Q	R
1	Test1	Test2	Test3		Analysis of variance (Anova):							Anova: Single Factor						
2	1.11	3.77	0.97		we use the difference among sample means													
3	3.77	5.94	4.33		to estimate the population's variance							SUMMARY						
4	5.94	2.90	5.35									Groups	Count	Sum	Average	Variance		
5	2.90	5.35	2.30		If all samples come from the same population,							Column 1	6	18.99	3.165	3.60195		
6	1.04	2.30	1.19		then small differences between sample means							Column 2	10	31.63	3.163	3.1471344		
7	4.23	1.19	3.88									Column 3	8	25.23	3.15375	2.4237411		
8		1.11	3.12		between-groups variance:													
9		3.77	4.09		variance of the groups means						Sum of Squared Measurements or squared SDs. The function is called DEVSQ.							
10		0.97			within-groups variance:													
11		4.33			variance of all individuals							Source of Variation	SS	df	MS	F	P-value	F crit
12												Between Groups	0.0005483	2	0.0002742	0.0001	0.999909	3.4667949
13					F = b-g variance / w-g variance							Within Groups	63.300148	21	3.0142927			
14															(6-1) + (10-1) + (8-1)			
15					Use ANOVA single factor ▶							Total	63.300696	23				
16																		
17	t-Test would require 3 tests: 1-2, 1-3, 2-3 (each with 5% error chance): 1-(1-0.05)^3 =																	
18	F-Test requires 1 test: b-g var / w-g var (with 1x 5% error chance)									0.142625								
19																		

Figure 5.68

It is quite a procedure to calculate all the steps needed for a *between-group* variance and a *within-group* variance—not to mention the final analysis. You can instead use the super-speedy *Anova* tool from the *Analysis Toolpak* instead:

1. Open the *Anova Single Factor* tool. It is a single factor analysis because each test measures one and the same property.

2. Use the following settings: *Input Range* A1:C11, *Grouped* by ⊙ *Columns*, ☑ *Labels in First Row*, *Alpha* 0.05, and *Output Range* L1.

3. Let *Anova* display all the basic information, such as counts, sums, and variances (L4:P7). Then it calculates the *between-groups* and *within-groups* variance (L11:R15).

4. Note

5. When the samples are not of equal size, the *sum of squares* (*SS*) should be used instead of variances.

6. Based on the *sum of squares* (which can also be found with the function DEVSQ) and the *degrees of freedom*, the *F*-value is calculated (cell P12).

What is your conclusion based on ANOVA? Because the *actual F*-value is well within the range of the *critical F*-value (cell R12) and thus has a high probability of occurring by mere chance (cell Q12), the samples do not differ significantly.

In Figure 5.69, the number of colonies on Petri dishes has been counted for two sets of conditions. This is called a *two-factor analysis with replication*. It is a *two-factor* analysis because it deals with the factor nutrient level (rows) as well as the factor pH (columns). It is considered to be a test *with replication* because there are several readings per combination of factors (there are actually 10). Using the *Analysis Toolpak* is your best bet. You need to set *Input Range* to A1:D21, *Rows per Sample* to 10, *Alpha* to 0.05, and *Output Range* to F1. This is what happens:

	A	B	C	D	E	F	G	H	I	J	K	L
1		pH<6	pH 6-8	pH>8		Anova: Two-Factor With Replication						
2		1	4	6								
3		2	5	7		SUMMARY	pH<6	pH 6-8	pH>8	Total		
4		2	5	7		<2000 mg						
5		3	6	8		Count	10	10	10	30		
6		3	6	8		Sum	30	60	80	170		
7	<2000 mg	3	6	8		Average	3	6	8	5.667		
8		3	6	8		Variance	1.333	1.333333	1.333	5.609		
9		4	7	9								
10		4	7	9		>2000 mg						
11		5	8	10		Count	10	10	10	30		
12		5	3	0		Sum	70	50	20	140		
13		6	4	1		Average	7	5	2	4.667		
14		6	4	1		Variance	1.333	1.333333	1.333	5.609		
15		7	5	2								
16		7	5	2		Total						
17	>2000 mg	7	5	2		Count	20	20	20			
18		7	5	2		Sum	100	110	100			
19		8	6	3		Average	5	5.5	5			
20		8	6	3		Variance	5.474	1.526316	10.74		Nutrient level makes	
21		9	7	4							significant difference	
22												
23						ANOVA						
24						Source of Variatio	SS	df	MS	F	P-value	F crit
25						Sample	15	1	15	11.25	0.001462	4.01954
26						Columns	3.333	2	1.667	1.25	0.294662	3.16825
27						Interaction	250	2	125	93.75	2.73E-18	3.16825
28						Within	72	54	1.333			
29											Interaction makes	
30						Total	340.3	59			significant difference	
31												
32												

Figure 5.69

First there is a summary table with the categories of each factor. They speak for themselves.

At the bottom is a table that includes *F*-values and *p*-values (for probabilities, not proportions):

- The first row (called *Sample*) represents the impact of the first factor, nutrient level. You find here the *between-rows* variance (*B-R SS*).

- The second row (called *Columns*) stands for the effect of the second factor, *pH*. It displays the *between-columns* variance (*B-C SS*)

- The third row shows their interaction, which is explained later in this chapter.

- The fourth row (called *Within*) is for the *within-group variance* (W-G SS).

- The *between-group variance* (*B-G SS*) is missing.

What does the interaction stand for? The *B-G SS* is usually larger than the combination of *B-R SS* and *B-C SS*. The remaining part is due to the combined effects of rows and columns—which is the *interaction* of both variables. That's what the third row is about.

The conclusion is three-fold:

- The differences for nutrient level are significant (*11.25>4*).

- The differences for pH are **not** significant (*1.25<3.2*).

- The interaction between both factors is significant (*93.75>3.2*).

However, you should go for the conclusion that corresponds with your preexisting *alternative* hypothesis because each conclusion comes with a 5% error chance:

- If you are testing the effect of nutrient levels, you did find a significant one!
- If you are interested as to whether there is an optimum combination of level and pH, the answer is yes!
- But don't draw both conclusions at the same time because that would result in a 9.75% error!

Figure 5.70 revisits an example from Chapter 55. It is a situation where `T.TEST` would fail. Earlier, you used `CHISQ.TEST` to do the job, but it was not a very good solution. Would the *Anova* tool be a good alternative? When you apply the *Anova* tool, you notice that there is definitely not a great match here with the *Chi*-test. Why not? Because *Anova* has its own requirements:

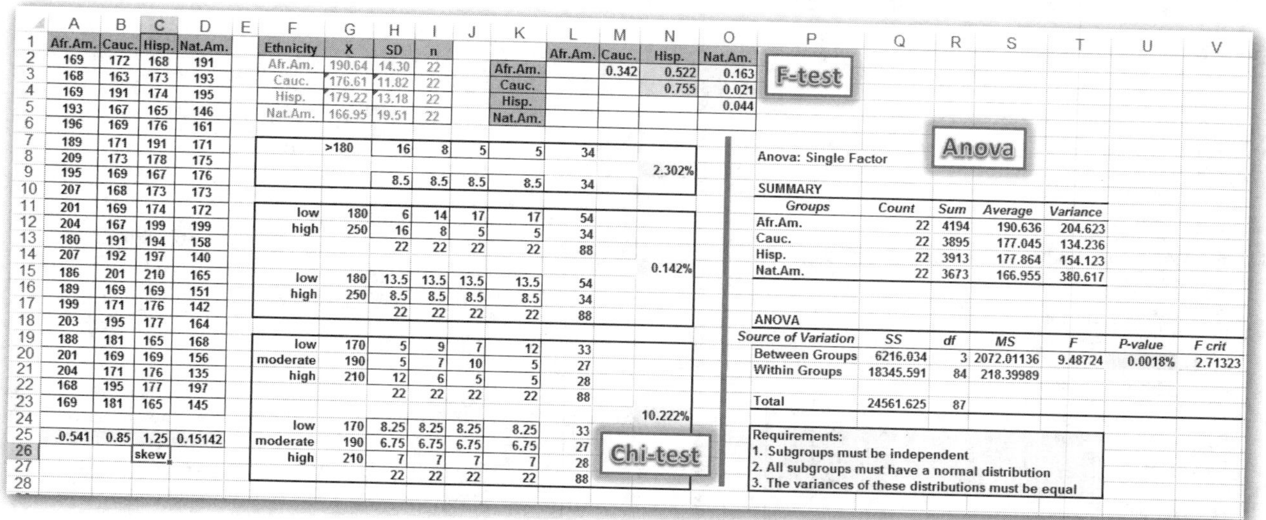

Row	Afr.Am.	Cauc.	Hisp.	Nat.Am.
2	169	172	168	191
3	168	163	173	193
4	169	191	174	195
5	193	167	165	146
6	196	169	176	161
7	189	171	191	171
8	209	173	178	175
9	195	169	167	176
10	207	168	173	173
11	201	169	174	172
12	204	167	199	199
13	180	191	194	158
14	207	192	197	140
15	186	201	210	165
16	189	169	169	151
17	199	171	176	142
18	203	195	177	164
19	188	181	165	168
20	201	169	169	156
21	204	171	176	135
22	168	195	177	197
23	169	181	165	145
25	-0.541	0.85	1.25	0.15142
26			skew	

Ethnicity	X	SD	n
Afr.Am.	190.64	14.30	22
Cauc.	176.61	11.82	22
Hisp.	179.22	13.18	22
Nat.Am.	166.95	19.51	22

	Afr.Am.	Cauc.	Hisp.	Nat.Am.
Afr.Am.		0.342	0.522	0.163
Cauc.			0.755	0.021
Hisp.				0.044
Nat.Am.				

F-test

	>180	16	8	5	5	34	
							2.302%
		8.5	8.5	8.5	8.5	34	
low	180	6	14	17	17	54	
high	250	16	8	5	5	34	
		22	22	22	22	88	
							0.142%
low	180	13.5	13.5	13.5	13.5	54	
high	250	8.5	8.5	8.5	8.5	34	
		22	22	22	22	88	
low	170	5	9	7	12	33	
moderate	190	5	7	10	5	27	
high	210	12	6	5	5	28	
		22	22	22	22	88	
							10.222%
low	170	8.25	8.25	8.25	8.25	33	
moderate	190	6.75	6.75	6.75	6.75	27	
high	210	7	7	7	7	28	
		22	22	22	22	88	

Chi-test

Anova: Single Factor

Anova

SUMMARY

Groups	Count	Sum	Average	Variance
Afr.Am.	22	4194	190.636	204.623
Cauc.	22	3895	177.045	134.236
Hisp.	22	3913	177.864	154.123
Nat.Am.	22	3673	166.955	380.617

ANOVA

Source of Variation	SS	df	MS	F	P-value	F crit
Between Groups	6216.034	3	2072.01136	9.48724	0.0018%	2.71323
Within Groups	18345.591	84	218.39989			
Total	24561.625	87				

Requirements:
1. Subgroups must be independent
2. All subgroups must have a normal distribution
3. The variances of these distributions must be equal

Figure 5.670

- Every subgroup must be independent (which is okay in this case).
- Every subgroup must have a *normal* distribution (which is **not** okay in this case).
- The variances of these distributions must be equal (which is **not** okay in this case).

So the *Chi*-test may still be your best bet for a case like the one shown in Figure 5.69. You need to make sure, though, to set up your categories ahead of time so you don't manipulate them afterward in order to force a favorable verdict.

We have come to a close. In addition to what you have learned in this book, there are many more issues you should know in statistics. This book is not a handbook on statistics, so you need to gather more detailed statistical knowledge somewhere else. Even if you don't opt to learn more about statistics, Excel may still be an excellent and much needed tool for applying your statistical knowledge in all your scientific work.

Part 5 Exercises

You can download all the files used in this book from www.genesispc.com/Science2013.htm, where you can find each file in its original version (to work on) and in its finished version (to check your solutions).

1. Types of Distributions

   1.1. Use the proper *normal* distribution functions in columns B and E.

   1.2. Use the proper *normal* distribution functions in columns I, J, and M, based on a specific mean (cell K2) and a specific SE (cell K3).

   1.3. Test changes in the settings of cells K2 and/or K3.

	A	B	C	D	E	F	G	H	I	J	K	L	M
1													
2		Use a normal distribution (NORM...)								**Mean**	50		
3										**SE**	5.9		
4													
5									non-cumul.	cumul.			
6	**Z**	**Probability**		**Probability**	**Z**			**Value**	**Probability**			**Probability**	**Value**
7	-4.0	0.003%		0.003%	-4.0			26.4	0.002%	0.003%		0.003%	26.4
8	-3.5	0.023%		0.023%	-3.5			29.4	0.015%	0.023%		0.023%	29.4
9	-3.0	0.135%		0.135%	-3.0			32.3	0.075%	0.135%		0.135%	32.3
10	-2.5	0.621%		0.621%	-2.5			35.3	0.297%	0.621%		0.621%	35.3
11	-2.0	2.275%		2.275%	-2.0			38.2	0.915%	2.275%		2.275%	38.2
12	-1.5	6.681%		6.681%	-1.5			41.2	2.195%	6.681%		6.681%	41.2
13	-1.0	15.866%		15.866%	-1.0			44.1	4.101%	15.866%		15.866%	44.1
14	-0.5	30.854%		30.854%	-0.5			47.1	5.967%	30.854%		30.854%	47.0
15	0.0	50.000%		50.000%	0.0			50.0	6.762%	50.000%		50.000%	50.0
16	0.5	69.146%		69.146%	0.5			53.0	5.967%	69.146%		69.146%	53.0
17	1.0	84.134%		84.134%	1.0			55.9	4.101%	84.134%		84.134%	55.9
18	1.5	93.319%		93.319%	1.5			58.9	2.195%	93.319%		93.319%	58.8
19	2.0	97.725%		97.725%	2.0			61.8	0.915%	97.725%		97.725%	61.8
20	2.5	99.379%		99.379%	2.5			64.8	0.297%	99.379%		99.379%	64.7
21	3.0	99.865%		99.865%	3.0			67.7	0.075%	99.865%		99.865%	67.7
22	3.5	99.977%		99.977%	3.5			70.7	0.015%	99.977%		99.977%	70.6
23	4.0	99.997%		99.997%	4.0			73.6	0.002%	99.997%		99.997%	73.6
24													

2. Simulating Distributions

2.1. Calculate the values in column B by using the proper function.

2.2. Create a formula for the values in column C based on a certain *significance* level in cell C1. (You need the functions IF, ABS, NORM.S.INV, and NA combined.)

2.3. Make changes to cell C1 and watch their effect.

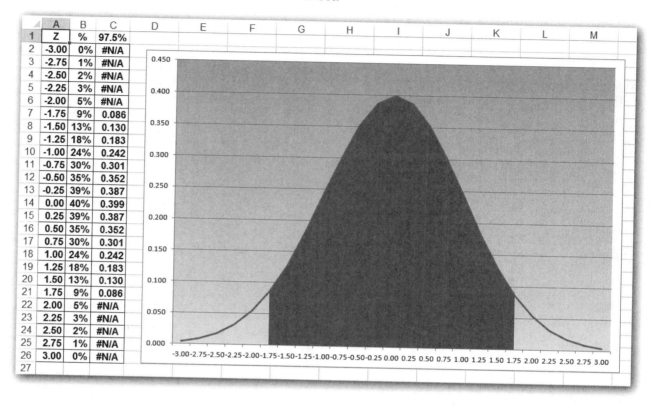

	A	B	C
1	Z	%	97.5%
2	-3.00	0%	#N/A
3	-2.75	1%	#N/A
4	-2.50	2%	#N/A
5	-2.25	3%	#N/A
6	-2.00	5%	#N/A
7	-1.75	9%	0.086
8	-1.50	13%	0.130
9	-1.25	18%	0.183
10	-1.00	24%	0.242
11	-0.75	30%	0.301
12	-0.50	35%	0.352
13	-0.25	39%	0.387
14	0.00	40%	0.399
15	0.25	39%	0.387
16	0.50	35%	0.352
17	0.75	30%	0.301
18	1.00	24%	0.242
19	1.25	18%	0.183
20	1.50	13%	0.130
21	1.75	9%	0.086
22	2.00	5%	#N/A
23	2.25	3%	#N/A
24	2.50	2%	#N/A
25	2.75	1%	#N/A
26	3.00	0%	#N/A
27			

3. Sampling Techniques

3.1. In the table on the left, use a *binomial* function to calculate how often you find exactly X cases (column A) of high blood pressure in samples of size Y (row 5), given the fact that 9% of the population is known to have high blood pressure (A1).

3.2. In the table on the right, use a *Poisson* function for similar calculations.

	A	B	C	D	E	F	G	H	I	J	K	L	M	N
1	9%	of population has high blood pressure												
2														
3			in samples of size Y, how often do exactly X cases have a high SBP											
4														
5		10	15	20	25	30			10	15	20	25	30	sample size
6	0	38.9%	24.3%	15.2%	9.5%	5.9%		0	40.7%	25.9%	16.5%	10.5%	6.7%	
7	1	38.5%	36.1%	30.0%	23.4%	17.5%		1	36.6%	35.0%	29.8%	23.7%	18.1%	
8	2	17.1%	25.0%	28.2%	27.8%	25.1%		2	16.5%	23.6%	26.8%	26.7%	24.5%	
9	3	4.5%	10.7%	16.7%	21.1%	23.2%		3	4.9%	10.6%	16.1%	20.0%	22.0%	
10	4	0.8%	3.2%	7.0%	11.5%	15.5%		4	1.1%	3.6%	7.2%	11.3%	14.9%	
11	5	0.1%	0.7%	2.2%	4.8%	8.0%		5	0.2%	1.0%	2.6%	5.1%	8.0%	
12	6	0.0%	0.1%	0.6%	1.6%	3.3%		6	0.0%	0.2%	0.8%	1.9%	3.6%	
13	7	0.0%	0.0%	0.1%	0.4%	1.1%		7	0.0%	0.0%	0.2%	0.6%	1.4%	
14	8	0.0%	0.0%	0.0%	0.1%	0.3%		8	0.0%	0.0%	0.0%	0.2%	0.5%	
15	9	0.0%	0.0%	0.0%	0.0%	0.1%		9	0.0%	0.0%	0.0%	0.0%	0.1%	
16	10	0.0%	0.0%	0.0%	0.0%	0.0%		10	0.0%	0.0%	0.0%	0.0%	0.0%	
17	#SBP high													
18														

4. Sampling Techniques

4.1. Calculate in column B what the probability is of finding X% defects (column A) in a sample of 10 (cell A3) from a batch of 100 (cell B3).

4.2. Calculate in column E what the probability is of finding X% defects in a sample of 20 from a batch of 200.

4.3. Do the previous step also in column H, for a sample of 100 from a batch of 1,000 – and you will see that sample size is all that matters.

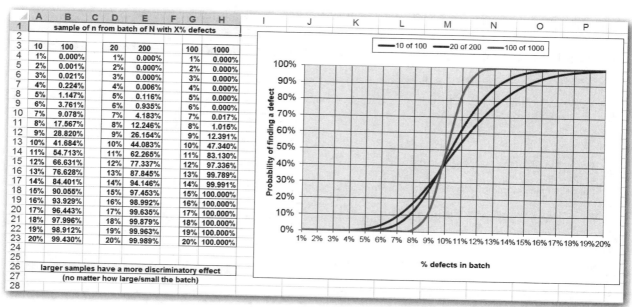

10	100		20	200		100	1000
1%	0.000%		1%	0.000%		1%	0.000%
2%	0.001%		2%	0.000%		2%	0.000%
3%	0.021%		3%	0.000%		3%	0.000%
4%	0.224%		4%	0.006%		4%	0.000%
5%	1.147%		5%	0.116%		5%	0.000%
6%	3.761%		6%	0.935%		6%	0.000%
7%	9.078%		7%	4.183%		7%	0.017%
8%	17.567%		8%	12.246%		8%	1.015%
9%	28.820%		9%	26.154%		9%	12.391%
10%	41.684%		10%	44.083%		10%	47.340%
11%	54.713%		11%	62.265%		11%	83.130%
12%	66.631%		12%	77.337%		12%	97.336%
13%	76.628%		13%	87.845%		13%	99.789%
14%	84.401%		14%	94.146%		14%	99.991%
15%	90.055%		15%	97.453%		15%	100.000%
16%	93.929%		16%	98.992%		16%	100.000%
17%	96.443%		17%	99.635%		17%	100.000%
18%	97.996%		18%	99.879%		18%	100.000%
19%	98.912%		19%	99.963%		19%	100.000%
20%	99.430%		20%	99.989%		20%	100.000%

sample of n from batch of N with X% defects

larger samples have a more discriminatory effect
(no matter how large/small the batch)

5. Some Conditions

5.1. Calculate the *SE* of the sampling distribution in G5 and J5.

5.2. What is the probability of being -1.96 SE units away from 56 in G7 and J7?

5.3. Calculate the *Z* or *t* value that has a 5% chance of occurring (in G9 and J9).

5.4. Find the *Z* or *t* value that covers 95% of the cases (in G11 and J11).

5.5. Calculate how far away 50 is from 56 in SE units. (Don't use a function to do this.)

5.6. Which cells change when you change the mean in cells G1 and J1 from 56 to 50?

	A	B	C	D	E	F	G	H	I	J
1						Mean	56		Mean	56
2						SD	11		SD	11
3						Size	20		Size	20
4										
5	What is the SE of the sampling distribution?						2.460			2.460
6										
7	The probability of being -1.96 SE-Units away from 56 is:						2.50%			3.24%
8										
9	Which Z or t value has a 5% chance of occurring?						-1.645			1.729
10										
11	Which Z or t value covers 95% of the cases?						1.645			1.729
12										
13	How many SE-units is 50 away from 56? (don't use a function)						2.439			2.439
14										
15	Which cells change when you change the mean on top from 56 to 54?						none			none
16										
17	Make both sample sizes 49									
18										
19	Make both sample sizes 20									
20										

6. Estimating Means

6.1. Calculate the 95% *confidence intervals* (or *margins of error*) for row 9 by using *Z* and *SE*.

6.2. Calculate the 95% *confidence intervals* (or *margins of error*) for row 10 by using the function CONFIDENCE.

6.3. Calculate the 95% *confidence intervals* (or *margins of error*) for row 15 by using *t* and SE.

6.4. Use CONFIDENCE.T in cell K16.

	A	B	C	D	E	F	G	H	I	J	K	L	M	N
1														
2										confidence limit				confidence intervals
3		SAMPLES					Confidence						Mean	
4	Feature	Mean	SD	Count		Level	2-tails	1-tail	Z or t	StErr	Margin	Min	Max	
5														
6														
7		size over 30								Z	use *Normal* Distribution			
8														
9	pH	6.80	0.04	50		95%	5%	2.5%	-1.96	0.006	0.011	6.789	6.811	
10									Confidence uses 5%+SD:		0.011	6.789	6.811	
11														
12														
13		size under 30								t	use t-table: *t*-Distribution			
14														
15	pH	6.80	0.04	15		95%	5%	2.5%	2.14	0.010	0.022	6.778	6.822	
16									Confidence uses 5%+SD:		0.022	6.778	6.822	
17														

7. Estimating Means

7.1. Calculate the *confidence margin* in cell B5 based on the data in B1:B3.

7.2. Calculate in cell B6 the upper and lower margin combined.

7.3. Use this formula to calculate the margins in C7:G15 for various *SD*s (B7:B15) and various sample sizes (C6:G6). Use Excel's *Data Table* tool to create the calculations.

	A	B	C	D	E	F	G	H
1	Mean	4.5						
2	SD	0.7						
3	Size	35						
4	2-tailed error level	5%						
5	Confidence margin	0.23						
6	95% conf. margin	4.27 to 4.73	30	35	40	45	50	Size
7		0.2	4.43 to 4.57	4.43 to 4.57	4.44 to 4.56	4.44 to 4.56	4.44 to 4.56	
8		0.3	4.39 to 4.61	4.4 to 4.6	4.41 to 4.59	4.41 to 4.59	4.42 to 4.58	
9		0.4	4.36 to 4.64	4.37 to 4.63	4.38 to 4.62	4.38 to 4.62	4.39 to 4.61	
10		0.5	4.32 to 4.68	4.33 to 4.67	4.35 to 4.65	4.35 to 4.65	4.36 to 4.64	
11		0.6	4.29 to 4.71	4.3 to 4.7	4.31 to 4.69	4.32 to 4.68	4.33 to 4.67	
12		0.7	4.25 to 4.75	4.27 to 4.73	4.28 to 4.72	4.3 to 4.7	4.31 to 4.69	
13		0.8	4.21 to 4.79	4.23 to 4.77	4.25 to 4.75	4.27 to 4.73	4.28 to 4.72	
14		0.9	4.18 to 4.82	4.2 to 4.8	4.22 to 4.78	4.24 to 4.76	4.25 to 4.75	
15		1.0	4.14 to 4.86	4.17 to 4.83	4.19 to 4.81	4.21 to 4.79	4.22 to 4.78	
16		SD						
17								

8. Estimating Proportions

8.1. Assume you flip a coin six times (rows 2:8), but there are 4 different coins (columns C:F), each one having a different chance of showing "heads" (X). Only the coin in column F is a "fair" coin.

8.2. In C2:F8, calculate your chances of hitting "heads" from 0 to 6 times for these 4 different coins.

8.3. In C11:F17, simulate random results ("X" or "O") for these 4 coins flipped 6 times. Use IF and RAND combined.

8.4. Count in row 18 the percentage of "heads" in C11:F17. These numbers should change each time you press (*Sh+*) *F9*.

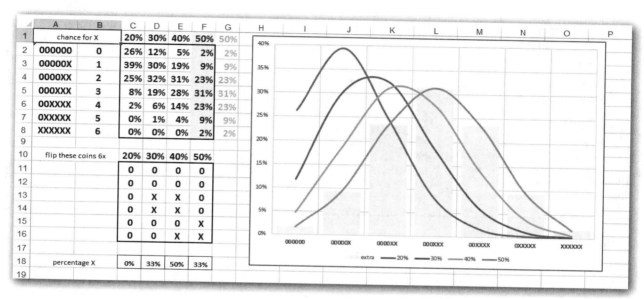

	A	B	C	D	E	F	G
1	chance for X		20%	30%	40%	50%	50%
2	000000	0	26%	12%	5%	2%	2%
3	00000X	1	39%	30%	19%	9%	9%
4	0000XX	2	25%	32%	31%	23%	23%
5	000XXX	3	8%	19%	28%	31%	31%
6	00XXXX	4	2%	6%	14%	23%	23%
7	0XXXXX	5	0%	1%	4%	9%	9%
8	XXXXXX	6	0%	0%	0%	2%	2%
9							
10	flip these coins 6x		20%	30%	40%	50%	
11			0	0	0	0	
12			0	0	0	0	
13			0	X	X	0	
14			0	X	X	0	
15			0	0	0	X	
16			0	0	X	X	
17							
18	percentage X		0%	33%	50%	33%	
19							

9. Estimating Proportions

9.1. Calculate in columns B and C the minimum and maximum number of affected cases if being affected has various proportions (column A), given a certain sample size (cell B1) and a certain *confidence* level (cell G1).

9.2. Move the scroll-bar *controls* and watch the results of changes in sample size and *confidence* level.

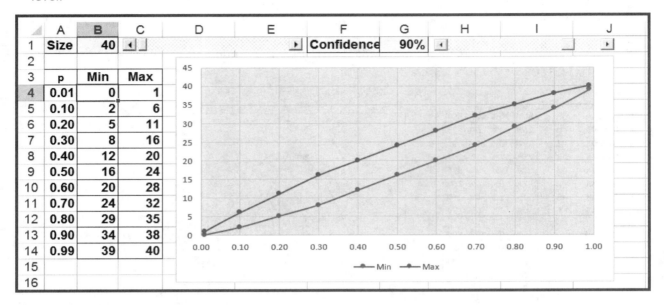

A	B	C
Size	40	

Confidence 90%

p	Min	Max
0.01	0	1
0.10	2	6
0.20	5	11
0.30	8	16
0.40	12	20
0.50	16	24
0.60	20	28
0.70	24	32
0.80	29	35
0.90	34	38
0.99	39	40

10. Significant Means

10.1. Calculate in column D the differences before and after some treatment for each strain.

10.2. Calculate the main statistics in G3:G10.

10.3. Use T.TEST in cell G12 and use its result to calculate the actual *t*-value again in cell G13 (it should be the same as in cell G8).

	A	B	C	D	E	F		G
1		Treated	Non-treated	Diff.		Null Hypothesis: Difference is random		
2	Strain1	1.11	0.97	0.14				
3	Strain2	3.77	4.33	-0.56		mean of diff.		0.16
4	Strain3	5.94	5.35	0.59		stdev of diff.		0.45
5	Strain4	2.90	2.30	0.60		n		6
6	Strain5	1.04	1.19	-0.15		level of probability		5%
7	Strain6	4.23	3.88	0.35		stderror		0.19
8						actual t-value		0.87
9						critical t-value		2.57
10						verdict on Null Hypothesis		Random
11								
12						t-Test paired probability		42.274%
13						actual t-value		0.872713
14								

11. Significant Means

11.1. Simulate 100 random numbers in column A with a mean of 10 and *SD* of 2.

11.2. In column D, calculate the mean of the first 3 items, 6 items, 10 items, etc. (according to column C). Use AVERAGE combined with a nested INDEX function.

11.3. Calculate in column E the *SD* for these different sample sizes and in column G their *SE*.

11.4. Calculate in column F the differences between each observed mean and the expected mean of 10.

11.5. Column H shows significant outcomes based on a 40% level (H1).

11.6. Calculate *skewness* in column I.

11.7. Mark in column J which sample is significantly skewed.

	A	B	C	D	E	F	G	H	I	J
1	15.87351		sample size	mean	SD	mean-10	SE	40%	skew	skewed
2	10.35599		3	12.622	2.888	2.622	1.667	signif.	1.357	
3	11.63672		6	11.309	2.702	1.309	1.103	signif.	0.937	
4	8.952764		10	10.213	2.579	0.213	0.816		1.177	
5	12.49734		15	9.963	2.322	0.037	0.600		1.115	
6	8.537568		20	9.837	2.056	0.163	0.460		1.308	yes
7	9.477241		25	9.784	1.965	0.216	0.393		1.218	yes
8	7.278783		30	9.693	1.887	0.307	0.344		1.241	yes
9	9.946114		35	9.684	1.954	0.316	0.330		0.681	
10	7.576644		50	9.941	1.821	0.059	0.258		0.429	
11	11.04361		100	9.918	1.718	0.082	0.172		0.327	
12	8.221822									
13	7.201487									
14	11.59766									
15	9.244264									

12. Significant Means

12.1. Calculate in column B the probability of missing a real difference (*beta*) with the function NORM.S.DIST twice: once with "actual Z + critical Z" minus once with "actual Z − critical Z."

12.2. Calculate in column C the probability of detecting a real difference (Power= 1 − β).

12.3. Check the impact of changing *alpha* (in cell B1).

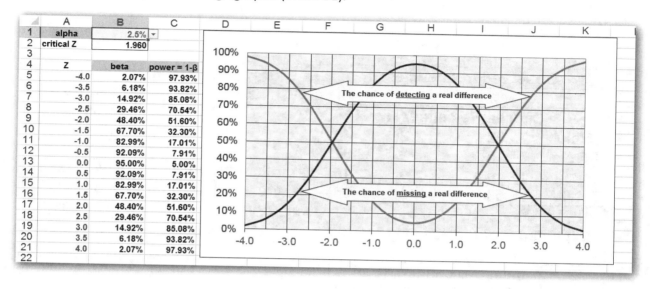

	A	B	C
1	alpha	2.5%	
2	critical Z	1.960	
3			
4	Z	beta	power = 1-β
5	-4.0	2.07%	97.93%
6	-3.5	6.18%	93.82%
7	-3.0	14.92%	85.08%
8	-2.5	29.46%	70.54%
9	-2.0	48.40%	51.60%
10	-1.5	67.70%	32.30%
11	-1.0	82.99%	17.01%
12	-0.5	92.09%	7.91%
13	0.0	95.00%	5.00%
14	0.5	92.09%	7.91%
15	1.0	82.99%	17.01%
16	1.5	67.70%	32.30%
17	2.0	48.40%	51.60%
18	2.5	29.46%	70.54%
19	3.0	14.92%	85.08%
20	3.5	6.18%	93.82%
21	4.0	2.07%	97.93%
22			

13. Significant Frequencies

13.1. Calculate the expected frequencies in B12:C14.

13.2. Calculate the statistics in column G.

13.3. Are all conditions for a *Chi*-test fulfilled here?

13.4. Could you think of a confounding factor?

	A	B	C	D	E	F	G
1	**Observed frequencies:**					**Null Hypothesis: independence**	
2						**CHITEST**	**0.646%**
3		**Cancer**	**No cancer**	**Total**		**5.0%**	**significant**
4	**>5 cig**	32	12	44		**1.0%**	**highly**
5	**1-5 cig**	15	22	37			
6	**no cig**	6	9	15		**critical CHIINV**	**5.9914645**
7	**Total**	53	43	96		**actual CHIINV**	**10.082974**
8						**CHIDIST**	**0.646%**
9	**Expected frequencies (if indep.):**						
10							
11		**Cancer**	**No cancer**	**Total**			
12	**>5 cig**	24.292	19.70833	44			
13	**1-5 cig**	20.427	16.57292	37			
14	**no cig**	8.2813	6.71875	15			
15	**Total**	53	43	96			
16							
17	**>5 cig./Cancer**						
18	=Subtotal$_{>5 cig.}$ * Subtotal$_{Cancer}$ / Total						
19							

14. Analysis of Variance

14.1. Use the *Anova* tool from the *Analysis Toolpak* for the table on the left.

14.2. Is there any significant outcome?

	A	B	C	D	E	F	G	H	I	J	K	L
1		50 ng/mL	25 ng/mL	10 ng/mL		Anova: Two-Factor With Replication						
2	Frozen	47.3	23.0	8.9								
3		48.8	24.0	9.2		SUMMARY	50 ng/mL	25 ng/mL	10 ng/mL	Total		
4		51.1	24.6	8.8		Frozen						
5		50.7	25.2	10.0		Count	7	7	7	21		
6		56.1	26.7	9.4		Sum	360	168.333333	65.6333333	593.966667		
7		51.9	22.6	9.8		Average	51.4285714	24.047619	9.37619048	28.284127		
8		54.1	22.2	9.5		Variance	8.96238095	2.52587302	0.19730159	322.398847		
9	Fresh	50.1	21.9	10.0								
10		49.9	23.2	9.1		Fresh						
11		49.8	23.6	9.1		Count	7	7	7	21		
12		49.6	25.7	11.1		Sum	352.733333	166.7	68.7666667	588.2		
13		53.7	27.7	9.8		Average	50.3904762	23.8142857	9.82380952	28.0095238		
14		49.2	22.5	10.2		Variance	2.2784127	4.56809524	0.49619048	299.432349		
15		50.4	22.1	9.5								
16						Total						
17						Count	14	14	14			
18						Sum	712.733333	335.033333	134.4			
19						Average	50.9095238	23.9309524	9.6			
20						Variance	5.47819292	3.28879731	0.37401709			
21												
22												
23						ANOVA						
24						Source of Variat	SS	df	MS	F	P-value	F crit
25						Sample	0.79177249	1	0.79177249	0.24966216	0.6203534	4.11316522
26						Columns	12318.5826	2	6159.2913	1942.15128	2.1562E-37	3.25944631
27						Interaction	3.87179894	2	1.93589947	0.61042894	0.54864345	3.25944631
28						Within	114.169524	36	3.17137566			
29												
30						Total	12437.4157	41				
31												

15. Analysis of Variance

15.1. Use the *Anova* tool from the *Analysis Toolpak* for the table on the left.

15.2. Make sure you choose the correct version of *Anova*.

15.3. What is your conclusion?

	A	B	C	D	E
1	HbA1C after 3 months				Anova: Single Factor
2	Insulin	Diet	Exercise		
3	5.8	6.0	6.2		SUMMARY
4	6.0	6.2	6.0		Groups
5	6.0	6.3	6.5		Insulin
6	6.2	6.5	7.0		Diet
7	6.3	6.2	6.8		Exercise
8					
9					
10					ANOVA
11					Source of Variation
12					Between Groups
13					Within Groups
14					
15					Total
16					

Index

Symbols

#NA. *See* NA

A

AGGREGATE 73
alpha. *See* error
ampersand (&) 26
Analysis of Variance 290
Analysis Toolpak 177, 185, 188, 191, 244, 252, 254, 275, 290
AND 16
ANOVA 290
array formula 9
  multi-cell 64
  operators 73
  single-cell 69

B

Boltzmann model 182
Box-Cox transformation 288

C

charts and graphs
  broken axis 114
  data source 104
  default 116
  error bars 126
  histogram 109
  secondary axis 122
  template 116
  types 97
CHISQ.TEST 281
circular reference 194
colinearity 188, 191
conditional formatting 41
confidence 264
controls 203
copying
  Ctrl+Enter 6
  fill handle 5, 76
  formulas 7, 8, 62
correlation coefficient 183, 187
Ctrl+Enter 6
Ctrl+Shift+Enter 27
Cumulative Distribution Factor 290
curve fitting 174, 260
custom list 6

D

DATEDIF 76
degrees of freedom 239, 282
developer tab 203

D-function. *See* function
distribution
  INV vs. DIST 237
  sample 232
  sampling 232
  types 235
duplicates 35, 38, 41

E

EC50 determination 54, 181, 214
error
  Type I (alpha) 271
  Type II (beta) 271

F

factor
  confounding 189, 283
  dependent 161
  independent 161
fill handle 5
filtering 33
  advanced 45
  computed filter 34
FREQUENCY 64
F.TEST 274
function
  D-function 33
  INV vs. DIST 237
  nested 15, 273
  user-defined (UDF) 206
  worksheetfunction in VBA 212

G

Goal Seek 199, 264

H

hypothesis
  alternative 270
  null 270, 285

I

IC50 determination. *See* EC50 determination
IFERROR 72
INDEX 51, 66, 139
INDIRECT 12, 51
interaction 193, 292
interpolation 135, 165
interval
  confidence 184
  prediction 183
ISERROR 34, 72
ISFORMULA 44

Written by a Scientist for Scientists

Dr. Gerard Verschuuren

Excel 2013 For Scientists

A complete course for Scientists

This self-paced course will teach you Excel's features for science. Over 1900 pages in full color.

MREXCEL.COM

With over 1900 slides, this self-paced training package is loaded with informative samples from the world of science plus frequent self-tests to enhance your learning

"Excel Simulations: Solve Problems with Excel"
by Dr. Gerard Verschuuren.

"This title offers a solid introduction to using Microsoft Excel Simulations
in the disciplines of Business, Science, and Casino Gaming."